Recent Advances of Discrete Optimization and Scheduling

Recent Advances of Discrete Optimization and Scheduling

Editors

Alexander A. Lazarev
Frank Werner
Bertrand M.T. Lin

Basel • Beijing • Wuhan • Barcelona • Belgrade • Novi Sad • Cluj • Manchester

Editors

Alexander A. Lazarev
Institute of Control Sciences
Russian Academy of Sciences
Moscow
Russia

Frank Werner
Otto-von-Guericke-University
Magdeburg
Germany

Bertrand M.T. Lin
National Yang Ming Chiao
Tung University
Taipei
Taiwan, China

Editorial Office
MDPI
St. Alban-Anlage 66
4052 Basel, Switzerland

This is a reprint of articles from the Special Issue published online in the open access journal *Mathematics* (ISSN 2227-7390) (available at: https://www.mdpi.com/journal/mathematics/special_issues/recent_advances_discrete_optimization_and_scheduling).

For citation purposes, cite each article independently as indicated on the article page online and as indicated below:

Lastname, A.A.; Lastname, B.B. Article Title. *Journal Name* **Year**, *Volume Number*, Page Range.

ISBN 978-3-7258-0673-7 (Hbk)
ISBN 978-3-7258-0674-4 (PDF)
doi.org/10.3390/books978-3-7258-0674-4

© 2024 by the authors. Articles in this book are Open Access and distributed under the Creative Commons Attribution (CC BY) license. The book as a whole is distributed by MDPI under the terms and conditions of the Creative Commons Attribution-NonCommercial-NoDerivs (CC BY-NC-ND) license.

Contents

About the Editors vii

Preface ix

Alexander A. Lazarev, Frank Werner and Bertrand M.T. Lin
Special Issue "Recent Advances of Discrete Optimization and Scheduling"
Reprinted from: *Mathematics* **2024**, *12*, 793, doi:10.3390/math12060793 1

Jae Won Jang, Yong Jae Kim and Byung Soo Kim
A Three-Stage ACO-Based Algorithm for Parallel Batch Loading and Scheduling Problem with Batch Deterioration and Rate-Modifying Activities
Reprinted from: *Mathematics* **2022**, *10*, 657, doi:10.3390/math10040657 4

Dinesh Karunanidy, Subramanian Ramalingam, Ankur Dumka, Rajesh Singh, Mamoon Rashid, Anita Gehlot, et al.
JMA: Nature-Inspired Java Macaque Algorithm for Optimization Problem
Reprinted from: *Mathematics* **2022**, *10*, 688, doi:10.3390/math10050688 30

Alexander Alekseevich Lazarev, Darya Vladimirovna Lemtyuzhnikova and Mikhail Lvovich Somov
Decomposition of the Knapsack Problem for Increasing the Capacity of Operating Rooms
Reprinted from: *Mathematics* **2022**, *10*, 784, doi:10.3390/math10050784 58

Tatiana Makarovskikh and Anatoly Panyukov
Special Type Routing Problems in Plane Graphs
Reprinted from: *Mathematics* **2022**, *10*, 795, doi:10.3390/math10050795 76

Lev G. Afraimovich and Maxim D. Emelin
Complexity of Solutions Combination for the Three-Index Axial Assignment Problem
Reprinted from: *Mathematics* **2022**, *10*, 1062, doi:10.3390/math10071062 98

Vladimir Galuzin, Anastasia Galitskaya, Sergey Grachev, Vladimir Larukhin, Dmitry Novichkov, Petr Skobelev, et al.
Autonomous Digital Twin of Enterprise: Method and Toolset for Knowledge-Based Multi-Agent Adaptive Management of Tasks and Resources in Real Time
Reprinted from: *Mathematics* **2022**, *10*, 1662, doi:10.3390/math10101662 108

Navid Behmanesh-Fard, Hossein Yazdanjouei, Mohammad Shokouhifar and Frank Werner
Mathematical Circuit Root Simplification Using an Ensemble Heuristic–Metaheuristic Algorithm
Reprinted from: *Mathematics* **2023**, *11*, 1498, doi:10.3390/math11061498 135

Man-Ting Chao and Bertrand M. T. Lin
Scheduling of Software Test to Minimize the Total Completion Time
Reprinted from: *Mathematics* **2023**, *11*, 4705, doi:10.3390/math11224705 157

Shuhui Shen and Xiaojun Zhang
Several Goethals–Seidel Sequences with Special Structures
Reprinted from: *Mathematics* **2024**, *12*, 530, doi:10.3390/math12040530 174

Alexander Lazarev, Nikolay Pravdivets and Egor Barashov
Approximation of the Objective Function of Single-Machine Scheduling Problem
Reprinted from: *Mathematics* **2024**, *12*, 699, doi:10.3390/math12050699 187

About the Editors

Alexander A. Lazarev

Alexander A. Lazarev was born in 1958. In 1980, he graduated from Kazan University. In 1990, he defended his PhD thesis in Minsk under the scientific supervision of Academician V.S. Tanaev. In 2007, he defended his doctor Habilitation dissertation in Moscow. He has been acting as a professor since 2009. He got married in 1983 (in Moldova) and has three children. Area of scientific interests: scheduling theory and discrete optimization, construction of effective metrics for these problems, with the help of which algorithms are constructed for finding approximate solutions with a guaranteed absolute error of the objective function. These methods were practically utilized for the Cosmonaut Training Center and the Russian Railways company.

Frank Werner

Frank Werner studied mathematics from 1975 to 1980 and graduated from the Technical University of Magdeburg (Germany) with a distinction. He received a Ph.D. degree (with summa cum laude) in Mathematics in 1984 and defended his habilitation thesis in 1989. From this, he worked at the Faculty of Mathematics at the Otto-von-Guericke University Magdeburg in Germany, and since 1998, as an extraordinary professor. In 1992, he received a grant from the Alexander von Humboldt Foundation. He was a manager of several research projects, supported by the German Research Society (DFG) and the European Union (INTAS). Since 2019, he has been the Editor-in-Chief of the journal *Algorithms*. He is also an Associate Editor of *The International Journal of Production Research* since 2012, and of *The Journal of Scheduling* since 2014, as well a member of the editorial/advisory boards of 18 further international journals. He has been a guest editor of Special Issues in ten international journals, and has served as a member of the program committee of more than 140 international conferences. Frank Werner is an author/editor of 14 books, among them, the textbooks *Mathematics of Economics and Business* and *A Refresher Course in Mathematics*. In addition, he has co-edited three proceedings volumes of the SIMULTECH conferences and published more than 300 journal and conference papers, e.g., in *The International Journal of Production Research*, *Computers & Operations Research*, *The Journal of Scheduling*, *Applied Mathematical Modelling*, or *The European Journal of Operational Research*. He received Best Paper Awards from *The International Journal of Production Research* (2016) and *IISE Transactions* (2021). His main research subjects are scheduling, discrete optimization, graph theory, and mathematical problems in operations research.

Bertrand M.T. Lin

Bertrand M.T. Lin is a professor (and the director) at the Institute of Information Management at the National Yang Ming Chiao Tung University, Taiwan. Dr. Lin received his B.S. in Computer Science (1986), M.S. in Computer and Information Science (1988), and Ph.D. in Computer Science and Information Engineering (1991), all from National Chiao Tung University, Taiwan. After his Ph.D. study, Dr. Lin served military duty as a second lieutenant at ROC (Taiwan) Air Force Headquarters. In 1994, his academic career started at the Department of Information Management at Ming Chuan University, where he later founded the Department of Computer Science. In 2001, Dr. Lin joined the Department of Information Management, National Chi Nan University. He also acted as the director of the Office of Extension Education and Industrial Development and the Chair of the Department of Computer Science. Dr. Lin joined the National Chiao Tung University in 2004. He visited several institutions, such as the Hong Kong Institute of Advanced Studies, IBM Watson Research Center, New Jersey Institute of Technology, The Hong Kong Polytechnic University, University of Technology Sydney, the University of Michigan, and Warwick Business School as a visiting scholar/professor. Dr. Lin's research interests are mainly in scheduling theory and discrete optimization, in terms of both theory and applications. Dr. Lin serves the professional community as an Associate Editor of *The Journal of Scheduling*, *The Journal of Industrial and Management Optimization*, and *The Asia Pacific Journal of Operational Research*, and an Area Editor of *Computers and Industrial Engineering and NTU Management Review*. He has published over 100 papers in such professional journals as *IIE Transactions*, *Management Science*, *Naval Research Logistics*, *SIAM Journal on Optimization*, among others.

Preface

This is the printed edition of a Special Issue published in the *Mathematics* journal. We received 20 submissions for this issue, representing a broad spectrum in the field of discrete optimization and scheduling. In addition to the Editorial, this book contains ten research papers focusing on these issues. Among the subjects addressed in this book, we can mention nature-inspired optimization algorithms, routing problems in plane graphs, decomposition approaches for scheduling surgeries, the three-index axial assignment problem, autonomous digital twins, or single machine scheduling problems, to name a few.

Finally, we extend our gratitude to all who have contributed to the success of this issue, including, but not limited to, authors from eight countries, many referees from all over the world, and the staff of the *Mathematics* journal. I hope that the readers of this Special Issue find many stimulating ideas for their own future research in this challenging field of discrete optimization and scheduling.

Alexander A. Lazarev, Frank Werner, and Bertrand M.T. Lin
Editors

Editorial

Special Issue "Recent Advances of Discrete Optimization and Scheduling"

Alexander A. Lazarev [1], Frank Werner [2,*] and Bertrand M. T. Lin [3]

1. V.A. Trapeznikov Institute of Control Sciences of Russian Academy of Sciences, 65 Profsoyuznaya Street, 117997 Moscow, Russia; jobmath@mail.ru
2. Faculty of Mathematics, Otto-von-Guericke University Magdeburg, 39106 Magdeburg, Germany
3. Institute of Information Management, National Yang Ming Chiao Tung University, Hsinchu 300, Taiwan; bmtlin@nycu.edu.tw
* Correspondence: frank.werner@ovgu.de; Tel.: +49-391-675-2025

MSC: 90B35; 90C27; 90C10

This Special Issue of the journal Mathematics is dedicated to new results on the topic of discrete optimization and scheduling. We particularly invited submissions for articles aimed at solving problems in practical applications, e.g., optimization problems related to the management of medical institutions, cargo transportation, or production planning, to name a few. Both structural investigations as well as investigations on algorithm efficiency were welcome.

After a careful peer-review process, 10 papers were selected for this Issue, which represent a broad spectrum of research fields in discrete optimization and scheduling. As a rule, all submissions were reviewed by two or more experts from the corresponding area. Subsequently, the papers were then surveyed in increasing order of their publication dates.

The first accepted paper, written by Jang et al., deals with a batch loading and scheduling problem on parallel machines with the objective to minimize the makespan. In particular, the authors suggest a three-stage ant colony algorithm which can find optimal solutions for instances of small size. For large-sized instances, the algorithm was found to be superior to a genetic algorithm as well as a particle swarm algorithm.

The second paper of this Issue, written by Karunanidy et al., suggests a novel Java macaque algorithm, which mimics the natural behaviour of the Java macaque monkeys and uses a promising social hierarchy-based selection process. The algorithm presented in this paper is extensively tested on various benchmark functions for a continuous optimization problem and on the traveling salesman problem as a frequently considered discrete optimization problem. The presented algorithm was found to be efficient compared to existing dominant optimization algorithms.

In contribution 3, Lazarev at al. conducted a study concerning scheduling surgeries in operating rooms. They suggested a model that uses a variation of the bin packing problem with the primary goal of increasing patient throughput. Since the suggested mixed-integer model is computationally extensive, two approximation algorithms based on decomposition are also presented. Using the Gurobi solver, experiments were performed using real historical data for surgeries in a Russian neurosurgical center.

Makarovskikh and Panyukov carried out research pertaining to routing problems on plane graphs with the goal to solve the industrial control problems of cutting machines. Polynomial algorithms were developed to determine listed routes with the minimum number of covering paths and the minimum length of transitions, between the end of the current path and the beginning of the next path. It was concluded that the obtained solutions can improve the quality of the technological preparation of such cutting processes in CAD/CAM systems.

The work of Afraimovich and Emelin concerns the three-index axial assignment problem, which is NP-hard. The problem of combining feasible solutions is investigated,

---

Citation: Lazarev, A.A.; Werner, F.; Lin, B.M.T. Special Issue "Recent Advances of Discrete Optimization and Scheduling". *Mathematics* **2024**, *12*, 793. https://doi.org/10.3390/math12060793

Received: 29 February 2024
Accepted: 1 March 2024
Published: 8 March 2024

Copyright: © 2024 by the authors. Licensee MDPI, Basel, Switzerland. This article is an open access article distributed under the terms and conditions of the Creative Commons Attribution (CC BY) license (https://creativecommons.org/licenses/by/4.0/).

and approaches for the solution of such combination problems are considered. It is proven that the resulting problem is already NP-hard in the case of combining four solutions.

The sixth published paper by Galuzin et al. presents an autonomous digital twin of an enterprise with the goal to provide the knowledge-based multi-agent adaptive allocation, scheduling, optimization, monitoring, and control of tasks and resources in real time. Formalized ontological and multi-agent models for developing such digital twins are presented. The developed approaches and toolset were found to be successful in terms of efficiency as well as savings in time and delivery costs.

Behmanesh-Fard et al. present a mathematical model for symbolic pole/zero simplification in operational transconductance amplifiers. After solving the circuit symbolically and applying an improved root-splitting method, a hybrid algorithm is used and combined with a simulated annealing metaheuristic method for the simplification of the derived symbolic roots. The developed approach is tested on three amplifiers, and the approach determines accurate simplified expressions with low complexity.

In the next paper, Chao and Lin attempt to solve a single-machine scheduling problem with shared common setup operations resulting from a software test. The authors suggest sequence-based and position-based integer programming models as well as a branch and bound algorithm. To obtain an upper bound for the latter algorithm, an ant colony algorithm is used. Detailed numerical results for a dataset with up to 50 jobs and 45 setup operations are presented.

Shen and Zhang present a novel method to construct so-called Goethals–Seidel sequences with special structures. They present significant results that allow users to potentially construct all of such sequences more efficiently. Moreover, some of their examples are considered to verify the obtained theoretical results.

In contribution 10, as the last accepted paper, Lazarev et al. target the single-machine scheduling problem so as to minimize total weighted completion times. They assume that the objective coefficients are unknown, but the set of optimal schedules is given. The problem can be reduced to a system of linear inequalities for the coefficients. For the case of simultaneous job release times, the authors present an algorithm for solving this system, which is the base for a polynomial algorithm to find the weight coefficients belonging to the given optimal schedules.

It is our pleasure to thank all authors for submitting their recent works, all reviewers for their timely and insightful reports, and the staff of the Editorial Office for their support in preparing this Issue. We hope that the readers of this Issue will find stimulating ideas to initiate new research in this challenging research field.

Conflicts of Interest: The authors declare no conflicts of interest.

List of Contributions

1. Jang, J.W.; Kim, Y.J.; Kim, B.S. A Three-Stage ACO-Based Algorithm for Parallel Batch Loading and Scheduling Problem with Batch Deterioation and Rate-Modifying Activities. *Mathematics* **2022**, *10*, 657.
2. Karamanidy,D.; Ramalingam, S.; Dumka, C.; Singh, R.; Rashid, M.; Gehlot, A.; Alshamrani, S.S.; AlGhamdi, A.S. JMA: Nature-Inspired Java Macaque Algorithm for Optimization Problem. *Mathematics* **2022**, *10*, 688.
3. Lazarev, A.A.; Lemtyuzhnikova, D.V.; Somov, M.L. Decomposition of the Knapsack Problem for Increasing the Capacity of Operating Rooms. *Mathematics* **2022**, *10*, 784.
4. Makarovskikh, T.; Panyukov, A. Special Type Routing Problems in Plane Graphs. *Mathematics* **2022**, *10*, 795.
5. Afraimovich, L.G.; Emelin, M.D. Complexity of Solutions Combination for the Three-Index Axial Assignment Problem. *Mathematics* **2022**, *10*, 1062.
6. Galuzin, V.; Galitskaya, A.; Grachev, S.; Larukhin, V.; Novichkov, D.; Skobelev, P.; Zhilyaev, A. Autonomous Digital Twin of Enterprise: Method and Toolset for Knowledge-Based Multi-Agent Adaptive Management of Tasks and Resources in Real Time. *Mathematics* **2022**, *10*, 1662.

7. Behmanesh-Fard, N.; Yazdanjouei, H.; Shokouhifar, M.; Werner, F. Mathematical Circuit Root Simplification Using an Ensemble Heuristic-Metaheuristic Algorithm. *Mathematics* **2023**, *11*, 1498.
8. Chao, M.-T.; Lin B.M.T. Scheduling of Software Test to Minimize the Total Completion Time. *Mathematics* **2023**, *11*, 4705.
9. Shen, S.; Zhang, X. Several Goethals-Seidel Sequences with Special Structures. *Mathematics* **2024**, *12*, 530.
10. Lazarev, A.A.; Pravdivets, A.N.; Barashov, E.B. Approximation of the Objective Function of Single-Machine Scheduling Problem. *Mathematics* **2024**, *12*, 699.

Disclaimer/Publisher's Note: The statements, opinions and data contained in all publications are solely those of the individual author(s) and contributor(s) and not of MDPI and/or the editor(s). MDPI and/or the editor(s) disclaim responsibility for any injury to people or property resulting from any ideas, methods, instructions or products referred to in the content.

Article

A Three-Stage ACO-Based Algorithm for Parallel Batch Loading and Scheduling Problem with Batch Deterioration and Rate-Modifying Activities

Jae Won Jang, Yong Jae Kim and Byung Soo Kim *

Department of Industrial and Management Engineering, Incheon National University, 119 Academy-ro, Yeonsu-gu, Incheon 22012, Korea; 8chris8@inu.ac.kr (J.W.J.); yongjae@inu.ac.kr (Y.J.K.)
* Correspondence: bskim@inu.ac.kr

Abstract: This paper addresses a batch loading and scheduling problem of minimizing the makespan on parallel batch processing machines. For batch loading, jobs with compatible families can be assigned to the same batch process even if they differ in size; however, batches can only be formed from jobs within the same family, and the batch production time is determined by the family. During the batch scheduling, the deterioration effects are continuously added to batches processed in each parallel machine so that the batch production times become deteriorated. The deteriorated processing time of batches can be recovered to the original processing times of batches by a maintenance or cleaning process of machines. In this problem, we sequentially determine the batching of jobs and the scheduling of batches. Due to the complexity of the problem, we proposed a three-stage ant colony optimization algorithm. The proposed algorithm found an optimal solution for small-sized problems and achieved near-optimal solutions and better performance than a genetic algorithm or a particle swarm optimization for large-sized problems.

Keywords: scheduling; batching; ant colony optimization; mixed linear integer programming; deterioration; rate-modifying activity

Citation: Jang, J.W.; Kim, Y.J.; Kim, B.S. A Three-Stage ACO-Based Algorithm for Parallel Batch Loading and Scheduling Problem with Batch Deterioration and Rate-Modifying Activities. *Mathematics* **2022**, *10*, 657. https://doi.org/10.3390/math10040657

Academic Editors: Alexander A. Lazarev, Frank Werner and Bertrand M. T. Lin

Received: 23 January 2022
Accepted: 16 February 2022
Published: 20 February 2022

Publisher's Note: MDPI stays neutral with regard to jurisdictional claims in published maps and institutional affiliations.

Copyright: © 2022 by the authors. Licensee MDPI, Basel, Switzerland. This article is an open access article distributed under the terms and conditions of the Creative Commons Attribution (CC BY) license (https://creativecommons.org/licenses/by/4.0/).

1. Introduction

Batch-processing machines (BPMs) have been applied to numerous manufacturing industries such as ceramics, steel, and integrated circuits industries to enhance the productivity of production. Due to this reason, several BPM scheduling problems have been studied in recent years. In general, the BPM sequentially processes batches, a group of jobs processed together in the same machine. The job is the smallest unit of an order requested by a customer. In this paper, we deal with the batch loading and scheduling problem (BLSP) at the diffusion operation in the semiconductor industry [1,2]. In addition to general batching, the concept of job family processing the same operation is adopted. Owing to the chemical nature of the diffusion operation in the semiconductor industry, only jobs with the same family can be assigned to the same batch. Thus, in this manufacturing environment, the batch production time is determined by the family type. In most batch scheduling studies, the batch production time is assumed to be constant. However, for a real-world scheduling problem, the batch production times increase due to the inclusion of activities such as the loading/unloading of jobs and alignment/calibration of tools. The increased batch production times can be recovered to the original production times of each batch by a maintenance or cleaning process of machines. The recovering process is called rate-modifying activity (RMA) [3]; multiple RMAs are considered in the schedule. The RMA time is assumed to be constant, and the RMA can be scheduled between batches. In this paper, the deterioration of batch production time linearly depends on the consecutive batch production runs without the RMA. Thus, it can be formulated as a linear function of the interval between the starting time of the first batch after the previous RMA and the completion time of the last batch before the recent RMA. The interval between RMAs including periods before the first and after the last RMAs is called a bucket, which is defined in Joo and Kim [4].

In this paper, we address BLSP with incompatible job families in parallel BPMs subject to time-dependent batch deterioration and RMAs applied between batches. The BLSP can be decomposed into the two sub-problems of batch loading and batch scheduling [5–7]. In the example of a batch loading problem shown in Figure 1a, 11 jobs belonging to three families are shown. All of the jobs must be formed in batches, which can only be assigned to batches within the same family. For example, batch 1 is formed from jobs 1 and 6, which have the same family type. The sum of their job sizes does not exceed the batch capacity. In Figure 1a, job 1–4, 5–8, and 9–11 belong to family 1, 2, and 3, respectively. The size of job is (0.43, 0.49, 0.34, 0.40, 0.49, 0.54, 0.43, 0.66, 0.37, 0.40, 0.46). The machine capacity is 1. The sum of job sizes in a batch does not exceed the batch capacity. For example, the sum of job sizes of job 1 and 4 is 0.83 ($S_1 + S_4 = 0.43 + 0.40 = 0.83 \leq 1$). After batches have been formed from all of the jobs, the batches must be scheduled to machines, which is referred to as the batch scheduling procedure.

Here, the problem with batch deterioration and RMAs during batch scheduling is considered. An illustrative example of the batch scheduling problem is shown in Figure 1b. As the batch production time including the deterioration increases, the assigning of RMAs between batches should be considered. Since the problem becomes complex, the batch scheduling problem is decomposed into three stages using buckets. The bucket is the set of batches between RMAs. The first stage is to determine the number of buckets. The second stage is to assign batches to each bucket. The last stage is to schedule the buckets to machines. In Figure 1b, the number of buckets is set to 3. The processing time for family is (44, 36, 52). Since batch 1–2, 3–5, and 6–7 consist of jobs for family 1, 2, and 3, respectively, the processing time of batch 1–2, 3–5, and 6–7 is 44, 36, and 52, respectively. The number of machines is 2. The deterioration rate is 0.25 and the processing time of RMA is 30. As a batch is processed, time is added equally to the difference between the last RMA completion time and the batch start time multiplied by the deterioration rate. For example, when batch 4 is processed in bucket 1, since the processing time of batch 2 has elapsed without RMA, 11 ($= 44 \times 0.25$) is added to the original processing time of batch 4. On the other hand, batch 6 of bucket 3 is not affected by deterioration because there is an RMA immediately before it. Once the batches have been assigned and sequenced in three buckets, the buckets are scheduled to the corresponding machines. As a result, the makespan can be calculated.

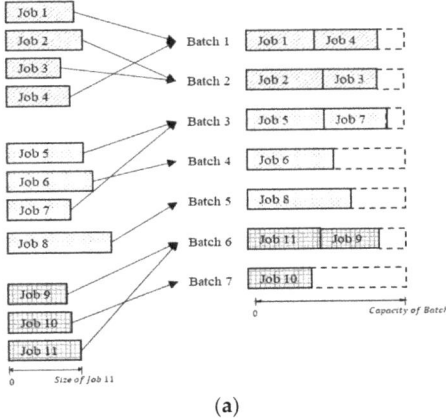

(a)

Figure 1. *Cont.*

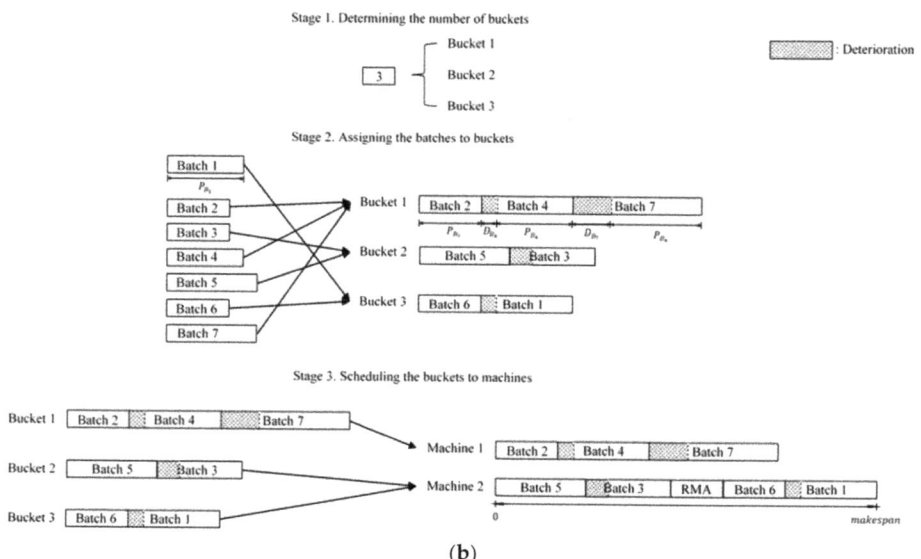

Figure 1. Batch loading and scheduling problem. (**a**) Batch loading procedure. (**b**) Batch scheduling procedure.

The BLSP with no deterioration was addressed by Jia et al. [2], who proposed ant colony optimization (ACO) and the multi-fit (MF) algorithm for solving the batch loading and batch scheduling problems, respectively. We proposed the same algorithm for the batch loading problem, but the MF algorithm cannot be used in our problem because batch deterioration and RMAs impose complexity on the batch scheduling problem. Therefore, we decompose the batch scheduling problem into the three stages mentioned above. In the first stage, the number of buckets is determined between the lower and upper bounds. The fixed number of buckets determines the positions of the RMAs and helps to reduce the search space. In the second stage, a rule-based ACO is applied to assign batches to the buckets defined in the preceding stage. In the last stage, the buckets are scheduled to machines using a dispatching rule.

The remainder of this paper is organized as follows. A previous related work is reviewed in Section 2. Section 3 presents our mixed-integer programming (MIP) model. In Sections 4–6, the overall batch scheduling algorithm is proposed, with the MF algorithm applying the RMA scheduling rule developed in Section 4, the ACO-based three-stage algorithm proposed in Section 5, and the genetic algorithm (GA) and particle swarm optimization (PSO) approaches proposed in Section 6. Section 7 presents our experimental results and, finally, the conclusions are presented in Section 8.

2. Literature Review

To enhance productivity, many BPM studies have attracted the attention of various production areas such as ceramics, steel, and integrated circuit industries. For reviewing the related studies on BPM, we divided BPM studies into seven categories: manufacturing system, production methods, family constraint, job sizes, deterioration constant, recovering process, method, and objective function. The initial studies on BPMs assumed the size of jobs in a batch to be identical. The batch scheduling problem was first introduced by Ikura and Gimple [8]. They proposed a polynomial-time algorithm for minimizing the makespan under an assumption of identical job sizes. In this problem, the total job size in each batch must not exceed the batch capacity. For solving the BLSP with identical job sizes, Lee et al. [9] proposed dynamic programming algorithms to minimize the maximum tardiness and the number of tardy jobs. Cheng et al. [10] proposed a novel ACO for minimizing the makespan. Subsequent studies have extended this approach to single BPMs with non-identical job sizes. Uzsoy [11] proposed the use of heuristics and a B&B algorithm to minimize the total weighted completion time. Two heuristics for solving this problem were proposed by Dupont and Ghazvini [5]. Later studies extended this to the problem of parallel BPMs with non-identical job sizes. Jia et al. [12] considered parallel BPMs with arbitrary capacities carrying out jobs of arbitrary sizes with dynamic arrival times. They proposed the use of two meta-heuristics based on ACO to minimize the makespan. Ozturk et al. [13] considered the problem of parallel BPMs with identical job sizes and release dates. They proposed a branch and bound (B&B) algorithm to minimize the makespan. Zhou et al. [6] considered parallel BPMs with arbitrary release times and non-identical job sizes. They presented different heuristics for solving batch loading and batch scheduling problems. The batch loading problem is tractable under the application of GA, ACO, and greedy randomized adaptive search procedure algorithms. Jia et al. [14] proposed a fuzzy ACO for minimizing the makespans for parallel batch processing machines with jobs having non-identical sizes and fuzzy processing times. Parallel BPM studies have also been extended to unrelated parallel BPMs. Arroyo and Leung [15,16] considered unrelated parallel batch machines with different capacities processing jobs with arbitrary sizes and non-zero ready times. They proposed several heuristics based on rules applying best-fit, first-fit, and meta-heuristic-based iterated greedy algorithms. Arroyo et al. [17] considered the use of unrelated parallel BPMs to minimize the total job flow time. They proposed a simple and effective iterated greedy algorithm and compared them to three meta-heuristic algorithms. Gao and Yuan [18] considered unbounded parallel batch scheduling problems involving jobs with agreeable release dates and processing times. They demonstrated that such problems are binary NP-hard. Zhou et al. [19] considered unrelated parallel BPM processing jobs with non-identical sizes and arbitrary release times. They proposed using a GA with a random key to schedule batches to the machines in such cases.

The studies described above focused on problems in which all jobs were compatible. However, the issue of incompatible jobs has occurred in actual situations. For instance, incompatibilities arise from a non-empty intersection on intervals and two-dimensional volumes for individual jobs [20,21]. Uzsoy [1] considered the problem of single BPM with incompatible families. He developed B&B and polynomial-time dynamic programming algorithms to minimize the makespan, lateness, and total weighted completion time. Azizoglu and Webster [22] considered a BPM with incompatible families, identical processing times, arbitrary job weights, and arbitrary job sizes. They proposed a B&B algorithm that can solve this problem with less than 25 jobs in a reasonable time. Dupont and Dhaenens-Flipo [7] considered a BPM with non-identical job sizes for minimizing the makespan. To solve problems with large numbers of jobs, they added two rules to a B&B algorithm to minimize the makespan. Yao et al. [23] considered single BPMs with incompatible job families and dynamic arrivals. They proposed a decomposed B&B algorithm for minimizing the total batch completion time and makespan. Jolai [24] considered BPMs with identical job sizes and incompatible families and applied a polynomial-time dynamic programming algorithm to minimize the number of tardy jobs. Parallel BPMs with incompatible families have also been extensively examined. Balasubramanian et al. [25] considered the problem of identical parallel BPMs with incompatible families. They proposed an approach in which the batch processing time is determined based on the family and developed two GAs for scheduling jobs to batches and machines, respectively. Li et al. [26] further considered the problem of incompatible families and proposed a method for determining the batch processing time based on the length of the longest job. For parallel BPMs with incompatible job families and release times, constraint programming and apparent tardiness cost approaches were presented [27,28].

In previous studies on the BLSP, the processing time was assumed to be constant and known in advance. In several real-world industry situations, however, the processing time increases due to the deterioration phenomenon. The concept of a deteriorating job was introduced by Gupta and Gupta [29], who considered a single BPM governed by a linear deterioration function. The literature on deterioration follows two general tracks: sequence and time-dependent deterioration. The case of parallel machine scheduling under sequence dependent deterioration was addressed by Ding et al. [30], who proposed an ejection chain algorithm for minimizing the completion-time-based criteria. The case of time-dependent deterioration was first introduced by Browne and Yechiali [31]. Soleimani et al. [32] proposed cat swarm optimization on unrelated parallel machine scheduling problems with time-dependent deterioration. In general, the degree of deterioration increases with the length of the job process. To recover the inefficient execution of processes under deterioration, it is necessary to carry out the recovering processes called RMAs by Lee and Leon [3]. RMAs return a machine to its initial state. Joo and Kim [33] considered a single BPM with time-dependent deterioration to which RMAs are applied and proposed hybrid meta-heuristic algorithms to minimize the makespan. Woo et al. [34] considered unrelated parallel BLSPs with time-dependent deterioration and RMAs, proposing a GA with a random key to solve the problem. Abdullah and Süer [35] considered the decision-making on the selection of a manufacturing strategy between the classical assembly line and seru according to the skill levels of the operator. Liu et al. [36] proposed exact solutions and heuristic algorithms to minimize the makespan and balance the worker's workload of divisional and rotating seru in the seru production system. Gai et al. [37] presented an accurate dimensionality reduction algorithm to minimize makespan. It is also compared to the greedy algorithm to verify it.

As a problem becomes more complex, it becomes increasingly important to decompose it. The meta-heuristic approaches developed in previous studies generally decompose a BLSP into sub-problems. Dupont and Dhaenens-Flipo [7] considered unrelated parallel BPMs with non-identically sized jobs. They developed an approach for decomposing the BLSP into two sub-problems of forming and scheduling batches to improve performance. Determining which algorithm to apply to each sub-problem following division is another important challenge. Dupont and Ghazvini [5] assessed GA, ACO, and greedy adaptive search heuristic algorithms as methods for addressing the batch scheduling problem and compared their performances on batch loading situations fixed using the same algorithm. Similarly, Zhou et al. [19] proposed a GA with a random key for solving the batch scheduling problem. In this paper, the BLSP for processes with time-dependent batch deterioration for which RMAs are applied between batches is considered. To the best of our knowledge, this is the first paper to address this problem.

A list of recent studies on BLSPs and scheduling problems under deterioration is provided in Table 1. The recent studies are categorized by manufacturing system, production methods, family constraint, job sizes, deterioration constant, recovery process, method, and objective function. To the best of our knowledge, none of the studies dealt with the BLSP simultaneously considering parallel BPMs, incompatible job families, non-identical job sizes, time-dependent deterioration, and RMAs. Among the research, Jia et al. [2] proposed the ACO and MF algorithm for addressing, respectively, the batch loading and batch scheduling problems for parallel BPMs with incompatible families and arbitrary job sizes. For our problem, we adopted the ACO by Jia et al. [2] to solve the batch loading problem. However, the MF algorithm cannot provide the near-optimal makespan during the batch scheduling because time-dependent deterioration and RMAs increase the complexity of the problem. Therefore, in this paper, we decompose the batch scheduling problem into three stages and propose an ACO-based three-stage algorithm for solving the scheduling problem.

Table 1. The comparisons between recent studies.

	Mfg. System	Production Methods	Family Constraint	Job sizes	Deterioration Constraint	Recovery Process	Method	Objective
Woo et al. [34]	Parallel	Single	No family	N/A	Time-dependent deterioration	RMA	GA	Makespan
Ding et al. [30]	Parallel	Single	No family	N/A	Sequence-dependent deterioration	No recovery	ECA	Completion time
Soleimani et al. [32]	Parallel	Single	No family	N/A	Time-dependent deterioration	No recovery	GA, CSO, IABC	Mean weighted tardiness
Ozturk et al. [13]	Parallel	Batch	No family	Identical	No deterioration	No recovery	B&B	Makespan
Jia et al. [14]	Parallel	Batch	No family	Non-identical	No deterioration	No recovery	ACO	Makespan
Jia et al. [12]	Parallel	Batch	No family	Non-identical	No deterioration	No recovery	ACO	Makespan
Arroyo et al. [17]	Parallel	Batch	No family	Non-identical	No deterioration	No recovery	Iterated greedy	Total flow time
Li et al. [26]	Parallel	Batch	Incompatible family	Non-identical	No deterioration	No recovery	LB	Lateness
Jia et al. [2]	Parallel	Batch	Incompatible family	Non-identical	No deterioration	No recovery	ACO	Makespan
This paper	**Parallel**	**Batch**	**Incompatible family**	**Non-identical**	**Time-dependent deterioration**	**RMA**	**ACO**	**Makespan**

3. Mixed-Integer Programming Model

The BLSP is the problem of scheduling jobs to machines. In this problem, we have to make two decisions. We need to determine which jobs to assign in which batches and then schedule the assigned batches and RMA to machines. This is called batch loading problem and batch scheduling problem. In this section, the BLSP for time-dependent deterioration with rate-modifying activities and incompatible families for minimizing the makespan is formulated using MIP. The following parameters and decision variables are used in the mathematical formulation:

Parameters

J	set of jobs
F	set of families
B	set of batches
K	set of buckets
M	set of machines
J^f	set of jobs not belongings to family $f \in F$
F_j	family type of job $j \in J$
F_b	family type of batch $b \in B$
S_j	size of job $j \in J$
P_b	processing time of batch $b \in B$
Q	processing time of RMA
DR	deterioration rate
L	large number
SC	size of machine

Decision variables

X_{jb}	Equals 1 if job $j \in J$ is assigned in batch $b \in B$
Y_{bkm}	Equals 1 if batch $b \in B$ is assigned to bucket $k \in K$ from machine $m \in M$
Z_{abkm}	Equals 1 if batch $a \in B$ precedes batch $b \in B$ in bucket $k \in K$ from machine $m \in M$

Dependent variables

MS	Makespan
C_k	Completion time of bucket $k \in K$
C_m	Completion time of machine $m \in M$
T_b	Time gap between starting time of batch $b \in B$ and completion time of recent RMA

Based on parameters and decision variables, the MIP is formulated as follows:

$$\text{Minimize } MS$$

Subject to

$$\sum_{b \in B} X_{jb} = 1, \ \forall j \in J \qquad (1)$$

$$X_{jb} = 0, \ \forall b \in B, \forall j \in J^{F_b}, \qquad (2)$$

$$\sum_{j \in J} S_j \cdot X_{jb} \leq SC, \ \forall b \in B \qquad (3)$$

$$\sum_{j \in J} X_{jb} \leq L \cdot \sum_{k \in K} \sum_{m \in M} Y_{bkm}, \ \forall b \in B \qquad (4)$$

$$\sum_{k \in K} \sum_{m \in M} Y_{bkm} \leq 1, \ \forall b \in B \qquad (5)$$

$$\sum_{k \in K} \sum_{m \in M} Z_{bbkm} \leq 1, \ \forall b \in B \qquad (6)$$

$$\sum_{a \in B} Z_{abkm} = Y_{bkm}, \ \forall b \in B, \forall k \in K, \forall m \in M \qquad (7)$$

$$\sum_{\substack{b \in B \\ b \neq a}} Z_{abkm} \leq Y_{akm}, \quad \forall b \in B, \, \forall a \in B, \forall k \in K, \forall m \in M \tag{8}$$

$$\sum_{b \in B} Z_{bbkm} \leq 1, \quad \forall k \in K, \forall m \in M \tag{9}$$

$$T_a \cdot (1+D) + P_a \leq T_b + L \cdot \left(1 - \sum_{k \in K} \sum_{m \in M} Z_{abkm}\right), \quad \forall a, b \in B, a \neq b \tag{10}$$

$$T_b \cdot (1+D) + P_b \leq C_k + L \cdot (1 - Y_{bkm}), \quad \forall b \in B, \forall k \in K, \forall m \in M \tag{11}$$

$$\sum_{k \in K} C_k + Q \cdot \left(\sum_{k \in K} \sum_{b \in B} Z_{bbkm}\right) - Q \leq MS, \quad \forall m \in M \tag{12}$$

The first decision we have to make is which job should be assigned to which batch by Constraint (1), (2) and (3). One job can be assigned to only one batch, and to be assigned to the same batch, the type of family must be the same and the size must not exceed the capacity. Constraints (1) and (2) confirm that each job is assigned to only one batch and that each batch comprises jobs within the same family. Constraint (3) ensures that the total job sizes assigned to each batch do not exceed the capacity of the batch. After all, once batches have been assigned, the assigned batches should be scheduled to the machine considering the RMA by constraint (4) to constraint (9). There are two ways to consider RMAs, i.e., considering scheduling between all batches, and assuming that RMAs are scheduled only between buckets. The bucket means a set of batches between buckets; hence the RMA does not exist between batches in the same bucket. In the batch scheduling problem, we determine which batch should be assigned to which bucket and the order of the batches in the bucket by constraint (4) to constraint (9). Constraints (4) and (5) ensure that each assigned batch is sequenced in one bucket. Constraints (6) and (8) ensure that there cannot be two first-sequence batches in a given bucket. Constraint (7) ensures that, except for the first batch in each bucket, any batches assigned to a bucket must be immediately preceded. Similarly, constraint (8) ensures that if a batch is assigned to a bucket, at most one batch can be performed immediately afterward. When all batches are scheduled, the makespan can be calculated by constraint (10) to constraint (12). Constraint (10) ensures the precedence relation among assigned batches in a bucket and calculates the starting time for each batch. Constraint (11) calculates the completion time of each bucket by computing the maximum time needed to complete each batch in the bucket. Constraint (12) determines the completion times of the machines needed to calculate the makespan.

4. Multi-Fit Batch Scheduling Algorithm with the RMA Scheduling Rule

The MF algorithm has demonstrated good performance in solving the batch scheduling problem with no deterioration [2]. Unlike previous approaches, however, the scheduling of RMAs must be considered in our problem. One of the ways to do so is to consider the scheduling between all batches. Whenever a batch is scheduled one by one, scheduling the RMA should be considered. To determine whether an RMA should be scheduled, an RMA scheduling rule is used. The RMA scheduling rule is that an RMA is scheduled if the deterioration is longer than the RMA processing time. The MF algorithm using this RMA scheduling rule is proposed in Algorithm 1 and the initial lower and upper bounds on completion time, LB_{ct} and UB_{ct}, can be calculated as

$$LB_{ct} = max\left\{\max_{b \in B} P_b, \left\lfloor \sum_{b \in B} \frac{P_b}{M} \right\rfloor\right\}, \tag{13}$$

$$UB_{ct} = max\left\{\max_{b \in B} P_b, \left\lceil \sum_{b \in B} \frac{P_b + Q}{M} \right\rceil\right\}. \tag{14}$$

Algorithm 1. Multi-fit algorithm with the RMA scheduling rule for the batch scheduling problem

Input:	The set of assigned batches B.
Output:	The makespan.
Begin:	Sort B in non-increasing order of processing times and obtain a batch set B'.
	Compute LB_{ct} and UB_{ct}, respectively.
	Let iteration $h = 1$.
	While ($h < 8$)
	$\quad A = (UB_{ct} + LB_{ct})/2$
	$\quad$ Let batch index $b = 1$.
	$\quad$ **While** ($b \leq |B'|$)
	$\quad\quad$ Select a batch with a sequence b in B'.
	$\quad\quad$ Schedule the batch to the machine according to the first-fit rule if the completion time does not exceed A.
	$\quad\quad$ **If** (Completion time of machine when the batch is scheduled > Completion time of machine when additionally scheduled RMA precedes the batch) **then**
	$\quad\quad\quad$ Schedule the RMA to precede the batch.
	$\quad\quad b = b + 1$.
	$\quad$ **End While**
	$\quad$ **If** (All batches in B' are scheduled) **then**
	$\quad\quad UB_{ct} = A$.
	$\quad$ **Else**
	$\quad\quad LB_{ct} = A$.
	$\quad h = h + 1$.
	End While
	Output the makespan of the global best solution.

Because the positioning of the RMAs and batches has a significant influence on the makespan, the MF algorithm does not perform well in solving this problem; therefore, we divide the batch scheduling problem into three stages and propose an ACO-based three-stage batch scheduling algorithm for solving it.

5. Ant Colony Optimization-Based Three-Stage Algorithm for Batch Scheduling Problem

The batch loading part of the BLSP referred to the solution of Jia et al. [2], and this section deals with the batch scheduling part. Determining the positioning of RMAs between all batches requires lots of calculations. If the number of buckets is pre-determined, however, the RMA positioning will be fixed between buckets. To reduce the computational complexity, we divide the batch scheduling problem into three stages, in which (1) the number of buckets is determined, (2) batches are assigned to the respective buckets, and (3) the buckets are dispatched to the machines.

5.1. Determining the Number of Buckets

In stage 1, the number of buckets is determined. Determining it fixes the positions of the RMAs between the buckets and it can range from zero to $|B| - 1$ in each machine. To reduce the range of this number, we calculate LB_k and UB_k, the lower and upper bounds, respectively, for the number of buckets during batch scheduling with the dispatching rule. The dispatching rule is the rule that selects the bucket with the shortest tentative completion time. Tentative completion time in each machine means the completion time if the current batch is assigned to the machine. The dispatching rule helps to search for the solution with good quality. A detailed explanation of the dispatching rule is given in Algorithm 2.

Algorithm 2. The dispatching rule

Input:	The processing time of batch P_b. The current completion time of buckets C_k.
Output:	Selected bucket k', which must be assigned by batch b

Begin:	Let bucket index $k = 1$
	While $(k \leq |K|)$
	    Calculate the tentative completion time using the RMA rule
	    $k = k + 1$
	End While
	Select the bucket k' with the smallest tentative completion time

To calculate the LB_k and UB_k in subsequent algorithm, we must calculate the minimum and the maximum numbers of batches that can be scheduled on one machine. We assume that the batch processing time can be determined between P_{min} and P_{max} during batch scheduling with the dispatching rule, then the minimum number of batches on a machine is calculated in Algorithm 3. P_{min} and P_{max} are the longest and shortest processing time of the given batches, respectively. In determining the minimum number of batches that can be scheduled to the first machine, the first machine should be assigned a minimum number of batches and the rest of the machines should be assigned as many batches as possible. To assign a small number of batches to the machine under the dispatching rule, the completion time of the machine should be tentatively set to a large value. Since the dispatching rule schedules a batch on a machine with a small tentatively completion time, the allocated batches in the first machine must be given the longest processing time as P_{max}. The lower bound on the number of batches input to the first machine is calculated using the dispatching rule in Algorithm 3.

Algorithm 3. Calculating the lower bound on the number of batches input to a machine

Input:	P_{min}; P_{max}; The number of batches; The number of machines.
Output:	Lower bound on the number of batches input to a machine.

Begin:	Let batch index $b = 1$
	While$(b \leq |B|)$
	    Select a machine m' using the dispatching rule.
	    If$(m' = 1)$ **then**
	        Assign a batch assuming the processing time is P_{max}.
	    Else
	        Assign a batch assuming the processing time is P_{min}.
	    $b = b + 1$.
	End While
	Output the number of batches in machine 1

Before calculating the LB_k using Algorithm 4, the batch deteriorations must be represented in order. A time-dependent batch deterioration can be represented as the product of DR and P_i. In this section, P_k and D_k represent the processing time and deterioration of a batch in sequence k, respectively. D_k and D_{k-1} can be represented by the processing time and the deterioration of previous batches as

$$D_k = DR \times \left(\sum_{i=1}^{k-1} P_i + \sum_{i=1}^{k-1} D_i \right), \tag{15}$$

$$D_{k-1} = DR \times \left(\sum_{i=1}^{k-2} P_i + \sum_{i=1}^{k-2} D_i \right). \tag{16}$$

By subtracting D_{k-1} from D_k, D_k can be given in terms of the processing time and the deterioration of the preceding batch as

$$D_k - D_{k-1} = DR \times (P_{k-1} + D_{k-1}), \tag{17}$$

and then D_k can be represented as

$$D_k = (1 + DR) \times D_{k-1} + DR \times P_{k-1}. \tag{18}$$

Using the above equations, the situation in which an RMA must be scheduled is defined through Proposition 1.

Proposition 1. *If the deterioration portion of a batch exceeds the processing time of an RMA scheduling an RMA before the batch will reduce the completion time of the bucket.*

Proof. Let $\widetilde{B}$ be a set of scheduled batches with no RMAs, which comprises $B_1, B_2 \ldots, B_n$. Let $\widetilde{B}'$ be a set of the same scheduled batches with one RMA, comprising $B'_1, B'_2 \ldots, B'_{l-1}$, RMA, $B'_l, \ldots, B'_n$. Deterioration of B'_i can be represented as D'_i. Except for the RMA in $\widetilde{B}'$, the processing time of batches in the same sequence as $\widetilde{B}$ are equal Thus, the sums of the deteriorations up to $l-1$ will be equal in both $\widetilde{B}$ and $\widetilde{B}'$ as follows:

$$\sum_{i=1}^{l-1} D_i = \sum_{i=1}^{l-1} D'_i. \tag{19}$$

As we assume that D_l is greater than Q, the sum of D'_l and Q is less than D_l:

$$D_l > D'_l + Q. \tag{20}$$

From Equation (19), the deteriorations of D_{l+1} and D'_{l+1} can be obtained as, respectively,

$$D_{l+1} = (1 + DR) \times D_l + DR \times P_l, \tag{21}$$

$$D'_{l+1} = (1 + DR) \times D'_l + DR \times P_l \tag{22}$$

Because the processing time of each batch is the same and $D'_l = 0$, D'_{l+1} is larger than D_{l+1}, repeating the above reasoning, D'_{l+2} is larger than D_{l+2}, D'_{l+3} is larger than D_{l+3}, ..., and D'_n is larger than D_n. Adding these deteriorations, we obtain

$$\sum_{i=l+1}^{n} D_i > \sum_{i=l+1}^{n} D'_i. \tag{23}$$

From Equations (20), (21) and (24), $D_1 + D_2 + \ldots + D_l + \ldots + D_n$ is larger than $D'_1 + D'_2 + \ldots + Q + D'_l + \ldots + D'_n$. Hence, the deterioration period of $\widetilde{B}$ is longer than that of $\widetilde{B}'$. □

The above proof gives the condition under which scheduling an RMA reduces the makespan. This can be used to find the minimum number of RMAs. If we set the processing time of each scheduled batch as P_{min}, then we can use Proposition 1 to schedule the RMAs starting from the first batch. The lower bound on the number of buckets can then be calculated based on the number of RMAs scheduled per machine using Algorithm 4.

Using these algorithms and propositions, we can obtain the LB_k for a machine. In a similar manner, UB_k can be calculated. Assuming a batch processing time of P_{min} for the first machine and P_{max} for the remaining machines in Algorithm 3, the upper bound on the number of batches per machine can be applied in Algorithm 4.

Algorithm 4. Calculating the lower bound on the number of buckets (LB_k)

Input:	P_{max}; the lower bound on the number of batches in a machine;
Output:	the lower bound on the number of RMAs required by a machine
Begin:	Let batch index $b = 1$
	Let RMA index $r = 0$
	While ($b \leq$ *The lower bound on the number of batches in a machine*)
	Calculate a tentative deterioration proportional to the gap between the preceding RMA and C_{b-1}
	If (Tentative deterioration $>$ Processing time of RMA) **then**
	Schedule RMA after C_{b-1}.
	$r = r + 1$.
	Else
	$C_b = (DR + 1) \times C_{b-1} + P_{max}$
	$b = b + 1$.
	End While
	Output $(r + 1) \times |M|$

5.2. Assigning Batches to Buckets

In stage 2, an ACO algorithm is used to assign batches to each bucket and then a rule is applied to determine the sequencing of the batches. Unlike the problem of assigning batches, the individual buckets do not have size capacities, and the objective function is the makespan. In this case, the batch deterioration has a significant influence on the makespan. Based on the number of buckets determined from stage 1, the batches must be scheduled using a load balancing among buckets.

To assign batches, an ACO algorithm called the min-max ant system (MMAS) is used. MMAS is a constructive meta-heuristic algorithm that builds solutions sequentially, i.e., to solve the batch assignment problem, the batches are assigned one by one. During the batch assignment, we make a probabilistic choice based on pheromone trails and heuristic information until no further batches are available. After assigning the batches, the minimum completion time of each bucket can be calculated using Proposition 2 (Section 5.2.5).

5.2.1. Pheromone Trails

The desirability of unscheduled batches can be calculated using a pheromone trail that gives the relationship between assigned batches. There is a pheromone trail value between all batches and a higher pheromone trail value indicates a higher probability that two batches will be allocated to the same bucket. Defining $\tau_{il}(t)$ as the pheromone trail between B_i and B_l in iteration t, $\tau_{il}(1)$ is initialized as

$$\tau_{il}(1) = ((1-\rho) \times LB_\tau)^{-1}, \qquad (24)$$

where ρ means evaporation rate and LB_τ is the lower bound given by

$$LB_\tau = \sum_{b \in B} \frac{P_b}{|M|} \qquad (25)$$

The desirability of a given batch is calculated using the pheromone trails between the given batch and batches, $B_k(t)$, that have already been assigned to the selected bucket in iteration t. The desirability of assigning batch i into the current bucket k during iteration t can be represented as

$$\theta_{ik}(t) = \sum_{B_l \in B_k(t)} \frac{\tau_{il}(t)}{|B_k(t)|}. \qquad (26)$$

5.2.2. Heuristic Information

The load balance of each bucket is important because the deterioration increases rapidly when many batches are allocated per bucket. The heuristic information between batch i and bucket k during iteration t can be represented by

$$\eta_{ik}(t) = \frac{1}{|\max\{c_k(t)\} - c_{k+i}(t)| + p_{max}}, \tag{27}$$

where $c_{k+i}(h)$ is the completion time of bucket k calculated after assigning batch i to it during iteration t.

5.2.3. Forming the Buckets

The pheromone trails and heuristic information are used together to calculate the probability that each batch can be formed. The probability that batch i can be assigned to bucket k during iteration t is expressed as $P_{ik}(t)$, which represents the desirability of the batches assigned to bucket k as follows:

$$P_{ik}(t) = \begin{cases} \frac{\theta_{ik}(t) \times \eta_{ik}(t)^\beta}{\sum_{B_i \in U_k} \theta_{ik}(t) \times \eta_{ik}(t)^\beta}, & \text{if } B_i \in U_k \\ 0, & \text{otherwise} \end{cases}, \tag{28}$$

where β represents the relative importance of heuristic information and U_k represents the set of unscheduled batches.

5.2.4. Updating the Pheromone Trails

In MMAS, the use of pheromone trails leads to solutions based on experience. Thus, updating the pheromone trails has a significant effect on the performance of the algorithm. Global- and iteration-best solutions are used to update the pheromone trails. Representing the frequency with which jobs i and l are placed in the same batch as m_{il}, the pheromone trail updating process can be defined as follows:

$$\tau_{il}(t+1) = (1-\rho) \times \tau_{il}(t) + m_{il} \times \Delta\tau_{il}(t), \tag{29}$$

$$\Delta\tau_{il}(t) = \frac{Q}{Makespan_{iteration\ best}(t)}. \tag{30}$$

The solutions corresponding to pheromone trails that are too extreme cannot be found easily. Under MMAS, pheromone trail lower and upper bounds are defined as τ_{min} and τ_{max}, respectively, and when the trails are updated, they are modulated as follows:

$$\tau_{il}(t+1) = \begin{cases} \tau_{min}, & \tau_{il}(t+1) < \tau_{min} \\ \tau_{il}(t+1), & \tau_{min} \le \tau_{il}(t+1) \le \tau_{max} \\ \tau_{max}, & \tau_{il}(t+1) > \tau_{max} \end{cases}, \tag{31}$$

$$\tau_{max} = \left((1-\rho) \times Makespan_{global\ best}(t)\right)^{-1}, \tag{32}$$

$$\tau_{min} = \frac{\tau_{max} \times \left(1 - \sqrt[|B|]{0.05}\right)}{\left(\frac{|B|}{2} - 1\right) \times \sqrt[|B|]{0.05}}. \tag{33}$$

5.2.5. Rule-Based Batch Sequencing

After assigning the batches to the buckets, the completion time of each bucket can be minimized using Proposition 2.

Proposition 2. *Let B be the set of batches in one bucket. Then, scheduling B in ascending order of processing time minimizes the completion time of each bucket.*

Proof. As the starting time of the first batch is zero, we have

$$D_1 = 0. \tag{34}$$

By applying the previous deterioration to Equation (16), we obtain

$$\begin{aligned} D_2 &= DR \times P_1 + (1+DR) \times D_1 \\ &= DR \times P_1, \end{aligned} \tag{35}$$

$$\begin{aligned} D_3 &= DR \times P_2 + (1+DR) \times D_2 \\ &= DR \times P_2 + (1+DR) \times DR \times P_1, \end{aligned} \tag{36}$$

$$\begin{aligned} D_4 &= DR \times P_3 + (1+DR) \times D_3 \\ &= DR \times P_3 + (1+DR) \times DR \times P_2 + (1+DR)^2 \times DR \times P_1, \end{aligned} \tag{37}$$

$$\begin{aligned} D_n &= DR \times P_{n-1} + (1+DR) \times DR \times P_{n-2} + \ldots + (1+DR)^{n-2} \times DR \times P_1 \\ &= \sum_{i=1}^{n-1} (1+DR)^{n-1-i} \times DR \times P_i. \end{aligned} \tag{38}$$

By using the generalized formula above, D_n, the sum of the deteriorations, can be represented as

$$\begin{aligned} \sum_{i=1}^{n} D_i &= D_2 + D_3 + D_4 + \ldots + D_n \\ &= [DR \times P_1] + [DR \times P_2 + (1+DR) \times DR \times P_1] + \ldots \\ &\quad + \sum_{i=1}^{n-1} (1+DR)^{n-1-i} \times DR \times P_i \\ &= \left[1 + (1+DR) + (1+DR)^2 + \ldots + (1+DR)^{n-2}\right] \times DR \times P_1 \\ &\quad + \left[1 + (1+DR) + (1+DR)^2 + \ldots + (1+DR)^{n-3}\right] \times DR \times P_2 \\ &\quad + \ldots + [1 + (1+DR)] \times DR \times P_{n-2} + DR \times P_{n-1} \\ &= \sum_{i=0}^{n-2} (1+DR)^i \times DR \times P_1 + \sum_{i=0}^{n-3} (1+DR)^i \times DR \times P_2 + \ldots \\ &\quad + \sum_{i=0}^{1} (1+DR)^i \times DR \times P_{n-2} + DR \times P_{n-1} \end{aligned} \tag{39}$$

In Equation (39), P_k, the processing time of a batch in sequence k, is multiplied by $\sum_{i=0}^{n-1-k}(1+DR)^i$. $\sum_{i=0}^{n-1-k}(1+DR)^i$ increases as the sequence become slower. As the batch we have to schedule is fixed, the total deterioration can be minimized by scheduling the batches with longer processing times in faster sequences. □

Using the above proof, we can obtain the shortest completion for each bucket. After all, once the shortest completion time of buckets is calculated, buckets must be scheduled to the machines.

5.3. Scheduling Buckets to Machines

In stage 3, buckets are scheduled to machines using the dispatching rule. Tentative timings are used to determine the completion time at which the current batch is scheduled using the RMA rule as Algorithm 2 (Section 5.1). To balance the load among the machines, therefore, the current batch should be scheduled to the machine with the shortest tentative completion time.

5.4. Overall Algorithm

Using the algorithms defined for the three stages in the preceding sections, the ACO-based three-stage algorithm can be defined as Algorithm 5.

Algorithm 5. ACO-based three-stage algorithm for batch scheduling problem

Input:	The set of assigned batches.
Output:	The makespan
	Compute the LB_K and UB_K, respectively.
	Compute the LB_τ and $\tau_{il}(1)$, respectively.
Begin:	Initialize pheromone trails.
	Let index of iteration $t = 1$
	While$(t \leq t_{max})$
	Let index of iteration $a = 1$
	While $(a \leq a_{max})$
	Select the number of buckets between LB_K and UB_K.
	While$(U_B \neq \varnothing)$
	Select bucket k using the dispatching rule.
	If (Bucket k has no assigned batches) **then**
	Select a batch b randomly.
	Assigned the batch b to bucket k.
	Else
	Select a batch b using pheromone trail and heuristic information.
	Assign the batch b to bucket k.
	End While
	Minimize the completion time of the buckets by sequencing the batches.
	Dispatch the buckets to machines.
	Calculate the makespan.
	Update the iteration and global best solutions
	$a = a + 1$
	End While
	Compute τ_{max} and τ_{min}.
	Update $\Delta \tau_{il}(h)$ and $\tau_{il}(h)$.
	$t = t + 1$
	End While
	Output the makespan of the global best solution

The algorithm divides the batch scheduling problem into three-stage. In stage 1, LB_K and UB_K are used for fast convergence. To demonstrate that LB_K and UB_K affect the performance of the algorithm, an ACO with no bound (ACO_NB) is proposed.

6. Genetic Algorithm- and Particle Swarm Optimization-Based Batch Scheduling Algorithms

In this section, two population-based meta-heuristic algorithms for solving the batch scheduling problem—a GA-based three-stage algorithm and a PSO-based three-stage algorithm—are proposed. Unlike constructively generated ACO solutions, these two algorithms search solutions to develop an encoded solution that is represented using a random key. The two proposed population-based meta-heuristic algorithms (Algorithms 6 and 7) are defined as follows.

Algorithm 6. GA-based three-stage algorithm for batch scheduling problem

Input:	The set of assigned batches from the batch loading problem
Output:	The makespan

Begin:	Compute the LB_K and UB_K respectively.
	Set the initial decoded solution.
	Let index of generation $t = 1$
	While $(t \leq t_{max})$
	    Let index of chromosome $c = 1$
	    While $(c \leq c_{max})$
	        Select the number of buckets between LB_K and UB_K.
	        Let random value $r_1 = Unif(0,1)$.
	        Let random value $r_2 = Unif(0,1)$.
	        Select two parent chromosomes, c, and $c+1$, in sequence.
	        If $(r_1 <$ Crossover rate) **then**
	            Do one-point crossover operations.
	        If $(r_2 <$ Mutation rate) **then**
	            Do swap mutation operation.
	        Decode the offspring chromosome c and calculate the makespan.
	        $c = c+1$
	    End While
	    Reproduce the next generation parents from current-generation offspring
	    Update the iteration and global best solutions
	    $t = t+1$
	End While
	Output the makespan of the global best solution

Algorithm 7. PSO-based three-stage algorithm for batch scheduling problem

Input:	The set of assigned batches from the batch loading problem
Output:	The makespan

Begin:	Compute the LB_K and UB_K, respectively.
	Set the initial solution.
	Let index of iteration $t = 1$
	While $(t \leq t_{max})$
	    Let index of particle $p = 1$
	    While $(p \leq p_{max})$
	        Select the number of buckets between LB_K and UB_K
	        Update the factor velocity
	        Update the factor position
	        Decode the particle p.
	        $p = p+1$
	    End While
	    Decode the particles.
	    Update the iteration and global best solutions;
	    $t = t+1$
	End While
	Output the makespan of global best solution

7. Computational Experiments

To evaluate the performance of the ACO-based three-stage batch scheduling algorithm, extensive computational experiments were conducted using the solutions obtained by an ACO-based batch loading algorithm presented in Jia et al. [2]. In the first experiment, the absolute differences between the optimal solutions produced by CPLEX and the solutions produced by the ACO, ACO_NB, GA, PSO, and MF algorithms were compared for small-sized problems. In the second experiment, ACO and ACO_NB were compared to validate the LB_k and UB_k used in the proposed algorithm. In the third experiment, the relative differences between the solutions obtained by ACO and other meta-heuristic algorithms,

GA and PSO, were compared for large-sized problems. All meta-heuristic algorithms are implemented in C#.

7.1. Problem Parameter Settings

In the experiments, BLSPs corresponding to the batch scheduling problem with varying complexity were randomly generated. The complexity of a batch scheduling problem with batch deterioration and RMAs is highly dependent on $|M|$, $|K|$, $|B|$, and $|F|$ [24–26]. Therefore, four problem parameters, $|M|$, $|K|/|M|$, $|B|/|K|$, and $|F|$, were used to generate problems with different complexities, where $|K|/|M|$ is the average number of buckets per machine and $|B|/|K|$ is the average number of batches per bucket. The machines and families were generated as $|M|$ and $|F|$, respectively, and the batches were generated using $|M| \times |K|/|M| \times |B|/|K|$. To assign $|B|/|K|$ batches to each bucket, Q was generated as $\frac{Q_{min}+Q_{max}}{2}$. As Q decreases, RMAs will occur more frequently and the number of batches per bucket will be reduced. To assign $|B|/|K|$ batches to each bucket, Q should be adjusted so that it falls between Q_{min} and Q_{max}, where those values mean the minimum and maximum sums of deteriorations that occur when there are $|B|/|K|$ batches, respectively. The sums can be calculated by assuming the processing time of batches as P_{min} and P_{max}, respectively. P_f is randomly generated in $[P_{min}, P_{max}]$ with P_{min} and P_{max} fixed at 40 and 60, respectively. D and $\overline{S_j}$ are fixed at 0.2 and 0.4, respectively. Using the four problem parameters defined above, two groups of problems (small-sized problems with fewer than 10 batches and large-sized problems with more than 10 batches) were randomly generated.

7.2. Algorithm Parameter Settings

To find the major parameters that affect the performance of algorithms, the Taguchi method was applied in this section. The method can be used to conduct experiments more rapidly than a full factorial experiment because the method can carry out experiments using fewer scenarios. Using the Taguchi method, five control factors for the ACO-based batch scheduling algorithm were analyzed. The levels of each control factor are listed in Table 2. The first factor, A, is the number of ants (Ant_{max}). When a problem becomes more complicated, more ants are needed to solve it. Therefore, we set Ant_{max} to increase according to the complexity of the problem; as the complexity was proportional to $|B|$, Ant_{max} is varied over the range $\{1.0 \times |B|, 1.5 \times |B|, 2.0 \times |B|, 2.5 \times |B|, 3.0 \times |B|\}$. The second factor, B, is the evaporation rate (ρ), which is used to calculate the initial pheromone trails and update later trails. Because the evaporation must be a real value between [0, 1] and values lower than 0.5 are relatively insignificant to the parameter settings, ρ is varied over $\{0.5, 0.6, 0.7, 0.8, 0.9\}$. The third factor, C, is the iteration limit (G), which indicates how many iterations are needed to reset a pheromone trail in the ACO. If there is no change in the global solution over G iterations, the trail must be reset and, therefore, smaller values of G mean that trails must be more often reset. In this paper, G is varied over $\{10, 30, 50, 70, 90\}$. The fourth factor, D, is the updating parameter (δ), which is used to update the pheromone trails. In a previous paper [2], δ performs better when it is based on LB_τ rather than a constant parameter. Therefore, δ is varied over $\{0.5 \times LB_\tau, 1.0 \times LB_\tau, 1.5 \times LB_\tau, 2.0 \times LB_\tau, 2.5 \times LB_\tau\}$. The final factor, E, is the relative importance of heuristic information (β), which is used in calculating desirability. β is varied over $\{4, 6, 8, 10, 12\}$.

Table 2. Factors levels for MMAS based three-stage batch scheduling algorithm.

Factor 1	Factor 2	Factor 3	Factor 4	Factor 5
Number of Ants	Evaporation Rate	Iteration Limit	Updating Parameter	Relative Importance of Heuristic Information
Ant_{max} (A)	ρ (B)	G (C)	δ (D)	β (E)
A (1): $1.0 \times |B|$	B (1): 0.5	C (1): 10	D (1): $0.5 \times LB_T$	E (1): 4
A (2): $1.5 \times |B|$	B (2): 0.6	C (2): 30	D (2): $1.0 \times LB_T$	E (2): 6
A (3): $2.0 \times |B|$	B (3): 0.7	C (3): 50	D (3): $1.5 \times LB_T$	E (3): 8
A (4): $2.5 \times |B|$	B (4): 0.8	C (4): 70	D (4): $2.0 \times LB_T$	E (4): 10
A (5): $3.0 \times |B|$	B (5): 0.9	C (5): 90	D (5): $2.5 \times LB_T$	E (5): 12

Using the control factors described above, an experiment involving 25 scenarios was conducted. The number of scenarios was chosen so that the best-fit design for five factors with five levels. Table 3 shows $L_{25}(5^5)$ orthogonal array. In each scenario, 12 test problems were solved three times each for a total of 900 runs for the experiment. Under the Taguchi method, variation in performance is measured using the mean signal-to-noise (S/N) ratio. Generally, the S/N ratio is expressed as $-10\log(objective\ function)^2$, but this formula was not directly applicable to this case because the experimental tests had varying objective functions and sizes. Therefore, we adopted the relative percentage deviation (RPD) of the objective function as follows:

$$RPD(\%) = \frac{OBJ_{sol} - OBJ_{best}}{OBJ_{best}} \times 100, \qquad (40)$$

where OBJ_{sol} is the objective function given by an algorithm and OBJ_{best} is the objective function of the best solution. Using the RPD, the S/N ratio can be computed as follows:

$$S/N\ ratio_k = -10\log\left(\frac{1}{12}\sum_{i=1}^{4}\sum_{j=1}^{3} RPD_{ijk}^2\right) \qquad \forall k \in 1,2,\ldots,2,D \qquad h\ the\ 12525. \qquad (41)$$

Table 3. Factor levels of array L_{25}.

Scenario No.	Factor Levels				
	A	B	C	D	E
1	A (1)	B (1)	C (1)	D (1)	E (1)
2	A (1)	B (2)	C (2)	D (2)	E (2)
3	A (1)	B (3)	C (3)	D (3)	E (3)
4	A (1)	B (4)	C (4)	D (4)	E (4)
5	A (1)	B (5)	C (5)	D (5)	E (5)
6	A (2)	B (1)	C (2)	D (3)	E (4)
7	A (2)	B (2)	C (3)	D (4)	E (5)
8	A (2)	B (3)	C (4)	D (5)	E (1)
9	A (2)	B (4)	C (5)	D (1)	E (2)
10	A (2)	B (5)	C (1)	D (2)	E (3)
11	A (3)	B (1)	C (3)	D (5)	E (2)
12	A (3)	B (2)	C (4)	D (1)	E (3)
13	A (3)	B (3)	C (5)	D (2)	E (4)
14	A (3)	B (4)	C (1)	D (3)	E (5)
15	A (3)	B (5)	C (2)	D (4)	E (1)
16	A (4)	B (1)	C (4)	D (2)	E (5)
17	A (4)	B (2)	C (5)	D (3)	E (1)
18	A (4)	B (3)	C (1)	D (4)	E (2)
19	A (4)	B (4)	C (2)	D (5)	E (3)

Table 3. *Cont.*

Scenario No.	Factor Levels				
	A	B	C	D	E
20	A (4)	B (5)	C (3)	D (1)	E (4)
21	A (5)	B (1)	C (5)	D (4)	E (3)
22	A (5)	B (2)	C (1)	D (5)	E (4)
23	A (5)	B (3)	C (2)	D (1)	E (5)
24	A (5)	B (4)	C (3)	D (2)	E (1)
25	A (5)	B (5)	C (4)	D (3)	E (2)

To analyze statistically significant factors, analysis of variance (ANOVA) was performed using the S/N ratio data. The factor D, which had the smallest sum squares (SS) was selected as the error term. After pooling this factor, ANOVA was performed, the results of which are listed in Table 4. Factors B and E exceeded the significance level, indicating that they had a large effect on the algorithm performance. The levels of these factors with the highest S/N ratios—B (5) and E (5)—were identified based on an examination of the S/N results in Figure 2. The factors and levels A (4), C (3), and D (1) had the least effect on the performance, as reflected by the *RPD* values shown in Figure 3. From these results, we identified an optimal combination of A (4), B (5), C (3), D (1), and E (5).

Table 4. Analysis of variance for the S/N ratio.

Factor	SS	df	V	F_0	*p*-Value
A	0.2593	4	0.0648	2.6456	0.1844
B	1.4578	4	0.3644	14.8721	0.0114
C	0.1809	4	0.0452	1.8459	0.2836
D(Error)	0.0980		0.0245		
E	0.2144	4	0.5360	21.8756	0.0055
Total	4.1404	20			

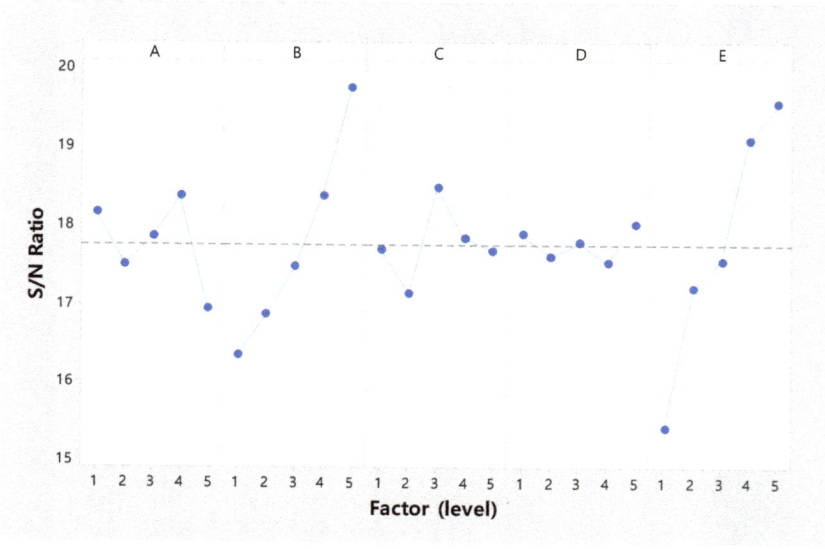

Figure 2. The mean S/N ratio plot for each level of the factor.

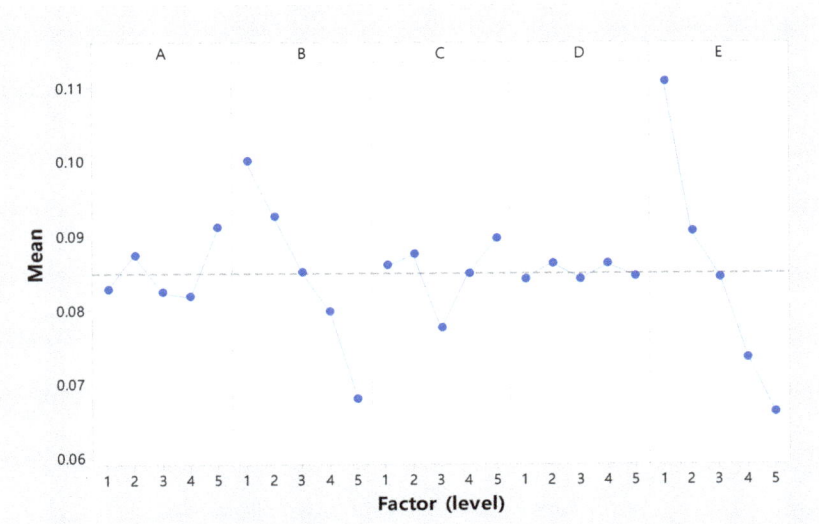

Figure 3. The mean RPD plot for each level of the factors.

The GA and PSO parameters were also set using the Taguchi method. For the GA, the parameters population size $= 3 \times |B|$, crossover rate $= 0.9$, and mutation rate $= 0.2$ were set. For the PSO, the parameters population size $= 3 \times |B|$, inertia weight $= 0.9$, social cognitive 1 $= 1.0$, and social cognitive 2 $= 0.5$ were set.

7.3. Experimental Results

Three experiments were conducted to validate the ACO-based three-stage batch scheduling algorithm. All of the experiments were carried out on a PC with an Intel Core i7-7700 CPU running at 3.6 GHz with 16 GB of memory. In each experiment, the batch scheduling problem with the same problem instance was solved using the same given solution obtained from the ACO-based batch loading algorithm. All the algorithms were run until iteration reached 1500 or performance did not increase for 100 iterations.

In the first experiment, the ACO, ACO_NB, GA, PSO, and MF algorithms were validated by comparing their solutions with optimal solutions produced by ILOG CPLEX. The experiment was conducted on eight small-sized problems with 30 replications, with the results summarized in Table 5. To compare the performance of the respective algorithms, the RPD values were calculated using the optimal solution obtained from CPLEX. In the table, "N/A" denotes cases in which CPLEX was unable to obtain the optimal solution before 7200s. The problems with more than eight batches could not be solved by ILOG CPLEX. For problems with fewer than eight batches, the average RPD values of ACO, ACO_NB, GA, and PSO were zero whereas the average for the MF algorithm was 2.16. The result indicates that the meta-heuristic algorithms provided optimal solutions to small-sized problems. However, the MF algorithm performed poorly even on small-sized problems.

In the second experiment, the relative performances of ACO and ACO_NB in solving large-sized problems were compared to validate the LB_k and UB_k values obtained in stage 1. The experiment was conducted on 36 large-sized problems with 30 replications. The results are summarized in Table 6. To validate the results, a paired t-test ($\alpha = 0.05$) was conducted to statistically evaluate the differences in performance between ACO and ACO_NB. The results of the paired t-tests are listed in Table 7. ACO significantly outperformed ACO_NB because it is seen from the table that all of the p-values are less than 0.05. The differences between the results obtained by ACO and ACO_NB are dependent upon the calculated values of LB_k and UB_k, respectively. To demonstrate that the use of LB_k and UB_k quickly converge $|K|$ and the makespan, the performance improvements obtained at different levels of $|F|$ are shown in Figure 4, in which the average makespan and $|K|$ are presented for five iterations of ACO and ACO_NB, respectively. The results demonstrate that the makespan converges faster under ACO than under ACO_NB because the $|K|$ from ACO rapidly converges to an optimal value between LB_k and UB_k.

Table 5. The test results of small-sized problems.

$|M|$	$\frac{|K|}{|M|}$	$\frac{|B|}{|K|}$	CPLEX		ACO		ACO_NB		GA		PSO		MF
			Opt.	Time	RPD	Time	RPD	Time	RPD	Time	RPD	Time	RPD
1	1	1	65	0.02	0.00	0.01	0.00	0.01	0.00	0.02	0.00	0.01	0.00
1	1	2	217.2	0.24	0.00	0.01	0.00	0.01	0.00	0.02	0.00	0.01	0.73
1	2	1	149	0.14	0.00	0.01	0.00	0.01	0.00	0.02	0.00	0.01	0.00
1	2	2	423	5.93	0.00	0.01	0.00	0.01	0.00	0.02	0.00	0.01	3.30
2	1	1	136	0.12	0.00	0.01	0.00	0.01	0.00	0.03	0.00	0.01	0.73
2	1	2	246	8.85	0.00	0.01	0.00	0.01	0.00	0.03	0.00	0.01	9.75
2	2	1	219	9.412	0.00	0.01	0.00	0.01	0.00	0.03	0.00	0.01	2.73
2	2	2	N/A	7200+	N/A		N/A		N/A		N/A		N/A
Avg.					0.00	0.01	0.00	0.01	0.00	0.02	0.00	0.01	2.16

Table 6. The test results of large-sized problems.

$|F|$	$|M|$	$\frac{|K|}{|M|}$	$\frac{|B|}{|K|}$	Best	ACO		ACO_NB		GA		PSO	
					RPD	Time	RPD	Time	RPD	Time	RPD	Time
4	3	3	3	964.68	0.08	0.50	0.08	0.48	0.59	0.22	2.16	0.15
4	3	3	4	1458.448	0.00	1.09	0.00	1.10	0.96	0.42	1.10	0.28
4	3	4	3	1402.04	0.29	1.19	0.29	1.17	0.07	0.55	1.55	0.39
4	3	4	4	1776.96	1.36	2.62	1.39	3.37	0.15	1.03	1.89	0.56
4	4	3	3	859.28	0.00	0.65	0.00	0.69	0.43	0.38	0.47	0.27
4	4	3	4	1498.52	0.22	3.49	0.30	3.23	0.48	1.21	2.73	0.60
4	4	4	3	1218.04	0.00	1.40	0.00	1.48	1.54	0.53	1.28	0.54
4	4	4	4	1806.64	0.51	7.96	0.53	6.81	0.14	2.34	1.80	1.28
4	5	3	3	953.6	0.00	1.00	0.00	1.14	0.39	0.72	0.39	0.46
4	5	3	4	1383.896	0.00	3.50	0.00	3.19	1.08	1.01	1.07	0.92
4	5	4	3	1324.6	0.64	3.72	0.67	3.74	0.10	1.97	1.96	0.94
4	5	4	4	1924.68	0.00	7.12	0.00	6.75	0.73	2.62	0.82	1.76
5	3	3	3	944	0.00	0.28	0.00	0.31	0.79	0.22	0.91	0.14
5	3	3	4	1347.904	0.08	1.28	0.09	1.30	0.32	0.53	2.29	0.25
5	3	4	3	1168.44	0.12	1.12	0.14	1.08	0.27	0.54	1.58	0.29
5	3	4	4	1922.64	0.00	3.32	0.01	2.91	0.86	1.17	1.03	0.58
5	4	3	3	966	0.00	0.64	0.00	0.78	0.56	0.43	0.59	0.27
5	4	3	4	1583.16	0.61	3.52	0.60	3.26	0.27	1.31	1.27	0.53
5	4	4	3	1206.48	0.00	1.86	0.00	1.94	1.42	0.56	1.13	0.55
5	4	4	4	1733.96	0.00	5.08	0.00	4.52	1.54	1.68	1.67	1.03
5	5	3	3	977.6	0.73	1.80	0.78	2.18	0.22	0.89	3.51	0.52
5	5	3	4	1360.248	0.06	5.22	0.10	5.39	1.05	2.51	2.31	0.97
5	5	4	3	1152	0.00	2.76	0.00	2.98	1.06	0.89	0.73	0.90
5	5	4	4	1827.6	0.11	15.07	0.16	14.06	0.10	4.65	1.64	2.09
6	3	3	3	990.92	0.72	0.55	0.73	0.57	0.36	0.31	2.20	0.16
6	3	3	4	1449.64	0.06	1.47	0.07	1.52	0.31	0.66	0.92	0.27
6	3	4	3	1300.6	0.00	0.62	0.00	0.71	0.45	0.39	0.52	0.28
6	3	4	4	1932.56	0.02	3.25	0.02	2.99	0.80	1.43	0.95	0.53
6	4	3	3	915.04	0.08	1.14	0.11	0.95	0.25	0.54	1.72	0.26
6	4	3	4	1382.528	0.26	3.27	0.27	3.73	1.48	1.35	2.98	0.52
6	4	4	3	1286.6	0.00	1.52	0.00	1.67	0.35	0.93	0.41	0.66
6	4	4	4	1959.84	0.06	8.84	0.08	7.50	1.33	3.27	2.65	1.33
6	5	3	3	962.8	0.00	1.35	0.01	1.66	0.64	0.73	0.67	0.47
6	5	3	4	1437.832	0.32	5.16	0.38	5.81	1.74	1.83	2.33	0.90
6	5	4	3	1306.64	0.06	4.24	0.06	4.35	0.21	1.90	1.19	1.02
6	5	4	4	1919.76	0.08	13.48	0.09	12.55	0.40	4.64	1.88	1.91
Avg.					0.18	3.36	0.19	3.27	0.65	1.29	1.51	0.68

Table 7. Paired *t*-test between ACO_NB-ACO.

	N	Mean	St. Dev.	St. e. Mean	Lower	*t*-Value	*p*-Value
Paired *t*-test for ACO_NB-ACO					0.16	3.75	0.001
ACO_NB	36	1386.2	337.0	56.2			
ACO	36	1385.8	336.8	56.1			
Difference	36	0.35	0.56	0.09			

In the third experiment, the results produced by ACO, GA, and PSO in solving large-sized problems were relatively compared. The experiment was conducted on the same large-sized problems used in the second experiment, and the average RPD values obtained by ACO, GA, and PSO were 0.18, 0.65, and 1.51 in Table 6, respectively. These results indicate that ACO obtained better RPD values than GA and PSO. However, it took more computing time for it to obtain the best feasible solutions because, despite the fact that the algorithm generally converges quickly to the best solution, ACO requires a considerable amount of computing time to execute the proposed MMAS algorithm within one pheromone search iteration. In our batch scheduling problem, the calculation of desirability under the MMAS algorithm exponentially increases the algorithm running time when $|B|/|K|$ increases.

To determine whether the application of GA or PSO could result in an improved solution, an additional experiment in which the computing times for GA and PSO were extended until the ACO solution converged was conducted. Using the input data from the large-sized problem, GA and PSO were retested, with the results summarized in Table 8. The average RPD values produced by ACO, GA, and PSO were 0.33, 0.48, 1.55, respectively, indicating that applying GA and PSO could not improve the ACO solution quality even if they were provided with additional computing time. To statistically validate the results in Table 8, *t*-tests were conducted to verify the differences in performance between ACO and the other meta-heuristics. As the same instance of the problem was used in each case, a paired *t*-test ($\alpha = 0.05$) was conducted. The results of paired *t*-testing between PSO-ACO and GA-ACO are shown in Table 9. In both cases, the *p*-values are less than 0.05, suggesting that ACO performed significantly better than either PSO or GA.

Table 8. The mean RPD of large-sized problems with an equal running time.

|F|	ACO	GA	PSO
4	0.35	0.51	1.36
5	0.40	0.42	1.66
6	0.23	0.51	1.63
Average	0.33	0.48	1.55

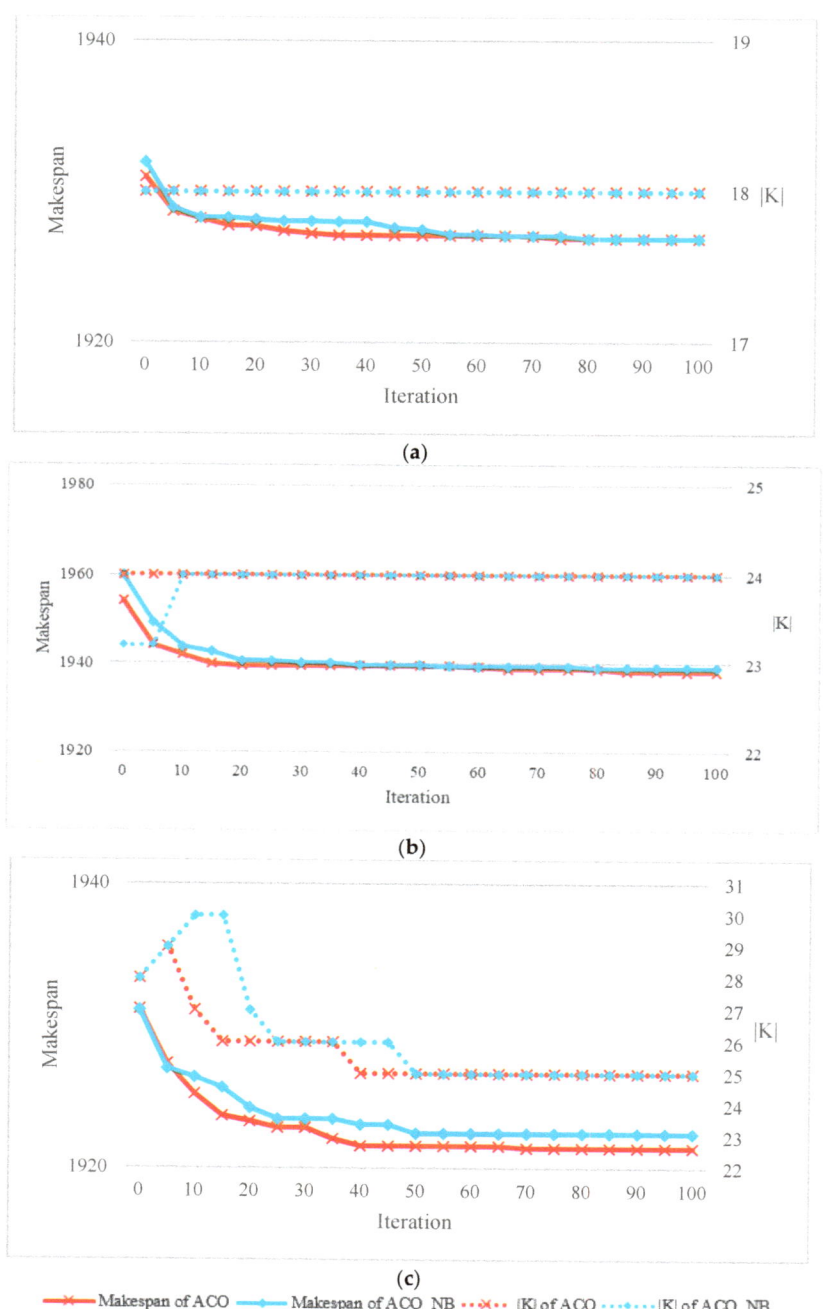

Figure 4. Convergence of ACO and ACO_NB in each level for $|F|$. (**a**) Convergence of algorithms with the instance as $|F| = 4$. (**b**) Convergence of algorithms with the instance as $|F| = 5$. (**c**) Convergence of algorithms with the instance as $|F| = 6$.

Table 9. Paired t-test between PSO-ACO and GA-ACO.

	N	Mean	St. Dev.	St. e. Mean	Lower	t-Value	p-Value
Paired t-test for PSO-ACO					15.577	18.04	0.000
PSO	180	1403.6	339.0	25.3			
ACO	180	1386.1	332.6	24.8			
Difference	180	17.490	13.009	0.970			
Paired t-test for GA-ACO					0.209	2.21	0.029
GA	180	1388.1	332.5	24.8			
ACO	180	1386.1	332.6	24.8			
Difference	180	1.987	12.090	0.901			

8. Conclusions

In this paper, we considered a BLSP for parallel BPMs with batch deterioration and applied RMAs. In the proposed BLSP, the time-dependent deterioration occurring during batch processing and the need to schedule RMAs between all batches increases the complexity of the batch scheduling problem. As an MF algorithm from a previous paper could not find an optimal solution to even small-sized versions of this problem, we solved the batch scheduling problem by dividing it into three stages, determining the number of buckets, assigning the batches to buckets, and scheduling the buckets to machines. Determining the number of buckets fixes the position of the RMAs and reduces the complexity of the batch scheduling problem. The lower and upper bounds of the number of buckets, LB_k and UB_k, respectively, are calculated to improve the solution performance and increase the speed of convergence. To schedule batches into a fixed number of buckets, an ACO is used to assign batches and a derived rule is used to sequence the batches. In solving the batch assignment problem, the ACO outperformed both GA and PSO. Finally, a dispatching rule is used to schedule buckets to the machines. Using this three-stage ACO-based batch scheduling algorithm, the proposed method finds optimal solutions for small-sized problems and provides better-quality solutions for large-size problems than can be obtained using other meta-heuristics.

Author Contributions: Conceptualization, B.S.K.; methodology, J.W.J.; software, J.W.J.; validation, B.S.K.; formal analysis, J.W.J.; investigation, B.S.K. and J.W.J.; resources, B.S.K.; project administration: B.S.K.; data curation, J.W.J.; writing—original draft preparation, J.W.J.; writing—review and editing, B.S.K. and Y.J.K.; visualization, J.W.J. and Y.J.K.; supervision, B.S.K. All authors have read and agreed to the published version of the manuscript.

Funding: This research was supported by the Basic Science Research Program through the National Research Foundation of Korea (NRF) funded by the Ministry of Science, ICT and Future Planning (grant number NRF-2019R1F1A1056119).

Institutional Review Board Statement: Not applicable.

Informed Consent Statement: Not applicable.

Data Availability Statement: Not applicable.

Conflicts of Interest: The authors declare no conflict of interest.

References

1. Uzsoy, R. Scheduling batch processing machines with incompatible job families. *Int. J. Prod. Res.* **1995**, *33*, 2685–2708. [CrossRef]
2. Jia, Z.; Wang, C.; Leung, J.Y.T. An ACO algorithm for makespan minimization in parallel batch machines with non-identical job sizes and incompatible job families. *Appl. Soft Comput.* **2016**, *38*, 395–404. [CrossRef]
3. Lee, C.Y.; Leon, V.J. Machine scheduling with a rate-modifying activity. *Eur. J. Oper. Res.* **2001**, *128*, 119–128. [CrossRef]
4. Joo, C.M.; Kim, B.S. Genetic algorithms for single machine scheduling with time-dependent deterioration and rate-modifying activities. *Expert Syst. Appl.* **2013**, *40*, 3036–3043. [CrossRef]

5. Dupont, L.; Ghazvini, F.J. Minimizing makespan on a single batch processing machine with non-identical job sizes. *J. Eur. Des Systèmes Autom.* **1998**, *32*, 431–440.
6. Zhou, S.; Chen, H.; Li, X. Distance matrix based heuristics to minimize makespan of parallel batch processing machines with arbitrary job sizes and release times. *Appl. Soft Comput. J.* **2017**, *52*, 630–641. [CrossRef]
7. Dupont, L.; Dhaenens-Flipo, C. Minimizing the makespan on a batch machine with non-identical job sizes: An exact procedure. *Comput. Oper. Res.* **2002**, *29*, 807–819. [CrossRef]
8. Ikura, Y.; Gimple, M. Efficient scheduling algorithms for a single batch processing machine. *Oper. Res. Lett.* **1986**, *5*, 61–65. [CrossRef]
9. Lee, C.Y.; Uzsoy, R.; Martin-Vega, L.A. Efficient algorithms for scheduling semiconductor burn-in operations. *Oper. Res.* **1992**, *40*, 764–775. [CrossRef]
10. Cheng, B.; Wang, Q.; Yang, S.; Hu, X. An improved ant colony optimization for scheduling identical parallel batching machines with arbitrary job sizes. *Appl. Soft Comput. J.* **2013**, *13*, 765–772. [CrossRef]
11. Uzsoy, R. Scheduling a single batch processing machine with non-identical job sizes. *Int. J. Prod. Res.* **1994**, *32*, 1615–1635. [CrossRef]
12. Jia, Z.; Li, X.; Leung, J.Y.T. Minimizing makespan for arbitrary size jobs with release times on P-batch machines with arbitrary capacities. *Future Gener. Comput. Syst.* **2017**, *67*, 22–34. [CrossRef]
13. Ozturk, O.; Begen, M.A.; Zaric, G.S. A branch and bound algorithm for scheduling unit size jobs on parallel batching machines to minimize makespan. *Int. J. Prod. Res.* **2017**, *55*, 1815–1831. [CrossRef]
14. Jia, Z.; Yan, J.; Leung, J.Y.T.; Li, K.; Chen, H. Ant colony optimization algorithm for scheduling jobs with fuzzy processing time on parallel batch machines with different capacities. *Appl. Soft Comput. J.* **2019**, *75*, 548–561. [CrossRef]
15. Arroyo, J.E.C.; Leung, J.Y.T. Scheduling unrelated parallel batch processing machines with non-identical job sizes and unequal ready times. *Comput. Oper. Res.* **2017**, *78*, 117–128. [CrossRef]
16. Arroyo, J.E.C.; Leung, J.Y.T. An effective iterated greedy algorithm for scheduling unrelated parallel batch machines with non-identical capacities and unequal ready times. *Comput. Ind. Eng.* **2017**, *105*, 84–100. [CrossRef]
17. Arroyo, J.E.C.; Leung, J.Y.T.; Tavares, R.G. An iterated greedy algorithm for total flow time minimization in unrelated parallel batch machines with unequal job release times. *Eng. Appl. Artif. Intell.* **2019**, *77*, 239–254. [CrossRef]
18. Gao, Y.; Yuan, J. Unbounded parallel-batch scheduling under agreeable release and processing to minimize total weighted number of tardy jobs. *J. Comb. Optim.* **2019**, *38*, 698–711. [CrossRef]
19. Zhou, S.; Xie, J.; Du, N.; Pang, Y. A random-keys genetic algorithm for scheduling unrelated parallel batch processing machines with different capacities and arbitrary job sizes. *Appl. Math. Comput.* **2018**, *334*, 254–268. [CrossRef]
20. Li, X.; Zhang, K. Single batch processing machine scheduling with two-dimensional bin packing constraints. *Int. J. Prod. Econ.* **2018**, *196*, 113–121. [CrossRef]
21. Fu, R.; Tian, J.; Li, S.; Yuan, J. An optimal online algorithm for the parallel-batch scheduling with job processing time compatibilities. *J. Comb. Optim.* **2017**, *34*, 1187–1197. [CrossRef]
22. Azizoglu, M.; Webster, S. Scheduling a batch processing machine with incompatible job families. *Comput. Ind. Eng.* **2001**, *39*, 325–335. [CrossRef]
23. Yao, S.; Jiang, Z.; Li, N. A branch and bound algorithm for minimizing total completion time on a single batch machine with incompatible job families and dynamic arrivals. *Comput. Oper. Res.* **2012**, *39*, 939–951. [CrossRef]
24. Jolai, F. Minimizing number of tardy jobs on a batch processing machine with incompatible job families. *Eur. J. Oper. Res.* **2005**, *162*, 184–190. [CrossRef]
25. Balasubramanian, H.; Mönch, L.; Fowler, J.; Pfund, M. Genetic algorithm based scheduling of parallel batch machines with incompatible job families to minimize total weighted tardiness. *Int. J. Prod. Res.* **2004**, *42*, 1621–1638. [CrossRef]
26. Li, X.L.; Li, Y.P.; Huang, Y.L. Heuristics for minimizing maximum lateness on a batch processing machine with incompatible job families. *Comput. Oper. Res.* **2019**, *106*, 91–101. [CrossRef]
27. Ham, A.; Fowler, J.W.; Cakici, E. Constraint programming approach for scheduling jobs with release times, non-identical sizes, and incompatible families on parallel batching machines. *IEEE Trans. Semicond. Manuf.* **2017**, *30*, 500–507. [CrossRef]
28. Vimala Rani, M.; Mathirajan, M. Performance evaluation of ATC based greedy heuristic algorithms in scheduling diffusion furnace in wafer fabrication. *J. Inf. Optim. Sci.* **2016**, *37*, 717–762. [CrossRef]
29. Gupta, J.N.D.; Gupta, S.K. Single facility scheduling with nonlinear processing times. *Comput. Industiral Eng.* **1988**, *14*, 387–393. [CrossRef]
30. Ding, J.; Shen, L.; Lü, Z.; Peng, B. Parallel machine scheduling with completion-time-based criteria and sequence-dependent deterioration. *Comput. Oper. Res.* **2019**, *103*, 35–45. [CrossRef]
31. Browne, S.; Yechiali, U. Scheduling deteriorating jobs on a single processor. *Oper. Res.* **1990**, *38*, 495–498. [CrossRef]
32. Soleimani, H.; Ghaderi, H.; Tsai, P.W.; Zarbakhshnia, N.; Maleki, M. Scheduling of unrelated parallel machines considering sequence-related setup time, start time-dependent deterioration, position-dependent learning and power consumption minimization. *J. Clean. Prod.* **2020**, *249*, 119428. [CrossRef]
33. Joo, C.M.; Kim, B.S. Machine scheduling of time-dependent deteriorating jobs with determining the optimal number of rate modifying activities and the position of the activities. *J. Adv. Mech. Des. Syst. Manuf.* **2015**, *9*, JAMDSM0007. [CrossRef]

4. Woo, Y.B.; Jung, S.W.; Kim, B.S. A rule-based genetic algorithm with an improvement heuristic for unrelated parallel machine scheduling problem with time-dependent deterioration and multiple rate-modifying activities. *Comput. Ind. Eng.* **2017**, *109*, 179–190. [CrossRef]
5. Abdullah, M.; Süer, G.A. Consideration of skills in assembly lines and seru production systems. *Asian J. Manag. Sci. Appl.* **2019**, *4*, 99–123. [CrossRef]
6. Gai, Y.; Yin, Y.; Tang, J.; Liu, S. Minimizing makespan of a production batch within concurrent systems: Seru production perspective. *J. Manag. Sci. Eng.* **2020**, in press. [CrossRef]
7. Liu, F.; Niu, B.; Xing, M.; Wu, L.; Feng, Y. Optimal cross-trained worker assignment for a hybrid seru production system to minimize makespan and workload imbalance. *Comput. Ind. Eng.* **2021**, *160*, 107552. [CrossRef]

Article

JMA: Nature-Inspired Java Macaque Algorithm for Optimization Problem

Dinesh Karunanidy [1], Subramanian Ramalingam [2], Ankur Dumka [3], Rajesh Singh [4], Mamoon Rashid [5,*], Anita Gehlot [4], Sultan S. Alshamrani [6] and Ahmed Saeed AlGhamdi [7]

[1] Department of Computer Science & Technology, Madanapalle Institute of Technology and Science, Madanapalle 517325, India; drdineshk@mits.ac.in
[2] Department of Computer Science & Engineering, Pondicherry University, Puducherry 605014, India; drrajakumarr@mits.ac.in
[3] Department of Computer Science and Engineering, Women's Institute of Technology, Dehradun 248007, India; ankurdumka2@gmail.com
[4] Department of Research and Development, Uttaranchal Institute of Technology, Uttaranchal University, Dehradun 248007, India; drrajeshsingh004@gmail.com (R.S.); dranitagehlot@gmail.com (A.G.)
[5] Department of Computer Engineering, Faculty of Science and Technology, Vishwakarma University, Pune 411048, India
[6] Department of Information Technology, College of Computer and Information Technology, Taif University, P.O. Box 11099, Taif 21944, Saudi Arabia; susamash@tu.edu.sa
[7] Department of Computer Engineering, College of Computer and Information Technology, Taif University, P.O. Box 11099, Taif 21994, Saudi Arabia; asjannah@tu.edu.sa
* Correspondence: mamoon.rashid@vupune.ac.in; Tel.: +91-7814346505

Abstract: In recent years, optimization problems have been intriguing in the field of computation and engineering due to various conflicting objectives. The complexity of the optimization problem also dramatically increases with respect to a complex search space. Nature-Inspired Optimization Algorithms (NIOAs) are becoming dominant algorithms because of their flexibility and simplicity in solving the different kinds of optimization problems. Hence, the NIOAs may be struck with local optima due to an imbalance in selection strategy, and which is difficult when stabilizing exploration and exploitation in the search space. To tackle this problem, we propose a novel Java macaque algorithm that mimics the natural behavior of the Java macaque monkeys. The Java macaque algorithm uses a promising social hierarchy-based selection process and also achieves well-balanced exploration and exploitation by using multiple search agents with a multi-group population, male replacement, and learning processes. Then, the proposed algorithm extensively experimented with the benchmark function, including unimodal, multimodal, and fixed-dimension multimodal functions for the continuous optimization problem, and the Travelling Salesman Problem (TSP) was utilized for the discrete optimization problem. The experimental outcome depicts the efficiency of the proposed Java macaque algorithm over the existing dominant optimization algorithms.

Keywords: continuous optimization problem; discrete optimization problem; grey wolf optimizer; Java macaque algorithm; nature-inspired algorithm

MSC: 68U01

Citation: Karunanidy, D.; Ramalingam, S.; Dumka, A.; Singh, R.; Rashid, M.; Gehlot, A.; Alshamrani, S.S.; AlGhamdi, A.S. JMA: Nature-Inspired Java Macaque Algorithm for Optimization Problem. *Mathematics* **2022**, *10*, 688. https://doi.org/10.3390/math10050688

Academic Editors: Alexander A Lazarev, Frank Werner and Bertrand M.T. Lin

Received: 25 December 2021
Accepted: 12 February 2022
Published: 23 February 2022

Publisher's Note: MDPI stays neutral with regard to jurisdictional claims in published maps and institutional affiliations.

Copyright: © 2022 by the authors. Licensee MDPI, Basel, Switzerland. This article is an open access article distributed under the terms and conditions of the Creative Commons Attribution (CC BY) license (https://creativecommons.org/licenses/by/4.0/).

1. Introduction

Nature-Inspired Optimization Algorithms (NIOAs) are one of the dominant techniques used due to their simplicity and flexibility in solving large-scale optimization problems [1]. The search process of the nature-inspired optimization algorithms was developed based on the behavior or processes encountered from nature. Notably, the NIOAs have emphasised the significant collection of algorithms, like the evolutionary algorithm (EA), swarm intelligence (SI), physical algorithm, and bio-inspired algorithm. These algorithms have illustrated their efficiency in solving wide variants of real-world problems [2]. A variety of nature-inspired optimization algorithms, such as the Genetic Algorithm (GA) [3], Differential Evolution (DE) [4], Ant Colony Optimization (ACO) [5] Artificial Bee Colony (ABC) [6], Particle Swarm Optimization (PSO) [7], Firefly Algorithm (FA) [8], Cuckoo Search (CO) [9], Bat Algorithm [10], Monkey Algorithm (MA) [11], Spider Monkey Algorithm (SMO) [12], Reptile Search Algorithm (RSA) [13], Membrane Computing (MC) [2], and whale optimization [14] use simple local searches for convoluted learning procedures to tackle complex real-world problems.

The complexity of real-world problems increases with the current scenario. Hence, the nature-inspired optimization algorithm has to find the best feasible solution with respect to the decision and objective space of the optimization problem. The increase in a decision variable may directly increase the size of the problem space. Then the complexity of the search space is also exponentially increased due to an increase in decision variables. Similarly, the search space will also increase due to an increase in the number of objectives [1]. Thus, the performance of the optimization algorithms will depend on two major components, as follows [15]: (i) the exploration used to generate the candidate solution to explore the search space globally; and (ii) the exploitation used to focus on exploiting the search space in the local region to find the optimal solution in the particular region. Thus, it is of essential importance for the optimization algorithm to acquire an equilibrium between the exploitation and exploration for solving different kinds of the optimization problem [16].

2. Literature Survey

Many optimization algorithms in the literature have been modified from the initial version to a hybrid model in order to tackle the balance between exploration and exploitation [17,18]. For example, we consider the most famous nature-inspired optimizations, such as GA, PSO, DE, ABC, and the most recent algorithms, such as the grey wolf-optimizer, reptile search algorithm, Spider Monkey Algorithm, and whale optimization algorithm. The main operators of the genetic algorithm are selection, crossover, and mutation [19]. Many authors [20] in the literature have proposed novel crossover operators in order to adjust the exploration capability of the genetic algorithm. Then, the selection process [21] and mutation operators [22,23] have been modified by authors in order to maintain a diverse and converged population. The author in the Ref. [24] proposed a special chromosome design based on a mixed-graph model to address the complex scheduling problem, and this technique enhances the heuristic behaviour of a genetic algorithm. Further, the genetic algorithm is combined with other techniques in order to improve its performance, such as a self-organization map [25,26], adaptive techniques [27], and other optimization algorithms [28]. These operators help to attain a balance over convergence and randomness to find the optimal results [29]. However, the convergence depends on the mutation operator because of its dual nature, that is, it either slows down the convergence or attains the global optima. Thus, fine-tuning the operators concerning the optimization problem is quite difficult [30].

The next feasible approach for solving the optimization problem is differential evolution. It also uses vector-based operators in the search process. However, the mutation operator shows its dominance over the search process by contributing to the weighted divergence between two individuals. The selection procedures of the DE have a crucial impact on the search process and also influences diversity among the parents and offspring [31]. However, the author in the Ref. [32] developed a new technique based on self-adaptive differential evolution with weighted strategies to address these large-scale problems. In the Particle Swarm Optimizer (PSO) [7], the selection process of a global best seems to play a vital role in finding the global optimal solution—that is, it can accelerate the convergence, or it can lead to premature convergence. ACO is based on the pheromone trails, such as trail-leaving and trail-after practices of ants, in which every ant sees synthetic pheromone fixations on the earth, and acts by probabilistic selecting bearings focused around the accessible pheromone fixation. However, the search process of the ACO is well-suited for exploration, whereas the exploitation has considerably lower importance [33].

The Artificial Immune System (AIS) [34] is mimicked by the biological behavior of the immune system. The AIS uses the unsupervised learning technique obtained from the immune cell over the infected cells. Hence, the algorithm suits cluster-oriented optimization problems well, and strong exploitation and learning processes are intensified at the poor level [35]. The bacterial foraging algorithm (BFA) was developed by Passino [36], which works on the basic principle of the natural selection of bacteria. It is also a non-gradient optimization algorithm that mimicks the foraging behavior of the bacteria from the landscape towards the available nutrients [37]. However, the algorithm has different kinds of operators, where it depicts less convergence over complex optimization problems [38]. The Krill Herd (KH) is a bio-inspired optimization algorithm which imitates the behavior of krill [39]. The basic underlying concept of a krill herd is to reduce the distance between the food and each individual krill in the population. However, the author of the Ref. [40] stated that the KH algorithm does not maintain a steady process between exploration and exploitation.

The dominant author in the field of NIA, Yang [41], proposed the Firefly Algorithm (FA). The lighting behavior of fireflies during the food acquirement process is the primary ideology of the firefly algorithm [42]. Thus, the search process of the firefly algorithm is well-suited for solving multi-model optimization using a multi-population [8]. However, the cuckoo search well-utilises the random walk process that explores the search in an efficient manner, which may lead to slow convergence [43]. Further, the bat algorithm finds difficulty in the optimal adjustment of the frequency for an echo process, which helps to attain the optimal solution in the search process [9].

The various types of algorithms evolved in the literature based on the behavior of monkeys, such as the monkey algorithm (MA), monkey king evolution (MKO), and spider monkey algorithm (SMO). The initial solution was brought into existence via a random process, and it completes the local search process using the limb process and also performs a somersault process for the global search operation. Further, an improved version of the monkey algorithm was proposed in the Ref. [11], which includes the evolutionary speed factor to dynamically change the climb process and aggregation degree to dynamically assist somersault distance. The Spider Monkey Algorithm (SMO) was developed based on the swarm behavior of monkeys, and performs well with regard to the local search problem. The SMO also incorporates a fitness-based position update to enhance the convergence rate [44]. The Ageist Spider Monkey Algorithm (ASMO) includes features of agility and swiftness based on their age groups, which work based on the age differences present in the spider monkey population [12]. However, the algorithm performance decreases during the global search operation.

An empirical study from the literature [45] clearly shows the importance of a diverse population to attain the best solutions worldwide. Hence, a recent advancement in the field of an optimization algorithm incorporated multi-population methods where the population was subdivided into many sub-populations to avert the local optima and maintain diversity among the population [46]. Thus, multi-population methods guide the search process either in exploiting or exploring the search space. The significance of a multi-population has been incorporated in several dominant optimization algorithms [8,47].

Though multi-population-based algorithms have attained viable advantages in exploring and exploiting the search space, it has some consequences in designing the algorithm, such as the number of sub-populations, and communication and strategy among the sub-population [48]. Firstly, the number of sub-populations helps to spread the individuals over the search space. In fact, the small number of sub-populations leads to local optima, whereas the increase in the number of sub-populations leads to a wastage of computation resources and also extends the convergence [49]. The next important issue is the communication handling procedure between sub-populations, such as communication rates and policy [50]. The communication rate determines the number of individuals in a sub-population who have to interact with other sub-populations, and a communication policy is subjected to the replacement of individuals with other sub-populations.

The above discussion clearly illustrates the importance of balanced exploration and exploitation in the search process. Most of the optimization algorithms have problems in tuning the search operators and with diversity among the individuals. On the other hand, the multi-population-based algorithm amply shows its efficiency in maintaining a diverse population. However, it also requires some attention towards communication strategies between the sub-population. Hence, this motivated our research to develop a novel optimization algorithm with well-balanced exploration and exploitation. In particular, the Java macaque is also the vital primitive among the monkeys family and is widely available in South-Asian countries. Thus, the Java macaques have suitable behavior for balancing the exploration and exploitation search process.

The novel contribution of the proposed Java macaque algorithm is described as follows:

(1) We introduced the novel optimization algorithm based on the behavior of Java macaque monkeys for balancing the search operation. The balance is achieved by modeling the behavioral nature of Java macaque monkeys, such as multi-group behavior, multiple search agents, a social hierarchy-based selection strategy, mating, male replacement, and learning process.
(2) The multi-group population with multiple search agents as male and female monkeys helps to explore the different search spaces and also maintain diversity.
(3) This algorithm utilises the dominance hierarchy-based mating process to explore the complex search spaces.
(4) In order to address the communication issues in a multi-group population, the Java monkeys have unique behavior, called male replacement.
(5) The exploitation phase of the proposed algorithm is achieved by the learning process.
(6) This algorithm utilises a multi-leader approach using male and female search agents, which consists of an alpha male and alpha female in each group, and also remains as the best solution globally. Thus, the multi-leader approach assists in a smooth transition from the exploration phase to exploitation phase [50]. Further, the social hierarchy-based selecting strategy helps in maintaining both an improved converged and diverse solution in each group, as well as in the population.

Further in this paper, Section 3 describes the brief behavior analysis of the Java macaque monkey. Section 4 formulates the algorithmic compounds using the Java macaque behavior model. Then, Section 3.1 explores the stability of Java macaque behavior, and Section 4 introduces the generic version of the proposed Java macaque algorithm for the optimization problem. Further, Section 5 provides a brief experimentation of the continuous optimization problem, and Section 6 illustrates the detailed experimentation of discrete optimization. Finally, the paper is concluded in Section 8.

3. Behavior Analysis of the Java Macaque Monkey

The Java macaque monkey is an essential native breed that lives with a social structure, and it has almost 95% of gene similarity when compared with human beings [51]. The basic search agent of the java monkey is divided into male and female, where males are identified with a moustache and females with a beard. The average number of male and female individuals is 5.7 and 9.9 in each group, respectively. Usually, the Java macaque lives (with a group community of 20–40 monkeys) in an environment where macaques try to dominate over others in their region of living. Age, size and fighting skills are the factors used to determine social hierarchy among macaques [52]. The structure of social hierarchy has been followed among the java monkey groups where the lower-ranking individuals are dominated by the higher-ranking individuals when accessing food and resources [51,53]. The higher-ranking adult male and female macaques of a group are called the "Alpha Male" and "Alpha Female". Further, studies have shown that the alpha male has dominant access to females, which probably sires the offspring.

The number of female individuals is higher in comparison with the male individuals for every group. The next essential stage of the java monkey culture is mating. The mating operator depends on the hierarchical structure of the macaques, that is, the selection of male and female macaques is based on the social rank [54]. The male macaque attracts the female by creating a special noise and gesture for the reproduction. The higher-ranking male individuals are typically attracted to the female individual due to their social power and fitness. The male individual reaches sexual maturity approximately at the age of 6 years, while the female matures at the age of 4 years [55]. The newborn offspring or juvenile's social status depends on the parent's social rank and matrilineal hierarchy, which traces their descent through the female line. In detail, the offspring of the dominant macaque have a higher level of security when compared with offspring of lower-ranking individuals [56].

The male offspring are forced to leave their natal group after reaching sexual maturity and become stray males, whereas the female can populate in the same group based on their matrilineal status [53]. Hence, stray males have to join another social group, otherwise they are subjected to risk in the form of predators, disease, and injury. Male replacement is a process in which stray males can reside in another group in two ways—they either have to dominate the existing alpha male or sexually attract a female, and that way the macaque can convince another member to let the stray male into the group. Hence, the behavior of the Java macaque shows excellent skill in solving real-world problems in order to protect their group from challenging circumstances. Thus, the stray male can continuously learn from the dominant behavior of other macaques. Thus, the improvement in the ability of the Java macaque enhances its social ranking and provides higher access to food and protection. Further, the monkey can improve its ranking via a learning process and can also become the alpha monkey, which leads to the attainment of higher power within the group.

The behavior of Java macaque monkeys illustrates the characteristics of an optimization algorithm, such as selection, mating, maintaining elitism, and male replacement, finding the best position via learning from nature. The Java macaque exhibits population-based behavior with multiple groups in it and also adapts a dominant hierarchy. Then, each group can be divided into male and female search agents, which can be further divided into an adult, sub-adult, juvenile, and infant based on age. Next, an important characteristic of a java monkey is mating. In particular, the selection procedure for mating predominantly depends on the fitness hierarchy of the individuals. Further, the dominant individuals in a male and female population are maintained in each group of the population, known as the alpha male and female. The ageing factor is also considered to be an important deciding factor. The male monkey which attains sexual maturity at the age of 4 is forced to leave its natal group, and becomes a stray male. Thus, the stray male has to find another suitable group based on fitness ranking, and this process is known as male replacement. In addition to the above behavior, the monkey efficiently utilises the learning behavior from dominant individuals in order to attain the dominant ranking. The behavior of java monkeys does well to attain global optimal solutions in real-world problems. According to the observations from the above discussion, the behavior of java monkeys exhibits the following features: (1) the group behavior of individuals with different search agents helps in exploring a complex search space; (2) exploration and exploitation is performed using selection, mating, male replacement, and learning behavior; and (3) dominant monkeys are maintained within the group using an alpha male and female.

3.1. State Space Model for Java Macaque

Over the centuries, Java macaque monkeys have survived in this world because of their well-balanced behavior. This amply shows that the behavior of Java macaque monkeys has stability within the population. Then, the state space model for the Java macaque monkey in Figure 1 was designed using the demographic data shown in Table 1, obtained from the Ref. [57]. The demographic composition of the monkey population over the period of 1978 to 1982 was used to develop the state space model of the java monkey.

Table 1. Demographic composition of the monkey population (1978–1982).

Class	Age Years	1978	1979	1980	1981	1982
Adult Male	≥7	19	25	30(1)	39(3)	63(2)
Adult Female	≥5	51(1)	57(1)	68(1)	76(1)	91(1)
Subadult Male	4–6	25	45	48(1)	54	43
Subadult Female	4	7	12	9	16	25
Juvenile Male	1–3	55	43(2)	47(1)	54	75
Juvenile Female	1–4	39	50(2)	71(2)	82(1)	82(2)
Infant Male	<1	16(3)	15(3)	25(3)	36(2)	37(5)
Infant Unsexed	<2	25(1)	32(2)	28(1)	27(1)	38(5)
Infant Female	<3	0	0(2)	0(1)	0	0
Total		237	279	326	384	454
Infant Mortality 2		8.89	12.96	7.02	4.54	11.76
Noninfant Mortality 1		0.51	2.11	2.15	1.23	1.31

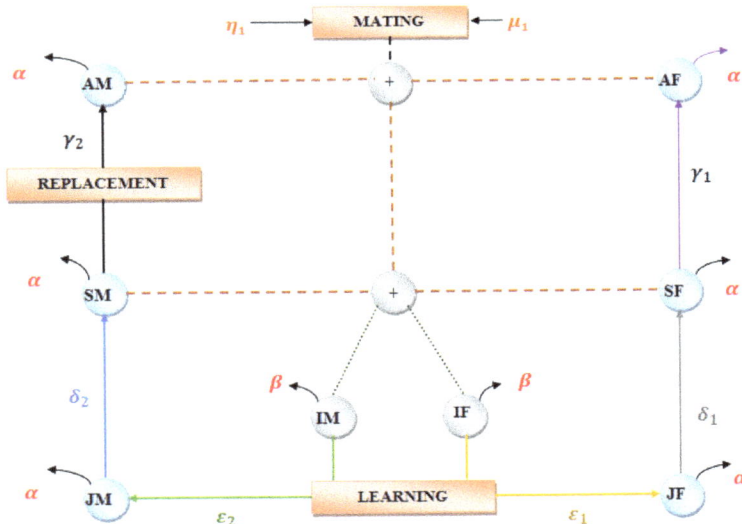

Figure 1. State space model of the Java macaque monkey.

The generalized equation for female individuals in the state space models are represented as:

$$AF^* = -\alpha AF + \gamma_1 SF \qquad (1)$$
$$SF^* = \delta_1 JF - \gamma_1 SF - \alpha SF \qquad (2)$$
$$JF^* = \varepsilon_1 IF - \delta_1 JF - \alpha JF \qquad (3)$$
$$IF^* = \eta_1 AM + \mu_1 AF - \varepsilon_1 IF - \beta IF \qquad (4)$$
$$\eta_1 = \frac{2}{3}\mu_1, \qquad (5)$$

where β, α are the death rate of the Infant (Offspring) and Non-Infant. Input variables $u(t)$ are $AF, SF, JF, IF,$ and the output variables $y(t)$ are AF^*, SF^*, JF^*, IF^* with respect to the state variable $\alpha_1, \beta_1, \gamma_1, \delta_1, \varepsilon_1, \mu_1, \eta_1$. Additionally, AF, SF, JF and IF indicates the adult, sub-adult, juvenile and infant females.

Similarly, the generalized equation for male individuals in the population are presented as:

$$AM^* = -\alpha AM + \gamma_2 SM \tag{6}$$
$$SM^* = \delta_2 JM - \gamma_2 SM - \alpha SM \tag{7}$$
$$JM^* = \varepsilon_2 IM - \delta_2 JM - \alpha JM \tag{8}$$
$$IM^* = \eta_2 AM + \mu_2 AF - \varepsilon_2 IM - \beta IM \tag{9}$$
$$\eta_2 = \frac{2}{3}\mu_2, \tag{10}$$

where β, α are the death rate of the Infant (Offspring) and Non-Infant. Input variables $u(t)$ are AM, SM, JM, IM and the output variable $y(t)$ are AM^*, SM^*, JM^*, IM^* with respect to state variable $\alpha_2, \beta_2, \gamma_2, \delta_2, \varepsilon_2, \mu_2, \eta_2$. Additionally, AM, SM, JM and IM indicate the adult sub-adult, or stray, juvenile, and infant males.

By using the state space model, we generated the transition matrix, which helps in proving the stability of the population using the α- diagonally dominant method, which has been clearly explained in the supplementary documents.

4. Java Macaque Monkey Algorithm Modeling

The Java Macaque Algorithm (JMA) is a meta-heuristic algorithm based on the genetic and social behavior of the java monkey. Initially, it starts with a population of the random solution and explores the search space to find the optimal. The life cycle of the Java macaque consists of selecting, mating, male replacement, and learning. Hence, the intelligent behavior of the java monkey does well to solve large-scale optimization problems Moreover, it also demonstrates the behavior of Java macaques, and exhibits their adaptive learning, genetic, and social behavior and how they often respond according to changes in their environment, which maintains the global order emerging from the interaction of the java monkey. Thus, the life cycle of the java monkey could be transformed as the algorithm model for solving the real-world optimization problem.

4.1. JMA—Preamble

In the primitive of the Java macaque monkey, the search agents are divided into two types, known as the 'Male' and 'Female' Java macaque. The nature of male and female search agents is to produce different cooperative behavior depending on its gender. Then, the Java macaque exhibits a multi-group population that is utilized to achieve the best performance.

The population of a Java macaque leaves in g-groups and N-individuals in the group.

$$POP = \{G_i\}_{i=1,2,\ldots,g}$$
$$= \{M_j\}_{j=1,2,\ldots,M_{size}} \bigcup \{F_k\}_{k=1,2,\ldots,F_{size}} \tag{11}$$
$$s.t \ (G_i \supset M, F : M \notin F),$$

where G_i presents the group i with M_{size} of male individuals and F_{size} of female individuals in the population. The initialization process starts with a minimum number of individuals in the group with respect to the problem size. Then the casual system is utilized to control the size of the population in every group. $|G_i|$, with a population size which consists of a number of male individuals M_{size} and female individuals F_{size}, is defined as:

$$M_{size} = floor[0.9 - rand(0.25, 0.4) * |G_i|] \tag{12}$$
$$F_{size} = floor[0.9 - rand(0.45, 0.6) * |G_i|] \tag{13}$$
$$M_{size} + F_{size} \Rightarrow Act_{size} : Act_{size} \in \mathbb{R}^*. \tag{14}$$

4.2. JMA—Fitness Evaluation

The Java macaque depends on the genetic and social behavior in which dominant individuals are likely to be a winner in a problem space. The fitness evaluation indicates how far the individual is converged concerning the problem space. Fitness evaluation predicts the probability and survival rate of the individual to be transferred to the next generation of the population and is defined as:

$$\begin{aligned} \text{minimize} \quad & F(\Psi) \\ \text{s.t} \quad & \Psi \in \mathbb{G}, \end{aligned} \quad (15)$$

where ψ denotes an individual of x-dimensional integer vector $\psi_i = (\psi_1, \psi_2, \ldots, \psi_x)$, $\mathbb{G}$ represent the feasible region of the search space, and $F \in \mathbb{R}$, where F is the optimization value.

4.3. JMA—Categorization

The basic structure of the java monkey follows the dominant hierarchy where the higher-ranking individuals dominate the remaining lower-ranking individuals in the group. The dominant male of the group also shows its dominance in accessing food, places, and other resources. Likewise, the dominant female of the group receives more access to resources and protection from a dominant male. Thus, the dominance hierarchy is based on evaluations of fitness value. Hence, the individuals are subdivided into higher-ranking or non-dominated (dominant) individuals and lower-ranking or dominated (non-dominant) individuals. Therefore, the individual ranking is based on the fitness value. The best individual in the group is known as the "Alpha" individual. Then, the 'Alpha Male' is the best male, and the 'Alpha Female' is the best female individual in the group. These are represented as follows:

$$AM_i = \min \quad \{F(\Psi_j \ | j \in \{M\}_i, i \in \{G_i\}\} \quad (16)$$

$$AF_i = \min \quad \{F(\Psi_j \ | j \in \{F\}_i, i \in \{G_i\}\}, \quad (17)$$

where AM_i and AF_i are the local optimal solution for the problem $\mathbb{X}$ from the group $\{G_i\}$. Therefore, the $AM_i, AF_i \in \mathbb{X}$, and it is better than other individuals from the set $\{M\}_i$ and $\{F\}_i$, where $(\forall AM_i, AF_i \in \mathbb{G} \Rightarrow (\forall AM, AF \in \mathbb{X} : F(AM_i) < \{M\}_i, F(AF_i) < \{F\}_i))$.

The global best individual from the set $\{AM\}$ and $\{AF\}$ are selected using:

$$[GM, GF] = \min\{\{AM\}, \{AF\}\}, \quad (18)$$

where $GM, GF \in \mathbb{X}$ are globally the best solution for the individual from the POP.

Then the set of dominant and non-dominant (subordinate) male and female individuals in the group can also be formulated using the fitness value.

$$\Psi, \Psi^* \in \{M\} \text{then} = \begin{cases} \Psi & \in \{DS\}, if F(\Psi) > F(\Psi^*) \\ \Psi^* & \in \{DS\}, \Psi \in \{NDS\}, otherwise, \end{cases} \quad (19)$$

$$\Psi, \Psi^* \in \{F\} \text{then} = \begin{cases} \Psi & \in \{NDS\}_F, if F(\Psi) > F(\Psi^*) \\ \Psi^* & \in \{NDS\}_F, \Psi \in \{DS\}_F, otherwise, \end{cases} \quad (20)$$

where both Ψ and Ψ^* are either distinct male or female individuals from the G_i. The non-dominant set of male and female individuals are represented as $\{NDS\}_M$ and $\{NDS\}_F$. Similarly, the dominant male and female individuals are presented as $\{DS\}_M$ and $\{DS\}_F$.

4.4. JMA—Mating

Mating is an important operator in the Java macaque algorithm that ensures group survival and also enables the exchange of genetic information and social behavior between individuals. In particular, the dominant males have the privilege of mating with dominant females. Hence, non-dominant males may also have a lesser chance of mating due to the special prerequisite of dominance. The selection of individuals in the mating process plays an important role in generating populations for the next generation. Specifically, if the selection process depends only on a dominant individual, this may lead to local optima and reduce population diversity. Thus, the non-dominant individuals are also selected to perform mating operations with the probability ratio, which maintains diversity among individuals. Mating is the search process which is used to exploit the problem space $\mathbb{X}$. Mating between males Ψ^m and females Ψ^f is either from the set {NDS} or {DS}. Then, new offspring Ψ_{off} are generated as follows:

$$\Psi^{off} = Mating(\Psi^m, \Psi^f) \quad s.t \quad \Psi_m, \Psi_f \in G_i, \quad (21)$$

where the uniform crossover is used for the discrete optimization problem, and the simulated binary crossover for the continuous optimization problem.

The age of the Infant Male (IM) and Infant Female (IF) is set at 0, who then undergo a learning process to improve their fitness. The offspring generated in each $\{G_i\}$ from the mating process reaches sexual maturity $\mathbb{S}$. Then the SM, SF and AF represent the Stray Male (subadult male), Subadult Female, and Adult Female, defined as the following:

$$\Psi^{IM} = \begin{cases} \Psi^{IM} \in \{JM\}, & if\, Age = 1 \\ \Psi^{IM} \in \{IM\}, & otherwise. \end{cases} \quad (22)$$

$$\Psi^{JM} = \begin{cases} \Psi^{JM} \in \{SM\}, & if\, Age = 4 \\ \Psi^{JM} \in \{JM\}, & otherwise. \end{cases} \quad (23)$$

$$\Psi^{IF} = \begin{cases} \Psi^{IF} \in \{JF\}, & if\, Age = 1 \\ \Psi^{IF} \in \{IF\}, & otherwise. \end{cases} \quad (24)$$

$$\Psi^{JF} = \begin{cases} \Psi^{JF} \in \{SF\}, & if\, Age = 3 \\ \Psi^{JF} \in \{JF\}, & otherwise; \end{cases} \quad (25)$$

$$\Psi^{SF} = \begin{cases} \Psi^{SF} \in \{AF\}, & if\, Age = 5 \\ \Psi^{SF} \in \{SF\}, & otherwise, \end{cases} \quad (26)$$

where Age indicates the age of the individual. Similarly, if the Age = 5, then the Juvenile Female (JF) is moved to the set of Adult Females (AFs).

4.5. JMA—Male Replacement

The new offspring generated from the mating operation undergo a learning process from the dominant individual and the circumstances of the environment. Male replacement plays an important role in the Java macaque algorithm where the stray male chooses another group to reside in and replace the existing dominant male in the group. This is also considered as swarm behavior, where the stray male has to find a suitable position in the ruling hierarchy of the male. On the contrary, if a stray male cannot find a suitable position, then it is subjected to the risk of death. According to the fitness of the stray male, the replacement strategy variation plays out in a different manner. The male replacement can be defined as:

$$MR = \begin{cases} REPLACE(\Psi_{sm}, \Psi_m), & if\, F(\Psi_{sm}) > F(\Psi_m) \\ \Psi_{sm} \in \{ES\}, & otherwise; \end{cases} \quad (27)$$

$$\exists \Psi_{sm} \in G_i || \Psi_m \in \{DS\}_M : (\Psi_m \in \{G_j\}_{j=1,2,\ldots,M}) | i \neq j,$$

where $REPLACE(\Psi_{sm}, \Psi_m)$ is the replacement process with the stray Ψ_{sm} and dominant Ψ_m male. Then $\{ES\}$ is the elimination set where the individuals are eliminated from the population.

4.6. JMA—Learning

In this stage, the individuals in the population set can improve their fitness to reach the dominant individual set. The efficiency of the individual is improved based on the environment and social behavior. However, the potential of this learning process is to increase efficiency when compared with the current dominant hierarchy. Exploration is achieved by the learning method which enhances the fitness of an individual and also attains the optimal solution. The learning method is applied to the Java macaque algorithm to attain the desired results in global optimum, and this can be represented as follows:

$$Learning = \{PoP, \mathbb{G}, \delta, L(\Psi), F(\Psi), \mathbb{X}\}, \quad (28)$$

where POP represents the set of the individual, $\mathbb{G}$ is the feasible search space of the solution, $F(\Psi)$ is the fitness function, $\mathbb{X}$ is the problem space of the optimization problem, and δ is referred to as the learning rate of the individual which is uniformly distributed ($0 \leq \delta \leq 1$). Then, the learning process is $L(\Psi_k, i, j) : \forall \Psi \in \mathbb{G} | \exists x \in \mathbb{X}$.

5. Continuous Optimization Problem

In the continuous optimization problem, each decision variable may take any value between the range of constraints. Thus, the search space of continuous optimization may exponentially increase with the associated constraints. The initial difference between the continuous and discrete optimization is the representation of the individual with regard to a continuous search space. The java macaque for the continuous optimization algorithm consists of significant features selection, categorization, mating, male replacement and learning behavior. The Algorithm 1 clearly describes the computational methodology of java macaque optimization algorithm.

Definition 1. *The individuals are mapped ($map : \mathbb{G} \to \mathbb{X}$) between the dimension vector of the search space $\mathbb{G}$ to a dimensional vector in the problem space $\mathbb{X}$. In the continuous optimization problem, the individuals are mapped to the number of decision variables (NOD) and represented as the dimension vector of the problem space.*

$$\vec{\Psi} = \{\psi_1, \psi_2, \ldots, \psi_{NOD}\} \quad \vec{\Psi}.\psi \in \mathbb{G}_i, \forall i \in 1, 2, \ldots, NOD, \quad (29)$$

$$\exists \vec{\Psi}.x \in \mathbb{X} : map(\vec{\Psi}.\psi) = \vec{\Psi}.x$$

where $\vec{\Psi}$ is a vector of decision variable $\{\psi_1, \psi_2, \ldots, \psi_{NOD}\}$ in the search space $\mathbb{G}$. Each individual for the continuous function is represented as $\Psi \in \mathbb{R}$ and $\mathbb{G} = \mathbb{X} \subseteq \mathbb{R}$. Then the next level of difference in the continuous optimization problem is the evaluation of the fitness value of the individual.

Definition 2. *The generic form of the fitness evaluation is presented as follows:*

$$Minimize \quad F(\vec{\Psi}) \quad (30)$$

$$S.t \quad \forall \vec{\Psi} \in \mathbb{X},$$

where $F(\vec{\Psi})$ is the fitness value of individuals with respect to the continuous optimization problem, and $\mathbb{X}$ is the decision space $\{F : \mathbb{X} \to \mathbb{R}^{NOC} : \vec{lb_i} \leq \vec{\Psi_i} \leq \vec{ub_i}\}$ with the upper bound (ub) and the lower bound (lb) of individual $\vec{\Psi}$.

Then the remaining processes, like selecting the alpha male, alpha female, global best individual, and subdividing the population into dominated and non-dominated individuals, are completed using the fitness value.

Definition 3. *Mating is an important search process of JMA which is used to exploit the continuous search space $\mathbb{G}$. Thus, the mating process is redefined with respect to the continuous search space. Mating between males $\vec{\Psi_m}$ and females $\vec{\Psi_f}$ is either from the set $\{DS\}$ or $\{NDS\}$. Therefore, A_i and*

I_i are obtained from $max(\psi_i^m, \psi_i^f)$ and $min(\psi_i^m, \psi_i^f)$. Then, new offspring $\overrightarrow{\Psi_{off}}$ are generated as follows [58–60]:

$$\overrightarrow{\Psi_{off}} = Mating(\overrightarrow{\Psi_m}, \overrightarrow{\Psi_f}) \quad s.t \quad \overrightarrow{\Psi_m}, \overrightarrow{\Psi_f} \in G_i \qquad (31)$$

$$|off| = \{P(A) * (|G_i| - Act_{size}\}$$

$$\overrightarrow{\Psi_{off}^0} = 0.5[(A_i + I_i) - \theta_0 \times (A_i - I_i)] \qquad (32)$$

$$\overrightarrow{\Psi_{off}^1} = 0.5[(A_i + I_i) + \theta_1 \times (A_i - I_i)], \qquad (33)$$

where $\overrightarrow{\Psi_{off}^0}$ and $\overrightarrow{\Psi_{off}^1}$ are two new offspring generated from the crossover, and $\theta_j (j = 0, 1)$ can be incurred as

$$\theta_j = \begin{cases} (C_j \times D_j)^{\frac{1}{\zeta+1}}, & \text{if } C_j \leq 1/D_j \\ (\frac{1}{2-C_j \times D_j})^{\frac{1}{\zeta+1}}, & \text{otherwise,} \end{cases} \qquad (34)$$

where C_j is a uniformly distributed random number between [0,1] and θ is the distributed crossover index of offspring related to the parent's natal code. Then $D_j (j = 0, 1)$ is generated by the assumption $A_i \neq I_i$:

$$D_j = \begin{cases} 2 - (\frac{A_i - I_i}{A_i + I_i - 2lb_i})^{(\zeta+1)} & j = 0 \\ 2 - (\frac{A_i - I_i}{2ub_i - A_i - I_i})^{(\zeta+1)} & j = 1, \end{cases} \qquad (35)$$

where lb_i and ub_i indicate the upper and lower bound of the decision variable.

Definition 4. *The learning process is adopted to improve the fitness value of the individual with respect to the problem space. Then, the learning process of the Java macaque may change with respect to the environment. Then the learning model for the continuous optimization problem is defined as follows:*

$$Learning = \{PoP, \mathbb{G}, \overrightarrow{\delta}, L(\overrightarrow{\Psi_k}), F(\overrightarrow{\Psi}), \mathbb{X}\} \qquad (36)$$

where POP represents the set of individuals, $\mathbb{G}$ is the feasible search space of solutions, $F(\overrightarrow{\Psi})$ is the fitness function, and $\overrightarrow{\delta}$ indicates the learning rate of the individual in linear decreasing order $(0 \leq \overrightarrow{\delta} \leq 1)$. Then, the learning process of the individual is given by

$$\overrightarrow{L_1}(\overrightarrow{\Psi_{GM}}, \overrightarrow{\Psi_k}) := \overrightarrow{\Psi_{GM}} - (2 \cdot \overrightarrow{\delta} \cdot \overrightarrow{r_1} - \overrightarrow{\delta})|2 \cdot \overrightarrow{r_2} \cdot \overrightarrow{\Psi_{GM}} - \overrightarrow{\Psi_k}|, \qquad (37)$$

where $\overrightarrow{r_1}, \overrightarrow{r_2}$ are the random vectors between [0,1]. Similarly, the learning process of the individual $\overrightarrow{\Psi_k}$ is performed between the global best female $\overrightarrow{L_2}(\overrightarrow{\Psi_{GF}}, \overrightarrow{\Psi_k})$, alpha male $\overrightarrow{L_3}(\overrightarrow{\Psi_{AM}}, \overrightarrow{\Psi_k})$ and alpha female $\overrightarrow{L_4}(\overrightarrow{\Psi_{AF}}, \overrightarrow{\Psi_k})$. Then, the individual $\overrightarrow{\Psi_k}$ is modified as follows:

$$\overrightarrow{\Psi_k} = \frac{\overrightarrow{L_1} + \overrightarrow{L_2} + \overrightarrow{L_3} + \overrightarrow{L_4}}{4}, \qquad (38)$$

where $\overrightarrow{\Psi_i}$ is the individual obtained from the learning process and replaced in the POP.

Algorithm 1 JMAC: Java Macaque Algorithm for Continuous Optimization Problem.

Input: N number of individuals, g number of groups, F is the fitness function.
Output: GB_{AM}, GB_{FM}, POP
Step 1: [Initialization] The initial Population is initialized using a random seeding technique using Equation (29).
Step 2: [Evaluation] Each individual in the population is evaluated using the fitness function, as represented in Equation (30).
Step 3: The various categories of search agents are classified as:
    (a) [Alpha Individual] Determine the AlphaMale and AlphaFemale in each group using Equations (16) and (17).
    (b) [GB-Alpha Individual] Select the best individual from the AlphaMale and AlphaFemale sets using Equation (18).
    (c) [NDS and DS] Male and Female individual sets are further divided into dominant and non-dominant solutions using Equations (19) and (20).
Step 4: [Mating] Then the new offsprings are generated using the mating process, defined as in Equation (31).
Step 5: [Evaluation of Offspring] The fitness values of offspring are evaluated and the stray male and female are determined.
Step 6: [Male Replacement] The stray male finds a suitable group to replace the dominant male.
Step 7: [Learning] The fitness value of the individual is improved by moving the global best and alpha individuals by Equation (36).
Step 8: [Termination] The population is maintained by using Equation (11) and the above process is repeated from Step 2 until termination criteria are satisfied.

5.1. Experimentation and Result Analysis of Continuous Optimization Problem

In this section of experimentation, the benchmark function is taken from the popular literature [61,62] and used for analyzing the performance of the Java macaque algorithm. The performance of the proposed Java macaque algorithm is measured on 23 benchmark functions. The benchmark function utilized for the experimentation process consists of the 7 unimodal functions, 6 multimodal functions, and 10 fixed-dimension multimodal functions, where the dimension of the function is indicated in Dim, the upper and lower bound of the search space is referred to using Range, and finally, the optimal value of the benchmark function is indicated using the f_{min}.

In the experimentation process, the proposed JMA is compared with the dominant algorithm from the literature, such as the grey wolf optimization (GWO) technique [61] and spider monkey algorithm (SMO) [12]. For all the algorithms, the population size was fixed as 200, stopping criteria were set as 100 iterations, and the primary population was produced using the random population seeding techniques. Every algorithm executed the 30 independent runs for each benchmark function, and the evaluation of the algorithm was measured using statistical measures such as the mean and standard deviation, as referred to in the literature [61,62]. Further, the best result is mentioned in bold font for reference in the respective table.

5.1.1. Result Analysis for Unimodal Benchmark Functions

The unimodal benchmark functions are suitable for analyzing the exploitation capability of the algorithm because it contains only one global optimum. Table 2 clearly shows a list of unimodal benchmark functions which is used for the experimentation process, and the function has different properties, like convex and non-convex shaped, non-differentiable, discontinuous, scalable, separable, and non-separable properties. Table 3 clearly shows the results of SMO, GWO and JMA on the unimodal benchmark functions. The performance of the proposed Java macaque optimization algorithm has clear dominance over the other two algorithms. In particular, the JMA attains the best results in both means and standard deviation on all the unimodel instances. GWO typically performs well in F5 and F6 in terms of means value, but struggles to outperform JMA. The Figure 2 facilitates the clear illustration that JMA dominates the other algorithm in terms of better convergence. The JMA has a dominant exploitation capability and can achieve a well-converged population. Further, it can clearly be depicted via standard deviations.

Table 2. Benchmark Function.

Function	Dim	Range	f_{min}
$f_1(x) = \sum_{i=1}^{n} x_i^2$	30	$[-100, 100]$	0
$f_2(x) = \sum_{i=1}^{n} |x_i| + \prod_{i=1}^{n} |x_i|$	30	$[-10, 10]$	0
$f_3(x) = \sum_{i=1}^{n} \left(\sum_{j=1}^{i} x_j \right)^2$	30	$[-100, 100]$	0
$f_4(x) = maximum_i\{|x_i|, 1 \leq i \leq n\}$	30	$[-100, 100]$	0
$f_5(x) = \sum_{i=1}^{n} \left| 100(x_{i+1} - x_i^2)^2 + (x_i - 1)^2 \right|$	30	$[-30, 30]$	0
$f_6(x) = \sum_{i=1}^{n} (|x_i + 0.5|)^2$	30	$[-100, 100]$	0
$f_7(x) = \sum_{i=1}^{n} i x_i^4 + U(0, 1)$	30	$[-1.28, 1.28]$	0

Table 3. Experimental results of unimodal benchmark function.

Function	Technique	Optimal Value	Best	SD
F1	SMO	0	9.64E-02	1.09E+04
	GWO		1.21E-07	7.92E+03
	JMA		**1.06E-30**	**1.47E+03**
F2	SMO	0	8.96E-01	2.45E+10
	GWO		3.18E-05	9.84E+08
	JMA		**2.50E-17**	**1.40E+02**
F3	SMO	0	1.28E+02	1.83E+04
	GWO		3.28E-01	1.67E+04
	JMA		**5.43E-24**	**5.21E+03**
F4	SMO	0	1.15E+00	1.93E+01
	GWO		3.31E-02	1.75E+01
	JMA		**4.75E-14**	**6.63E+00**
F5	SMO	0	8.85E+01	2.67E+07
	GWO		2.58E+01	2.20E+07
	JMA		**2.81E+01**	**1.80E+06**
F6	SMO	0	1.21E-01	1.23E+04
	GWO		3.89E-04	7.57E+03
	JMA		**3.98E-04**	**2.09E+03**
F7	SMO	0	3.15E-01	1.78E+01
	GWO		1.76E-03	7.61E+00
	JMA		**1.15E-03**	**6.35E-01**

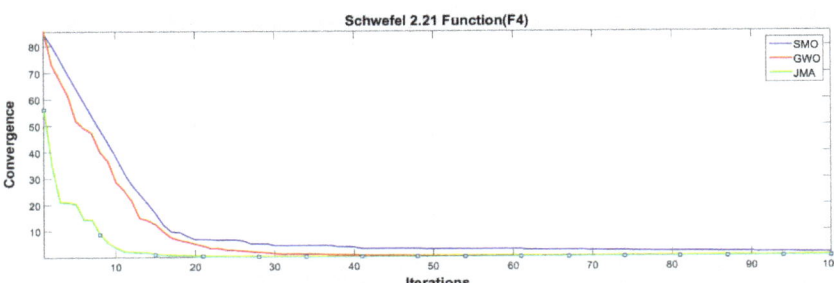

Figure 2. Convergence Curve for Schwefel 2.21 Function (F4).

5.1.2. Multimodal Benchmark Function

The next important set of test functions used for the experimentation process is multimodal benchmark functions. The multimodal functions are utilized for analyzing the exploration potential of the algorithm because of its multiple local minima. Further, the benchmark function measures the global exploration capability of the algorithm, and an increase in dimension exponentially increases the number of local optima in the search space. Table 4 shows the list of multimodal benchmark functions for the experimentation.

Table 4. Multimodal benchmark function.

Function	Dim	Range	f_{min}
$f_8(x) = \sum_{i=1}^{n} -x_i \sin\left(\sqrt{|x_i|}\right)$	30	$[-500, 500]$	-418.9829×5
$f_9(x) = \sum_{i=1}^{n} \left\| x_i^2 - 10\cos(2\pi x_i) + 10 \right\|$	30	$[-5.12, 5.12]$	0
$f_{10}(x) = -20\exp\left(-0.2\sqrt{\frac{1}{n}\sum_{i=1}^{n} x_i^2}\right) - \exp\left(\frac{1}{n}\sum_{i=1}^{n} \cos(2\pi x_i)\right) + 20 + e$	30	$[-32, 32]$	0
$f_{11}(x) = \frac{1}{4000}\sum_{i=1}^{n} x_i^2 - \prod_{i=1}^{n} \cos\left(\frac{x_i}{\sqrt{i}}\right) + 1$	30	$[-600, 600]$	0
$f_{12}(x) = \frac{\pi}{n}\left\{10\sin(\pi y_1) + \sum_{i=1}^{n-1}(y_i-1)^2[1+10\sin^2(\pi y_{i+1})] + (y_n-1)^2\right\} + \sum_{i=1}^{n} u(x_i, 10, 100, 4)$ $y_i = 1 + \frac{x_i+1}{4} u(x_i, a, k, m) = \begin{cases} k(x_i-a)^m & x_i > a \\ 0-a & <x_i<a \\ k(-x_i-a)^m & x_i < -a \end{cases}$	30	$[-50, 50]$	0
$f_{13}(x) = 0.1\left\{\sin^2(3\pi x_1) + \sum_{i=1}^{n}(x_i-1)^2\left[1+\sin^2(3\pi x_i+1)\right] + (x_n-1)^2\left[1+\sin^2(2\pi x_n)\right]\right\} + \sum_{i=1}^{n} u(x_i, 5, 100, 4)$	30	$[-50, 50]$	0

The result illustrated in Table 5 and Figure 3 exhibits the performance of existing and proposed algorithms in terms of means and standard deviation. From the table observation, it is clearly shown that the performance of JMA rules out the other two algorithms. The JMA demonstrates its significance in mean value as 0.00E+00, 8.88E-16, 0.00E+00, 3.87E-05 and 3.21E-04 for the instance of F9 to F13, whereas the GWO achieves only 8.74E+00, 7.69E-05, 1.45E-07, 6.52E-03 and 4.83E-04. Similarly, the performance of standard deviation also demonstrates the dominance of the proposed algorithm over the GWO and SMO. Hence, this observation clearly provides the proof that the exploring capability of the proposed algorithm is superior to the existing algorithms.

Table 5. Experimental results of the multimodal benchmark function.

Function	Technique	Optimal Value	Best	SD
F8	SMO GWO JMA	−12569.5	−4706.47 −4374.35 **−3384.65**	2.60E+02 1.18E+03 **1.26E+01**
F9	SMO GWO JMA	0	7.81E+01 8.74E+00 **0.00E+00**	6.70E+01 9.46E+01 **5.04E+01**
F10	SMO GWO JMA	0	3.78E-01 7.69E-05 **8.88E-16**	3.77E+00 4.85E+00 **2.94E+00**
F11	SMO GWO JMA	0	2.78E+00 1.45E-07 **0.00E+00**	1.76E+02 6.94E+01 **1.46E+01**
F12	SMO GWO JMA	0	1.36E-03 6.52E-03 **3.87E-05**	5.15E+07 7.12E+07 **2.61E+06**
F13	SMO GWO JMA	0	5.45E-02 4.83E-04 **3.21E-04**	1.07E+08 9.37E+07 **9.53E+06**

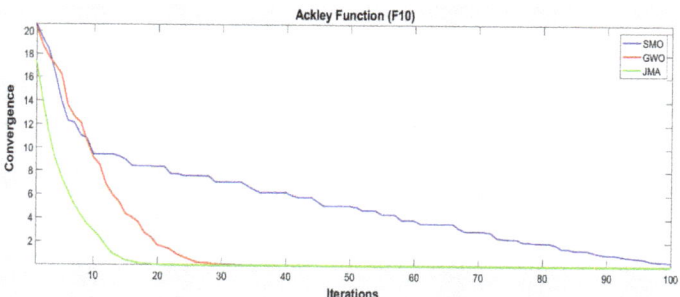

Figure 3. Convergence curve for the Ackley function (F10).

5.1.3. Fixed-Dimension Multimodal Benchmark Function

The final experimentation for a continuous Java macaque algorithm is experimented with using the fixed-dimension multimodal benchmark functions. In this test function, the dimension of the benchmark function is fixed, which is used to analyze the performance of the algorithm in terms of exploration, exploitation, and also to avoid the local minima. The list of benchmark functions used for experimentation is shown in Table 6.

The results described in Table 7 clearly show that the JMA attains better values for the performance measures by comparing the GWO and SMO. The mean values of JMA and GWO are same as 1 for the instance F14, but the JMA shows its dominance in the SD value as 0.194221, whereas the GWO reaches only 1.737368. Similarly, Table 7 portrays how the performance of the three algorithms are almost the same as for the instance F18, but the proposed algorithm dominates in standard deviation. On the other hand, the performance of JMA lacks in terms of standard deviation for the instances F20 and F22 by GWO, and F17 and F21 by SMO. However, the JMA algorithm outperformed the GWO and SMO in terms of mean value for instances like f14, F16, F18, F19, F20, F21, F22 and F23. The fixed-dimension multi-modal benchmark function is utilized for analysis in the performance of the algorithm due to its multiple local minima, exploitation, and exploration capabilities.

Table 6. Fixed-dimension multimodal benchmark function.

Function	Dim	Range	f_{min}
$f_{14}(x) = \left(\frac{1}{500} + \sum_{j=1}^{25} \frac{1}{j + \sum_{i=1}^{2}(x_i - a_{ij})^6}\right)^{-1}$	2	[−65, 65]	1
$f_{15}(x) = \sum_{i=1}^{11}\left[a_i - \frac{x_1(b_i^2 + b_i x_2)}{b_i^2 + b_i x_3 + x_4}\right]^2$	4	[−5, 5]	0.00030
$f_{16}(x) = 4x_1^2 - 2.1x_1^4 + \frac{1}{3}x_1^6 + x_1 x_2 - 4x_2^2 + 4x_2^4$	2	[−5, 5]	−1.0316
$f_{17}(x) = \left(x_2 - \frac{5.1}{4\pi^2}x_1^2 + \frac{5}{\pi}x_1 - 6\right)^2 + 10\left(1 - \frac{1}{8\pi}\right)\cos x_1 + 10$	2	[−5, 5]	0.398
$f_{18}(x) = \left[1 + (x_1 + x_2 + 1)^2(19 - 14x_1 + 3x_1^2 - 14x_2 + 6x_1 x_2 + 3x_2^2)\right]$ $\times \left[30 + (2x_1 - 3x_2)^2 \times (18 - 32x_1 + 12x_1^2 + 48x_2 - 36x_1 x_2 + 27x_2^2)\right]$	2	[−2, 2]	3
$f_{19}(x) = -\sum_{i=1}^{4} c_i \exp\left(-\sum_{j=1}^{3} a_{ij}(x_j - p_{ij})^2\right)$	3	[1, 3]	−3.86
$f_{20}(x) = -\sum_{i=1}^{4} c_i \exp\left(-\sum_{j=1}^{6} a_{ij}(x_j - p_{ij})^2\right)$	6	[0, 1]	−3.32
$f_{21}(x) = -\sum_{i=1}^{5}\left[(X - a_i)(X - a_i)^T + c_i\right]^{-1}$	4	[0, 10]	−10.1532
$f_{22}(x) = -\sum_{i=1}^{7}\left[(X - a_i)(X - a_i)^T + c_i\right]^{-1}$	4	[0, 10]	−10.4028
$f_{23}(x) = -\sum_{i=1}^{10}\left[(X - a_i)(X - a_i)^T + c_i\right]^{-1}$	4	[0, 10]	−10.5363

Table 7. Experimental results of the fixed-dimension multimodal benchmark function.

Function	Technique	Optimal Value	Best	SD
F14	SMO	1	1.08E+00	1.13E+00
	GWO		1.00E+00	1.74E+00
	JMA		**1.00E+00**	**1.94E-01**
F15	SMO	0.0003	4.26E-04	4.18E-03
	GWO		**3.08E-04**	**5.26E-04**
	JMA		3.23E-04	9.30E-03
F16	SMO	−1.0316	−1.03E+00	1.87E-02
	GWO		−1.03E+00	6.11E-02
	JMA		**−1.03E+00**	**7.90E-03**
F17	SMO	0.398	**3.98E-01**	**3.81E-02**
	GWO		3.98E-01	7.42E-02
	JMA		3.98E-01	4.15E-02
F18	SMO	3	3.00E+00	8.54E-01
	GWO		3.00E+00	1.85E+00
	JMA		**3.00E+00**	**6.43E-01**
F19	SMO	−3.86	**−3.86E+00**	3.67E-02
	GWO		**−3.86E+00**	3.11E-02
	JMA		**−3.86E+00**	**2.45E-02**
F20	SMO	−3.22	−3.32E+00	1.28E-01
	GWO		−3.32E+00	**5.63E-02**
	JMA		−3.07E+00	1.43E-01
F21	SMO	−10.1532	−1.02E+01	**2.13E+00**
	GWO		−1.01E+01	2.38E+00
	JMA		**−1.02E+01**	2.65E+00
F22	SMO	−10.4028	−1.04E+01	3.40E+00
	GWO		−1.04E+01	**2.42E+00**
	JMA		**−1.04E+01**	3.03E+00
F23	SMO	−10.5363	−1.05E+01	2.71E+00
	GWO		−1.05E+01	2.87E+00
	JMA		**−1.05E+01**	**2.52E+00**

The result shown in Table 8 and sample Figure 4 helps to analyze the experimentation in terms of convergence. The means value of 30 independent runs for the best convergence value in iterations 1, 10, and 25 illustrates the search ability of algorithms. The best value obtained from the iteration limit of 1 clearly demonstrated stronger convergence behavior of the JMA over the GWO and SMO in terms of all the unimodal instances. Further, the JMA was able to attain a near-optimal value in just 25 iterations for instances like F1, F2, F3, F4 and F7 with respective values 8.56E-04, 1.09E-02, 2.76E-01, 1.16E-01, and 7.76E-04, respectively. Additionally, in the case of the multimodal benchmark function, the proposed JMA led to the existing algorithm by all means. Correspondingly, in terms of the fixed dimensional multimodal function, the proposed JMA outperforms the existing algorithm in almost all instances, except F17, F21, and F22. The SMO algorithm shows better performance in terms of F17 and F21, whereas the GWO dominates only in F22. This observation shows that the potential behavior of the proposed JMA prevails over the existing algorithm in terms of avoiding local optima and achieving exploitation, exploration and strong convergence in minimum iteration.

Table 8. Best values obtained by JMA, GWO and SMO in Iterations 1, 10, and 25.

Function	Technique	Iteration 1	Iteration 10	Iteration 25	Function	Technique	Iteration 1	Iteration 10	Iteration 25
F1	SMO	5.66E+04	1.28E+04	2.29E+02	F13	SMO	9.37E+08	3.10E+05	3.31E+01
	GWO	5.73E+04	2.23E+03	1.84E+00		GWO	8.34E+08	6.01E+04	2.27E+00
	JMA	**1.11E+04**	**2.58E+01**	**8.56E-04**		JMA	**9.58E+07**	**7.49E+00**	**2.52E+00**
F2	SMO	2.46E+11	6.32E+01	3.81E+01	F14	SMO	1.04E+01	1.00E+00	9.98E-01
	GWO	9.89E+09	1.34E+01	3.73E-01		GWO	1.09E+01	2.07E+00	9.99E-01
	JMA	**1.41E+03**	**2.11E+00**	**1.09E-02**		JMA	**2.10E+00**	**1.20E+00**	**9.98E-01**
F3	SMO	1.01E+05	2.45E+04	2.97E+03	F15	SMO	4.12E-02	4.70E-03	8.52E-04
	GWO	1.05E+05	2.27E+04	2.25E+03		GWO	3.47E-03	1.05E-03	7.26E-04
	JMA	**3.93E+04**	**1.56E+03**	**2.76E-01**		JMA	**9.36E-02**	**7.02E-04**	**7.02E-04**
F4	SMO	8.89E+01	4.00E+01	7.37E+00	F16	SMO	−8.52E-01	−1.03E+00	−1.03E+00
	GWO	7.72E+01	3.25E+01	4.02E+00		GWO	−4.18E-01	−1.03E+00	−1.03E+00
	JMA	**4.18E+01**	**5.90E+00**	**1.16E-01**		JMA	**−9.76E-01**	**−1.03E+00**	**−1.03E+00**
F5	SMO	2.51E+08	8.24E+05	7.85E+04	F17	SMO	7.74E-01	4.00E-01	3.98E-01
	GWO	1.90E+08	4.18E+05	1.34E+02		GWO	6.84E-01	5.56E-01	3.99E-01
	JMA	**1.71E+07**	**1.44E+03**	**2.88E+01**		JMA	**6.49E-01**	**4.49E-01**	**4.02E-01**
F6	SMO	6.48E+04	1.06E+04	1.59E+02	F18	SMO	1.16E+01	3.14E+00	3.00E+00
	GWO	5.74E+04	7.93E+02	2.20E+00		GWO	2.16E+01	3.01E+00	3.00E+00
	JMA	**2.00E+04**	**4.51E+01**	**3.43E+00**		JMA	**9.42E+00**	**3.00E+00**	**3.00E+00**
F7	SMO	8.82E+01	4.04E+01	4.04E+01	F19	SMO	−3.50E+00	−3.85E+00	−3.86E+00
	GWO	6.81E+01	5.55E-01	6.53E-03		GWO	−3.67E+00	−3.84E+00	−3.85E+00
	JMA	**5.17E+00**	**1.10E-02**	**7.76E-04**		JMA	**−3.63E+00**	**−3.84E+00**	**−3.86E+00**
F8	SMO	−3.25E+03	−3.70E+03	−4.15E+03	F20	SMO	−2.13E+00	−3.01E+00	−3.11E+00
	GWO	−2.85E+03	−3.83E+03	−3.83E+03		GWO	−2.92E+00	−3.11E+00	−3.18E+00
	JMA	**−2.83E+03**	**−2.96E+03**	**−2.96E+03**		JMA	**−2.22E+00**	**−3.23E+00**	**−3.29E+00**
F9	SMO	4.03E+02	3.25E+02	3.18E+02	F21	SMO	−7.42E-01	−4.67E+00	−9.36E+00
	GWO	4.11E+02	2.12E+02	6.19E+01		GWO	−7.32E-01	−2.91E+00	−6.09E+00
	JMA	**3.08E+02**	**7.21E+01**	**5.99E-03**		JMA	**−5.13E-01**	**−3.82E+00**	**−4.25E+00**
F10	SMO	2.04E+01	1.04E+01	6.81E+00	F22	SMO	−9.54E-01	−1.95E+00	−5.23E+00
	GWO	2.05E+01	1.04E+01	6.82E-01		GWO	−8.49E-01	−3.89E+00	−6.45E+00
	JMA	**1.77E+01**	**2.73E+00**	**5.31E-03**		JMA	**−8.38E-01**	**−2.38E+00**	**−4.20E+00**
F11	SMO	5.89E+02	4.79E+02	3.15E+02	F23	SMO	−1.11E+00	−4.74E+00	−7.82E+00
	GWO	5.56E+02	1.04E+01	9.28E-01		GWO	−1.49E+00	−6.06E+00	−8.27E+00
	JMA	**1.25E+02**	**1.17E+00**	**7.83E-04**		JMA	**−1.39E+00**	**−2.96E+00**	**−3.93E+00**
F12	SMO	4.65E+08	2.10E+01	4.39E+00					
	GWO	6.06E+08	2.46E+04	2.70E-01					
	JMA	**2.62E+07**	**1.23E+00**	**5.28E-01**					

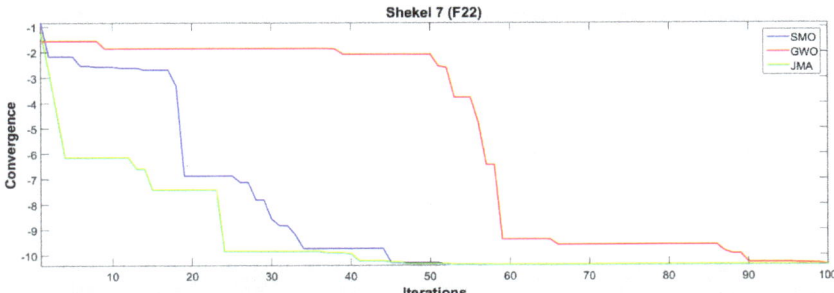

Figure 4. Convergence curve for Shekel 7 Function (F22).

6. Discrete Optimization Problem

The problem space of a discrete optimization problem is represented as the set of all feasible solutions that satisfy the constraint and the fitness function, which maps each element to the problem space. Thus, the discrete or combinatorial optimization problem searches for the optimal solution from the set of feasible solutions.

The generic form of the discrete optimization problem is represented as follows [63]:

$$Minimize \quad F(\Psi) \tag{39}$$

$$subject\ to \quad \forall \Psi \in \mathbb{G},$$

where $F : \mathbb{G} \to \mathbb{Z}$ is the objective function with discrete problem space, which maps each individual in the search space $\mathbb{G}$ to the problem space $\mathbb{X}$ and the set of feasible solutions is $\mathbb{G} \subset \mathbb{X}$.

The individuals were generated with the mapping ($map : \mathbb{G} \to \mathbb{X}$) between the dimensional vector of the search space $\mathbb{G}$ to the dimensional vector in the problem space $\mathbb{X}$. In the discrete optimization problem, the total number of elements (NOC) is represented as the dimensional vector of the problem space, and it must be mapped as the element of search spaces of individual.

$$\Psi = \{c_1, c_2, \ldots, c_{NOC}\} \quad \forall \Psi.c \in \mathbb{G}, \exists \Psi.x \in \mathbb{X} : map(\Psi.c) = \Psi.x, \tag{40}$$

where Ψ is an individual, represented as a tuple ($\Psi.c, \Psi.x$) of a dimensional vector $\Psi.c$ in the search space $\mathbb{G}$ and the corresponding dimensional vector $\Psi.x = \Psi.c$ in the problem space $\mathbb{X}$. G_i presents the group i with M_{size} of male individuals and F_{size} of female individuals in the population. The initialization process starts with a minimum number of individuals in the group with respect to the problem size.

The learning process is a mechanism which adapts the learning model for enhancing individual fitness. However, it increases individual fitness by exploiting the search space with respect to the problem space. The individual Ψ in the POP should improve its fitness value $F(\Psi)$ via learning and increase the probability of attaining a global optimum. Then, the learning for discrete optimization is defined as:

$$Learning = \{PoP, \mathbb{G}, \delta, L(\Psi_k, i, j), F(\Psi), \mathbb{X}\}, \tag{41}$$

where POP represents the set of individuals, $\mathbb{G}$ is the feasible search space of solutions, $F(\Psi)$ is the fitness function, and δ is referred to as the learning rate of the individual between ($0 \leq \delta \leq 1$).

Then, $L(\Psi_k, i, j)$ is the learning process $L(\Psi_k, i, j) : \Psi \to \mathbb{G}, \forall i, j \in \Psi$.

$$[i, j] = sort[ceil(x * rand(\delta, 2))], \tag{42}$$

where the two values are randomly generated for i and j. Thus, the x is in linear decreasing order, generated between max to 3 ($max \Longleftarrow \mathbb{G}$).

$$(Case\ 1): L_1(\Psi, [i,j]) = L(\Psi, [j,i]) \tag{43}$$
$$(Case\ 2): L_2(\Psi, i, j) = L(\Psi, j: -1: i) \tag{44}$$
$$(Case\ 3): L_3(\Psi, i, j) = L(\Psi, [i+1: ji]) \tag{45}$$
$$(Case\ 4): L_4(\Psi, i, j) = L(\Psi, i, j) \tag{46}$$

$$\Psi^* = best\{F(L_1), F(L_2), F(L_3), F(L_4)\} \text{ where } \Psi^* \in POP, \tag{47}$$

where Ψ^* is the best individual obtained from the different learning process and replaced Ψ_k in the POP.

6.1. Experimentation and Result Analysis of Travelling Salesman Problem

The mathematical model for the travelling salesman problem is formulated as:

$$F = \min \sum_{i=1}^{NOC-1} D(C_i, C_{i+1}) + D(C_{NOC}, C_1), \tag{48}$$

where $D(C_i, C_{i+1})$ is the distance between two cities C_i and C_{i+1} and $D(C_{NOC}, C_1)$ indicate the tour between the last city C_{NOC} and first city C_1.

The standard experimental setup for the proposed Java macaque algorithm is as follows: (i) the initial population was randomly generated with 60 individuals in each group (m = 60); (ii) the number of groups (n = 5); (iii) executed up to 1000 iterations. The performance of the proposed JMA is correlated with an Imperialist Competitive Algorithm with a particle swarm optimization (ICA-PSO) [64], Fast Opposite Gradient Search with Ant Colony Optimization (FOGS-ACO) (Saenphon et al., 2014 [65]), and effective hybrid genetic algorithm (ECOGA) (Li and Zhang, 2007 [66]). Each algorithm was run on each instance 25 times, and hence, the best among the 25 runs was considered for analysis and validation purposes.

6.2. Parameter for Performance Assessment

This section briefly explains the list of parameters which evaluates the performance of the proposed Java macaque algorithm with the existing algorithm. It also helps to explore the efficiency of the proposed algorithm in various aspects. The various types of investigation parameters are the convergence rate, error rate, convergence diversity, and average convergence from the population. Thus, the parameter for the performance assessment is summarized as follows [3,67]:

Best Convergence Rate: In the experimentation, the best convergence rate measures the quality of the best individual obtained from the population in terms of percentage with regard to the optimal value. It can be measured as follows:

$$BestConv.(\%) = 1 - \frac{F(\Psi_{best}) - Opt.Fit.}{Opt.Fit.} \times 100, \tag{49}$$

where $F(\Psi_{best})$ is the fitness of the best individual in the population and $Opt.Fit.$ indicates the optimal fitness value of the instances.

Average Convergence Rate: The average percentage of the fitness value of the individual in the population with regard to the optimal fitness value is known as the average convergence rate. This can be calculated as:

$$AvgConv.(\%) = 1 - \frac{F(POP_{avg}) - Opt.Fit.}{Opt.Fit.} \times 100, \tag{50}$$

where $F(POP_{avg})$ indicates the average fitness of all the individuals in the population.

Worst Convergence Rate: This parameter measures the percentage fitness of the worst individual in the population with regard to optimal fitness. It can be represented as:

$$WorstConv.(\%) = 1 - \frac{F(\Psi_{worst}) - Opt.Fit.}{Opt.Fit.} \times 100, \quad (51)$$

where $F(\Psi_{worst})$ indicates the worst fitness value of the individual in the population.

Error rate: The error rate measures the percentage difference between the fitness value of the best individual and the optimal value of the instances. It can be given as:

$$Errorrate(\%) = \frac{F(\Psi_{best}) - Opt.Fit.}{Opt.Fit.} \times 100. \quad (52)$$

Convergence diversity: Measures the difference between the convergence rate of the dominant individual and worst individuals found in the population. It can be represented as

$$Conv.Div(\%) = BestConv. - WorstConv. \quad (53)$$

7. Result Analysis and Discussion

The computational results of the experimentation results are illustrated in this section. The Table 9 consists of the small-scale TSP instance, Table 10 has the results of the medium-scale TSP instance, and finally, Table 11 shows the results of large-scale instances. Thus, the experimentation were directed to evaluate the performance of the proposed JMA with other existing FOGS–ACO, ECO–GA and ICA–PSO. Consider, the sample instance eil51 for the result evaluation. The best convergence rate for ICA–PSO is 94.35%, FOGS–ACO is 92.88%, and ECO–GA is 97%, but the convergence rate of JMA is 100% for the instance eil76. Then the average convergence rate for ICA–PSO, FOGS–ACO, ECO–GA, and JMA are 65.64%, 80.39%, 70.94%, and 85.5%, respectively. On the other hand, this pattern of dominance is maintained in terms of error rate for all instances in Table 9. Further, the Table 11 depicts that the convergence rate of the proposed algorithm is above 99% for all the large-scale instances except rat575, whereas the existing ICA–PSO, FOGS–ACO, and ECO–GA are achieved above 90%, 93%, and 96% for the same. It can be observed from the Tables that the existing algorithm values for the average convergence rate is lower than the proposed JMA in most of the instances. The examination of the proposed algorithm dominated the existing ones in all the performance assessment parameters, except that the convergence diversity of ECO–GA is better than the proposed algorithm, but the proposed algorithm maintained well-balanced diversity in order to achieve optimal results.

Table 9. Small-scale TSP instances.

S. No	TSP Instance	Technique	Optimum Value	Fitness			Convergence Rate (%)			Error Rate (%)			Convergence Diversity
				Best	Average	Worst	Best	Average	Worst	Best	Average	Worst	
1	eil51	ICA-PSO	426	510.94	558.26	614.47	80.06	68.95	55.76	19.94	31.05	44.24	24.30
		FOGS–ACO		441.78	488.62	543.04	96.30	85.30	72.53	3.70	14.70	27.47	23.77
		ECO-GA		426.00	544.48	608.42	100.00	72.19	57.18	0.00	27.81	42.82	42.82
		JMA		426.00	485.84	538.78	100.00	85.95	73.53	0.00	14.05	26.47	26.47
2	eil76	ICA-PSO	538	568.42	722.84	773.84	94.35	65.64	56.16	5.65	34.36	43.84	38.18
		FOGS–ACO		576.28	643.52	694.00	92.88	80.39	71.00	7.12	19.61	29.00	21.88
		ECO-GA		554.14	694.32	767.32	97.00	70.94	57.38	3.00	29.06	42.62	39.62
		JMA		538.00	616.00	691.00	100.00	85.50	71.56	0.00	14.50	28.44	28.44
3	pr76	ICA-PSO	108159	145,811.11	162,142.84	179,175.19	65.19	50.09	34.34	34.81	49.91	65.66	30.85
		FOGS–ACO		142,578.34	147,127.58	159,215.06	68.18	63.97	52.80	31.82	36.03	47.20	15.38
		ECO-GA		139,373.57	161,178.25	176,905.82	71.14	50.98	36.44	28.86	49.02	63.56	34.70
		JMA		136,028.80	145,945.99	157,854.23	74.23	65.06	54.05	25.77	34.94	45.95	20.18
4	pr144	ICA-PSO	58,537	66,674.33	76,240.43	85,508.90	86.10	69.76	53.92	13.90	30.24	46.08	32.18
		FOGS–ACO		65,018.22	68,055.25	76,407.75	88.93	83.74	69.47	11.07	16.26	30.53	19.46
		ECO-GA		63,225.11	75,659.14	83,172.31	91.99	70.75	57.91	8.01	29.25	42.09	34.08
		JMA		61,496.00	67,479.88	74,562.87	94.95	84.72	72.62	5.05	15.28	27.38	22.32

Table 10. Medium-scale TSP instances.

S. No	TSP Instance	Technique	Optimum Value	Fitness			Convergence Rate (%)			Error Rate (%)			Convergence Diversity
				Best	Average	Worst	Best	Average	Worst	Best	Average	Worst	
5	tsp225	ICA-PSO	3919	4217.98	5084.07	5782.75	92.37	70.27	52.44	7.63	29.73	47.56	39.93
		FOGS–ACO		4164.41	4547.41	5199.74	93.74	83.97	67.32	6.26	16.03	32.68	26.42
		ECO-GA		4056.84	5015.69	5671.25	96.48	72.02	55.29	3.52	27.98	44.71	41.19
		JMA		3979.27	4477.03	5121.15	98.46	85.76	69.33	1.54	14.24	30.67	29.14
6	pr264	ICA-PSO	49201	59,574.21	64,837.84	73,339.96	78.92	68.22	50.94	21.08	31.78	49.06	27.98
		FOGS–ACO		51,675.05	57,959.70	66,105.45	94.97	82.20	65.64	5.03	17.80	34.36	29.33
		ECO-GA		49,254.00	63,845.90	72,011.25	99.89	70.23	53.64	0.11	29.77	46.36	46.25
		JMA		49,215.00	56,967.00	65,121.15	99.84	84.06	67.46	0.16	15.94	32.54	32.37
7	lin318	ICA-PSO	42,029	53,514.61	58,841.06	63,104.28	72.67	60.00	49.86	27.33	40.00	50.14	22.82
		FOGS–ACO		52,319.74	52,967.00	55,780.78	75.52	73.98	67.28	24.48	26.02	32.72	8.23
		ECO-GA		51,091.87	58,861.06	61,755.46	78.44	59.95	53.06	21.56	40.05	46.94	25.37
		JMA		49,797.00	52,957.00	54,785.00	81.52	74.00	69.65	18.48	26.00	30.35	11.87
8	fl417	ICA-PSO	11,861	14,331.81	15,644.21	17,201.57	79.17	68.10	54.97	20.83	31.90	45.03	24.19
		FOGS–ACO		12,448.05	13,973.67	15,458.00	95.05	82.19	69.67	4.95	17.81	30.33	25.38
		ECO-GA		11,861.00	15,535.60	17,118.54	100.00	69.02	55.67	0.00	30.98	44.33	44.33
		JMA		11,861.00	13,845.06	15,458.00	100.00	83.27	69.67	0.00	16.73	30.33	30.33
9	d493	ICA-PSO	35,002	44,419.18	49,475.36	54,273.86	73.10	58.65	44.94	26.90	41.35	55.06	28.15
		FOGS–ACO		43,449.12	44,565.08	48,190.98	75.87	72.68	62.32	24.13	27.32	37.68	13.55
		ECO-GA		42,389.06	48,025.28	53,152.86	78.90	62.79	48.14	21.10	37.21	51.86	30.75
		JMA		41,358.00	43,134.00	47,364.00	81.84	76.77	64.68	18.16	23.23	35.32	17.16

Table 11. Large-scale TSP instances.

S. No	TSP Instance	Technique	Optimum Value	Fitness			Convergence Rate (%)			Error Rate (%)			Convergence Diversity
				Best	Average	Worst	Best	Average	Worst	Best	Average	Worst	
10	rat575	ICA-PSO	6773	8294.57	9630.68	10,568.23	77.53	57.81	43.97	22.47	42.19	56.03	33.57
		FOGS–ACO		8083.38	8687.46	9436.00	80.65	71.73	60.68	19.35	28.27	39.32	19.97
		ECO-GA		7884.19	9489.22	10,511.34	83.59	59.90	44.81	16.41	40.10	55.19	38.79
		JMA		7686.00	8537.00	9436.00	86.52	73.96	60.68	13.48	26.04	39.32	25.84
11	u724	ICA-PSO	41910	45,757.90	56,315.70	62,157.88	90.82	65.63	51.69	9.18	34.37	48.31	39.13
		FOGS–ACO		44,512.60	50,428.30	55,927.52	93.79	79.67	66.55	6.21	20.33	33.45	27.24
		ECO-GA		43,251.30	55,138.40	60,126.32	96.80	68.44	56.53	3.20	31.56	43.47	40.26
		JMA		41,988.00	49,161.00	54,248.00	99.81	82.70	70.56	0.19	17.30	29.44	29.25
12	pr1002	ICA-PSO	259,045	313,554.45	358,324.65	413,357.62	78.96	61.67	40.43	21.04	38.33	59.57	38.53
		FOGS–ACO		272,002.25	322,458.35	375,264.00	95.00	75.52	55.14	5.00	24.48	44.86	39.86
		ECO-GA		259,121.00	350,743.30	411,544.30	99.97	64.60	41.13	0.03	35.40	58.87	58.84
		JMA		259,145	314,587.00	375,264.00	99.96	78.56	55.14	0.04	21.44	44.86	44.83
13	u1060	ICA-PSO	224,094	245,345.46	292,904.92	316,853.79	90.52	69.29	58.61	9.48	30.71	41.39	31.91
		FOGS–ACO		237,510.64	261,491.76	283,448.30	94.01	83.31	73.51	5.99	16.69	26.49	20.50
		ECO-GA		231,877.82	283,841.16	310,468.10	96.53	73.34	61.46	3.47	26.66	38.54	35.07
		JMA		225,165	252,428.00	278,945.00	99.52	87.36	75.52	0.48	12.64	24.48	24.00

7.1. Analyzes Based on Best Convergence Rate

The best convergence rate reflects the effectiveness of the population-generated by optimization algorithm. Figure 5 depicts a comparison of the proposed algorithm to the existing algorithm in terms of convergence rate. The JMA holds lesser value as 74.23% for pr76 in small-scale instances. For medium-scale instances, the JMA holds 100% for the instance fl417. Then, the ECO–GA has the highest value of 99.97%, and JMA achieves convergence of 99.96% for the instance pr1002. As a result, on a medium scale, the instance lin318 has the lowest value of a 72.67% convergence rate in the ICA–PSO and the highest of 81.52 % for the JMA and 75.52 % for the FOGS–ACO, while the ECO–GA comes in second with a value of 78.44 %. In terms of convergence rate, the proposed Java macaque algorithm outperforms the existing algorithm.

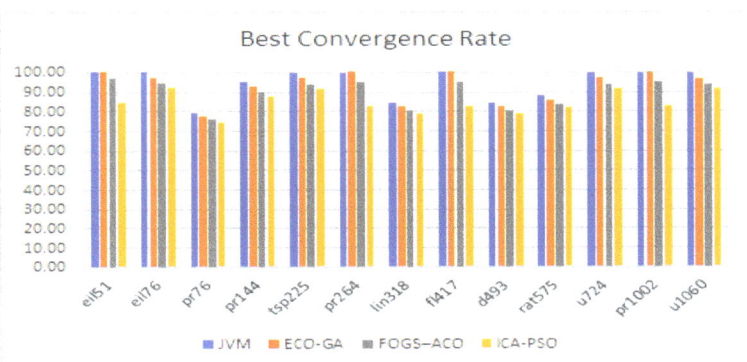

Figure 5. Best convergence rate.

7.2. Analyzes Based on Average Convergence Rate

Figure 6 depicts the results of an average convergence rate comparison between the proposed algorithm and existing algorithms. As an outcome, the investigation in terms of average convergence for JMA revealed that it outperformed the other algorithm. The average convergence rate of JMA has to attain a value above 65%, but the FOGS–ACO, ECO–GA, and ICA–PSO obtained values above 64%, 51%, and 50%. The JMA achieved a maximum value of 87.36% for u1060, while the FOGS–ACO achieved 88.74% for pr144, and ECO–GA reached an average convergence of 73.34% for u1060, and lastly, the ICA–PSO attained a maximum of 70.02%, for instance, tsp225, respectively. While comparing the performance of JMA and FOGS–ACO for the average convergence rate, both algorithms perform quite well, but JMA dominates in many cases.

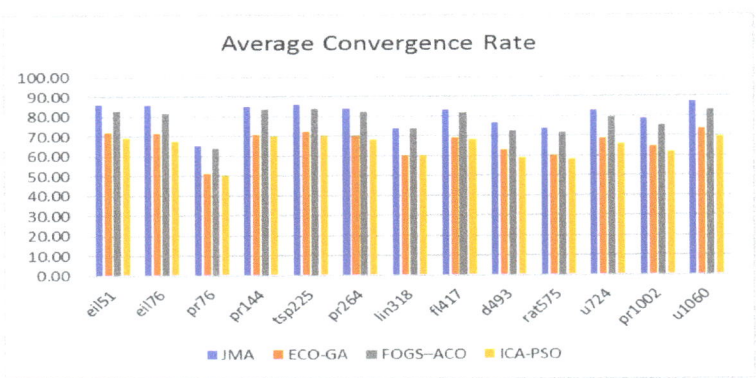

Figure 6. Average convergence rate.

7.3. Analyzes Based on the Worst Convergence Rate

Figure 7 shows the performance of the experimentation with regard to the worst convergence rate. The proposed Java macaque algorithm dominated the existing algorithm by all means. For example, by acknowledging the occurrence of instance pr144, the ICA–PSO, FOGS–ACO, ECO–GA, and JMA obtained the worst convergence rates of 53.92%, 69.47%, 57.21%, and 72.62%, respectively. Then, by considering the pr1002 instance from a large-scale dataset, the proposed JMA and FOGS–ACO held an equal value of 55.14%, which was followed by an ECO–GA value of 41.13%, and the lowest value of 40.43% was attained by ICA–PSO. Further, in terms of medium–scale instances, the proposed Java macaque algorithm also shows its superiority over the existing algorithm, such as FOGS–ACO, ECO–GA, and ICA–PSO.

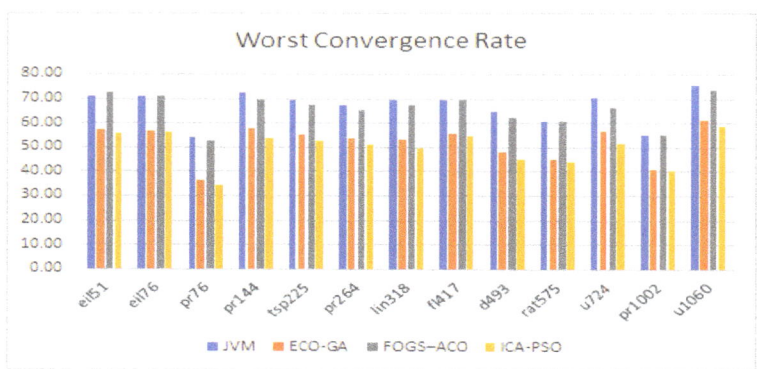

Figure 7. Worst convergence rate.

7.4. Analyzes Based on Error Rate

Figure 8 depicts the algorithm's performance in terms of error rate. The best error rate shows how far the best individual's convergence rate deviates from the optimal fitness value, whereas the worst error rate shows the difference between the worst individual's convergence rate and the optimal solution.

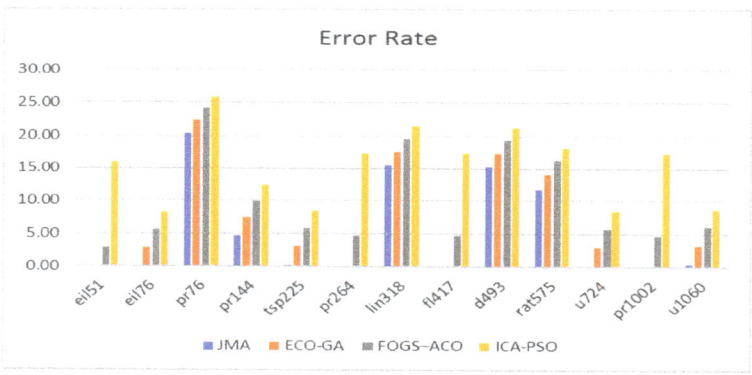

Figure 8. Error rate.

Consequently, the maximum error rate of 25.83 percent for particle swarm optimization, 24.14 percent for ant colony optimization, 22.37 percent for genetic algorithm, Java macaque algorithm is 20.52 percent, and in that order. Meanwhile, the least error rate value for JMA was 0% for instances such as eil51, eil76, tsp225, pr264, fl417, u724, pr1002 and u1060, whereas the genetic algorithm had 0% for instances eil51, fl417 and the particle swarm optimization had an approximate value of 8% for instances eil76, tsp225 and u724, and FOGS–ACO has less than 3% for instance eil51, respectively. JMA obtained better performance compared with the existing algorithm.

7.5. Analyzes Based on Convergence Diversity

One of the important assessment criteria that provides a concrete evidence of the optimal solution is convergence diversity. According to Figure 9, the performance of the existing ECO–GA surpassed the other algorithms in terms of diversity. For the sample instance u1060, the exisiting FOGS–ACO has a convergence diversity of 10.58%, the JMA has a convergence diversity for the instance as 12.19%, then the ICA–PSO has a value of 22%, whereas the ECO–GA achieved a highest value of 23.31%. The proposed JMA dominated the existing FOGS–ACO and was dominated by the other existing techniques, such as ECO–GA and ICA–PSO. Thus, the proposed JMA maintained the satisfactory level of convergence diversity among the population, and also achieved the best performance in terms of convergence with the existing algorithm.

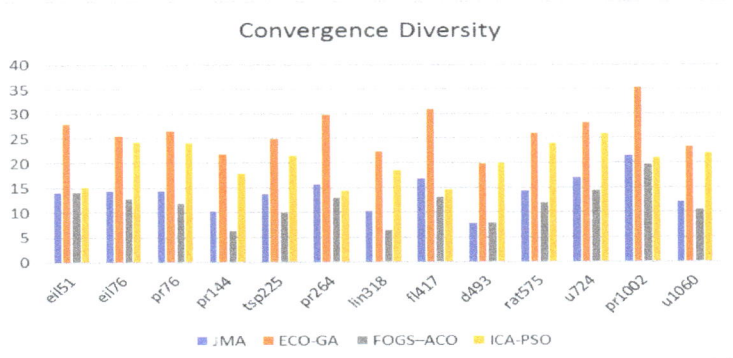

Figure 9. Convergence diversity.

8. Conclusions

The research proposed in this paper was motivated by the natural behavior of Java macaque monkeys and is suitable for solving real-world optimization problems. Thus, the Java macaque poses peculiar behavior with natural intelligence and a social hierarchy in an optimized way that well-suits the modeling of the novel Java macaque optimization algorithm. It was developed using the selection, categorisation, mating, male replacement, and learning behavior of the Java macaque. The important strategy exhibited by the population of the Java macaque is a dominance hierarchy, and that was incorporated with the JMA as a selection process. Hence, the individuals with higher social ranking dominated other individuals in the population and mostly gained preference in the mating process. Further, it helped the individuals with dominant status to gain a higher probability of generating new infants when considered with low-ranking individuals. Then, the algorithm also utilises the male replacement model, which increases the adaptive search capability of the JMA. Further, the JMA utilises the learning model that enhances the performance of the individual by increasing fitness, which proportionally upgrades social status. Hence, the JMA utilises the different search operations, which maintains well-balanced exploration and exploitation in finding the optimal solution. The performance of the proposed algorithm was analyzed with discrete and continuous optimization problems. The experimentation of continuous optimization was extensively conducted on 23 benchmark functions with unimodal, multimodal and fixed-dimension multimodal functions, and the proposed JMA depicts its dominant performance over the GWO and SMO. The outcomes of the experimentation were discussed as follows: (1) The unimodal functions are suitable for analyzing the exploitation capability of the algorithm because they contain only one global optimum. Thus, the result from Table 3 clearly depicts the dominance of JMA over other techniques. Hence, the JMA is well-suited for solving problems with exploitation behavior. (2) The multimodal functions are utilized for analyzing the exploration potential of the algorithm because of its multiple local minima, that is, the global exploration capability of the algorithm increases with an exponential increase in the number of local optima in the search space. Further, the performance of the experimentation illustrated from Table 5 also shows the dominance of the proposed system. (3) The final experimentation for the continuous Java macaque algorithm was experimented using the fixed-dimension multimodal benchmark functions. In this, the dimension of the benchmark function is fixed, which is used to analyze the performance of the algorithm in terms of exploration and exploitation. The results described in Table 7 clearly show that the JMA is well-suited to maintain the balance between exploration and exploitation. Further, the experimentation conducted over a discrete optimization problem by using the travelling salesman problem has to maintain balanced exploration and exploration with a quality selection process to achieve an optimal result. Thus, the results evidently show the performance of JMA over the existing dominant algorithm, such as FOGS–ACO, ECO–GA and ICA–PSO. Thus, the robustness of the JMA over the continuous and discrete search space clearly illustrates its potential over the optimization problem.

9. Future Enhancements

Future research will be focused on the development of the novel Java macaque algorithm with a hyper-optimization-based parameter-controlling casual system which efficiently explores and exploits the search space. Hence, the algorithm utilises social hierarchy-based selection, mating, male replacement, and a learning process as the operation of JMA. On the other hand, the grooming behavior of females and aggression behavior of males can also be incorporated with the JMA for enhancing the search process in the future. This algorithm enhancement may indeed improve the efficiency of the proposed algorithm for solving different kinds of real-world problems.

Author Contributions: Conceptualization, S.R.; methodology, A.D.; validation, R.S. and M.R.; formal analysis, D.K.; writing—original draft preparation, D.K.; writing—review and editing, M.R. and A.G.; supervision, S.S.A. and A.S.A.; funding acquisition, S.S.A. All authors have read and agreed to the published version of the manuscript.

Funding: This research was supported by Taif University, Research Supporting Project Number (TURSP-2020/215), Taif University, Taif, Saudi Arabia.

Institutional Review Board Statement: Not applicable.

Informed Consent Statement: Not applicable.

Data Availability Statement: Data available on request due to restrictions.

Conflicts of Interest: The authors declare no conflict of interest.

Abbreviations

The following abbreviations are used in this manuscript:

NIOAs	Nature-Inspired Optimization Algorithms
TSP	Travelling Salesman Problem
EA	Evolutionary Algorithm
SI	Swarm Intelligence
GA	Genetic Algorithm
DE	Differential Evolution
ACO	Ant Colony Optimization
ABC	Artificial Bee Colony
PSO	Particle Swarm Optimization
FA	Firefly Algorithm
CS	Cuckoo Search
MA	Monkey Algorithm
SMO	Spider Monkey Algorithm
ASMO	Ageist Spider Monkey Algorithm
GWO	Grey Wolf Optimization
JMA	Java macaque Algorithm
KH	Krill Herd
BFA	Bacterial foraging algorithm
AIS	rtificial Immune System
CA	Culture Algorithm

RA	Reptile Algorithm
ICA-PSO	Imperialist Competitive Algorithm with particle swarm optimization
FOGS-ACO	Fast Opposite Gradient Search with Ant Colony Optimization
ECOGA	SEffective hybrid genetic algorithm
AM	Adult Male
SM	Sub-Adult Male
JM	Juvenile Male
IM	Infant Male
AF	Adult Female
SF	Sub-Adult Female
JF	Juvenile Female
IF	Infant Female
α	Death rate of Infant
β	Death rate of Non-Infant
POP	Population of Java macaque
$\{G_i\}$	presents the Group i
M_{size}	Male individuals in the population
F_{size}	female individuals in the population
$F(\Psi)$	Fitness evaluation individuals
GM, GF	Global best male and female
{DS}	Dominant set of individuals
{NDS}	Non-Dominant set of individuals
δ	Learning rate of the individual

References

1. Uniyal, N.; Pant, S.; Kumar, A.; Pant, P. Nature-inspired metaheuristic algorithms for optimization. *Meta-Heuristic Optim. Tech. Appl. Eng.* **2022**, *10*, 1. [CrossRef]
2. Alsalibi, B.; Mirjalili, S.; Abualigah, L.; Gandomi, A.H. A Comprehensive Survey on the Recent Variants and Applications of Membrane-Inspired Evolutionary Algorithms. *Arch. Comput. Methods Eng.* **2022**, 1–17. [CrossRef]
3. Dinesh, K.; Amudhavel, J.; Rajakumar, R.; Dhavachelvan, P.; Subramanian, R. A novel self-organisation model for improving the performance of permutation coded genetic algorithm. *Int. J. Adv. Intell. Paradig.* **2020**, *17*, 299–322. [CrossRef]
4. Storn, R.; Price, K. Differential evolution—A simple and efficient heuristic for global optimization over continuous spaces. *J. Glob. Optim.* **1997**, *11*, 341–359. [CrossRef]
5. Liu, C.; Wu, L.; Huang, X.; Xiao, W. Improved dynamic adaptive ant colony optimization algorithm to solve pipe routing design. *Knowl.-Based Syst.* **2022**, *237*, 107846. [CrossRef]
6. Karaboga, D.; Basturk, B. A powerful and efficient algorithm for numerical function optimization: Artificial bee colony (ABC) algorithm. *J. Glob. Optim.* **2007**, *39*, 459–471. [CrossRef]
7. Latchoumi, T.; Balamurugan, K.; Dinesh, K.; Ezhilarasi, T. Particle swarm optimization approach for waterjet cavitation peening. *Measurement* **2019**, *141*, 184–189. [CrossRef]
8. Cao, L.; Ben, K.; Peng, H.; Zhang, X. Enhancing firefly algorithm with adaptive multi-group mechanism. *Appl. Intell.* **2022**, 1–21. [CrossRef]
9. Tang, C.; Song, S.; Ji, J.; Tang, Y.; Tang, Z.; Todo, Y. A cuckoo search algorithm with scale-free population topology. *Expert Syst. Appl.* **2022**, *188*, 116049. [CrossRef]
10. Yılmaz, S.; Küçüksille, E.U. A new modification approach on bat algorithm for solving optimization problems. *Appl. Soft Comput.* **2015**, *28*, 259–275. [CrossRef]
11. Ahmed, O.; Hu, M.; Ren, F. PEDTARA: Priority-Based Energy Efficient, Delay and Temperature Aware Routing Algorithm Using Multi-Objective Genetic Chaotic Spider Monkey Optimization for Critical Data Transmission in WBANs. *Electronics* **2022**, *11*, 68. [CrossRef]
12. Tarawneh, H.; Alhadid, I.; Khwaldeh, S.; Afaneh, S. An Intelligent Cloud Service Composition Optimization Using Spider Monkey and Multistage Forward Search Algorithms. *Symmetry* **2022**, *14*, 82. [CrossRef]
13. Abualigah, L.; Abd Elaziz, M.; Sumari, P.; Geem, Z.W.; Gandomi, A.H. Reptile Search Algorithm (RSA): A nature-inspired meta-heuristic optimizer. *Expert Syst. Appl.* **2022**, *191*, 116158. [CrossRef]
14. Jain, S. Mammals: Whale, Gray Wolf, and Bat Optimization. In *Nature-Inspired Optimization Algorithms with Java*; Apress: Berkeley, CA, USA, 2022; [CrossRef]
15. Yang, X.S. Mathematical Analysis of Nature-Inspired Algorithms. In *Nature-Inspired Algorithms and Applied Optimization*; Springer: Cham, Switzerland, 2018; Volume 744. [CrossRef]
16. Karunanidy, D.; Ramalingam, R.; Dumka, A.; Singh, R.; Alsukayti, I.; Anand, D.; Hamam, H.; Ibrahim, M. An Intelligent Optimized Route-Discovery Model for IoT-Based VANETs. *Processes* **2021**, *9*, 2171. [CrossRef]

17. Qin, S.; Pi, D.; Shao, Z.; Xu, Y. Hybrid collaborative multi-objective fruit fly optimization algorithm for scheduling workflow in cloud environment. *Swarm Evol. Comput.* **2022**, *68*, 101008. [CrossRef]
18. dos Anjos, J.C.S.; Gross, J.L.G.; Matteussi, K.J.; González, G.V.; Leithardt, V.R.Q.; Geyer, C.F.R. An Algorithm to Minimize Energy Consumption and Elapsed Time for IoT Workloads in a Hybrid Architecture. *Sensors* **2021**, *21*, 2914. [CrossRef]
19. Dinesh, K.; Subramanian, R.; Dweib, I.; Nandhini, M.; Mohamed, M.Y.N.; Rajakumar, R. Bi-directional self-organization technique for enhancing the genetic algorithm. In Proceedings of the 6th International Conference on Information Technology: IoT and Smart City, Hong Kong, 29 December 2018–31 December 2019; pp. 251–255. [CrossRef]
20. Jana, S.; Dey, A.; Maji, A.K.; Pal, R.K. Solving Sudoku Using Neighbourhood-Based Mutation Approach of Genetic Algorithm. In *Advanced Computing and Systems for Security: Volume 13*; Springer: Singapore, 2022; pp. 153–167. [CrossRef]
21. Al-Sharhan, S.; Bimba, A. Adaptive multi-parent crossover GA for feature optimization in epileptic seizure identification. *Appl. Soft Comput.* **2019**, *75*, 575–587. [CrossRef]
22. Manicassamy, J.; Karunanidhi, D.; Pothula, S.; Thirumal, V.; Ponnurangam, D.; Ramalingam, S. GPS: A constraint-based gene position procurement in chromosome for solving large-scale multiobjective multiple knapsack problems. *Front. Comput. Sci.* **2018**, *12*, 101–121. [CrossRef]
23. Zhang, P.; Yao, H.; Li, M.; Liu, Y. Virtual network embedding based on modified genetic algorithm. *Peer-to-Peer Netw. Appl.* **2019**, *12*, 481–492. [CrossRef]
24. Gholami, O.; Sotskov, Y.N.; Werner, F. A genetic algorithm for hybrid job-shop scheduling problems with minimizing the makespan or mean flow time. *J. Adv. Manuf. Syst.* **2018**, *17*, 461–486. [CrossRef]
25. Karunanidy, D.; Amudhavel, J.; Datchinamurthy, T.S.; Ramalingam, S. A Novel Java macaque Algorithm For Travelling Salesman Problem. *IIOAB J.* **2017**, *8*, 252–261.
26. Dinesh, K.; Rajakumar, R.; Subramanian, R. Self-organisation migration technique for enhancing the permutation coded genetic algorithm. *Int. J. Appl. Manag. Sci.* **2021**, *13*, 15–36. [CrossRef]
27. Santos, J.; Ferreira, A.; Flintsch, G. An adaptive hybrid genetic algorithm for pavement management. *Int. J. Pavement Eng.* **2019**, *20*, 266–286. [CrossRef]
28. Luan, J.; Yao, Z.; Zhao, F.; Song, X. A novel method to solve supplier selection problem: Hybrid algorithm of genetic algorithm and ant colony optimization. *Math. Comput. Simul.* **2019**, *156*, 294–309. [CrossRef]
29. Bujok, P.; Tvrdík, J.; Poláková, R. Comparison of nature-inspired population-based algorithms on continuous optimisation problems. *Swarm Evol. Comput.* **2019**, *50*, 100490. [CrossRef]
30. Ramos-Figueroa, O.; Quiroz-Castellanos, M.; Mezura-Montes, E.; Kharel, R. Variation operators for grouping genetic algorithms: A review. *Swarm Evol. Comput.* **2021**, *60*, 100796. [CrossRef]
31. Opara, K.R.; Arabas, J. Differential Evolution: A survey of theoretical analyzes. *Swarm Evol. Comput.* **2019**, *44*, 546–558. [CrossRef]
32. Wang, X.; Wang, Y.; Wong, K.C.; Li, X. A self-adaptive weighted differential evolution approach for large-scale feature selection. *Knowl.-Based Syst.* **2022**, *235*, 107633. [CrossRef]
33. Müller, F.M.; Bonilha, I.S. Hyper-Heuristic Based on ACO and Local Search for Dynamic Optimization Problems. *Algorithms* **2022**, *15*, 9. [CrossRef]
34. Mahmoodi, L.; Aliyari Shoorehdeli, M. Comments on "A Novel Fault Diagnostics and Prediction Scheme Using a Nonlinear Observer With Artificial Immune System as an Online Approximator". *IEEE Trans. Control. Syst. Technol.* **2017**, *25*, 2243–2246. [CrossRef]
35. Coulter, N.; Moncayo, H. Artificial Immune System Optimized Support Vector Machine for Satellite Fault Detection. In Proceedings of the AIAA SCITECH 2022 Forum, San Diego, CA, USA, 3–7 January 2022; p. 1713. [CrossRef]
36. Passino, K.M. Biomimicry of bacterial foraging for distributed optimization and control. *IEEE Control. Syst.* **2002**, *22*, 52–67.
37. Hernández-Ocaña, B.; Chávez-Bosquez, O.; Hernández-Torruco, J.; Canul-Reich, J.; Pozos-Parra, P. Bacterial Foraging Optimization Algorithm for menu planning. *IEEE Access* **2018**, *6*, 8619–8629. [CrossRef]
38. Awad, H.; Hafez, A. Optimal operation of under-frequency load shedding relays by hybrid optimization of particle swarm and bacterial foraging algorithms. *Alex. Eng. J.* **2022**, *61*, 763–774. [CrossRef]
39. Wang, G.G.; Gandomi, A.H.; Alavi, A.H.; Deb, S. A hybrid method based on krill herd and quantum-behaved particle swarm optimization. *Neural Comput. Appl.* **2016**, *27*, 989–1006. [CrossRef]
40. Saravanan, D.; Janakiraman, S.; Harshavardhanan, P.; Kumar, S.A.; Sathian, D. Enhanced Binary Krill Herd Algorithm for Effective Data Propagation in VANET. In *Secure Communication for 5G and IoT Networks*; Springer: Cham, Switzerland, 2022; pp. 221–235. [CrossRef]
41. Yang, X.S.; He, X. Firefly algorithm: Recent advances and applications. *Int. J. Swarm Intell.* **2013**, *1*, 36–50. [CrossRef]
42. Cheng, Z.; Song, H.; Chang, T.; Wang, J. An improved mixed-coded hybrid firefly algorithm for the mixed-discrete SSCGR problem. *Expert Syst. Appl.* **2022**, *188*, 116050. [CrossRef]
43. Mohanty, P.P.; Nayak, S.K. A Modified Cuckoo Search Algorithm for Data Clustering. *Int. J. Appl. Metaheuristic Comput. (IJAMC)* **2022**, *13*, 1–32. [CrossRef]
44. Kumar, S.; Kumari, R. Modified position update in spider monkey optimization algorithm. *Int. J. Emerg. Technol. Comput. Appl. Sci. (IJETCAS)* **2014**, *2*, 198–204.
45. Wu, G.; Mallipeddi, R.; Suganthan, P.N.; Wang, R.; Chen, H. Differential evolution with multi-population based ensemble of mutation strategies. *Inf. Sci.* **2016**, *329*, 329–345. [CrossRef]

26. Ma, H.; Shen, S.; Yu, M.; Yang, Z.; Fei, M.; Zhou, H. Multi-population techniques in nature inspired optimization algorithms: A comprehensive survey. *Swarm Evol. Comput.* **2019**, *44*, 365–387. [CrossRef]
27. Xu, Z.; Liu, X.; Zhang, K.; He, J. Cultural transmission based multi-objective evolution strategy for evolutionary multitasking. *Inf. Sci.* **2022**, *582*, 215–242. [CrossRef]
28. Warwas, K.; Tengler, S. Multi-population Genetic Algorithm with the Actor Model Approach to Determine Optimal Braking Torques of the Articulated Vehicle. In *Intelligent Computing*; Springer: Cham, Switzerland, 2022; Volume 283, pp. 56–74. [CrossRef]
29. Hesar, A.S.; Kamel, S.R.; Houshmand, M. A quantum multi-objective optimization algorithm based on harmony search method. *Soft Comput.* **2021**, *25*, 9427–9439. [CrossRef]
30. Zhang, Y.; Li, J.; Li, L. A Reward Population-Based Differential Genetic Harmony Search Algorithm. *Algorithms* **2022**, *15*, 23. [CrossRef]
31. Van den Bercken, J.; Cools, A. Information-statistical analysis of factors determining ongoing behaviour and social interaction in Java monkeys (Macaca fascicularis). *Anim. Behav.* **1980**, *28*, 189–200. [CrossRef]
32. Veenema, H.C.; Spruijt, B.M.; Gispen, W.H.; Van Hooff, J. Aging, dominance history, and social behavior in Java-monkeys (Macaca fascicularis). *Neurobiol. Aging* **1997**, *18*, 509–515. [CrossRef]
33. Dewsbury, D.A. Dominance rank, copulatory behavior, and differential reproduction. *Q. Rev. Biol.* **1982**, *57*, 135–159. [CrossRef] [PubMed]
34. Engelhardt, A.; Pfeifer, J.B.; Heistermann, M.; Niemitz, C.; van Hooff, J.A.; Hodges, J.K. Assessment of female reproductive status by male longtailed macaques, Macaca fascicularis, under natural conditions. *Anim. Behav.* **2004**, *67*, 915–924. [CrossRef]
35. Sprague, D.S. Age, dominance rank, natal status, and tenure among male macaques. *Am. J. Phys. Anthropol.* **1998**, *105*, 511–521. [CrossRef]
36. Dasser, V. A social concept in Java monkeys. *Anim. Behav.* **1988**, *36*, 225–230. [CrossRef]
37. Paul, A.; Thommen, D. Timing of birth, female reproductive success and infant sex ratio in semifree-ranging Barbary macaques (Macaca sylvanus). *Folia Primatol.* **1984**, *42*, 2–16. [CrossRef]
38. Durillo, J.J.; Nebro, A.J. jMetal: A Java framework for multi-objective optimization. *Adv. Eng. Softw.* **2011**, *42*, 760–771. [CrossRef]
39. Deb, K.; Beyer, H.G. Self-Adaptive Genetic Algorithms with Simulated Binary Crossover. *Evol. Comput.* **2001**, *9*, 197–221. [CrossRef]
40. Lin, Q.; Chen, J.; Zhan, Z.H.; Chen, W.N.; Coello, C.A.C.; Yin, Y.; Lin, C.M.; Zhang, J. A hybrid evolutionary immune algorithm for multiobjective optimization problems. *IEEE Trans. Evol. Comput.* **2016**, *20*, 711–729. [CrossRef]
41. Meidani, K.; Hemmasian, A.; Mirjalili, S.; Barati Farimani, A. Adaptive grey wolf optimizer. *Neural Comput. Appl.* **2022**, 1–21. [CrossRef]
42. Zhang, L.; Liu, L.; Yang, X.S.; Dai, Y. A novel hybrid firefly algorithm for global optimization. *PLoS ONE* **2016**, *11*, e0163230. [CrossRef] [PubMed]
43. Di Gaspero, L.; Schaerf, A.; Cadoli, M.; Slany, W.; Falaschi, M. Local Search Techniques for Scheduling Problems: Algorithms and Software Tool. Ph.D. Thesis, Università degli Studi di Udine, Udine, Italy, 2003.
44. Idoumghar, L.; Chérin, N.; Siarry, P.; Roche, R.; Miraoui, A. Hybrid ICA–PSO algorithm for continuous optimization. *Appl. Math. Comput.* **2013**, *219*, 11149–11170. [CrossRef]
45. Saenphon, T.; Phimoltares, S.; Lursinsap, C. Combining new fast opposite gradient search with ant colony optimization for solving travelling salesman problem. *Eng. Appl. Artif. Intell.* **2014**, *35*, 324–334. [CrossRef]
46. Li, L.; Zhang, Y. An improved genetic algorithm for the traveling salesman problem. In *International Conference on Intelligent Computing*; Springer: Berlin/Heidelberg, Germany, 2007; Volume 2, pp. 208–216. [CrossRef]
47. Paul, P.V.; Moganarangan, N.; Kumar, S.S.; Raju, R.; Vengattaraman, T.; Dhavachelvan, P. Performance analyzes over population seeding techniques of the permutation-coded genetic algorithm: An empirical study based on traveling salesman problems. *Appl. Soft Comput.* **2015**, *32*, 383–402. [CrossRef]

Article

Decomposition of the Knapsack Problem for Increasing the Capacity of Operating Rooms[†]

Alexander Alekseevich Lazarev [1], Darya Vladimirovna Lemtyuzhnikova [1,2] and Mikhail Lvovich Somov [1,*]

[1] Institute of Control Sciences, 65 Profsoyuznaya Street, 117997 Moscow, Russia; jobmath@mail.ru (A.A.L.); darabbt@gmail.com (D.V.L.)
[2] Moscow Aviation Institute, 4, Volokolamskoe Shosse, 125993 Moscow, Russia
* Correspondence: somovml1999@gmail.com
[†] This paper is an extended version of our paper published in Proceedings of the International Conference on Learning and Intelligent Optimization, Springer: Cham, Germany, 2020; pp. 289–302.

Abstract: This paper is aimed at the problem of scheduling surgeries in operating rooms. To solve this problem, we suggest using some variation of the bin packing problem. The model is based on the actual operation of 10 operating rooms, each of which belongs to a specific department of the hospital. Departments are unevenly loaded, so operations can be moved to operating rooms in other departments. The main goal is to increase patient throughput. It is also necessary to measure how many operations take place in other departments with the proposed solution. The preferred solution is a solution with fewer such operations, all other things being equal. Due to the fact that the mixed-integer linear programming model turned out to be computationally complex, two approximation algorithms were also proposed. They are based on decomposition. The complexity of the proposed algorithms is estimated, and arguments are made regarding their accuracy from a theoretical point of view. To assess the practical accuracy of the algorithms, the Gurobi solver is used. Experiments were conducted on real historical data on surgeries obtained from the Burdenko Neurosurgical Center. Two decomposition algorithms were constructed and a comparative analysis was performed for 10 operating rooms based on real data.

Keywords: health scheduling; approximation algorithms; decomposition; capacity increase; bin packing problem; scheduling problem

1. Introduction

Health scheduling is an essential component for medicine automation. The development of scheduling models and algorithms has gained particular relevance in connection with the COVID-19 pandemic. In particular, there is a high demand for scheduling operating rooms. In Russia, many operations can be done free of charge according to a government quota. If the operation is considered urgent, the patient might agree to a paid service and later apply for compensation. Each surgical department has its own peculiarities of functioning. This is the time and principles of the work of anesthesiologists, the possibility of performing operations in other departments and associated overlays, the scheduling and rotation of doctors, and much more. For a multidisciplinary surgical hospital, an unbalanced operation of the surgical department is a limiting factor for the overall functioning of the organization. This is especially important for neurosurgical clinics, where individual surgical rooms are specialized and equipped to carry out certain types of surgery.

Due to modern technology, medical care is becoming automated. Therefore, the study of optimizing service processes is relevant. There are many publications on health scheduling. Let us consider some papers for the investigated problem of optimizing surgery rooms. The papers [1,2] are dedicated to an analysis of OR (operating room) and surgery scheduling. They highlight three decision levels in OR scheduling and planning: strategic, tactical, and operational. The strategic level covers long-term decisions, such as capacity planning and allocation, which typically take a long time. In such problems, the amount of time a given OR is dedicated to a surgical specialty is determined in order to optimize profit/cost over a long period. Problems with cyclic OR schedules, such as master surgical scheduling, are categorized at the tactical level. Moreover, the last decision level, the operational level, is the shortest and involves decisions such as resource allocation, surgical cases, and advanced scheduling. Our problem belongs to the operational level, our main goal is to distribute elective surgeries in operating rooms. There are also three well-known scheduling strategies/booking systems that dedicate OR-time to surgical groups: open scheduling strategy, block scheduling strategy, and modified block scheduling strategy. In reference [3], the authors used the block scheduling strategy, and tried to maximize the occupation of the ORs and respect the order of patients in the waiting list as much as possible. They used normal distribution for the duration of surgeries and cleaning time. In an objective function, the authors identified three criteria. The first is to maximize the expected surgery time in each block. The second criteria sets the probability that the total work duration of each time block does not exceed the available time. Furthermore, the last criteria ensures that preference is given to the first patients in the waiting list. However, they do not take into account differences between operating rooms. We also put patients from the waiting list to ORs using a block scheduling strategy but in our model different ORs belong to different departments, and we have to take this into account. Paper [4] shows the operating room scheduling problem, such as the bin packing problem. The authors look for a schedule with all n activities programmed to run in a container such that the container capacity is not exceeded and the downtime is minimal. Since the number of possible schedules grows exponentially, the complexity of solving these problems is due to the number of combinations that a large set of activities generate. This fact often leads to delays in the scheduling process, as the ease of finding an efficient schedule is reduced. To solve the problem, they developed a genetic algorithm. Genes are used to model time spaces in which jobs can be scheduled. Each gene has a length that cannot be exceeded. A chromosome contains a group of genes. In other words, each chromosome represents a possible schedule of work. In this representation, chromosomes may vary in size depending on the number of operating rooms used in the solution. We decided to use the bin packing problem with a homogeneous capacity in our model. The authors of paper [5] compare batched and online scheduling in surgery scheduling; in our model we use batched scheduling, the waiting list is updated every week, and patients are scheduled for the following week. The policy in batch schedules works as follows: it ignores new arrivals when the schedule is over. Thus, this class only cares about the result within the time horizon. Optimal solution methods for such schedules may include mixed-integer linear programming (MILPs) solvers. These can be optimal solvers based on branching and cutting methods or metaheuristics. Batch scheduling works as follows: when a certain number of people in a batch is recruited, a schedule is made for the current day. People who have already been enrolled are removed from the upcoming batch, and new patients and those not yet enrolled are put into the next batch scheduling for the next day. Batch scheduling problems are often simpler, but can involve many different constraints. Paper [6] solves a problem close to ours. In that paper, the authors present an optimization framework for batch scheduling within a block-booking system that maximizes the expected utilization of operating room resources subject to a set of probabilistic capacity constraints. To understand whether a given schedule is feasible or not, the scheduler uses an estimate provided by the surgeon and an estimate based on historical data. If the sum of the point estimates of the duration of the operations assigned to the same schedule block and the intermediate cleaning time does not exceed the block length, then the block assignment is considered feasible. Note that we use historical data of a hospital too. The main purpose of this strategy is to ensure that all scheduled surgeries can be finished within the allotted block length, avoiding overtime. They solved the problem with mixed-integer programming and we also use this method. The authors develop an algorithm based on a normal approximation for the sum of the surgery duration to provide near-optimal solutions to the stochastic scheduling problem. The primary aim of paper [7] is the effective and balanced use of equipment and resources in hospital operating rooms. In this context, datasets from a state hospital were used via the goal programming and constraint programming methods. Now, we consider more contemporary papers in surgery scheduling. In research [8] from 2021, the authors use a weekly surgery schedule with an open scheduling strategy. In our work, we also construct a weekly schedule. The objective is to minimize the total operating cost while maximizing the utilization of the operating rooms, while also minimizing overtime use. Their mathematical model can provide optimal solutions for a surgery size of up to 110 surgical cases. Furthermore, the authors proposed two modified heuristics, based on the earliest due date and longest processing time rules, to quickly find feasible solutions. In article [9] from 2021, the authors find the optimal schedule of surgeries by minimizing operating rooms' idle times (in our paper we minimizing idle times too) while maximizing the number of scheduled surgeries during the most effective and desirable time windows. Surgeries during ideal time windows are encouraged by assigning bonus weights in the objective function. The stated and implied benefits of this strategy include mitigating financial loss, complications, and death rate due to a reduction in surgery delays. They introduce a binary programming model for scheduling operating rooms and a mixed-integer binary program for planning and scheduling both operating and recovery rooms for elected patients under deterministic conditions. The authors apply an open scheduling strategy for assigning operating rooms to surgeons and a Lagrangian relaxation method for finding promising solutions. Consider another article, namely [10] from 2021, which is similar to ours. In this paper, the authors allocate elective patients and resources (i.e., operating rooms, surgeons, and anesthetists) to days, assign resources to patients, and sequence patients in each day. They consider patients' due dates, resource eligibility, the heterogeneous performances of resources, downstream unit requirements, and lag times between resources. The goal is to create a weekly surgery schedule that minimizes fixed and overtime costs. To efficiently and effectively solve the problems of MILP models, the authors develop new multi-featured logic-based Benders decomposition approaches. Furthermore, a lot of works, such as [11–13], have an uncertain duration of surgery, and we plan to include this complication. In this paper, we do not consider the uncertainty. Our work is organized as follows: We consider the mathematical model in Section 2. Section 3 reviews the computational experiments. The decomposition algorithms are shown in Section 4. Section 5 presents the results of the algorithms compared to the MILP. Furthermore, some remarks are presented in the Conclusion section.

2. Mathematical Model

2.1. Problematic

The goal is to increase throughput according to two factors: reducing gaps in schedules and increasing the operation time in ORs. We can use the information system of the Burdenko Neurosurgical Center and doctors' expert evaluations to solve the problem. Experts identify subproblems such as hospitalization, surgical department manipulations, and the monitoring of surgery rooms. The problem is divided into three subproblems: The first is the problem of allocating specialists to the appropriate rooms at a certain time. The second problem is to create a schedule for receiving patients for surgery. The third one is the problem of predicting the idle times of surgery rooms.

In this paper, we consider only assignment patients to ORs. There are 10 departments in the Burdenko Neurosurgical Center, and each department has its own operating room. Incoming patients are always assigned to one of these departments. We will consider only elective patients. The Burdenko Neurosurgical Center information system includes information about a patient's hospitalization, the principles of their treatment, and the work of the department, including occupied beds and the work of the surgical department, etc. For each patient, information about their operations is generated in the system. This creates a table that consists of the following columns: number of the patient; date; the host department; surgery room ID; complexity category of surgery; start of surgery; end of surgery. Based on this table, we can conclude that the usage periods of ORs usually have gaps, which greatly reduces the efficiency of ORs. According to examples for each surgery, we know the duration, number, and the department in which it should be performed. By using these examples, we created the frequency dictionary of various parameters and used it in the generation. Each department has its operating room. However, we can try to allocate some operations of the busy departments to the operating rooms of less busy departments.

2.2. Model

Let $M = 1, 2, ..., m$–set of operating rooms, $O = 1, 2, ..., o$–set of departments, and $J = 1, 2, ..., n$–set of surgeries. We consider 10 operating rooms $m_i \in M$ that work 4 days a week for 11 h every day (from 9:00 to 20:00). Our main goal is to decrease the gaps in these operating rooms. Gaps there mean that the operating room is not busy at these moments. Analyzing the hospital report, we can see that the duration of surgeries is quite long. Let us assume that if the surgery ends at 17:00, then there will be no others after it because there is a high risk of overtime work. Because of this, there are gaps in the schedule. To solve this problem, we suggest using some variation of the bin packing problem, as containers will be operating rooms, the capacity of which is determined by the number of hours during which the surgeries can be performed (11 h). This model does not include urgent patients. We receive a patient waiting list at the end of each week and make a schedule for the next working week. In this case, the schedule is not a specific time for the start of operations, but only the distribution of surgeries in the ORs and days. The main goal is to decrease the number of gaps in the OR's schedule for the whole working week. Furthermore, an important criterion is a department where the patient is treated, because each department $o_i \in O$ has its own OR m_i (10 departments), and it is undesirable to operate the patient in an external OR. In our previous work on this topic [14], we approached this problem in terms of schedule theory, and we assigned patients strictly to their operating rooms. However, in this work, for this purpose, a weight matrix W has been added to the model, where $w_{ij} = w_0$ ($w_0 > 1$), if the surgery j is performed in "its" OR m_i, and $w_{ij} = 1$ in the other case. The definition of a guest surgery and a home surgery is introduced; we will call the surgery "home" if it is performed in "its" operating room, and we will call the surgery "guest" if it is performed in another operating room. Let us construct a mathematical model. The parameters of the model are:

- p_j—processing time of surgery j, $\forall j \in J$;
- w_{ij}—weight of surgery j, if it is being performed in OR i, $\forall i \in M$;
- D—set of days when you can perform the surgery. In our case it is $d = 1, 2, 3, 4$ (Monday, Tuesday, Wednesday, Thursday);
- A—operating room hours per day (11 h).

The variables of the model are:

- $x_{ij}^d = 1$, iff surgery j assigned to OR i on day d, and equal 0 otherwise.

Objective function:

$$\sum_{d \in D} \sum_{i \in M} \sum_{j \in J} x_{ij}^d p_j w_{ij} \to \max \qquad (1)$$

Subject to:

$$\sum_{d \in D} \sum_{i \in M} x_{ij}^d \leq 1, \quad \forall j \in J; \qquad (2)$$

$$\sum_{j \in J} p_j x_{ij}^d \leq A, \quad \forall i \in M, \forall d \in D. \qquad (3)$$

The objective function (1) maximizes the weighted number of operating hours during the week, which, accordingly, minimizes gap hours. Constraint (2) ensures that one operation is not scheduled more than once. Furthermore, constraint (3) guarantees that the total duration of all surgeries in one OR on one day does not exceed the operating time of that room; in our case all operating rooms work the same number of hours. It is also necessary to note that this problem is NP-hard and cannot be solved in polynomial time.

3. Computational Experiments

Experiments will be conducted on pseudo-real data. Surgical data were provided to us by Burdenko Neurosurgical Center. The Burdenko National Medical Research Center for Neurosurgery is the leading neurosurgical hospital in the Russian Federation and the world's leading neurosurgical clinic, with a rich history, state-of-the-art equipment, and a unique professional team. Every year the National Center performs about 10,000 neurosurgical surgeries for the widest range of diseases of the nervous system. The structure of the center includes 10 clinical departments with 10 main operating rooms. We have data on all surgery operations made in 2014. It is also important to note that some operating rooms are busier than others. In other words, operations are assigned to operating rooms unevenly. The duration of surgical operations is generated randomly, with a variation of one hour from the average duration of surgeries in a given department. Thus, our dataset contains the department to which the surgery is attached and the duration of this surgery. The MILP model in all experiments is solved using Gurobi with an academic license in a Python environment. We decided to use Gurobi since it is the most powerful mathematical optimization solver.

The simulation scheme is as follows:

1. At the beginning of the week, N of generated surgeries is added to the waiting list;
2. The problem of mixed-integer linear programming with the above-described constraints and objective functions is solved by Gurobi in Python. That is, the optimal schedule for a given week is made, and the surgeries that could not be assigned remain in the waiting list and are transferred to the next week;
3. Furthermore, this cycle is repeated.

The number of surgeries N that we add to the waiting list every week is important. On average, about 130–140 surgeries are performed per week. Accordingly, if we take N much more than this value, the operations will accumulate in the waiting list, and with each week the gaps will become smaller because there will be a large selection of surgeries to schedule. However, the queue will keep steadily growing.

We need to minimize the total gap hours concerning the fact that guest surgeries are undesirable. Then, we need to check the dependency of OR's gap hours, and the number of guest surgeries, depending on the choice of weight w_0. The planning period is chosen to be two weeks and the number of surgeries $N = 150$, so that a large number of surgeries would not accumulate. We tested the experiments on five different generated data, where only the duration of surgeries changes randomly. We took the average values of the total gap duration and the number of guest surgeries for each experiment.

Figure 1 shows a sharp jump at the beginning. In Figure 2 with the increased scale, you can see that the jump occurs when the weight coefficients w_0 are from 1 to 4. Next, with the further increasing of weights, the value of the total gaps stabilizes at approximately 11 h.

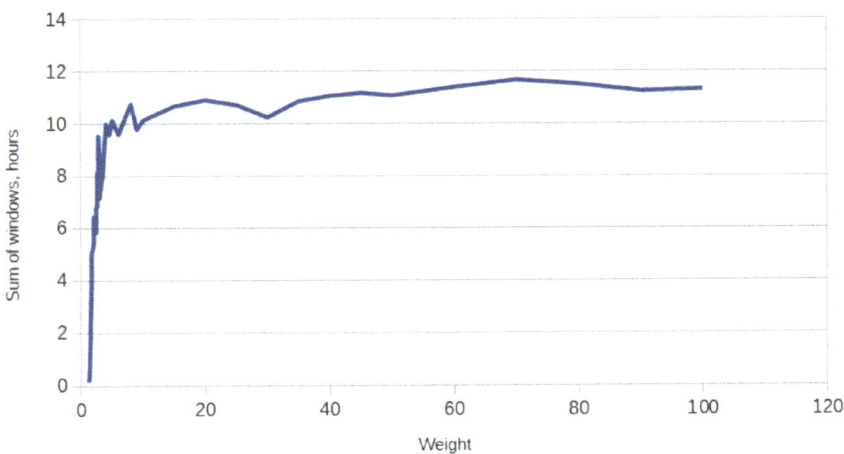

Figure 1. The dependency of the total duration of all schedule gaps on the weight w_0, $1 \leq w_o \leq 100$.

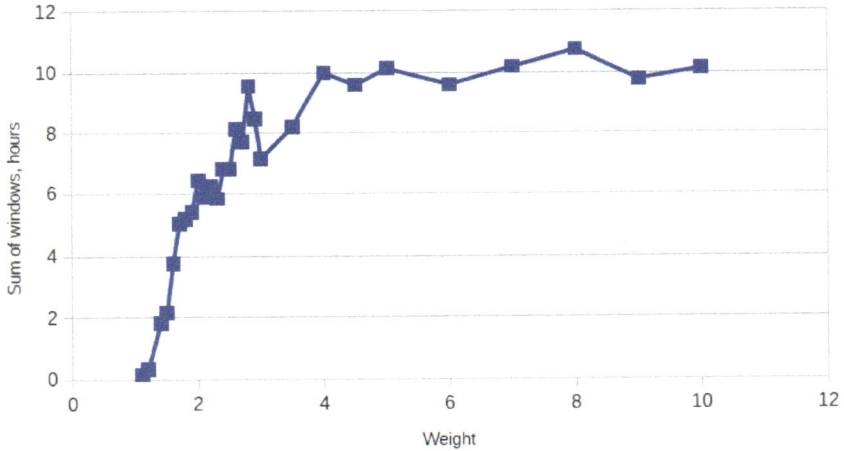

Figure 2. More detailed dependency diagram of the total duration of all schedule gaps on the weight w_0, $1 \leq w_o \leq 10$.

Now, let us consider the graph of dependence of the number of guest surgeries on the same w_0 weighting coefficients (Figures 3 and 4). This graph behaves almost in the same way; there is a sharp jump down with small values of w_0. Next, with the further increasing of weights, the number of the guest surgeries becomes stable, starting with the same values of w_0 as in the previous graph. The following conclusion can be drawn from these graphs: Even if it is very important to perform home surgeries ($w_0 \gg 1$), we need to assign some guest surgeries (Figure 4) to make an optimal schedule. Furthermore, it appeared that the total duration of gaps also does not change at large values of w_0. The problem appeared to be computationally difficult for weights, at which there is a sharp jump in the graphics. That is the reason for adding a time limit to the experiment. If for a certain weight w_0 it takes a long time to calculate the result, then we skip this value and proceed with the next value of weight.

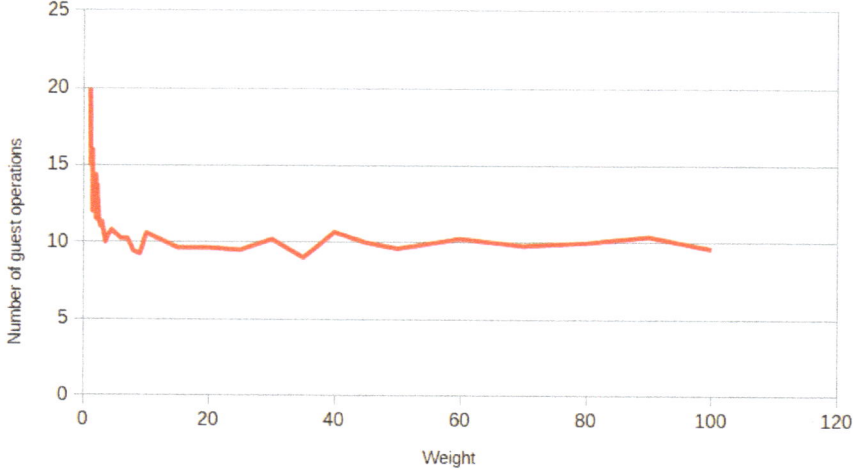

Figure 3. The dependency of the number of guest surgeries on the weight w_0, $1 \leq w_o \leq 100$.

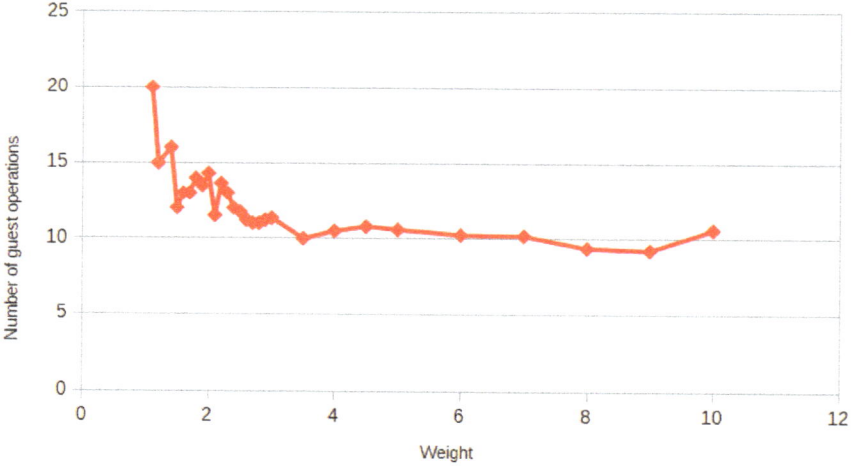

Figure 4. More detailed dependency diagram of the number of guest surgeries on the weight w_0, $1 \leq w_o \leq 10$.

4. Algorithms

Since our MILP model is computationally difficult, we consider two approximate algorithms and compare them with each other. First, the algorithm constructs a schedule for each department separately, and after that, it changes some surgeries to more optimal solutions. In the second algorithm, we construct a decomposition graph to divide departments into groups and solve the MILP problem for each group.

4.1. Vertex Decomposition with Balanced Distribution

Vertex decomposition with balanced distribution further in the text will be called Algorithm 1. The main idea of this algorithm is to assign patients to ORs in their departments at first. This is the first stage. After this distribution, we have a schedule without guest surgeries and some patients remained on the waiting list. Next, at the second stage, we check if the patients from the waiting list can be assigned to any OR on any day of the week. Next, at the third stage, our algorithm checks if it is possible to assign patients from the waiting list to the OR if the surgery with the minimum duration is removed from it. Removed surgeries are added back to the waiting list and all steps of the algorithm are repeated for these surgeries. The third stage of the algorithm may be repeated several times. We look at the maximum value of the following values for all operation rooms and for all days: the remaining hours in the operating room if we remove the surgery with the minimum duration. Furthermore, this value is compared to the duration of the minimal surgeries on the waiting list; if it is more than the duration of two or one surgeries, we repeat the third stage twice or once, respectively. In our case, we always get one repetition of the third stage. As a reminder, our main goal is to minimize gaps in all ORs during the week. At first, we need to set a problem for the first step, whereby we construct a schedule without guest surgeries. It is a MILP model with the following parameters, objective functions, and constraints:

- p_j—processing time of surgery j, $\forall j \in J$;
- D—set of days when you can perform the surgery. In our case it is $d = 1, 2, 3, 4$ (Monday, Tuesday, Wednesday, Thursday);
- A—operating room hours per day (11 h).

The variables of the model are:

- $x_j^d = 1$, iff surgery j assigned to OR on day d, and equal 0 otherwise.

Objective function:

$$\sum_{d \in D} \sum_{j \in J} x_j^d p_j \to \max \qquad (4)$$

Subject to:

$$\sum_{d \in D} x_j^d \leq 1, \qquad \forall j \in J; \qquad (5)$$

$$\sum_{j \in J} p_j x_j^d \leq A, \qquad \forall d \in D. \qquad (6)$$

The solution of this MILP model presents an optimal weekly schedule for one department if there are no guest surgeries. We solve this problem 10 times for each department (for each OR) and put all unassigned patients in the general waiting list. For a better understanding, we present the pseudocode of our Algorithm 1.

In our first experiment, we constructed a schedule for two weeks. Now we need to construct a schedule for two weeks for this algorithm. To achieve this, it is necessary to use the algorithm twice, but the second time the waiting list will not be empty, it will remain from the previous week. Furthermore, we can construct a schedule for N weeks, we just need to perform this algorithm N times and add unscheduled surgeries from previous weeks to the waiting list.

Remark 1. *At the third stage, we have restriction remains_hours[i] > T, which means that we consider only ORs with more than T hours left for surgeries. Here, we took $T = 1$ h, but in future works, we will find the cost of an operational hour and the cost of one guest surgery, and then calculate T based on these considerations, because T affects gap hours and the number of guest surgeries.*

Algorithm 1: pseudocode

Departments = 10
surgeries = []
remains_hours = []
waiting_list = []
guest_surgeries = 0
for $i = 1$ **to** *Departments* **do**
    // The first stage:
    Solve MILP model with Gurobi for department i;
    surgeries += surgeries[i]
    remains_hours += remains_hours[i]
    waiting_list += waiting_list[i]
    // Solution of MILP model return remains_hours[i], it is an array with four elements, and each element shows the unused hours of the operating room on one day of the work week (4 working days per week). It also returns waiting_list[i], which have the durations of surgeries that are not scheduled for this week. Furthermore, it returns surgeries[i]; it is the array with four arrays inside that contain surgeries, which are scheduled on one day(four arrays because of 4 working days per week).
end
for $j = 1$ **to** *waiting_list.length* **do**
    // For each surgery on the waiting list:
    for $i = 1$ **to** *remains_hours.length* **do**
        // for each day in each department
        // The second stage:
        if *waiting_list[j]* $\leq$ *remains_hours[i]* **then**
            remains_hours[i] $-=$ waiting_list[j]
            // If the surgery can be put on that day in the OR of this department, we deduct from the remaining unused time of that OR on that day's duration of surgeries:
            guest_surgeries $+= 1$
            // We add one to the counter of guest surgeries because this surgery is not scheduled in its department:
            waiting_list[j] := 0
        else
        end
        // The third stage:
        if *waiting_list[j]* $\leq$ *remains_hours[i]* + *min(surgeries[i])* AND *waiting_list[j]* $\geq$ *min(surgeries[i])* AND *remains_hours[i]* $\geq$ 1 hour **then**
            remains_hours[i] $-=$ waiting_list[j]
            // Do the same things, but now we remove the surgery with the minimum duration, which was scheduled on that day in this OR. Furthermore, the last restriction in the condition is needed so that there are not many guest surgeries in the final schedule.
            guest_surgeries $+= 1$
            waiting_list[j] := 0
            waiting_list $+=$ min(surgeries[i])
            // We need to add removed surgery to the waiting list.
        else
        end
    end
end

4.2. Graph Decomposition

Graph decomposition further in the text will be called Algorithm 2. Furthermore, we consider another approach to solve this problem. It is based on the mathematical model (1)–(3) (our exact approach); however, there, we break down the departments into groups. In other words, we solve several of the same problems with a smaller set of variables instead of one big problem with 10 departments. We can use the historical data of surgeries of each department and see which departments are overloaded and which are not, and combine them into groups. It can be represented with a graph (Figure 5): vertexes are the departments, one department can operate on patients from another department if there is an edge between them. We also solve this problem for N times to do the schedule for N weeks. In our case $N = 2$.

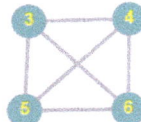
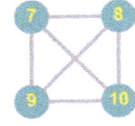

Figure 5. Decomposition graph.

So we need to solve our MILP model for every component of this graph. Now, we can compare three approaches on the same generated data in terms of the number of guest operations, the amount of unused work time in two weeks, and computing time. Below is the pseudocode of this algorithm.

Algorithm 2: pseudocode

Departments_blocks = $[[1], [2], [3,4,5,6], [7,8,9,10]]$
gaps_hours = $[]$
waiting_list = $[]$
guest_surgeries = 0
for i **in** Departments_blocks **do**
    // Solve MILP model with Gurobi for Departments_blocks[i]
    gaps_hours += gaps_hours[i]
    waiting_list += waiting_list[i]
    guest_surgeries += guest_surgeries[i]
    // Solution of MILP model return objective function in gaps_hours[i] for a given block of operating rooms, It also returns waiting_list[i], which have the duration of surgeries that are not scheduled for this week. Furthermore, it returns guest_surgeries[i] – a number of guest surgeries in a given block of ORs.
end

4.3. Complexity of the Algorithms

In general, the upper bound of the efficiency of our MILP problem using the exact approach is brute force: 2^n. In our case, n is equal to the number of binary variables x_{ij}^d, $n = N \cdot M \cdot D$, where N—the number of the surgeries, M—the number of the operation rooms, and D—the number of workdays in a week. Let the efficiency estimate of the algorithm for solving a discrete optimization problem with n binary variables be:

$$\phi(n) = 2^n. \tag{7}$$

Furthermore, let there be a tree that divides the problem into r blocks. It is argued that when decomposing the problem into blocks, the efficiency estimate of the entire problem will be equal to:

$$\sum_{i \in r} \phi(n_i) = \sum_{i \in r} 2^{n_i}, \qquad (8)$$

where $n = n_1 + n_2 + \ldots + n_r$.

Property 1. *The estimate (8) is better than (7).*

Proof. Using the well-known inequality $2^{x+y} > 2^x + 2^y$, $x, y > 1$ we can write the following chain of inequalities:

$$2^{n_1+n_2+\ldots+n_r} > 2^{n_1} + 2^{n_2+\ldots+n_r} > \ldots > 2^{n_1} + 2^{n_2} + \ldots + 2^{n_r}. \qquad (9)$$

As a result, we observe that the decomposition increases the efficiency of the algorithm. □

In Algorithm 2, we decompose our problem into four subproblems: $n = n_1 + n_2 + n_3 + n_4$. Furthermore, the MILP problem becomes much easier, because the efficiency estimate now is equal to $2^{n_1} + 2^{n_2} + 2^{n_3} + 2^{n_4}$, and with Property 1, it is better than 2^n. In Algorithm 1, we decompose the problem into 10 subproblems $n = n_1 + n_2 + \ldots + n_{10}$, but in each subproblem the dimension of the variable is reduced by one: $x_{ij}^d \to x_j^d$. $n_1 = D \cdot N_1$, $n_2 = D \cdot N_2, \ldots, n_{10} = D \cdot N_{10}$, where N_i is the number of surgeries in i-th department and $N = \sum_{i \in I} N_i$. So let us find the complexity of Algorithm 1 exclusive of the complexity of Gurobi. At the first stage, we solve the MILP problem by Gurobi for each department. At the second stage, we check for each surgery on the waiting list to see if it can be placed in an operating room on any given day. In the worst case, the number of surgeries on the waiting list can be N, then the complexity of the second stage is $O(D \cdot M \cdot N)$. At the third stage, we check for each surgery on the waiting list to see if it can be changed with the scheduled surgery with a minimum duration in an operating room on any given day. Furthermore, the complexity of this stage is the same as the second stage. The complexity of Algorithm 1, exclusive of the complexity of Gurobi, is $O(D \cdot N \cdot M)$ and it is less than $\sum_{i \in I} 2^{D \cdot N_i}$. Therefore, the efficiency estimate of Algorithm 1 is equal $\sum_{i \in I} 2^{n_i}$ and with Property 1, it is better than 2^n.

4.4. Algorithms Accuracy Estimation

Now, let consider evaluating the accuracy of our algorithms. Let us discuss this question using the following examples:

Example 1. *To illustrate the accuracy of Algorithm 1, consider a simple example. Let $p_1 = [2, 5, 2]$, $p_2 = [4, 3, 4]$, $p_3 = [3, 4, 3]$, and $p_4 = [2, 1, 3]$, where p_i is the processing time in hours of surgeries that are related to department i. There are a total of four departments and four operating rooms. Let each operating room work only 9 h and only one day. The total duration of all surgeries is 36 h. The optimal solution of this problem using model (1)–(3) constructs the schedule without gaps, all operations are scheduled, all 36 of the 36 h of operating time is used, and the number of guest surgeries is equal to three. To use Algorithm 1 for this example, we construct a schedule for each department using model (4)–(6) and then rearrange some surgeries if they will increase the objective function, according to Algorithm 1. We get the following results: 33 of the 36 h of operating time is used and only one guest surgery. Thus, the relative error of the objective function of Algorithm 1 for this example is 8.3%.*

Example 2. *To illustrate the accuracy of Algorithm 1, consider the same example as for the Algorithm 1. To use Algorithm 2 for this example, we break down the departments into groups and solve model (1)–(3) for each group. In this example, the total processing time of the surgeries for each department are 9 h, 11 h, 10 h, and 6 h, respectively. Thus, in the worst case we can divide the departments into the following groups: $[1, 4]$ and $[2, 3]$. Let me remind you that this means that* surgeries can only be transferred from one department to another within its group. After scheduling each group using model (1)–(3), we get the following results: only 32 of the 36 h of operating time were used and the number of guest surgeries is equal to two. Since our main criterion is the total duration of surgeries, Algorithm 2 gives a relative error equal to 11.1% of the optimal solution in this example.

In order to measure the accuracy of Algorithm 2, it is necessary to take the model (1)–(3), and according to the decomposition in Figure 5, construct a special example using additional parameters. These parameters must be related to the number of generated operations N described in the beginning of Section 3. It is necessary to describe these parameters in such a way that this special case is the worst case for the Algorithm 2. The estimate of the accuracy in the worst case will be the accuracy of the algorithm. For Algorithm 1, everything is done similarly, but instead of a decomposition graph, each operation is considered separately and then there is a balancing process according to Steps 2 and 3 of Algorithm 1.

Worst case of Algorithm 1. The problem of calculating the absolute error for the NP-hard problem is quite time consuming. The study of this problem is planned to be covered in future papers. However, let us show a rough estimation of the algorithm accuracy without taking into account some restrictions existing in practice. Let us neglect the restriction on the total number of operations and the number of operations that are assigned to each operation to construct the worst case of the problem. The exact algorithm allows for an even distribution of operations between operations, so we will construct the worst-case example so that the distribution of operations is unequal. Furthermore, the exact algorithm allows you to go through all possible combinations, to construct the worst case so that the approximate algorithm works least accurately due to the order of operations of the different durations. To increase the error of the approximate algorithm we will use only the minimum and maximum operations. In our case, the minimum duration of the operation is $h = 1$ h, and the maximum is $H = 6$ h. We took these durations based on historical data. Furthermore, we use the restriction on the size of one day in the operating room–$A = 11$ h of work. We construct the jobs in such a way that by using the largest duration of the surgery in each working day we get the gaps of a maximum size. Let the next set of surgeries be assigned to the first department for this week: eight surgeries with a duration of $A/2$ h, 180 surgeries with a duration of h hours, and 36 surgeries with a duration of H hours. Furthermore, the rest of the departments are empty. Following the exact approach, the schedule will be constructed as follows: all surgeries of $A/2$ h will be assigned to the first operating room (two surgeries for each day). Furthermore, the rest of the operating rooms will have one surgery of a duration of H and five surgeries of a duration of h on each day. Thus, there will be no gaps in the schedule at all. Applying the first algorithm to this example yields the following results: Since at the first step of the algorithm we construct the schedule for all departments separately, all surgeries of $A/2$ h will be assigned to the first operating room, but then all other surgeries will be on the waiting list. According to the second and third steps of Algorithm 1 on page 9, the operations from the waiting list will be distributed as follows: operating rooms number 2, 3, 4, and 5 will be "packed" with surgeries of a duration of $h = 1$ h, this will require $\frac{4 \cdot A \cdot D}{h} = 176$ surgeries, where $D = 4$ days. The remaining four surgeries of a duration of h will be assigned to OR six on the first day. Finally, one surgery of a duration of H will be assigned to operating room numbers 6, 7, 8, 9, and 10 for each day. So, it turns out that the number of gap hours is equal to $M' \cdot D \cdot (A - H) - 4 = 96$ h, where $M' = 5$ it is the number of not-fully-filled operating rooms. As a result, we obtain that a rough estimate of the absolute error of Algorithm 1 is 96 h.

Worst case of Algorithm 2. To construct the worst case for Algorithm 2, we introduce an additional restriction: 10 to 20 patients must be admitted to each department. Without this restriction, Algorithm 2 does not make much sense for extreme cases. To construct the worst case, we distribute the surgeries as follows: In each department of the first subgraph of the decomposition graph in Figure 5, we place 10 surgeries of duration $(A - H) = 5$ h.

Furthermore, in each department of the second subgraph we place 10 surgeries of duration $H = 6$ h. We also place 10 surgeries of duration $(A - H)$ hours and 10 surgeries of duration H hours, respectively, in department one and two. Thus, the exact approach would give an optimal solution with the number of gap hours equal to zero: each operating room would have one surgery of duration $(A - H)$ and one surgery of duration H on each day. Furthermore, following Algorithm 2, we obtain that half of the operating rooms for each day have one surgery of duration H, and the other half of the operating rooms for each day have two surgeries of duration $(A - H)$. We get the following estimate of the absolute error of gap hours for Algorithm 2:

$$Gap_{abs} = \frac{M}{2} \cdot D \cdot (A - H) + \frac{M}{2} \cdot D \cdot (A - 2(A - H)) = \frac{M}{2} \cdot D \cdot H = 120, \quad (10)$$

where M = 10—the number of operating rooms.

The result is that a rough estimate of the absolute error of Algorithm 2 is 120 h. However, although Algorithm 2 has a worse accuracy estimate, Algorithm 1 performs worse on average, as will be shown in the results below.

Our problem is a generalization of the 0–1 multiple knapsack problem. This problem is NP-hard, and it is shown in [15], where our problem is called LEGAP—a special case of the generalized assignment problem. Since it is NP-hard, it is not possible to obtain theoretical estimates for these algorithms. To estimate the practical accuracy of the algorithms, the extreme cases of the examples were constructed. In the first case, the surgeries with the minimum variation in the duration of surgeries were taken, and in the second case, with the maximum variation. As shown in [16,17], for examples with a large scatter of surgery duration, the core-type algorithms work badly, and for examples with a small scatter of surgery duration, the graphical-type algorithms work badly. For this experiment, the data were divided into two types. In the first case, the duration of the surgeries varies from 1.5 h to 9 h, with a uniform distribution. That is, the duration of surgeries has a very large scatter. In the second case, the duration of surgeries varies from 4.5 to 5.5 h, also with a uniform distribution. Using this experiment, we analyze the accuracy estimate of our algorithms depending on the width of the range of the duration of the surgeries. The other parameters of data remained the same as for the previous experiments. The assignment of surgeries to each of the 10 departments for each case is the same. However, in this experiment, half of the working week was taken, i.e., 2 days. Accordingly, half as many surgeries were taken. This was done so that the MILP solver could solve all the examples in a reasonable time. For each type, 100 examples were generated and tested for each of our approaches. Figures 6 and 7 show a graph of the dependence of the gap hours in the examples with a small variation of the duration of surgeries and on the examples with a large variation of the duration, accordingly. In Figure 6, it can be seen that Algorithm 1 performs better in almost all examples compared to Algorithm 2. The absolute error of the algorithms compared to the exact approach is not very large for surgeries with a small scatter, while it is already significantly larger for surgeries with a large scatter. Furthermore, it can be noticed that the scatter of the gap hours in Figure 6 is smaller than in Figure 7, which is quite logical, since the examples in Figure 6 are close to each other.

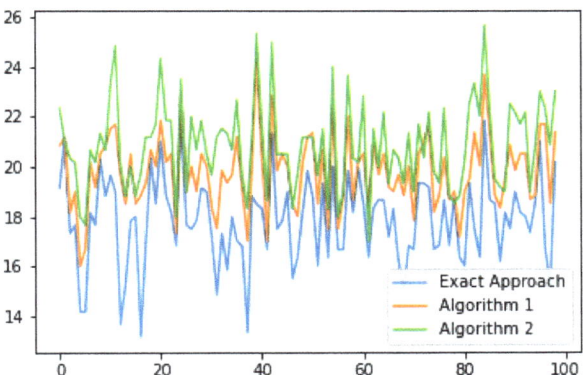

Figure 6. Graph of the dependence of the gap hours on the examples with a small variation of the duration.

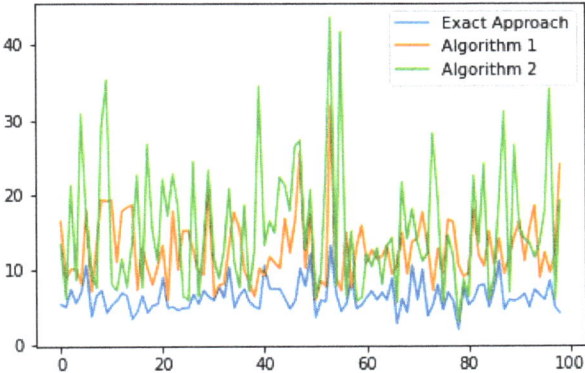

Figure 7. Graph of the dependence of the gap hours on the examples with a large variation of the duration.

The average values of the objective function and the number of guest surgeries are shown in Table 1. In the case of surgeries with a wide variation of duration, the absolute error of the gap hours for Algorithm 1 is 7.2 h, and for Algorithm 2 it is 8.9 h, while the number of guest surgeries for each approach is about the same. Now consider the case of surgeries with a small variation of duration. The absolute error of the gap hours for Algorithm 1 is only 0.2 h, and for Algorithm 2 it is 2.1 h. However, the average number of guest surgeries is different for each approach. For the exact approach, the average number of guest surgeries is equal to one. This can be explained by the fact that in each department the duration of the surgeries is almost the same. In Algorithm 2, the number of guest surgeries is not too large either, but Algorithm 1 has an average of 12 guest surgeries. This is due to the fact that in the second and third steps of Algorithm 1, surgeries are transferred from one department to another, even with a small improvement in the objective function. To summarize, our approaches work better for surgeries with a wide range of duration. This is a good factor for us, since in real life, the durations of surgeries are very different.

Table 1. Average values.

Data Type	Average	Exact Approach	Algorithm 1	Algorithm 2
Surgeries with a wide variation in duration	Gap hours, hours	5.7	12.9	14.6
	Guest surgeries	10.2	12.1	8.8
Surgeries with a small variation in duration	Gap hours, hours	17.7	17.9	20.8
	Guest surgeries	1.0	11.9	4.0

5. Results

Now we need to compare all approaches on the same data. All results are present in Tables 2–5; "-" means that the solve time limit is exceeded. The time limit is 30 min. All 10 examples were generated in the same way described in Section 3. Furthermore, we present an example schedule with the help of Gantt charts in Figure 8. Guest surgeries are marked in black.

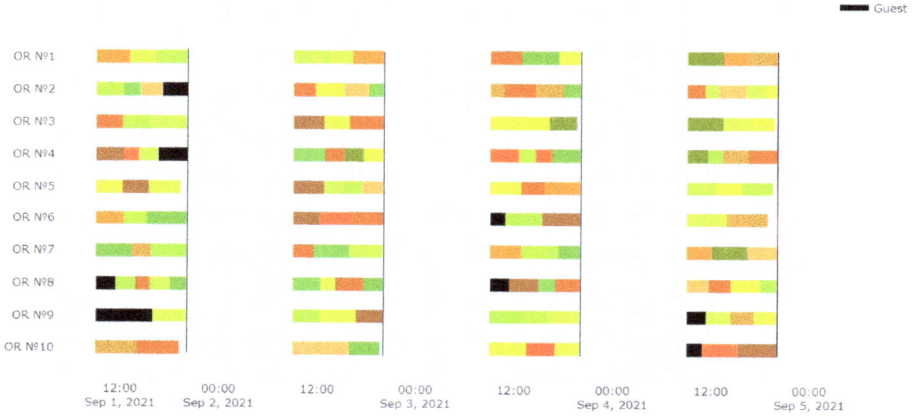

Figure 8. Example of schedule for exact approach.

Figure 8 presents that there are not many guest surgeries, and the duration of the surgeries is widely scattered.

Table 2. Computing Time.

Experiment	Exact Approach, sec	Algorithm 1, sec	Algorithm 2, sec
1	1500	1.92	7
2	340	1.97	13
3	1350	2.35	31
4	310	2.99	21
5	150	1.91	9
6	-	2.16	13
7	-	2.15	7
8	-	2.3	11
9	-	2.2	48
10	-	2.5	15

Table 2 shows the computing times for each approach for different examples. The computational time for the exact approach is extremely data-dependent. Furthermore, some examples cannot be solved at all within the time limits we set. Furthermore, the examples that are solved are solved long enough. Algorithms 1 and 2 solve the problem faster. In particular, Algorithm 1 is on average several times faster than Algorithm 2.

Table 3. Gap hours (objective function).

Experiment	Exact Approach, Hours	Algorithm 1, Hours	Algorithm 2, Hours
1	8	18.5	9
2	6	23	16
3	7.7	22	13
4	7	20.5	11.5
5	4.8	16	9
6	-	21.5	12.5
7	-	15.5	7
8	-	17	12.5
9	-	25	13
10	-	23	8

Table 3 compares the total number of gap hours for each approach. The results obtained by the exact algorithm show that the gaps range from 4.8 to 8 h for the groups of examples considered, but the results obtained by Algorithm 1 on average differ by 13.1 h compared to the exact approach. At the same time, the gaps obtained for the examples that the exact algorithm was unable to calculate averaged 20.4 h for Algorithm 1. Algorithm 2 in turn differs from the exact solution by 5.1 h for the first five examples. Furthermore, for the following examples, which do not have an exact solution, the gaps average 10.6 h for Algorithm 2.

Table 4. Guest surgeries.

Experiment	Exact Approach	Algorithm 1	Algorithm 2
1	17	15	9
2	12	20	13
3	16	26	13
4	13	16	13
5	14	26	7
6	-	31	12
7	-	22	13
8	-	20	13
9	-	18	8
10	-	19	10

Table 4 shows the number of guest surgeries. We have chosen the parameters so that the number of guest surgeries would be acceptable for each approach. It can be seen that for Algorithm 2, guest surgeries on average turn out even less than the exact approach; this is due to the decomposition of the problem into several groups of departments, while Algorithm 1 has more guest surgeries than the exact approach, because in it we transfer surgeries from one department to another at steps 2 and 3 of the algorithm.

Table 5. Average values.

Average	Exact Approach	Algorithm 1	Algorithm 2
Computing time, sec	730	2.2	17.5
Gap hours, hours	6.7	20.2	11.1
Guest surgeries	14.4	21.3	11.2

It can be seen that the exact approach can not find the optimal solution within the time limit for all generated examples. Thus, it can be observed that algorithms have a much shorter computation time, and at the same time do not lose much in the objective function. As we can see in Table 4, Algorithm 1 is the fastest, but Algorithm 2 has a running time not much longer and the objective function is half the size of Algorithm 1. However, pay attention to the gap hours relative to all available work times of all ORs in these two weeks. There are 880 h of work time. Furthermore, even in Algorithm 1, the gap hours are only 2.3% of all work time. It is not much different from the optimal solution with 0.8%.

6. Conclusions

This paper presents a formal statement of the problem of the predictive planning of surgery units in a large medical hospital and outlines the methods for its optimal solution. The experiments were carried out on real data that was generated based on data provided by the Burdenko Institute. The managerial insights of this work are to implement a program for scheduling operating rooms to automate this process and increase patient throughput at the Burdenko Neurosurgical Center. To achieve this, the plan is to make the existing model more complex, so that it is as similar as possible to the real situation in the hospital. In future works, we plan to add the uncertainty of the duration of surgery, urgent patients and the work of anesthesiologists.

The hospital report shows some departments are busier than others. Furthermore, our model implies the possibility of transferring the patients to the operating rooms of other departments if they are not busy. Our main goal was to increase patient throughput. This can be achieved by maximizing the number of operating hours. Operating rooms should be out of work for as little time as possible. The MILP model allows us to construct a long-term schedule with fewer gaps. Since we have to make a new schedule every time a patient is removed or added to the waiting list, a new schedule should be made in a short period of time. Furthermore, since our model is computationally complex, two decomposition algorithms were presented that significantly reduce the time calculations.

This paper shows that the complexity of the proposed algorithms is significantly reduced compared to the complexity of the exact approach. This thesis is confirmed in practice: the exact solution was obtained only in half of the cases. The problem with the exact approach is that for cases with the same number of applications but different distributions of surgery durations across operating rooms this approach may not find an exact solution in an acceptable time. Discussions are carried out regarding the theoretical estimation of the accuracy of the algorithms. For those examples for which the exact solution was obtained, the relative error of the solution was calculated. It can be seen that the first algorithm is further from the exact solution than the second. For further examples, in the accuracy of which has not been estimated we can also see this pattern. The objective function value obtained by the first algorithm is much higher than for the second. At the same time, we see that the computation time for the first algorithm is much less than for the second. This paper contributes to solving the problem of scheduling operating rooms. The peculiarity of the problem is that the operating rooms are multidisciplinary. That is, the operating rooms are assigned to certain departments where patients are admitted. The MILP model was invented for this problem. This problem is NP-hard. Therefore, it took a long time to construct the schedule. To solve this problem, two decomposition algorithms were developed to reduce the solution time. Furthermore, the complexities and rough estimates of the accuracies of these algorithms are given. In the future, we plan to expand the model for emergency patients and to add uncertainty, and we also will try a metric approach [18] for this case.

Author Contributions: Conceptualization, A.A.L. and D.V.L.; methodology, D.V.L.; software, M.L.S.; validation, M.L.S., D.V.L.; formal analysis, D.V.L.; investigation, A.A.L.; resources, M.L.S.; data curation, M.L.S.; writing—original draft preparation, D.V.L. and M.L.S.; writing—review and editing, M.L.S.; visualization, M.L.S.; supervision, A.A.L.; project administration, D.V.L.; funding acquisition, A.A.L. All authors have read and agreed to the published version of the manuscript.

Funding: This research was partially supported by Russian Foundation for Basic Grants, number 20-58-S52006.

Institutional Review Board Statement: Not applicable.

Informed Consent Statement: Not applicable.

Data Availability Statement: The pseudo-real data were generated from real data provided by the Burdenko Neurosurgical Center.

Conflicts of Interest: The authors declare no conflict of interest.

Abbreviations

The following abbreviations are used in this manuscript:

MILP   Mixed-integer linear problem
OR   Operating rooms

References

1. Zhu, S.; Fan, W.; Yang, S.; Pei, J.; Pardalos, P.M. Operating room planning and surgical case scheduling: A review of literature. *J. Comb. Optim.* **2019**, *37*, 757–805. [CrossRef]
2. Rahimi, I.; Gandomi, A.H. A Comprehensive Review and Analysis of Operating Room and Surgery Scheduling. *Arch. Comput. Methods Eng.* **2021**, *28*, 1667–1688. [CrossRef]
3. Clavel, D.; Mahulea, C.; Albareda, J.; Silva, M. A decision support system for elective surgery scheduling under uncertain durations. *Appl. Sci.* **2020**, *10*, 1937. [CrossRef]
4. Rivera, G.; Cisneros, L.; Sánchez-Solís, P.; Rangel-Valdez, N.; Rodas-Osollo, J. Genetic algorithm for scheduling optimization considering heterogeneous containers: A real-world case study. *Axioms* **2020**, *9*, 27. [CrossRef]
5. Allen, T.T.; Hernandez, O.K.; Roychowdhury, S.; Patterson, E.S. Practical Optimal Scheduling for Surgery. In *Proceedings of the International Symposium on Human Factors and Ergonomics in Health Care*; Sage: Los Angeles, CA, USA, 2020; Volume 9, pp. 1–14. [CrossRef]
6. Shylo, O.V.; Prokopyev, O.A.; Schaefer, A.J. Stochastic operating room scheduling for high-volume specialties under block booking. *INFORMS J. Comput.* **2013**, *25*, 682–692. [CrossRef]
7. Gür, Ş.; Eren, T.; Alakaş, H.M. Surgical operation scheduling with goal programming and constraint programming: A case study. *Mathematics* **2019**, *7*, 251. [CrossRef]
8. Lin, Y.K.; Li, M.Y. *Solving Operating Room Scheduling Problem Using Artificial Bee Colony Algorithm*; Healthcare Multidisciplinary Digital Publishing Institute: Basel, Switzerland, 2021; Volume 9, p. 152. [CrossRef]
9. Kayvanfar, V.; Akbari Jokar, M.R.; Rafiee, M.; Sheikh, S.; Iranzad, R. A new model for operating room scheduling with elective patient strategy. *INFOR Inf. Syst. Oper. Res.* **2021**, *59*, 309–332. [CrossRef]
10. Naderi, B.; Roshanaei, V.; Begen, M.A.; Aleman, D.M.; Urbach, D.R. Increased surgical capacity without additional resources: Generalized operating room planning and scheduling. *Prod. Oper. Manag.* **2021**, *30*, 2608–2635. [CrossRef]
11. Hans, E.; Wullink, G.; Van Houdenhoven, M.; Kazemier, G. Robust surgery loading. *Eur. J. Oper. Res.* **2008**, *185*, 1038–1050. [CrossRef]
12. Pang, B.; Xie, X.; Song, Y.; Luo, L. Surgery scheduling under case cancellation and surgery duration uncertainty. *IEEE Trans. Autom. Sci. Eng.* **2018**, *16*, 74–86. [CrossRef]
13. Liu, H.; Zhang, T.; Luo, S.; Xu, D. Operating room scheduling and surgeon assignment problem under surgery durations uncertainty. *Technol. Health Care* **2018**, *26*, 297–304. [CrossRef] [PubMed]
14. Lazarev, A.A.; Lemtyuzhnikova, D.V.; Mandel, A.S.; Pravdivets, N.A. The Problem of the Hospital Surgery Department Debottlenecking In *International Conference on Learning and Intelligent Optimization*; Springer: Cham, Germany, 2020; pp. 289–302. [CrossRef]
15. Ohlsson, M.; Pi, H. A study of the mean field approach to knapsack problems. *Neural Netw.* **1997**, *10*, 263–271. [CrossRef]
16. Hans, K.; Ulrich, P.; David, P. *Knapsack Problems*; Springer Science & Business Media: Berlin/Heidelberg, Germany, 2004; ISBN 10:3540402861/ISBN 13:9783540402862.
17. Lazarev, A.A.; Werner, F. A graphical realization of the dynamic programming method for solving NP-hard combinatorial problems. *Comput. Math. Appl.* **2009**, *58*, 619–631. [CrossRef]
18. Lazarev, A.A.; Lemtyuzhnikova, D.V.; Werner, F. A metric approach for scheduling problems with minimizing the maximum penalty. *Appl. Math. Model.* **2021**, *89*, 1163–1176. [CrossRef]

Article
Special Type Routing Problems in Plane Graphs

Tatiana Makarovskikh *,† and Anatoly Panyukov †

Department of System Programming, South Ural State University, 454080 Chelyabinsk, Russia;
paniukovav@susu.ru
* Correspondence: makarovskikh.t.a@susu.ru
† These authors contributed equally to this work.

Abstract: We considered routing problems for plane graphs to solve control problems of cutting machines in the industry. According to the cutting plan, we form its homeomorphic image in the form of a plane graph G. We determine the appropriate type of route for the given graph: OE-route represents an ordered sequence of chains satisfying the requirement that the part of the route that is not passed does not intersect the interior of its passed part, AOE-chain represents OE-chain consecutive edges which are incident to vertex v and they are neighbours in the cyclic order $O^{\pm}(v)$, NOE-route represents the non-intersecting OE-route, $PPOE$-route represents the Pierce Point NOE-route with allowable pierce points that are start points of OE-chains forming this route. We analyse the solvability of the listed routing problems in graph G. We developed the polynomial algorithms for obtaining listed routes with the minimum number of covering paths and the minimum length of transitions between the ending of the current path and the beginning of the next path. The solutions proposed in the article can improve the quality of technological preparation of cutting processes in CAD/CAM systems.

Keywords: routing; plane graph; polynomial algorithm

Citation: Makarovskikh, T.; Panyukov, A. Special Type Routing Problems in Plane Graphs. *Mathematics* **2022**, *10*, 795. https://doi.org/10.3390/math10050795

Academic Editor: Alexander A Lazarev

Received: 10 February 2022
Accepted: 26 February 2022
Published: 2 March 2022

Publisher's Note: MDPI stays neutral with regard to jurisdictional claims in published maps and institutional affiliations.

Copyright: © 2022 by the authors. Licensee MDPI, Basel, Switzerland. This article is an open access article distributed under the terms and conditions of the Creative Commons Attribution (CC BY) license (https://creativecommons.org/licenses/by/4.0/).

1. Introduction

Simulation of some control and automation design problems [1,2] explains interest in routing problems for CAD/CAM systems. Lots of them devoted to finding the routes satisfying certain constraints have arisen from specific practical situations. All kinds of trajectory problems are universal mathematical models of optimization and control tasks. The examples of them are the following: (1) heuristic algorithms for constructing routes (N.A. Eapen and R.B. Heckendorn [3], S.Q. Xie [4], Y. Jing and C. Zhige [5], M.K. Lee and K.B. Kwon [6], J. Hoeft and U.S. Palekar [7]); (2) trajectory stabilization of mobile robots (V.A. Utkin [8]); (3) management of routing process and optimization (A.A. Lazarev [9]); (4) problems of obtaining the routes in graphs (H. Fleischner [10]); (5) the routing problem for cutting blanks from sheet material (V.M. Kartak [11], A.A. Petunin [12,13], A.G. Chentsov [14,15], I. Landovskaya [16]).

The capabilities of modern equipment for cutting sheet material allow using the cutting plans with the combining of contours for cut-out of separate parts. This combining of cuts allows reducing the material loss, the cutting length and the number of idle passes.

Algorithms for obtaining the cutting plans for tasks with combined cuts do not fundamentally differ from algorithms that do not allow any combining. However, the algorithms for finding the routes of the cutter moving are fundamentally different. Therefore, the development of algorithms for finding the route of the cutter for plans allowing the combining of the cut parts contours is still an open task.

In this paper, we consider the routing problems in plane graphs. These graphs are homeomorphic images of cutting plans. The cutter path is defined as a path covering all the boundaries of the cut parts. The main constraint on this path is that the faces of the route's initial part do not intersect with the edges of the remaining part. For flame cutting, we need the following additional constraints on a path: (1) absence of self-intersections of the cutting path (NOE-condition), and (2) allowance to start cutting from allowable pierce vertices (PPOE-condition).

In practice, the most common approach does not involve a combination of the contours of the cut parts. This method is material and energy-consuming [13,17,18]. In one of such papers [3], the shapes are considered to be polygons. There are two different ways to cut each polygon: (1) entirely (complete cutting approach) or (2) partially (partial cutting approach) before cutting the next one. The authors of [3] proposed the approximation algorithm that uses such concepts as matching, spanning tree, and triangulation (MASTRI). This algorithm runs a time not greater than $O(n \log n)$, where n is the total number of all the polygons vertices. The cutting path computed by algorithm [3] is guaranteed to be within a factor of 3/2 of the optimum distance of the cutter. Hence, MASTRI algorithm can be used for computing cutting paths in industries like sheet metal cutting. It should be noted that the possibility of using concepts of matching, spanning tree, and triangulation was noted in our article [19].

The first attempts of constructing the routes in which the passed part of the route does not cover the edges of the remaining part were made in the work of U. Manber and S. Israni [20] where the image of the cutting plan is represented as an equivalent graph. The objective of this research is to cover this graph with a minimum number of chains starting in the pierce points or breakthroughs. Since the graph has $2k$ vertices of odd degree, then k pierce points are necessary and sufficient to traverse the graph. The cutter path problem formulation includes such parameters as manufacturing cost, efficiency, and distortion considerations. Some algorithms solving this task are considered in [20]. However, these algorithms do not have sufficient formalization, and the formulation of the problem does not take into account some technological constraints for flame cutting. Later, U. Manber and S.W. Bent [21] noted the need to construct a self-intersecting route and provided proof that this task belongs to the $\mathcal{NP}$ class. This proof is a compilation H. Fleischner's results [22] introducing the concept of an A-chain. This chain has the allowed transitions between edges, that are specified in a cyclic order at each vertex of the graph. H. Fleischner also proved that the task of constructing the A-chain is $\mathcal{NP}$-hard in general, but there are some special cases for which this task is solvable in polynomial time. One of such cases is a 4-regular graph. U. Manber and S.W. Bent in fact use A-chain instead of a self-intersecting chain. If we consider the partial case when the cutting plan is a plane Euler graph, then it is known that its dual face graph is bichromatic. For this case, S.B. Bely [23] proved the existence of an Euler cycle homeomorphic to a plane Jordan curve without self-intersections. However, it is unclear how to use this possibility for CAD/CAM systems for technological preparation of cutting processes.

The listed above problems have been solved by the authors. A rigorous formalization of these problems in terms of OE-chains is given in our paper [24]; however, the OE-chain allows the possibility of self-intersection of the trajectory. Representation of a plane Euler graph in the form of a self-intersecting Jordan curve has been announced at conferences [25,26]. We proved the necessary and sufficient conditions of $PPOE$-routes existence and built the polynomial algorithm $PPOE$-routing constructing such routes for any plane graph. The correctness of this algorithm has been announced at the conference [27]. The purpose of this article is to present the results obtained using a single terminology.

2. Methods
2.1. Abstracting the Cutting Plan to a Plane Graph

The information on the part shape is not used when we determine the sequence of cutting the fragments of the cutting. Hence, all the curves without self-intersections and contacts on the plane, representing the shape of the parts, are interpreted as the edges of the graph. All the points of intersection and contact are represented as the vertices of the graph. So, it is necessary to introduce additional functions on the set of vertices, faces and edges of the resulting graph to analyse the implementation of the given technological constraints.

We consider a plane S as a model of cutting plan, then a plane graph $G(V, E)$ with outer face $f_0 \subset S$ be the cutting plan model. The set of edges $E(G) \subset S$ of this graph is the Jordan curves with pairwise disjoint interiors and homeomorphic to open segments. Hence, the set of vertices $V(G) \subset S$ is the set of bounding points of these segments. For any part of the graph $J \subseteq G$, we denote the set-theoretic union of its interior faces (the union of all connected components of $S \setminus J$ that do not contain an outer face) by $\text{Int}(J)$. Then, $\text{Int}(J)$ can be interpreted as a part cut off a sheet. The sets of vertices, edges and faces of the graph G we denote as $V(G)$, $E(G)$ and $F(G)$, respectively. Since we consider graph G as a model of a cutting plan, there is no case when G is non-planar.

Theorem 1. *The topological representation of plane graph $G = (V, E)$ on plane S up to homeomorphism is defined by the following functions for each edge $e \in E$, $k = 1, 2$:*
- *$v_k(e)$ is the pair of vertices incident to e,*
- *$l_k(e)$ is the edges obtained by rotating edge e counter-clockwise around a vertex v_k,*
- *$r_k(e)$ is the edges obtained by rotating edge e clockwise around a vertex v_k,*
- *$f_k(e)$ is the face placed on the left when moving along the edge e from the vertex $v_k(e)$ to the vertex $v_{3-k}(e)$.*

Proof. An illustration of the functions from the Theorem 1 is given in Figure 1.

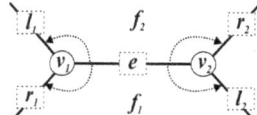

Figure 1. Functions representing graph edges.

Since functions $v_k(e), f_k(e), l_k(e), k = 1, 2$ for graph G edges define incident vertices, faces, and adjacent edges for each $e \in E(G)$ this statement is obvious. □

Figure 2 illustrates an example of a cutting plan. Its homeomorphic image is given in Figure 3 and the named functions for its computer representation are given in Table 1. We can interpret any path obtained in graph G as a trajectory of the cutter since we know the inverse images of all the vertices.

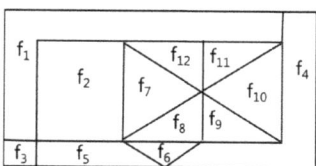

Figure 2. Example of cutting plan.

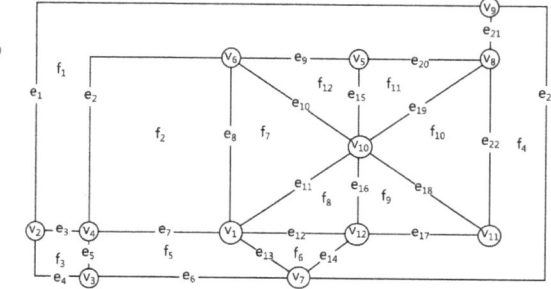

Figure 3. Geomorphic image of cutting plan in Figure 2.

Table 1. Encoding of the plane graph in Figure 3.

e	$v_1(e)$	$v_2(e)$	$l_1(e)$	$l_2(e)$	$r_1(e)$	$r_2(e)$	$f_1(e)$	$f_2(e)$
e_1	v_2	v_9	e_4	e_{21}	e_3	e_{23}	f_0	f_1
e_2	v_4	v_6	e_3	e_8	e_7	e_9	f_1	f_2
e_3	v_2	v_4	e_1	e_5	e_4	e_2	f_1	f_3
e_4	v_2	v_3	e_3	e_6	e_1	e_5	f_3	f_0
e_5	v_3	v_4	e_4	e_7	e_6	e_3	f_3	f_5
e_6	v_3	v_7	e_5	e_{23}	e_4	e_{13}	f_5	f_0
e_7	v_4	v_1	e_2	e_{13}	e_5	e_8	f_2	f_5
e_8	v_6	v_1	e_{10}	e_7	e_2	e_{11}	f_7	f_2
e_9	v_6	v_5	e_2	e_{15}	e_{10}	e_{20}	f_1	f_{12}
e_{10}	v_6	v_{10}	e_9	e_{11}	e_8	e_{15}	f_{12}	f_7
e_{11}	v_1	v_{10}	e_8	e_{16}	e_{12}	e_{10}	f_7	f_8
e_{12}	v_1	v_{12}	e_{11}	e_{14}	e_{13}	e_{16}	f_8	f_6
e_{13}	v_1	v_7	e_{12}	e_6	e_7	e_{14}	f_6	f_5
e_{14}	v_7	v_{12}	e_{13}	e_{17}	e_{23}	e_{12}	f_6	f_4
e_{15}	v_5	v_{10}	e_{20}	e_{10}	e_9	e_{19}	f_{11}	f_{12}
e_{16}	v_{10}	v_{12}	e_{18}	e_{12}	e_{11}	e_{17}	f_9	f_8
e_{17}	v_{12}	v_{11}	e_{16}	e_{22}	e_{14}	e_{18}	f_9	f_4
e_{18}	v_{10}	v_{11}	e_{19}	e_{17}	e_{16}	e_{22}	f_{10}	f_9
e_{19}	v_{10}	v_8	e_{15}	e_{22}	e_{18}	e_{20}	f_{11}	f_{10}
e_{20}	v_5	v_8	e_9	e_{19}	e_{15}	e_{21}	f_1	f_{11}
e_{21}	v_9	v_8	e_{23}	e_{20}	e_1	e_{22}	f_4	f_1
e_{22}	v_8	v_{11}	e_{21}	e_{18}	e_{19}	e_{17}	f_4	f_{10}
e_{23}	v_9	v_7	e_1	e_{14}	e_{21}	e_6	f_0	f_4

2.2. OE-Routing

2.2.1. Basic Definitions

Let us consider the formulation and solution of the problem for constructing the routes in a plane graph that satisfy the condition that the interior faces of any their initial parts do not intersect with the edges of the remaining part. Formally, such routes are defined as an ordered sequence of OE-chains (ordered enclosing chains) of the graph $G = (V, E)$ and form a class of OE-paths. The definitions, proofs and notations of the theory of routes with ordered enclosing (OE-routes) are introduced in [19]. Let us give these definitions to avoid the loss of generality.

Definition 1. *Chain $C = v_1 e_1 v_2 e_2 \ldots v_k$ in plane graph G has ordered enclosing (is an OE-chain), if for any its initial part $C_l = v_1 e_1 v_2 e_2 \ldots e_l$, $l \leq (|E|)$ the condition $\mathrm{Int}(C_l) \cap E = \emptyset$ holds.*

Theorem 2 ([19]). *Let $G = (V, E)$ be a plane Euler graph. For any vertex $v \in V(G)$ incident to outer (infinite) face of graph G there exists Euler OE-cycle $C = v e_1 v_1 e_2 v_2 \ldots v_{|E|-1} e_{|E|} v$.*

The proof of this theorem gives the recursive algorithm of OE-cycle constructing. This algorithm has computing complexity $O(|E|^2)$. However, there exists non-recursive approach with computing complexity $O(|V| \cdot \log |E|)$ [28].

Let's generalize Definition 1 up to the notion of OE-route plane graphs (it is possible non-Eulerian and disconnected).

Definition 2. *The ordered sequence of edge-disjoint OE-chains*

$$C^0 = v^0 e_1^0 v_1^0 e_2^0 \ldots e_{k_0}^0 v_{k_0}^0, \quad C^1 = v^1 e_1^1 v_1^1 e_2^1 \ldots e_{k_1}^1 v_{k_1}^1, \ldots,$$
$$C^{n-1} = v^{n-1} e_1^{n-1} v_1^{n-1} e_2^{n-1} \ldots e_{k_{n-1}}^{n-1} v_{k_{n-1}}^{n-1},$$

covering graph G and such that

$$(\forall m : m < n), \quad \left(\bigcup_{l=0}^{m-1} \mathrm{Int}(C^l)\right) \cap \left(\bigcup_{l=m}^{n-1} C^l\right) = \emptyset$$

is a route with ordered enclosing (OE-route).

Definition 3. *Let a route consisting of a minimal (in cardinality) ordered sequence of edge-disjoint OE-chains in a plane graph G be called an Euler route with ordered enclosing (Euler OE-route) and OE-chains forming it be the Euler OE-cover.*

Theorem 3 ([27])**.** *Let G connected plane graph, $V_{odd}(G)$ be the set of its odd vertices, then the cardinality N of Euler OE-cover of G satisfies the inequality*

$$k = \frac{|V_{odd}(G)|}{2} \leq N \leq |V_{odd}(G)| = 2k$$

holds. The upper and lower bounds are reachable.

The cover capacity is significantly influenced by the presence of bridges in the graph. In their absence, the lower bound is reached, in the case of the existence of vertices of odd degree incident to the outer face; or, if there are no such vertices, the cardinality of the cover is one higher than the lower bound.

The construction of the OE-route of the graph G solves the considered cutting problem in the absence of restrictions on self-intersections and the placement of starting (i.e., pierce) points for all chains.

2.2.2. Algorithms Constructing OE-Chains for Connected Graph G

Algorithms for constructing OE-routes in plane Eulerian graphs are known [28]. The possibility of constructing an OE route in an arbitrary plane graph demonstrates Theorem 4 [24].

Theorem 4. *Let $G = (V, E)$ be plane connected graph without bridges on S. There exists the set of edges $H : (H \cap S)\backslash V = \emptyset$ so that graph $\hat{G} = (V, E \cup H)$ be Euler, and there exists Euler cycle in graph $\hat{G}$, such that $C = v_1 e_1 v_2 e_2 ... e_n v_1$, $n = |E| + |H|$, for any its initial part $C_l = v_1 e_1 v_2 e_2 ... v_l$, $l \leq |E| + |H|$ the condition $\text{Int}(C_l) \cap G = \emptyset$ holds.*

We use the concept of the edge e rank while considering the algorithms of OE-routes constructing.

Definition 4. *The rank of edge $e \in E(G)$ be the value of function $\text{rank}(e) : E(G) \to \mathbb{N}$ recursively defined as following:*

- *let $E_1 = \{e \in E : e \subset f_0\}$ be the set of edges bounding outer face f_0 of graph $G(V, E)$, then $(\forall e \in E_1)(\text{rank}(e) = 1)$;*
- *let $E_k(G)$ be the set of edges of rank 1 for graph*

$$G_k \left(V, E \backslash \left(\bigcup_{l=1}^{k-1} E_l \right) \right),$$

then $(\forall e \in E_k)(\text{rank}(e) = k)$.

Definition 5 ([28])**.** *Let rank of face $f \in F(G)$ be a value of function $\text{rank} : F(G) \to \mathbb{N}_0$:*

$$\text{rank}(f) = \begin{cases} 0, & \text{if } f = f_0, \\ \min_{e \in E(f)} \text{rank}(e), & \text{otherwise,} \end{cases}$$

where $E(f)$ be a set of edges incident to outer face $f \in F$.

Definition 6 ([28])**.** *Let rank of vertex $v \in V(G)$ be a value of function $\text{rank} : V(G) \to \mathbb{N}$: $\text{rank}(v) = \min_{e \in E(v)} \text{rank}(e)$ where $E(v)$ is a set of edges incident to vertex $v \in V$.*

We developed the following polynomial time algorithms for constructing OE-routes for plane graphs:

- Euler OE-cycle in plane Euler graph (algorithm OE-CYCLE, computing complexity $O(|V|^2)$ [29]);
- connected OE-route of Chinese postman for any plane connected graph; removing retraversed edges will result in a OE-route; this route is not optimal either in terms of the number of covering chains or the length of idle passes (algorithm CPP_OE, computing complexity $O(|E(G)| \cdot |V(G)|)$ [30]);
- a route in plane connected graph without bridges being the OE-cover optimal by the number of chains, the length of idle passes may not be optimal (algorithm OECover, computing complexity $O(|E| \cdot \log |V|)$ [19]);
- OE-route in plane connected graph without bridges with additional edges, connecting the odd vertices (algorithm M-COVER with computing complexity $O(|E| \cdot \log |V|)$); this algorithm appended by algorithm of finding the shortest matching between odd vertices allows to obtain OE-cover with minimal summary length of additional edges (computing complexity $O(|E| \cdot \sqrt{|V|})$) [19].

In this paper, we describe in details those of them that are not published in open access for the convenience of the reader.

Algorithm 1 OECover covers the plane graph G by an ordered sequence of OE-chains. The graph G is encoded by the list of edges, and for each edge e the functions considered in Theorem 1 are defined.

Algorithm 1 Algorithm OECover

Require: $G = (V, E)$ be a plane graph; $V_{odd} \subseteq V$ be the set of odd vertices;
Ensure: $first \in E, last \in E, \text{mark}_1 : E \to E$;
 1: Initiate();   ▷ Assign the initial values of all used variables
 2: Order();   ▷ Define the ranks of edges, and form the ordered lists for vertices
 3: SortOdd();   ▷ Sorting of odd vertices by decreasing of their rank
 4: **if** $\{\exists v \in V_{odd} | v \in f_0\}$ **then**   ▷ Define the starting value of a chain
 5:   $v^0 \leftarrow \arg\max_{v \in V_{odd}} \text{rank}(v); \quad V_{odd} \leftarrow V_{odd} \setminus \{v^0\}$;
 6: **else** $v^0 \leftarrow v | v \in f_0$;
 7: **end if**
 8: **while** $(true)$ **do**
 9:   $v \leftarrow \text{FormChain}(v^0)$;   ▷ Form a chain from the defined vertex
10:   $V_{odd} \leftarrow V_{odd} \setminus \{v\}$;   ▷ Exclude the starting vertex of current chain from the list
11:   **if** (**then** $V_{odd} = \emptyset$)   ▷ Check the possibility to construct one more chain
12:     **break**;
13:   **end if**
14:   $v^0 \leftarrow \arg\max_{v \in V_{odd}} \text{rank}(v)$;
15: **end while**

In the body of the procedure Initiate, the initial values of all used variables are assigned, and the first edge $e_0 \in E$ belonging to the boundary of the outer face f_0 is defined.

Procedure Order Algorithm 2 functional purpose of the Order procedure is in:

(1) defining the value rank(e) for each edge $e \in E$ (note that the rank of any edge of a plane graph can be determined in time $O(|E|)$ using this procedure);

(2) forming the list $Q(v)$ of incident edges for each vertex (the edges are ordered in descending order of the rank() value).

Algorithm 2 Procedure Order

```
 1: procedure ORDER
 2:     while first ≠ ∞ do
 3:         while (mark(ne) = ∞) and (last ≠ ne) do
 4:             M1:                                    ▷ Forming the queue of M1-marked edges
 5:             rank(ne) ← k;                          ▷ Define the rank of an edge
 6:             mark₁(last) ← ne;
 7:             if v₂(ne) ≠ v then
 8:                 REPLACE(ne);
 9:             end if
10:             v ← v₁(ne); last ← ne; ne ← l₁(ne);
11:         end while
12:         e ← first; first ← mark₁(first); v ← v₂(e); ne ← l₂(e);
13:         M2:                         ▷ Placing the M1-marked edges to the lists of the corresponding vertices
14:         k ← rank(e) + 1; mark₁(e) ← Stack(v₁(e)); mark₂(e) ← Stack(v);
15:         if mark₁(e) ≠ 0 then
16:                                     ▷ Form queue of M1-marked edges of all unmarked edges bounding f₁(e)
17:             if v₁(e) = v₁(mark₁(e)) then
18:                 prev₁(mark₁(e)) ← e;
19:             else
20:                 prev₂(mark₁(e)) ← e;
21:             end if
22:         end if
23:         if mark₂(e) ≠ 0 then           ▷ Pushing of edge to stacks of vertices v₁(e) and v₂(e)
24:             if v = v₁(mark₂(e)) then
25:                 prev₁(mark₂(e)) ← e;
26:             else
27:                 prev₂(mark₂(e)) ← e;
28:             end if
29:             Stack(v) ← e; Stack(v₁(e)) ← e;
30:         end if
31:     end while
32: end procedure
```

After executing the Initiate and Order procedures, the odd vertices $v \in V_{odd}$ are ordered in ascending order of their rank using the SortOdd procedure. The rank of the vertex v is the value of the function $rank(Stack(v))$. Then, the loop do...while is executed using the FormChain procedure (see Algorithm 3). This cycle constructs a sequence of $|V_{odd}|/2$ simple paths between pairs of odd vertices. If none of the odd vertices is adjacent to the outer face, then it is necessary to construct a $|V_{odd}|/2 + 1$ chain, where the first of the constructed paths C^0 starts at vertex of even degree $v^0 \in f_0$, adjacent outer face, and ends at an odd vertex. All the chains of the cover $C^1, \ldots C^{n-1}$ are connecting the odd vertices, and the last one C^n starts at odd vertex, and ends at vertex $v^0 \in f_0$.

The aim of FormChain procedure is to obtain the OE-chain starting in a given vertex w and ending in some odd vertex $v \in V_{odd}, v \neq w$. As a result of the procedure, a simple chain will be obtained $C^i = v_0^i e_1^i v_1^i e_2^i \ldots e_k^i v_k^i$, for which $v_1^i, v_2^i, \ldots v_{k-1}^i \notin V_{odd}$, and for $i \neq 0$ and $i \neq n$ vertices $v_0^i, v_k^i \in V_{odd}$, if $i = 0$ vertex $v_k^i \in V_{odd}$, and if $i = n$ vertex $v_0^i \in V_{odd}$,

$$e_i = \arg\max_{e \in E(v_i) \setminus \{e_l | l < i\}} rank(e), \quad v_{i+1} = \overline{v_1}(e_i), \quad i = 1, 2, \ldots, k,$$

moreover, for any initial part $C_l = v^0 e_1 v_1 e_2 v_2 \ldots e_l$, $l \leq k$ and for any vertex $v \in V$ the inequality

$$\min_{e \in E(v) \cap E(C_l)} rank(e) > \max_{e \in E(v) \setminus E(C_l)} rank(e)$$

holds.

Algorithm 3 Procedure FormChain

```
 1: procedure FORMCHAIN(In: w starting vertex of a chain; Out: v ending vertex of a chain)
 2:     v ← w; e ← Q(v);
 3:     do
 4:         e₁ = arg max_{e∈Q(v)} rank(e);
 5:         e₂ = arg max_{e∈Q(v):f₁(e)=f₂(e)} rank(e);
 6:         if rank(e₁) = rank(e₂) then          ▷ Find the edge of maximal rank, a bridge if possible
 7:             e = e₂;
 8:         else
 9:             e = e₁;
10:         end if
11:         if v = v₁(e) then
12:             REPLACE(e);                      ▷ Change the indexes of functions for edge e from k to 3 − k, k = 1,2
13:         end if
14:         E(G) ← E(G) \ {e};                   ▷ Delete edge e and delete faces divided by edge e
15:         Trail ← Trail ∪ {e};
16:         v ← v₁(e);
17:     while (v ∉ V_odd & Q(v) ≠ ∅);
18:     return v;
19: end procedure
```

Theorem 5. *Let $G = (V, E)$ be a plane connected bridgeless graph on S, and $V_{odd} \subset V$ be the set of odd vertices. For any matching M on set V_{Odd} in graph $\tilde{G} = (V, E \cup M)$, there exists Euler cycle $C = v_1 e_1 v_2 e_2 ... e_n v_1$, $n = |E| + |M|$, for any initial part $C_l = v_1 e_1 v_2 e_2 ... v_l$, $l \leq |E| + |M|$ of which, the condition $\text{Int}(C_l) \cap G = \emptyset$ holds.*

The proof of Theorem 5 is constructive and consists in proving the efficiency of the algorithm M-Cover (see Algorithm 4) for constructing a cover for any matching on the set of odd vertices [19].

Algorithm 4 Algorithm M-Cover

Require: plane connected graph G, functions $v_k(e)$, $l_k(e)$, $e \in E(G)$, $k = 1,2$; vertex $v_0 \in V(G)$ incident to outer face; matching M on set of odd vertices V_{Odd}; boolean function $\text{Idle}_M : V_{Odd} \to \{\textbf{false}, \textbf{true}\}$ on set of odd vertices V_{Odd};
Ensure: almost ordered set C of OE-chains of graph G, being the OE-cover of graph G;

```
 1: Order (G);                              ▷ Define rank() for all e ∈ E(G), v ∈ V(G)
 2: v := v₀;                                ▷ Constructing
 3: while Q(v) ≠ ∅ do
 4:     FormChain(v, v);
 5:     if Idle_M(v) ∨ (Q(v) = ∅) then
 6:         u ← M(v);                       ▷ Vertex u is a pair for vertex v in matching M
 7:         V_Odd ← V_Odd \ {u, v}           ▷ Delete vertices u, v from V_Odd
 8:         v ← u;                          ▷ Finish constructing the current chain
 9:     end if
10: end while
11: End of algorithm
```

The main difference of this algorithm from OE-Cover is that for each vertex $v \in V_{Odd}$ the next one $u = M(v) \in V_{Odd}$ is fixed. It is the vertex to which the transition is made. Algorithm M-Cover can finish constructing the current chain both at the first visit to the vertex $v \in V_{Odd}$, and at the moment when the vertex becomes dead-end (i.e., $Q(v) = \emptyset$). To determine at what moment to finish the constructing of the chain, the values of

$$\text{Idle}_M(v) = (\text{rank}(v) \leq \text{rank}(M(v))) \wedge (f_{M(v)} \succeq f_v), v \in V_{Odd},$$

are used, where $f_w = \arg\min_{f:v\in f \subset F(G)} \text{rank}(f), w \in V_{Odd}$. Here $\succeq$ is partial ordering on $F(G)$ induced by tree $T_{f0}^{G'}$ of shortest paths to vertex $f_0 \in F$:

$$(f_i \succeq f_j) \leftrightarrow \left(f_j \text{ belongs to chain } T_{f0}^{G'} \text{ between } f_i \text{ and } f_0\right).$$

To construct the optimal cover (i.e., cover with a minimal length of additional edges) it is enough to take the shortest matching on set of odd vertices V_{odd} as M. This task is realized by the following Algorithm 5.

Algorithm 5 OptimalCover

Require: plane graph G represented by the list of edges with defined functions $v_k(e), l_k(e), f_k(e)$, $k = 1, 2$
Ensure: cover of graph G by OE-chains $C_j, j = 1, ..., |V_{odd}|/2$
1: Define the shortest matching M on set V_{odd}
2: Run algorithm M-Cover for graph G and matching M
3: Stop

Obviously, Algorithm 5 allows us to construct the optimal OE-cover, and its computing complexity is not greater than $O(|V|^3)$ (but by using special data structures and algorithms, it is possible to run this algorithm by the time not exceeding $O(|E(G)| \cdot \sqrt{|V(G)|})$). This estimation is defined by the computing complexity of Step 1.

2.3. Constructing of Routes Satisfying the Combination of Constraints

During the technological preparation of the cutting process, various constraints on the trajectory of the cutting tool may appear. One of them is the task considered above, where the cut off part of the sheet of the obtained route does not require additional cuts. However, in practice, it is required to fulfil additional constraints on the absence of intersection of cuts and on allowable pierce points that are start points of OE-chains forming this route.

To solve a problem of the cuts intersection absence at each vertex of the graph, a cyclic order of traversing the edges is specified, and the continuation of the traversal along the chain is carried out only by this cyclic order. In the general case, the problem of finding such a chain in a graph belongs to the class of $\mathcal{NP}$-complete problems, but there are effective algorithms of its solution for some special cases.

2.3.1. AOE-Routs

Let us consider Euler chain

$$T = v_0, k_1, v_1, \ldots, k_n, v_n, \ v_n = v_0$$

in graph $G = (V, E)$. Let we know the cyclic order $O^{\pm}(v)$ defining the transitions system $A_G(v) \subseteq O^{\pm}(v)$ for each vertex $v \in V$. In the case when $\forall v \in V(G) \ A_G(v) = O^{\pm}(v)$ the transitions system $A_G(v)$ is called the full transitions system, and chain satisfying this system is A_G-compatible.

Definition 7. *A_G-compatible chain T is called **A-chain**. Thus, consecutive edges in the chain T incident to vertex v are the neighbours in the cyclic order $O^{\pm}(v)$ [31].*

Definition 8. *The chain is called AOE-chain if it is OE-chain and A-chain simultaneously [32].*

Theorem 6. *If there is A-chain in a plane graph G then there is also AOE-chain in this graph [32].*

Theorem 7. *Plane connected 4-regular graph G has AOE-chain.*

To prove this theorem, we need to introduce some definitions and prove some propositions.

Definition 9. *The partial graph G_k of graph G for which $E(G_k) = \{e \in E(G) : \text{rank}(e) \geq k\}$ is called partial graph of rank k.*

Preliminarily, the "correct" splitting of all cut-vertices of partial graphs G_k is performed, so that as a result of the splitting, we get a graph for which any partial graph G_k has no cut-vertices. The vertices splitting is a local operation, hence the sequence of splitting does not affect the total result. The "correct" transition is one between arcs corresponding of a cyclic order and incident to the different pairs of faces (see Figure 4b)). The splitting result, in this case, is shown in Figure 4b).

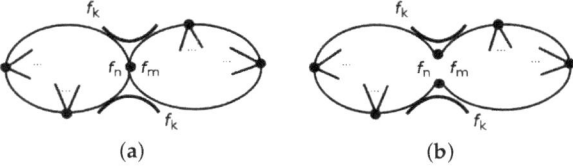

Figure 4. Splitting of cut-vertices of rank k. (**a**) The correct transitions system for splitting the cut-vertex of partial graph G_k. (**b**) Splitting according to the transitions system in cut-vertex for partial graph G_k.

These propositions imply the effectiveness of the CUT-POINT-SPLITTING Algorithm 6 running in time not greater than $O(|E(G)|\log|V(G)|)$.

Theorem 8. *Algorithm AOE-CHAIN constructs AOE-chain for plane connected 4-regular graph G any partial graph G_k, $k = 1, 2, \ldots$ of which has no cut-vertices. Algorithm solves the problem by the time $O(|E(G)| \cdot \log|V(G)|)$.*

The proof of this algorithm's effectiveness [32] finishes the proof of Theorem 7.

Proposition 1. *Vertex incident to four edges bounding outer face is cut-vertex.*

Proposition 2. *The outer face of a partial graph G_k is the union of all faces of rank k in graph G.*

Let us consider the Algorithm 7 for constructing the AOE-chain for plane connected 4-regular graph [32,33].

Algorithm 6 CUT-POINT-SPLITTING

Require: plane connected 4-regular graph $G = (V, E)$ represented for all $e \in E(G)$ by functions $v_s, l_s, r_s, s = 1, 2$.
Ensure: homeomorphic image of graph $G = (V, E)$ for which any partial graph G_k has no cut vertices.
Supplementary data $\forall v \in V(G)$:
point(v) is the array of pointers to one of edges incident to vertex v;
rank(v) is the array of vertices ranks;
count(v) is the counter of incident edges of one rank for each vertex;
Supplementary data $\forall f \in F(G)$: array rank(f).

1: Initiate():
2:   **for all** $v \in V(G)$ **do**   ▷ Zero the counter of edges of the same rank incident to a vertex
3:     point$(v) := 0$; count$(v) := 0$
4:   **end for**
5: Ranking(G)   ▷ Determining the rank of all vertices, edges and faces of a graph
6: Finding():   ▷ Defining the cut-vertices
7:   **for all** $e \in E(G)$ **do**
8:     point$(v_1(e))$: point$(v_2(e)) := e = e$
9:   **end for**
10:   **for all** $v \in V(G)$ **do**   ▷ To look through all the vertices
11:
12:     $e :=$ point(v); $k :=$ rank(v) ▷ Save the rank value k of the incident edge e
13:     **if** $v = v_1(e)$ **then**   ▷ Define the direction of edge e
14:       $s := 1$
15:     **else**
16:       $s := 2$
17:     **end if**
18:     $e := l_s(e)$ ▷ Counting the number of rank k edges incident to vertex v
19:     **for** $i = 1$ **up to** 4 **do**
20:       **if** rank$(e) = k$ **then**
21:         count$(v) :=$ count$(v) + 1$
22:         **if** $i < 4$ **then**
23:           $e := l_s(e)$
24:         **end if**
25:       **end if**
26:     **end for**
27:     **if** count$(v) = 4$ **then**   ▷ Split the vertex if it is cut-vertex
28:       **if** $(f_s(e) = f_s(l_s(e))$ **and** $f_{3-s}(e) = f_{3-s}(l_s(e)))$ **or**
29:         **or** $(f_s(e) = f_{3-s}(l_s(e))$ **and** $f_{3-s}(e) = f_s(l_s(e))))$ **then**
30:         $e^* := l_s(e), l_s(e) := r_s(e), r_s(r_s(e)) := e,$
31:         $r_s(e^*) := l_s(e^*), l_s(l_s(e^*)) := e^*$
32:       **else**
33:         $e^* := r_s(e), r_s(e) := l_s(e), l_s(l_s(e)) := e,$
34:         $l_s(e^*) := r_s(e^*), r_s(r_s(e^*)) := e^*$
35:       **end if**
36:     **end if**
37: **end for**

2.3.2. NOE-Routes

Algorithm 6 AOE-CHAIN is used for running the algorithm NOE-CHAIN (see Algorithm 8) to obtain the non-intersecting OE-chain for plane connected graph [26].

Definition 10 ([26]). *Let Eulerian cycle C of plane graph G be non-intersecting if it is homeomorphic to a closed Jordan curve without intersections obtained from graph G by applying of $O(|E(G)|)$ splittings of its vertices.*

Algorithm 7 Algorithm AOE-CHAIN

Require: plane connected 4-regular graph $G = (V, E)$ defined by functions $v_k, l_k, r_k, k = 1, 2$ (see Theorem 1); starting vertex $v \in V(f_0)$.
Ensure: $AChain$ – output stream containing AOE-chain obtained by the algorithm.
1: Initiate(G, v_0);
2: Ranking(G);
3: CUT_POINT_SPLITTING (G);   ▷ Deleting of cut-vertices in partial graphs of each rank
4:                               ▷ Constructing
5: $e = \arg\max_{e \in E(v)} \text{rank}(e)$ ▷ Choose the edge of maximal rank incident to vertex v
6: **repeat**
7:   **if** $v \neq v_1(e)$ **then**
8:     REPLACE(e)
9:   **end if**   ▷ If necessary, adjust the numbering of functions for the edge e
10: $AChain \leftarrow$ **Print**(v, e)   ▷ Add edge e to the resulting sequence $AChain$
11: mark(e) := **false**; counter:=counter+1; $v := v_2(e)$ ▷ Mark the current edge as passed
12: **if** (rank($r_2(e)$) $\geq$ rank($l_2(e)$)) **then**   ▷ Choose the next edge of maximal possible rank
13:    **if** mark($r_2(e)$) **then**   ▷ Check if the chosen edge is already passed
14:      $e := r_2(e)$ ▷ The passed edges have False value in the arra $mark$
15:    **else**
16:      $e := l_2(e)$
17:    **end if**
18: **else**
19:    **if** (mark($l_2(e)$)) **then**   ▷ Choose the not passed edge
20:      $e := l_2(e)$
21:    **else**
22:      $e := r_2(e)$
23:    **end if**
24: **end if**
25: **until** (counter $> |E(G)|$)   ▷ Finish the cycle when all the edges are scanned
26: **End of Algorithm**

Algorithm 8 NOE-CHAIN (G)

Require: plane Euler graph G defined by functions $v_k(e), l_k(e), r_k(e), f_k(e), k = 1, 2$ (see Theorem 1) and rank(e);
Ensure: C as NOE-chain in graph G;
1: $\widehat{G} =$ NonIntersecting(G);   ▷ Split all vertices of degree higher than 4
2: C^*=AOE_CHAIN($\widehat{G}$);   ▷ Obtain AOE-chain in graph $\widehat{G}$
3: C=Absorb(C^*);   ▷ Absorb all split vertices and obtain the resulting NOE-chain

---

Its execution means transforming the initial graph to a plane connected 4-regular graph by splitting the vertices of degree greater than 4. To obtain the Euler NOE-cycle in a plane Euler graph without given transitions system, we can act as follows. Let us define boolean function

$$\text{Checked}(v) = \begin{cases} \texttt{true}, & \text{if the vertex is viewed;} \\ \texttt{false}, & \text{otherwise;} \end{cases}$$

on the set of vertices $V(G)$. When performing initialization, declare all vertices not viewed. Function NonIntersecting (G) (Algorithm 9) splits all vertices $v \in V(G)$ of degree more than $2k - 1$ ($k \geq 3$) to k fictive vertices of degree 4 and introduces k fictive edges incident to the vertices obtained as a result of splitting and forming a cycle (see Figure 5).

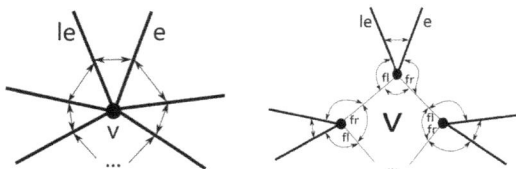

Figure 5. Splitting of vertex (the edges of graph G are bold lines, and the fictive ones are thick lines and modification of the pointers according to the splitting processed.

Algorithm 9 Function NonIntersecting (G)

Require: plane Euler graph G defined by functions $v_k(e), l_k(e), r_k(e), f_k(e), k = 1, 2$ (see Theorem 1 and rank(e);
Ensure: plane connected 4-regular graph G^* defined as the same;
1: **for all** $v \in V(G)$ **do**   ▷ Initialization of $Checked(v)$ function
2:   $Checked(v) := $ **false**;
3: **end for**
4: **for all** $(e \in E(G)$) **do**   ▷ Searching of vertices of degree greater than 4 and their splitting
5:   $k := 1$;   ▷ Consider vertex with index 1, then vertex with index 2
6:   **while** $(k \leq 2)$ **do**
7:     **if** $(!\ Checked(v_k(e)))$ **then**   ▷ Process only a previously unprocessed vertex
8:       **if** $(k = 2)$ **then**   ▷ Improve the indexes
9:         REPLACE(e);   ▷ Process vertices $v_1(e)$
10:      **end if**
11:      Handle (e);   ▷ Call the function to process vertex $v_1(e)$
12:      $Checked(v_1(e)) := $ **true**;   ▷ Mark the vertex as considered
13:    **end if**
14:    $k := k + 1$;
15: **end while**
16: **end for**
    End of function

In the body of function we use the procedure Handle (e, $v_k(e)$, k), which processes each unconsidered graph vertex.

Procedure Algorithm 10 during cycle repeat-until (lines 6–11) counts the degree d of current vertex v. If $d > 4$, then the second cycle repeat-until (lines 12–23) runs. Here the handled vertex is split to $d/2$ fictive vertices, and d fictive edges incident to these vertices. There fictive edges form a cycle.

In lines 18–23, we not only change the pointers to edges, but also create a new (fictive) face F, incident to all fictive vertices and edges, and also define the ranks of fictive edges [26].

Definition 11. *The rank of fictive edge (line 20) is equal to the rank of the initial graph face incident to the entered fictive edge.*

The introduced by Handle procedure $k/2$ fictive vertices and k fictive edges incident to these vertices are forming a cycle. As a result of processing all graph G vertices, we obtain the modified plane connected 4-regular graph G^*. Algorithm AOE-CHAIN() constructing AOE-chain T^* can be implemented to graph G^*. The considered procedure is realized in algorithm NonIntersecting (see Algorithm 9). If then in T^* all the fictive edges and the incident vertices obtained by splitting the vertex v are replaced by v, then we obtain the NOE-chain T in the original graph G.

Algorithm 10 Procedure Handle (*e*)

```
 1: procedure HANDLE(e)
 2:     v := v₁(e);                                      ▷ Splitting vertex
 3:     e_first := e;                                    ▷ Save the first considered edge
 4:     d := 0;                                          ▷ Initialization of a counter for vertex degree d
 5:     F := FaceNum() + 1;                              ▷ Define the number of a new face
 6:     repeat                                           ▷ Pass 1: Defining the degree of v
 7:         le := l₁(e);
 8:         if (v₁(le) ≠ v) then REPLACE(le);
 9:         end if                                       ▷ Change the indexing of functions if necessary
10:         e := le; d := d + 1;   ▷ Consider the edge when calculating the degree and move on to the
    next one
11:     until (e = e_first);                             ▷ Repeat until all edges incident v have been considered
12:     if (d > 4) then                                  ▷ If the degree of current vertex is greater than 4
13:         e := e_first;                                ▷ Begin from the first considered edge
14:         le := l_k(e);                                ▷ Define the number of its left neighbour
15:         e_next := l_k(le);                           ▷ Save the edge for the next iteration
16:         fl := new EDGE; fle := fl; e_first := e;     ▷ Introduce a fictive edge adjacent to le
17:         repeat                                       ▷ Put the pointers for edges
18:             e := e_next; le := l_k(e); fr := fl;
19:             f₁(fl) := F; f₂(fl) := f₂(e);            ▷ Define faces adjacent to a fictive edge
20:             rank(fl) := facerank(f₂(fl));            ▷ Define "rank" of fictive edge
21:                               ▷ Function facerank() defines the rank of a face according to the definition
22:             fl := new EDGE; e_next := l_k(le);
23:         until (l_k(le) = e_first);
24:     end if
25: end procedure
```

Theorem 9. *Algorithm* NOE-CHAIN *solves the task of constructing the NOE-chain for plane Euler graph by the time* $O(|E(G)|^2)$ *[26].*

Note that this algorithm constructs a *NOE*-chain in a plane Euler graph. In the case of a plane non-Euler (generally disconnected) graph *G*, it is necessary to split all vertices of degree higher than 4 by the Algorithm 10. As a result, we get a graph with vertex degrees equal to 3 or 4. For this graph, we apply the algorithm for constructing an *AOE*-cover. In the chains of the resulting cover, remove all artificial edges and absorb all split vertices. As a result, we get *NOE*-cover.

2.3.3. *PPOE*-Routes

Let us consider a problem arising in the case of intrusion of constraints on the location of pierce points. Obviously, the number of pierce points is determined by the number of covering chains. According to Theorem 3, the number of pierce points is at least $|V_{odd}|/2$. This problem can be formalized as following.

- Let faces $F_{in}(G) \subset F(G)$ allow piercing.
- Let odd vertices $v^- \in V_{in}(G) \subset V(G)$ be incident to face $F_{in}(G)$.
- Let for odd vertices $v^+ \in V_{out} = V_{odd} \setminus V_{in}$ piercing is forbidden.

If the constructed route in the graph is an *OE* route and all the initial vertices of the covering chains belong to $V_{in}(G)$, then this route can be used as a basis for constructing a route for the cutter trajectory for laser cutting process. Let these routes be called *PPOE*-routes [27].

Definition 12. *Let chain $C = v_1 e_1 v_2 e_2 \ldots v_k$ be called PPOE-**chain**, if it is OE-chain and starts from vertex $v_1 \in V_{in}(G)$.*

Definition 13. *Let PPOE-**cover** of graph G be such an OE-cover of G, consisting of PPOE chains.*

Definition 14. *An ordered sequence of edge-disjoint PPOE-chains in a plane graph G of the minimal cardinality is called an Euler PPOE-cover.*

The problem of determining the realizability of a cutting plan can be formulated as determining the existence of an Euler *PPOE*-cover for a plane graph that is a homeomorphic image of the corresponding cutting plan. Following the existing restrictions, we can formulate the following necessary condition for the existence of a *PPOE*-cover.

Theorem 10. *Plane connected graph $G(V, F, E)$ without bridges has PPOE-cover if and only if the cardinality of minimal $\{V_{in}, V_{out}\}$-cut is at least $|V_{out}|$.*

Proof. The validity of the necessary condition is obvious, sufficiency follows from the effectiveness of Algorithm 11 solves the problem of constructing *PPOE*-cover for a plane graph $G(V, E)$ without bridges. □

To find minimal $\{V_{in}, V_{out}\}$-cut let us construct a network

$$N(V \cup \{w\}, A \cup (\{w\} \times V_{in}))$$

(i.e., directed graph with source w), in which

- a pair of arcs $(u, v), (v, u) \in A(N)$ of capacity 1 corresponds to edge $e = \{u, v\} \in E(G)$;
- vertices $v^+ \in V_{out}(N)$, i.e., points of possible end of chain, are the sinks of a unit power flow;
- vertices $v^- \in V_{in}(N)$, i.e., possible pierce points, may be source of the unit.

Cardinality of minimal $\{V_{in}, V_{out}\}$-cut can be obtained as optimal value of problem

$$\sum_{(u,v) \in A(N)} x(u,v) \to \min, \quad (1)$$

$$\sum_{v:(u,v) \in A(N)} x(u,v) - \sum_{v:(v,u) \in A(N)} x(v,u) = 1, \quad u \in V_{out}(N), \quad (2)$$

$$-\sum_{v:(u,v) \in A(N)} x(u,v) + \sum_{v:(v,u) \in A(N)} x(v,u) = -x(w,u), \quad u \in V_{in}(N), \quad (3)$$

$$\sum_{v:(u,v) \in A(N)} x(u,v) - \sum_{v:(v,u) \in A(N)} x(v,u) = 0, \quad u \in V \setminus (V_{out}(N) \cup V_{in}(N)), \quad (4)$$

$$\sum_{v \in V_{in}(N)} x(w,v) = |V_{out}(N)|, \quad (5)$$

$$0 \leq x(u,v) \leq 1, \quad (u,v) \in A(N), \quad (6)$$

$$0 \leq x(w,u) \leq 1, \quad u \in V_{in}(N), \quad (7)$$

where w is a common source with capacity $|V_{out}|$ adjacent to all $v \in V_{in}$ to network N.

Let $x : A \to \{0, 1\}$ be optimal solution of problem (1)–(7). Let us construct a sequence of disjoint chains $C_1, C_2, \ldots C_{|V_{out}|}$, containing all the flow holders of x and only them. It is possible to «correctly» split each vertex $v \in V(G)$ to the dummy vertices with «correct» union of active arcs lists, while it is possible (i.e., taking into account the cyclic order on the set of arcs and their orientations). The examples of «correct» splitting and uniting are shown in Figure 6. The result of this step is a sequence of disjoint chains $C_1, C_2, \ldots C_{|V_{out}|}$, containing all the flow holders and only them. The above allows us to propose the Algorithm 11 PPOE-covering.

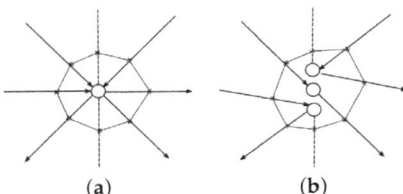

(a)   (b)

Figure 6. Example of the «correct» splitting, where $\to$ is flow hold arc, and $\dashrightarrow$ is arc without flow. (**a**) A vertex and arcs incident to it. (**b**) The «correct» splitting.

Algorithm 11 Algorithm *PPOE-covering*

Require: plane graph $G(V, F, E)$ without bridges, defined for all $e \in E(G)$
  functions $v_k(e), l_k(e), r_k(e), f_k(e), k = 1, 2$ (see Theorem 1) rank(e),
  functions rank(v), $v \in V(G)$, rank(f), $f \in F(G)$;
  subsets $V_{out}, V_{in} \subset V : |V_{in}| \geq |V_{out}|$;
  subset $\{F_{in} \subset F\}$ of faces that allow piercing.
Ensure: PPOE-cover of graph $G(V, E)$: $\tilde{C}_1, \tilde{C}_2, \ldots \tilde{C}_{|V_{out}|}, C_{|V_{out}|+1}, \ldots, C_M$.

1: Construct a network $N(V \cup \{w\}, A \cup (\{w\} \times V_{in}))$.
2: **if** ($V_{out} = \emptyset$) **then**
3:   Run Algorithm 5 OptimalCover for graph G
4:   **Return**(Cover of graph G by OE-chains $C_j, j = 1, \ldots, |V_{odd}(G)|/2$)
5: **end if**
6: **if** problem (2)–(7) is unsolvable **then**
7:   **Rteurn**(PPOE-cover does not exist)
8: **else**
9:   Let $x : A(N) \to \{0, 1\}$ be optimal solution of problem (2)–(7)
10: For each active arc $(u, v) : x(u, v) = 1$ create a list, including this arc and only it
11: Find a sequence of disjoint chains $C_1, C_2, \ldots C_{|V_{out}|}$, containing all the flow holders and only them with usage for each vertex $v \in V(G)$ of «correctly» splitting to the dummy vertices (see Figure 6)
12: Construct a partial graph

$$\tilde{G} = G \setminus \left(\bigcup_{i=1}^{|V_{out}|} C_i \right), E(\tilde{G}) = \left(E(G) \setminus \left(\bigcup_{i=1}^{|V_{out}|} C_i \right) \right),$$

in which all vertices $v \in V_{out}$, for which piercing is forbidden, are the vertices of even degree.
13: **end if**
14: For $\tilde{G}$ run algorithm OptimalCover 5. The result of this step is a sequence of disjoint chains

$$C_{|V_{out}|+1}, \ldots, C_{|V_{out}|+|M|}.$$

15: **Return**($\tilde{C}_1, \tilde{C}_2, \ldots \tilde{C}_{|V_{out}|}, C_{|V_{out}|+1}, \ldots, C_M$.)
16: **End of algorithm**

Theorem 11. *Algorithm PPOE-covering solves the problem of constructing PPOE-cover for a plane graph $G(V, E)$ without bridges by the time not exceeding $O(|V|^3)$.*

Proof. The route consisting of chains $C_1, C_2, \ldots C_{|V_{out}|}$ is the edge-disjoint OE-route (due to unit carrying capacity of arcs). Partial graph $\tilde{G}$ does not contain any edges belonging to chains C_i, $i = 1, \ldots, |V_{out}|$ by definition. All graph $\tilde{G}$ vertices avoiding piercing have even degree due to constructions. As a result of running Step 9, we get the continuation

$$C_{|V_{out}|+1}, \ldots, C_{|V_{out}|+|M|}$$

of route which is the OE-route in graph $\tilde{G}$ covering all edges of graph $\tilde{G}$, and starting vertex $v \in V_{in}$ of each chain C_i, $i = |V_{out}|+1, \ldots |V_{out}|+|M|$ is permissible for piercing. Hence the route

$$C_1, C_2, \ldots C_{|V_{out}|}, C_{|V_{out}|+1}, \ldots, C_{|V_{out}|+|M|}$$

is PPOE-cover of initial graph G.

Let us estimate the computing complexity of this algorithm. Step 1 allows to get the network by time $O(|E|)$. Step 2 verifies the condition and it is completed in $O(1)$. Circulation in step 3 may be obtained by time not exceeding $O(|V|^3)$ [34]. Step 4 verifies the condition and it is completed in $O(1)$. In step 5, we introduce a sequence of chains along with a set of active arcs. This operation is performed at a time not exceeding $O(|E|)$. In step 6, at each vertex v, a "merging" of lists is performed in a time not exceeding $O(|V| \cdot \deg(v))$. Thus, the computing complexity of step 6 does not exceed the value $O(|V| \cdot |E|)$. Step 7 runs by time not exceeding $O(|E|)$. The complexity of Step 7 is defined by the complexity of algorithm OE-Cover [19] and amounts to $O(|E(G)| \cdot \log_2 |V(G)|)$. Obtaining the partial graph $\tilde{G}$ at Step 7 claims the time not exceeding $O(|E|)$. The complexity of Step 9 does not exceed $O(|V|^3)$ used for the shortest matching obtaining. Thus, the complexity of algorithm PPOE-routing does not exceed the value of $O(|V|^3)$. □

Let us consider the application of algorithm PPOE-Routing to cutting plan in Figure 2 with geomorphic image presented in Figure 3 and in Table 1. We have $V_{out}(N) = \{v_1, v_5, V_{11}\}$, $V_{in}(N) = \{v_2, v_3, v_7, v_9\}$, $V(N)\setminus(V_{out}(N) \cup V_{in}(N)) = \{v_4, v_6, v_8, v_{10}, v_{12}\}$. Figure 7 demonstrates network $N(V \cup \{w\}, A \cup (\{w\} \times V_{in}))$ constructed in **Step 1** and optimal solution of problem (1)–(7) found in **Step 2**. Bold lines highlight carriers of non-zero flow.

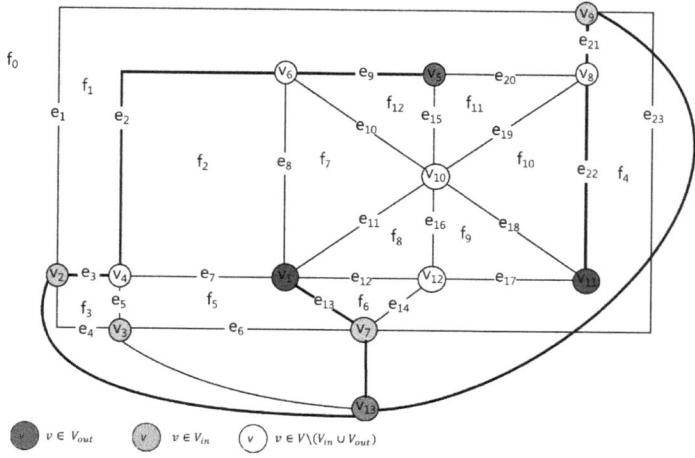

Figure 7. Network N for graph in Figure 3.

After running steps 3–6, we obtain the chains $C_1 = e_3e_2e_9$, $C_2 = e_{21}e_{22}$, $C_3 = e_{13}$. Partial graph constructed by step 7 is shown in Figure 8.

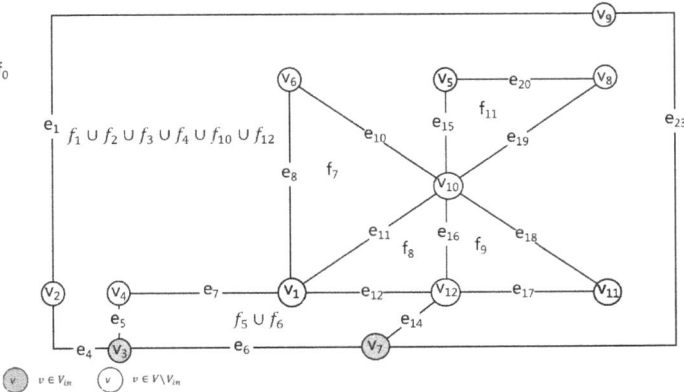

Figure 8. Rest of network N after running steps 3–6.

In this graph algorithm M-Cover constructs the only chain

$$C_4 = e_5e_7e_{11}e_{16}e_{12}e_8e_{10}e_{15}e_{20}e_{19}e_{18}e_{17}e_{14}e_{23}e_1e_4e_6.$$

So, the $PPOE$-cover for this graph is $\{C_1, C_2, C_3, C_4\}$.

Thus, the construction of the $PPOE$-cover of the G graph allows us to solve the problems of the cutter movement routing for a realizable cutting plan with restrictions on possible pierce points.

2.4. Algorithms for Disconnected Graphs

The problem of constructing OE-routes in disconnected graphs is also of practical value. In this case, the task of finding the OE-covering of the graph by chains can be reduced to several tasks of lower dimension (to construct a cover for each connected component separately). This approach is reasonable if the resulting graph does not contain nested components. However, in the presence of nesting of the connected components, the problem becomes somewhat more complicated and the following restrictions on the order of traversing the connected components arise: the connected components consisting of edges of higher rank must be traversed before the components consisting of edges of lower rank. To solve the problem in common for plane disconnected graph algorithms MultiComponent (computing complexity $O(|E(G)| \cdot \log_2 |V(G)|)$), Bridging, DoubleBridging) and FaceCutting (Figure 9) are developed.

The proofs of these results [19] are constructive and, in fact, are reduced to describing and proving the effectiveness of algorithms for constructing the desired cycles (routes).

Algorithms Bridging and DoubleBridging use the approach of reducing the initial disconnected graph to a connected one.

Definition 15. *Let face $f \in F(G)$ be called separating, if it is incident to two or more connected components.*

Let graph $\tilde{G}$ be obtained from graph G by adding bridges belonging to separating faces between the components. Obviously, the obtained graph $\tilde{G}$ be a plane connected graph and it is possible to construct the OE-route $R(\tilde{G})$ for it. This OE-route $R(G)$ can be obtained from route $R(\tilde{G})$ if vertices incident to the introduced bridges are to be the ends of the current chain and the beginnings of the next ones (i.e., introduced bridges are the idle passes).

Let us consider the way of constructing the bridges connecting graph G and having a minimal summary length (see Algorithm 12).

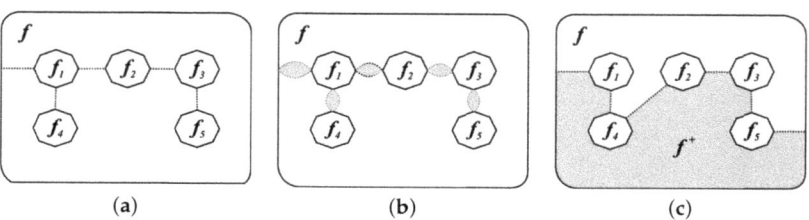

Figure 9. Examples of combining separated components. (**a**) Bridging; (**b**) DoubleBridging; (**c**) Face Cutting.

Algorithm 12 Bridging

Require: plane disconnected graph G
Ensure: plane connected graph $\tilde{G}$ and set B of introduced bridges
1: $\tilde{G} := G$; $B = \emptyset$;
2: Define the set C_F of all separating faces.
3: **for all** $f \in C_F$ **do**
4:     Find the set $S(f)$ of connected components of graph G incident to face f.
5:     Construct the full abstract graph $\mathcal{T}$ the vertices of which are the components $S(f)$, and lengths of edges are equal to the distance between the components.
6:     Obtain the minimal spanning tree $T(\mathcal{T})$ in $\mathcal{T}$.
7:     Add the edges of the obtained spanning tree to graph $\tilde{G}$: $E(\tilde{G}) := E(\tilde{G}) \cup E(T(\mathcal{T}))$, $B := B \cup E(T(\mathcal{T}))$.
8: **end for**
9: **end**

Plane graph $\tilde{G}$ obtained by algorithm Bridging contains bridges, hence it is possible to apply only algorithm CPP_OE [30] constructing the Chinese postman OE-route for plane graph [30]. Note that both the OECover algorithm and the M-Cover algorithm require no bridges in the graph. To avoid errors in the execution of the algorithms, it is necessary to add the edges of the spanning tree $T(\mathcal{T})$ to the graph twice (see line 6 of the Algorithm 12). The algorithm adjusted in this way is called DoubleBridging. The complexity of the Bridging and DoubleBridging algorithms is polynomial, depending on the method used to determine the distances between the connectivity components. If the distances are given it can be estimated as $O(|E(G)| \cdot \log |V(G)|)$.

Theorem 12. *If, for each component G_k of graph G, the degrees of vertices incident to separating faces of G are even, then the path of the minimal length of additional edges can be realized by algorithm DoubleBridging.*

Algorithm FaceCutting [35] is one other way to obtain graph $\tilde{G}$ without bridges. It consists in splitting the separating face using the Hamiltonian cycle. In fact, if for abstract graph $\mathcal{T}$ we use the minimal weight Hamiltonian cycle $H(\mathcal{T})$ instead of spanning tree $T(\mathcal{T})$, then the resulting graph $\tilde{G}$ does not contain any bridges and, hence, we can use algorithm M-Cover (see Algorithm 4) to obtain the OE-route with a minimal length of idle passes.

3. Discussion

In our article, we provide an overview of the plane graph routing problem statements since the 1980s. In the early works [20,21], the formalization of the tasks posed is not accurate enough, there is no classification of routes by the type of restrictions imposed. In this regard, mainly heuristic algorithms were developed. In the works of the authors (2007–2020), an exact formalization of some previously considered statements is given, classes of routes in plane graphs satisfying constraints are introduced, and polynomial exact algorithms for solving these problems are described.

Of particular note is the proof of the $\mathcal{NP}$-completeness of the problem of finding non-intersecting Euler chains [21], where the author takes an A-chain as a self-non-intersecting Euler chain. The authors have shown the existence of a polynomial algorithm for finding an Euler self-non-intersecting chain in a plane graph. The question of $\mathcal{NP}$-completeness of the problem of finding a self-non-intersecting chain remains open.

4. Conclusions

In our paper, we introduced a class of routes with ordered enclosing (OE-routes) in plane graphs. The routes of this class represent an ordered sequence of paths that satisfy the requirement that the inner edges of the traversed part of the route do not intersect with the edges of its non-traversed part.

We showed that the presence of bridges in the graph has a significant effect on the cover cardinality. If there are no bridges in a graph, the minimum number of OE-chains covering the graph is equal to the minimum number of paths covering the given graph (in the case of the existence of vertices of odd degree incident to the outer face). If there are no vertices of odd degree adjacent to the outer face, then the cardinality of the covering is one higher than the minimum number of paths covering the given graph. In general, the cardinality N of Euler OE-cover of graph G satisfies the inequality $k = \frac{|V_{odd}(G)|}{2} \leq N \leq |V_{odd}(G)| = 2k$. The upper and lower bounds are reachable.

We discussed the polynomial algorithms for constructing the OE-cover for different cases: plane Euler graph, any plane connected graph (CPP and OE-cover constructing problems), any disconnected plane graph. We developed the polynomial time algorithm for obtaining an OE-route with the minimum number of covering paths and an algorithm for constructing an OE-route with a minimum length of transitions between the end of the current path and the beginning of the next path.

To discover the chains with the complex groups of restrictions we introduced classes of AOE-chains, NOE-chains, and $PPOE$-chains. (1) Class of AOE-chains includes the chains with additional local restriction according to which the neighbouring edges need to satisfy the transitions system of A-chain. Algorithm AOE-CHAIN allows obtaining a chain belonging to class AOE for a plane connected 4-regular graph. The algorithm allows to obtain it by the time $O(|E(G)| \cdot \log |V(G)|)$. (2) Class of NOE is the extension of class AOE and contains all OE-chains with non-intersecting transitions. Algorithm Non-intersecting allows obtaining such a chain. Its implementation consists in reducing the original plane graph to a plane connected 4-regular graph by splitting vertices of degree higher than 4 and further executing the AOE-CHAIN algorithm. (3) Class of $PPOE$-chains contains OE-chains with fixed sets of starting and ending vertices, and algorithm $PPOE$-covering allows for correctly solving the problem of constructing this type of cover for a plane graph $G(V, E)$ without bridges by the time not exceeding $O(|V|^3)$ [36].

All our algorithms are implemented using the C++ programming language, and the initial data can be read either from text files with the table of functions for edges (see Theorem 1) or by conversion of JSON-files used in known CAD/CAM systems to the table of these functions [36].

Author Contributions: Conceptualization, T.M. and A.P.; Formal analysis, A.P.; Methodology, T.M.; Software, T.M.; Validation, A.P.; Writing—original draft, T.M.; Writing—review & editing, A.P. All authors have read and agreed to the published version of the manuscript.

Funding: The work was supported by Act 211 Government of the Russian Federation, contract No 02.A03.21.0011. The work was supported by the Ministry of Science and Higher Education of the Russian Federation (government order FENU-2020-0022).

Institutional Review Board Statement: Not applicable.

Informed Consent Statement: Not applicable.

Data Availability Statement: Not applicable.

Conflicts of Interest: The authors declare no conflict of interest.

References

1. Velayutham, K.; Waran, V.; Gurusamy, S. Optimisation of laser cutting of SS 430 plate using advanced Taguchi entropy weighted-based GRA methodology. *Int. J. Mechatron. Manuf. Syst.* **2018**, *11*, 148. [CrossRef]
2. Liang, F.; Kang, C.; Fang, F. Tool path planning on triangular mesh surfaces based on the shortest boundary path graph. *Int. J. Prod. Res.* **2021**, 1–20. [CrossRef]
3. Eapen, N.A.; Heckendorn, R.B. Cutting path optimization for an automatic cutter in polynomial time using a 3/2 approximation algorithm. *Int. J. Adv. Manuf. Technol.* **2021**, *113*, 3667–3679. [CrossRef]
4. Xie, S.; Gan, J. Optimal process planning for compound laser cutting and punch using Genetic Algorithms. *Int. J. Mechatron. Manuf. Syst.* **2009**, *2*, 20–38. [CrossRef]
5. Jing Y.; Chen, Z.C. An Optimized Algorithm of Numberical Cutting-Path Control in Garment Manufacturing. *Adv. Mater. Res.* **2013**, *796*, 454–457. [CrossRef]
6. Lee, M.K.; Kwon, K.B. Cutting path optimization in CNC cutting processes using a two-step genetic algorithm. *Int. J. Prod. Res.* **2006**, *44*, 5307–5326. [CrossRef]
7. Hoeft, J.; Palekar, U.S. Heuristics for the plate-cutting traveling salesman problem. *IIE Trans.* **1997**, *29*, 719–731. [CrossRef]
8. Kochetkov, S.A.; Utkin, V. Method of decomposition in mobile robot control. *Autom Remote Control* **2011**, *72*, 2084–2099. [CrossRef]
9. Arkhipov, D.; Battaia, O.; Lazarev, A. Long-term production planning problem: Scheduling, makespan estimation and bottleneck analysis. *IFAC-PapersOnLine* **2017**, *50*, 7970–7974. [CrossRef]
10. Fleischner, H. Eulerian Graphs and Related Topics. Part 2. *Ann. Discret. Math.* **1991**, *50*, 336.
11. Kartak, V.M.; Ripatti, A.V.; Scheithauer, G.; Kurz, S. Minimal proper non-IRUP instances of the one-dimensional Cutting Stock Problem. *Discret. Appl. Math.* **2015**, *187*, 120–129. [CrossRef]
12. Tavaeva, A.; Petunin, A.; Ukolov, S.; Krotov, V. A Cost Minimizing at Laser Cutting of Sheet Parts on CNC Machines. In *Mathematical Optimization Theory and Operations Research, Proceedings of the 18th International Conference, MOTOR 2019, Ekaterinburg, Russia, 8–12 July 2019*; Springer International Publishing: New York, NY, USA, 2019; Volume 1090, pp. 422–437. [CrossRef]
13. Petunin, A.A.; Polishchuk, E.G.; Ukolov, S.S. On the new Algorithm for Solving Continuous Cutting Problem. *IFAC-PapersOnLine* **2020**, *52*, 2320–2325. [CrossRef]
14. Chentsov, A.G.; Khachay, M.Y.; Khachay, D.M. Linear Time Algorithm for Precedence Constrained Asymmetric Generalized Traveling Salesman Problem. *IFAC-PapersOnLine* **2016**, *49*, 651–655. [CrossRef]
15. Chentsov, A.G.; Grigoryev, A.M.; Chentsov, A.A. Solving a Routing Problem with the Aid of an Independent Computations Scheme. *Bull. South Ural State Univ. Ser. Math. Model. Program. Comput. Softw.* **2018**, *11*, 60–74. [CrossRef]
16. Landovskaya, I. A processing algorithm of fabric particle interaction with solid object faces during computer simulation. *Proc. Russ. Higher Sch. Acad. Sci.* **2016**, *2*, 78–93. (In Russian) [CrossRef]
17. Dewil, R.; Vansteenwegen, P.; Cattrysse, D.; Laguna, M.; Vossen, T. An improvement heuristic framework for the laser cutting tool path problem. *Int. J. Prod. Res.* **2015**, *53*, 17611776. [CrossRef]
18. Dewil, R.; Vansteenwegen, P.; Cattrysse, D. A review of cutting algorithms for laser cutters. *Int. J. Manuf. Technol.* **2016**, *87*, 1865–1884. [CrossRef]
19. Panyukov, A.V.; Makarovskikh, T.A.; Savitskiy, E.A. Mathematical models and routing algorithms for economical cutting tool paths. *Int. J. Prod. Res.* **2018**, *56*, 1171–1188. [CrossRef]
20. Manber, U.; BentIsrani, S. Pierce Point Minimization and Optimal Torch Path Determination in Flame Cutting. *J. Manuf. Syst.* **1984**, *3*, 1. [CrossRef]
21. Manber, U.; Bent, S.W. On Non-intersecting Eulerian Circuits. *Discret. Appl. Math.* **1987**, *18*, 87–94.
22. Fleischner, H.; Beineke, L.; Wilson, R. *Selected Topics in Graph Theory. Part 2*; Academic Press: London, UK, 1983.
23. Bely, S. On self-non-intersecting and non-intersecting chain. *Math. Notes* **1983**, *34*, 625–628.
24. Panioukova, T. Eulerian cover with ordered enclosing for flat graphs. *Electron. Notes Discret. Math.* **2007**, *28*, 17–24. [CrossRef]
25. Makarovskikh, T.A.; Panyukov, A.V. The Cutter Trajectory Avoiding Intersections of Cuts. *IFAC PapersOnLine* **2017**, *50*, 2284–2289. [CrossRef]
26. Makarovskikh, T.A.; Panyukov, A.V. Mathematical model for a cutting path avoiding intersections. *IFAC-PapersOnLine* **2020**, *53*, 10455–10460. [CrossRef]

17. Makarovskikh, T.A.; Panyukov, A.V. Construction of a Technologically Feasible Cutting with Pierce Points Placement Constraints. *Commun. Comput. Inf. Sci.* **2020**, *1340*, 186–197. [CrossRef]
18. Panioukova, T. Chain sequences with ordered enclosing. *J. Comput. Syst. Sci. Int.* **2007**, *46*, 83–92. [CrossRef]
19. Panioukova, T.A.; Panyukov, A.V. Algorithms for Construction of Ordered Enclosing Traces in Planar Eulerian Graphs. In Proceedings of the International Workshop on Computer Science and Information Technologies' 2003, Ufa, Russia, 16–18 September 2003; Ufa State Technical University: Ufa, Russia, 2003; Volume 1, pp. 134–138.
20. Panyukova, T.A. Constructing of OE-postman Path for a Planar Graph. *Bull. South Ural State Univ. Ser. Math. Model. Program. Comput. Softw.* **2014**, *7*, 90–101. [CrossRef]
21. Fleischner, H. *Eulerian Graphs and Related Topics*; Elsevier Science Publishers B.V.: Amsterdam, The Netherlands, 1990; 450p.
22. Makarovskikh, T.A.; Panyukov, A.V. AOE-Trails Constructing for a Plane Connected 4-Regular Graph. In Proceedings of the Supplementary Proceedings of the 9th International Conference on Discrete Optimization and Operations Research and Scientific School (DOOR 2016), Vladivostok, Russia, 19–23 September 2016; Volume 1623, pp. 62–71.
23. Makarovskikh, T.A.; Panyukov, A.V. Algorithm for constructing AOE circuit in a connected flat 4-regular graph. In *Proceedings of the XII International Scientific Seminar "Discrete Mathematics and Its Applications" Academician Lupanov*; Mechanics and Mathematics Faculty of Moscow State University: Moscow, Russia, 2016, p. 293296. (In Russian)
24. Papadimitriou, C.H.; Steiglitz, K. *Combinatorial Optimization. Algorithms and Complexity*, Unabridged edition; Dover Publications: Mineola, NY, USA, 1998.
25. Makarovskikh, T.A.; Panyukov, A.V.; Savitskiy, E.A. Mathematical Models and Routing Algorithms for CAD Technological Preparation of Cutting Processes. *Autom. Remote Control* **2017**, *78*, 868–881. [CrossRef]
26. Makarovskikh, T.; Panyukov, A.; Savitsky, E. Software Development for Cutting Tool Routing Problems. *Procedia Manuf.* **2019**, *29*, 567–574. [CrossRef]

Article

Complexity of Solutions Combination for the Three-Index Axial Assignment Problem

Lev G. Afraimovich * and Maxim D. Emelin

Institute of Information Technology, Mathematics and Mechanics, Lobachevsky State University of Nizhny Novgorod, Nizhny Novgorod 603022, Russia; makcum888e@mail.ru
* Correspondence: lev.afraimovich@itmm.unn.ru

Abstract: In this work we consider the NP-hard three-index axial assignment problem. We formulate and investigate a problem of combining feasible solutions. Such combination can be applied in a wide range of heuristic and approximate algorithms for solving the assignment problem, instead of the commonly used strategy of selecting the best solution among the found feasible solutions. We discuss approaches to a solution of the combination problem and prove that it becomes NP-hard already in the case of combining four solutions.

Keywords: axial assignment problem; multi-index problem; approximate algorithms; NP-hardness

MSC: 90C10; 90C27; 90C59

Citation: Afraimovich, L.G.; Emelin, M.D. Complexity of Solutions Combination for the Three-Index Axial Assignment Problem. *Mathematics* **2022**, *10*, 1062. https://doi.org/10.3390/math10071062

Academic Editors: Alexander A Lazarev, Frank Werner and Bertrand M. T. Lin

Received: 4 March 2022
Accepted: 23 March 2022
Published: 25 March 2022

Publisher's Note: MDPI stays neutral with regard to jurisdictional claims in published maps and institutional affiliations.

Copyright: © 2022 by the authors. Licensee MDPI, Basel, Switzerland. This article is an open access article distributed under the terms and conditions of the Creative Commons Attribution (CC BY) license (https://creativecommons.org/licenses/by/4.0/).

1. Introduction

Multi-index axial assignment problems arise when it comes to solving a multitude of applied problems in the logistics and planning area [1–3]. An overview of the results obtained through analysis of the subclasses of multi-index assignment problems is given in [1]. The class of multi-index axial assignment problems is known to be NP-hard even in the three-index case [4]. In [5] it was proved that no polynomial ε-approximate algorithms for solving a three-index axial assignment problem (here ε is an arbitrary constant) exist, otherwise P = NP.

There are known approximate and heuristic algorithms for solving the NP-hard axial assignment problem [2,6–11]. As a rule, such algorithms construct a series of feasible solutions to the problem. The general approach in the final step of the algorithms is choosing the best solution from the constructed feasible solutions. As an improvement of the final step of such algorithms we propose building an optimal combination of the found feasible solutions instead of commonly applied selection of the best solution. The optimal combination of feasible solutions is an optimization problem where the fragments of the found feasible solutions need to be optimally combined. Obviously, such an optimal combination is no worse than a standard selection of the best solution. But, as we will demonstrate later, solutions combination outperforms (based on computational experiments) selection of the best solution while having comparable computational complexity.

The solutions combination problem was first formulated in our earlier paper [12]. In this work a linear complexity algorithm for optimal combining of a pair of feasible solutions was constructed. Heuristic algorithms for combining of three and a larger number of solutions were proposed in [13]. These heuristics are based on successive combination of pairs of solutions. An efficient algorithm for optimal combining of three and larger number of solutions was an open problem.

In this work we have proved that the solution combination problem is already NP-hard in the case of combining four solutions. Which means that there is already no polynomial algorithm for optimal combination in the case of four solutions, otherwise

$P = NP$. An efficient algorithm for optimal combining in the case of three solutions remains an open problem.

Further the article is organized as follows. In Section 2 we formulate the axial assignment problem and the corresponding solutions combination problem. Section 3 deals with the results of designing the algorithms for combining feasible solutions. Finally, in Section 4 the NP-hardness of combining four solutions is proved.

2. Solutions Combination Problem

Let I, J, K be the disjoint index sets, $I \cap J = \varnothing$, $I \cap K = \varnothing$, $J \cap K = \varnothing$ and $|I| = |J| = |K| = n$; c_{ijk}, $i \in I, j \in J, k \in K$ is the three-index cost matrix; and $x_{ijk}, i \in I$, $j \in J, k \in K$ is the three-index matrix of the variables. Then the three-index axial assignment problem is formulated as the following integer linear programming problem:

$$\sum_{i \in I}\sum_{j \in J} x_{ijk} = 1, k \in K, \quad (1)$$

$$\sum_{i \in I}\sum_{k \in K} x_{ijk} = 1, j \in J, \quad (2)$$

$$\sum_{j \in J}\sum_{k \in K} x_{ijk} = 1, i \in I, \quad (3)$$

$$x_{ijk} \in \{0,1\}, i \in I, j \in J, k \in K, \quad (4)$$

$$\sum_{i \in I}\sum_{j \in J}\sum_{k \in K} c_{ijk} x_{ijk} \to \min. \quad (5)$$

Next, let a set $W \subseteq I \times J \times K$ be given that defines a subset of the allowed assignments:

$$x_{ijk} = 0, (i,j,k) \notin W. \quad (6)$$

Then we consider an optimization problem with objective (5) subject to constraints (1)–(4) and denote it by $Z(W)$ for the given subset W. It is obvious that problem (1)–(5) corresponds to the problem $Z(I \times J \times K)$.

In the general case problem $Z(W)$ is NP-hard [1]. Moreover, the problem of feasibility check of system (1)–(4), (6) for an arbitrary set W is NP-complete [1]. We will further consider subsets W such that correspond to the assignments set of some feasible solutions of the problem (1)–(5).

We introduce auxiliary notations. Let x be a feasible solution to the system of constraints (1)–(4). Then $W(x)$ will be used to denote the following set of allowed assignments:

$$W(x) = \{(i,j,k) | x_{ijk} = 1, i \in I, j \in J, k \in K\}.$$

Let $x^1, x^2, \ldots, x^m$ be some arbitrary feasible solutions of the system (1)–(4). Denote $W(x^1, x^2, \ldots, x^m) = \bigcup_{t=1}^{m} W(x^t)$. Then the problem of optimal combining of m feasible solutions $x^1, x^2, \ldots, x^m$ takes the form $Z(W(x^1, x^2, \ldots, x^m))$.

A large number of known heuristic and approximate algorithms for solving the axial assignment problem yield, in the course of their operation, a certain set of feasible solutions (for convenience denoted by $x^1, x^2, \ldots, x^m$). Denote $C(x) = \sum_{i \in I}\sum_{j \in J}\sum_{k \in K} c_{ijk} x_{ijk}$. The general approach in the final step of these algorithms is choosing the best solution from the constructed feasible solutions, i.e., $C' = \min_{t=\overline{1,m}} C(x^t)$. As an improvement on the final step of such algorithms, i.e., selection of the best solution, we propose building an optimal combination of the found feasible solutions through solving the problem $Z(W(x^1, x^2, \ldots, x^m))$. In other words, we propose building a solution by combining the components of the found feasible solutions rather than only choosing the best one.

3. Solution Combination Algorithms

Let us consider algorithms for solutions combination problem $Z(W(x^1, x^2, \ldots, x^m))$ In our earlier paper [12] we constructed a linear complexity algorithm for solutions combination problem for the case $m = 2$.

It was proved in [12] that Algorithm 1 finds solution of the problem $Z(W(x^1, x^2))$ and requires $O(n)$ computational operations. Thus, in accordance with step 5 of Algorithm 1, the optimal value of the criterion for problem $Z(W(x^1, x^2))$ is defined as $\sum_{l=1}^{q} \min\left(\sum_{(i,j,k) \in D_l^1} c_{ijk}, \sum_{(i,j,k) \in D_l^2} c_{ijk} \right)$.

Algorithm 1. Ref. [12]. *Solution of problem $Z(W(x^1, x^2))$*

Step 1. Construct graph $G = (V, A)$, where
$V = \{I \cup J \cup K\}$, $A = \{(i,j), (i,k), (j,k) | (i,j,k) \in W(x^1, x^2)\}$.
Step 2. Find the connectivity components $V_l, l = \overline{1,q}$, of graph G and build subgraphs $G_l = (V_l, A_l), l = \overline{1,q}$, induced by the corresponding components of connectivity.
Step 3. Now, we build the following sets:
$$D_l^1 = \{(i,j,k) | (i,j,k) \in W(x^1), (i,j), (i,k), (j,k) \in A_l\},$$
$$D_l^2 = \{(i,j,k) | (i,j,k) \in W(x^2), (i,j), (i,k), (j,k) \in A_l\}.$$
Step 4. The optimal value of criterion of the problem $Z(W(x^1, x^2))$ is defined as
$$c^* = \sum_{l=1}^{q} \min\left(\sum_{(i,j,k) \in D_l^1} c_{ijk}, \sum_{(i,j,k) \in D_l^2} c_{ijk} \right).$$
Step 5. The optimal solution to the problem $Z(W(x^1, x^2))$ is constructed as follows. Initially let $x_{ijk} 0, i \in I, j \in J, k \in K$. Further, for each $l = \overline{1,q}$ perform
$$x_{ijk} 1, (i,j,k) \in D_l^{p^*}, \text{ where } p^* = \operatorname*{argmin}_{p \in \{1,2\}} \sum_{(i,j,k) \in D_l^p} c_{ijk}.$$

We have demonstrated in [13] that an algorithm based on successive optimal combination of feasible solutions pairs does not ensure an optimal solution for the problem $Z(W(x^1, x^2, \ldots, x^m))$ when $m = 3$. However, such a successive combination technique can be used as a heuristic algorithm for the problem $Z(W(x^1, x^2, \ldots, x^m))$ when $m \geq 3$. We provide the results of the computation experiments for a variety of successive combination strategies, which demonstrate the advantage of the proposed approach over the commonly used step of choosing the best feasible solution [13].

In [12,13] we presented comprehensive computational experiments for solutions combination algorithm for $m = 2$ and for solutions combination strategies for $m \geq 3$. Below we will giving a brief description of these computational results. In [5] an approximate algorithm was constructed for the axial assignment problems satisfying triangle inequality. This approximate algorithm constructs three feasible solutions and chooses the best among them. A collection of test problems for $n \in \{33, 66\}$ with the cost matrices satisfying triangle inequality was proposed in [5]. For the collection of the problems presented in [5] the solution combination algorithm gives 0.148% improvement compared to the original step of choosing the best solution by the approximate algorithm; for more details please see [12]. For a set of cost matrices whose entries were generated with integer values uniformly distributed at the interval $[0, 300]$ and for $n \in \{10, 11, \ldots, 19\}$ we randomly generated n^3 feasible solutions and applied the local optimization algorithm proposed in [6]. Based on computational results we demonstrated that applying of successive combination strategies to the locally optimized solution gives approximately 4–8% improvement compared to a standard approach of choosing the best solution; for more details please see [13].

4. Solutions Combination NP-Hardness

We will now show that the class of problems of the optimal combination of m feasible solutions is NP-hard even when $m = 4$. The proof is based on polynomial reduction of the well-known NP-hard class of 3-CNF problems [4]. Here 3-CNF is the problem of determining if a Boolean formula is satisfiable, where the Boolean formula is in conjunctive normal form with three variables per conjunct.

Theorem 1. *The class of 3-CNF problems is polynomially reduced to the class of 3-CNF problems without repeating variables in each clause.*

Proof of Theorem 1. Let us consider an arbitrary 3-CNF and apply the following algorithm to each clause of 3-CNF:

a. If a clause does not contain any repeating variables, it remains unchanged.
b. If a repeating variable is included into a clause only with or only without negation then a clause has the form $(x \cup x \cup y)$ or $(x \cup x \cup x)$, where x, y are the literals. A clause $u(x,y) = (x \cup x \cup y)$ is replaced by $u'(x,y,z) = (x \cup y \cup z) \cap (x \cup y \cup \bar{z})$, where z is the new Boolean variable. It is obvious that $u(x,y) = u'(x,y,z)$, $\forall z$. A clause $u(x) = (x \cup x \cup x)$ is replaced by $u'(x,z,w) = (x \cup z \cup w) \cap (x \cup z \cup \bar{w}) \cap (x \cup \bar{z} \cup w) \cap (x \cup \bar{z} \cup \bar{w})$, where z, w are the new Boolean variables. It is obvious that $u(x) = u'(x,z,w)$, $\forall z, w$.
c. If a repeating variable is included into a clause simultaneously with and without negation, this clause has the form $(x \cup \bar{x} \cup y)$, where x is the Boolean variable, y is the literal. Then $(x \cup \bar{x} \cup y) \equiv 1$, and the clause can be discarded from 3-CNF.

At this point we polynomially reduced the class of 3-CNF problems to the class of 3-CNF problems without repeating variables in each clause. The lemma is proved. □

Theorem 2. *The class of optimal combination of four solutions problems is NP-hard.*

Proof of Theorem 2. To prove the theorem, we will show that NP-hard class of 3-CNF problems [4] can be polynomially reduced to a class of optimal combination of four feasible solutions problems. □

Consider an arbitrary 3-CNF problem with N Boolean variables and M clauses. Let $L = \{1, \ldots, N\}$ be the set of indices of Boolean variables of the 3-CNF. According to theorem 1, without loss of generality we assume that there are no repeating variables in each clause. For convenience, we introduce the following notations:

- $l_1(s), l_2(s), l_3(s)$ are the indices of Boolean variables in the s-th clause;
- $L(s) = \{l_1(s) \cup l_2(s) \cup l_3(s)\}$ is the set of indices of the Boolean variables included into the s-th clause;
- $L^+(s) \subseteq L(s)$ is the set of indices of the Boolean variables included without negation into the s-th clause;
- $L^-(s) \subseteq L(s)$ is the set of indices of the Boolean variables included with negation into the s-th clause;
- $\bar{L}(s) = \{1, \ldots, N\} \setminus L(s)$ is the set of indices for the Boolean variables that are not included into the s-th clause,

$$s = \overline{1, M}.$$

Then we construct disjoint sets of indices I, J, K as follows; see Figure 1 for visualization of these sets:

- $I = \{a_{ls}^1 | l = \overline{1,N}, s = \overline{1,M}\} \cup \{d_s^1, q_s^1, w_s^1 | s = \overline{1,M}\} \cup \{e_{ls}^1 | l \in \bar{L}(s), s = \overline{1,M}\}$,
- $J = \{a_{ls}^2 | l = \overline{1,N}, s = \overline{1,M}\} \cup \{d_s^2, q_s^2, w_s^2 | s = \overline{1,M}\} \cup \{e_{ls}^2 | l \in \bar{L}(s), s = \overline{1,M}\}$,
- $K = \{b_{ls}^1, b_{ls}^2 | l = \overline{1,N}, s = \overline{1,M}\}$.

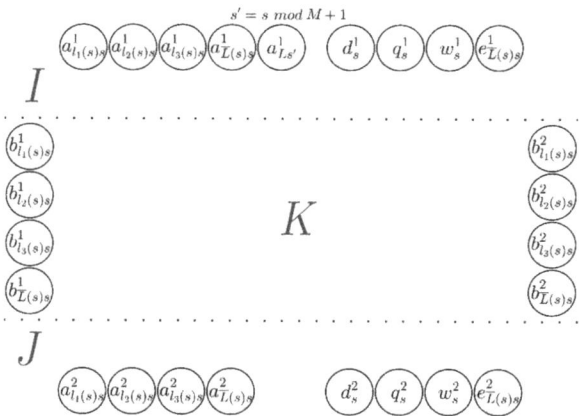

Figure 1. Scheme demonstrating subsets of indices I, J, K corresponding to a fixed s. A set of indices as a subscript of a node on the scheme (e.g., a_{Ls}^1) corresponds to a set of nodes.

According to above construction, $|I| = |J| = NM + 3M + (N-3)M = 2NM$, $|K| = 2NM$. Hence, $|I| = |J| = |K| = 2NM$.

Next, build a set $R \subseteq I \times J \times K$ to be used for defining a multi-index cost matrix of the axial assignment problem in the following form:

- $R_1 = \left\{ (a_{ls}^1, a_{ls}^2, b_{ls}^1), (a_{l(s \bmod M+1)}^1, a_{ls}^2, b_{ls}^2) \big| l = \overline{1,N}, s = \overline{1,M} \right\}$;
- $R_2 = \left\{ (d_s^1, d_s^2, b_{ls}^1) | l \in L^-(s), s = \overline{1,M} \right\} \cup \left\{ (d_s^1, d_s^2, b_{ls}^2) | l \in L^+(s), s = \overline{1,M} \right\}$;
- $R_3 = \left\{ (q_s^1, q_s^2, b_{l_1(s)s}^1), (q_s^1, q_s^2, b_{l_1(s)s}^2), (q_s^1, q_s^2, b_{l_2(s)s}^1), (q_s^1, q_s^2, b_{l_2(s)s}^2) \big| s = \overline{1,M} \right\}$;
- $R_4 = \left\{ (w_s^1, w_s^2, b_{l_2(s)s}^1), (w_s^1, w_s^2, b_{l_2(s)s}^2), (w_s^1, w_s^2, b_{l_3(s)s}^1), (w_s^1, w_s^2, b_{l_3(s)s}^2) \big| s = \overline{1,M} \right\}$;
- $R_5 = \left\{ (e_{ls}^1, e_{ls}^2, b_{ls}^1), (e_{ls}^1, e_{ls}^2, b_{ls}^2) | l \in \overline{L}(s), s = \overline{1,M} \right\}$;
- $R = R_1 \cup R_2 \cup R_3 \cup R_4 \cup R_5$.

Now we can define the three-index cost matrix as

$$c_{ijk} = \begin{cases} 0, & (i,j,k) \in R \\ 1, & \text{otherwise} \end{cases}, \ i \in I, j \in J, k \in K.$$

The constructed sets I, J, K and three-index cost matrix $\|c_{ijk}\|$ define the three-index axial assignment problem (1)–(5).

Further we build four subsets $P_1, P_2, P_3, P_4 \subseteq I \times J \times K$, that will determine four feasible solutions to problem (1)–(5); see Figures 2–5 for visualization of the sets P_1–P_4:

- $P_1 = \left\{ (a_{ls}^1, a_{ls}^2, b_{ls}^1) | l = \overline{1,N}, s = \overline{1,M} \right\} \cup \left\{ (q_s^1, q_s^2, b_{l_2(s)s}^2), (w_s^1, w_s^2, b_{l_3(s)s}^2) \big| s = \overline{1,M} \right\} \cup$
  $\left\{ (d_s^1, d_s^2, b_{l_1(s)s}^2) \big| s = \overline{1,M} \right\} \cup \left\{ (e_{ls}^1, e_{ls}^2, b_{ls}^2) | l \in \overline{L}(s), s = \overline{1,M} \right\}$;

- $P_2 = \left\{ (a_{l(s \bmod M+1)}^1, a_{ls}^2, b_{ls}^2) | l = \overline{1,N}, s = \overline{1,M} \right\} \cup \left\{ (q_s^1, q_s^2, b_{l_2(s)s}^1), (w_s^1, w_s^2, b_{l_3(s)s}^1) \big| s = \overline{1,M} \right\}$
  $\cup \left\{ (d_s^1, d_s^2, b_{l_1(s)s}^1) \big| s = \overline{1,M} \right\} \cup \left\{ (e_{ls}^1, e_{ls}^2, b_{ls}^1) | l \in \overline{L}(s), s = \overline{1,M} \right\}$;

- $P_3 = \left\{ (q_s^1, q_s^2, b_{l_1(s)s}^2), (w_s^1, w_s^2, b_{l_2(s)s}^2), (a_{l_1(s)s}^1, a_{l_1(s)s}^2, b_{l_1(s)s}^1) \big| s = \overline{1,M} \right\} \cup$
  $\left\{ (d_s^1, d_s^2, b_{l_2(s)s}^1), (a_{l_2(s)s}^1, a_{l_2(s)s}^2, b_{l_3(s)s}^1), (a_{l_3(s)s}^1, a_{l_3(s)s}^2, b_{l_3(s)s}^2) \big| l_2(s) \in L^-(s), s = \overline{1,M} \right\} \cup$
  $\left\{ (d_s^1, d_s^2, b_{l_3(s)s}^1), (a_{l_3(s)s}^1, a_{l_3(s)s}^2, b_{l_3(s)s}^1) \big| l_2(s) \in L^+(s), l_3(s) \in L^-(s), s = \overline{1,M} \right\} \cup$
  $\left\{ (d_s^1, d_s^2, b_{l_3(s)s}^2), (a_{l_3(s)s}^1, a_{l_3(s)s}^2, b_{l_3(s)s}^1) \big| l_2(s) \in L^+(s), l_3(s) \in L^+(s), s = \overline{1,M} \right\} \cup$
  $\left\{ (a_{l_2(s)s}^1, a_{l_2(s)s}^2, b_{l_2(s)s}^1) \big| l_2(s) \in L^+(s), s = \overline{1,M} \right\} \cup$
  $\left\{ (a_{ls}^1, a_{ls}^2, b_{ls}^1), (e_{ls}^1, e_{ls}^2, b_{ls}^2) | l \in \overline{L}(s), s = \overline{1,M} \right\}$;

- $P_4 = \left\{ (q_s^1, q_s^2, b_{l_1(s)s}^1), (w_s^1, w_s^2, b_{l_2(s)s}^1), (a_{l_1(s)s}^1, a_{l_1(s)s}^2, b_{l_1(s)s}^2) \big| s = \overline{1,M} \right\} \cup$
  $\left\{ (d_s^1, d_s^2, b_{l_2(s)s}^1), (a_{l_3(s)s}^1, a_{l_3(s)s}^2, b_{l_3(s)s}^1), (a_{l_2(s)s}^1, a_{l_2(s)s}^2, b_{l_3(s)s}^1) \big| l_2(s) \in L^+(s), s = \overline{1,M} \right\} \cup$

$$\left\{(d_s^1, d_s^2, b_{l_3(s)s}^1), (a_{l_3(s)s}^1, a_{l_3(s)s}^2, b_{l_3(s)s}^2) \bigg| l_2(s) \in L^-(s), l_3(s) \in L^-(s), s = \overline{1,M}\right\} \cup$$
$$\left\{(d_s^1, d_s^2, b_{l_3(s)s}^2), (a_{l_3(s)s}^1, a_{l_3(s)s}^2, b_{l_3(s)s}^1) \bigg| l_2(s) \in L^-(s), l_3(s) \in L^+(s), s = \overline{1,M}\right\} \cup$$
$$\left\{(a_{l_2(s)s}^1, a_{l_2(s)s}^2, b_{l_2(s)s}^2) \bigg| l_2(s) \in L^-(s), s = \overline{1,M}\right\} \cup \left\{(a_{ls}^1, a_{ls}^2, b_{ls}^2), (e_{ls}^1, e_{ls}^2, b_{ls}^1) \bigg| l \in \overline{L}(s), s = \overline{1,M}\right\}$$

The corresponding four feasible solutions x^1, x^2, x^3, x^4 will be defined as follows:

$$x_{ijk}^t = \begin{cases} 1, & \text{if } (i,j,k) \in P_t \\ 0, & \text{otherwise} \end{cases}, i \in I, j \in J, k \in K,$$

where $t \in \{1, 2, 3, 4\}$.

It is obvious that the criterion of the constructed solutions combination problem $Z(W(x^1, x^2, x^3, x^4))$ is nonnegative. Now we show that the optimal criterion value of $Z(W(x^1, x^2, x^3, x^4))$ is 0 if and only if the corresponding 3-CNF is satisfiable.

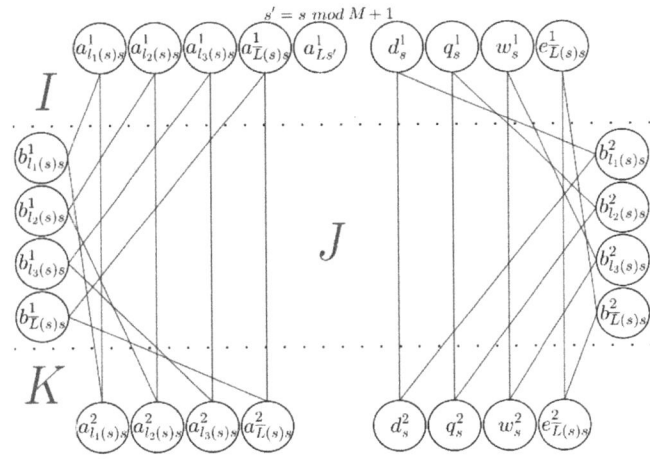

Figure 2. Scheme demonstrating the subset of triples of the set P_1, corresponding to a fixed s.

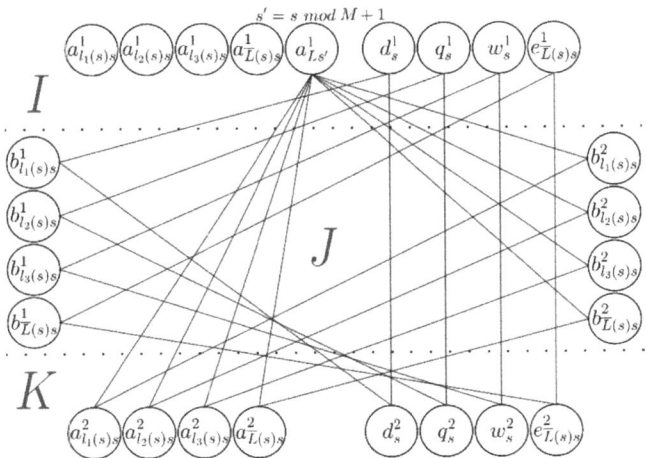

Figure 3. Scheme demonstrating the subset of triples of the set P_2, corresponding to a fixed s.

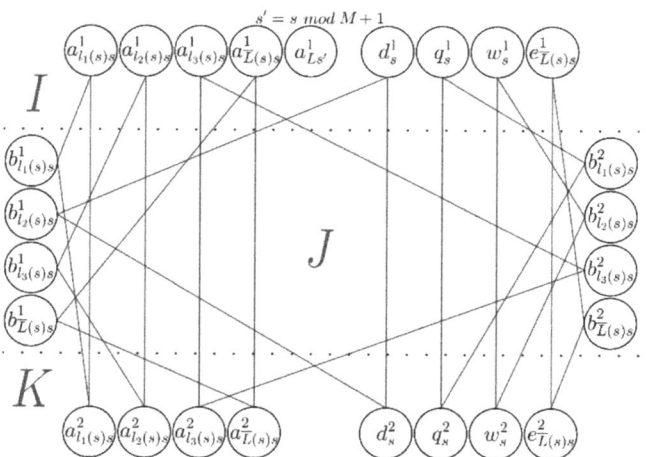

Figure 4. Scheme demonstrating the subset of triples of the set P_3, corresponding to a fixed s such that $l_2(s) \in L^-(s)$.

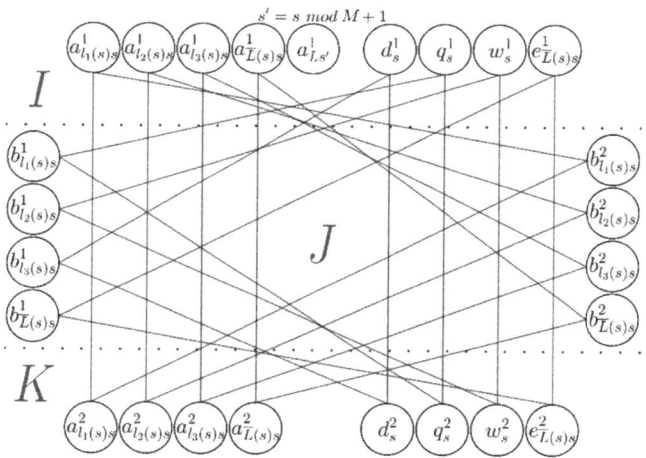

Figure 5. Scheme demonstrating the subset of triples of the sets P_4, corresponding to a fixed s such that $l_2(s) \in L^-(s), l_3(s) \in L^-(s)$.

1. Let x^* be the optimal solution to problem $Z\left(W(x^1, x^2, x^3, x^4)\right)$ and $C(x^*) = 0$. We build a set $W(x^*) = \left\{ (i,j,k) \middle| x^*_{ijk} = 1, i \in I, j \in J, k \in K \right\}$. Since x^* satisfies the system of constraints (1)–(4), we get $|W(x^*)| = 2NM$.

Now it is easily seen that for each $l \in \{1, 2, \ldots, N\}$ one of the following two conditions holds:

$$\left(a^1_{ls}, a^2_{ls}, b^1_{ls}\right) \in P(x^*), \ s = \overline{1, M}, \tag{7}$$

or

$$\left(a^1_{l(s \bmod M+1)}, a^2_{ls}, b^2_{ls}\right) \in P(x^*), \ s = \overline{1, M}. \tag{8}$$

Indeed, let us assume that for some $l \in \{1, 2, \ldots, N\}$ the condition $(a_{ls}^1, a_{ls}^2, b_{ls}^1) \in W(x^*)$ holds, but $\left(a_{l(s \bmod M+1)}^1, a_{l(s \bmod M+1)}^2, b_{l(s \bmod M+1)}^1\right) \notin W(x^*)$. By construction,

$$P \cap \left\{\left(a_{(l \bmod M+1)s}^1, j, k\right) \Big| j \in J, k \in K\right\}$$
$$= \left\{\left(a_{l(s \bmod M+1)}^1, a_{l(s \bmod M+1)}^2, b_{l(s \bmod M+1)}^1\right), \left(a_{l(s \bmod M+1)}^1, a_{ls}^2, b_{ls}^2\right)\right\}$$

Since $(a_{ls}^1, a_{ls}^2, b_{ls}^1) \in W(x^*)$ and x^* satisfies the system of constraints (1)–(4), then $\left(a_{l(s \bmod M+1)}^1, a_{ls}^2, b_{ls}^2\right) \notin W(x^*)$. Given $W(x^*) \subseteq P$, we finally obtain

$$W(x^*) \cap \left\{\left(a_{l(s \bmod M+1)}^1, j, k\right) \Big| j \in J, k \in K\right\} = \varnothing.$$

Then, $|W(x^*)| < 2NM$, which leads to contradiction and the above assumption is wrong. Hence, if $(a_{ls}^1, a_{ls}^2, b_{ls}^1) \in P(x^*)$, we get $\left(a_{l(s \bmod M+1)}^1, a_{l(s \bmod M+1)}^2, b_{l(s \bmod M+1)}^1\right) \in W(x^*)$. From here we conclude that, if $(a_{ls}^1, a_{ls}^2, b_{ls}^1) \in W(x^*)$ for some l, then condition (7) holds for l. If $(a_{ls}^1, a_{ls}^2, b_{ls}^1) \notin W(x^*)$ for some l, then $\left(a_{l(s \bmod M+1)}^1, a_{ls}^2, b_{ls}^2\right) \in W(x^*)$ and, similarly, we can prove that condition (8) holds for l.

Now we define vector X of the Boolean variables for the initial 3-CNF:

$$X_l = \begin{cases} true, & \text{if condition (7) holds for } l \\ false, & \text{if condition (8) holds for } l \end{cases}, l = \overline{1, N}.$$

By construction, each $s \in \{1, \ldots, M\}$ has a corresponding

$$l \in L^-(s) \text{ that } (d_s^1, d_s^2, b_{ls}^1) \in W(x^*),$$

or

$$l \in L^+(s) \text{ that } (d_s^1, d_s^2, b_{ls}^2) \in W(x^*).$$

Hence for each $s \in \{1, \ldots, M\}$ there exists

$$l \in L^+(s) \text{ that } X_l = true,$$

or

$$l \in L^-(s) \text{ that } X_l = false.$$

From this it follows that each clause takes the true value on Boolean vector X. Hence 3-CNF takes the true value on Boolean vector X and is satisfiable.

2. Let 3-CNF be satisfiable and X be the Boolean variables vector on which 3-CNF takes the true value. Then we build a set of allowed assignments, $P(X)$, that is to define the optimal solution to the combination problem $Z(W(x^1, x^2, x^3, x^4))$. Set $P(X)$ will be constructed by the following Algorithm 2:

Algorithm 2. *Constructing $P(X)$*

Step 1. Initialize $P(X) := \varnothing$.
Step 2. For each $l = \overline{1, N}$:
If $X_l = true$, then
$$P(X) := P(X) \cup \{(a_{ls}^1, a_{ls}^2, b_{ls}^1) | s = \overline{1, M}\} \cup \{(e_{ls}^1, e_{ls}^2, b_{ls}^2) | l \in \overline{L}(s), s = \overline{1, M}\};$$
else
$$P(X) := P(X) \cup \{(a_{l(s \bmod M+1)}^1, a_{ls}^2, b_{ls}^2) | s = \overline{1, M}\} \cup \{(e_{ls}^1, e_{ls}^2, b_{ls}^1) | l \in \overline{L}(s), s = \overline{1, M}\}.$$
Step 3. For each $s = \overline{1, M}$:
If $X_{l_1(s)} = true, l_1(s) \in L^+(s)$ or $X_{l_1(s)} = false, l_1(s) \in L^-(s)$, then
$$P(X) P(X) \cup$$
$$\cup \left\{ (d_s^1, d_s^2, b_{l_1(s)s}^2) \Big| X_{l_1(s)} = true \right\} \cup \left\{ (d_s^1, d_s^2, b_{l_1(s)s}^1) \Big| X_{l_1(s)} = false \right\} \cup$$
$$\cup \left\{ (q_s^1, q_s^2, b_{l_2(s)s}^2) \Big| X_{l_2(s)} = true \right\} \cup \left\{ (q_s^1, q_s^2, b_{l_2(s)s}^1) \Big| X_{l_2(s)} = false \right\} \cup$$
$$\cup \left\{ (w_s^1, w_s^2, b_{l_3(s)s}^2) \Big| X_{l_3(s)} = true \right\} \cup \left\{ (w_s^1, w_s^2, b_{l_3(s)s}^1) \Big| X_{l_3(s)} = false \right\};$$
else if $X_{l_2(s)} = true, l_2(s) \in L^+(s)$ or $X_{l_2(s)} = false, l_2(s) \in L^-(s)$, then
$$P(X) P(X) \cup$$
$$\cup \left\{ (d_s^1, d_s^2, b_{l_2(s)s}^2) \Big| X_{l_2(s)} = true \right\} \cup \left\{ (d_s^1, d_s^2, b_{l_2(s)s}^1) \Big| X_{l_2(s)} = false \right\} \cup$$
$$\cup \left\{ (q_s^1, q_s^2, b_{l_1(s)s}^2) \Big| X_{l_1(s)} = true \right\} \cup \left\{ (q_s^1, q_s^2, b_{l_1(s)s}^1) \Big| X_{l_1(s)} = false \right\} \cup$$
$$\cup \left\{ (w_s^1, w_s^2, b_{l_3(s)s}^2) \Big| X_{l_3(s)} = true \right\} \cup \left\{ (w_s^1, w_s^2, b_{l_3(s)s}^1) \Big| X_{l_3(s)} = false \right\};$$
else if $X_{l_3(s)} = true, l_3(s) \in L^+(s)$ or $X_{l_3(s)} = false, l_3(s) \in L^-(s)$, then
$$P(X) P(X) \cup$$
$$\cup \left\{ (d_s^1, d_s^2, b_{l_3(s)s}^2) \Big| X_{l_3(s)} = true \right\} \cup \left\{ (d_s^1, d_s^2, b_{l_3(s)s}^1) \Big| X_{l_3(s)} = false \right\} \cup$$
$$\cup \left\{ (q_s^1, q_s^2, b_{l_1(s)s}^2) \Big| X_{l_1(s)} = true \right\} \cup \left\{ (q_s^1, q_s^2, b_{l_1(s)s}^1) \Big| X_{l_1(s)} = false \right\} \cup$$
$$\cup \left\{ (w_s^1, w_s^2, b_{l_2(s)s}^2) \Big| X_{l_2(s)} = true \right\} \cup \left\{ (w_s^1, w_s^2, b_{l_2(s)s}^1) \Big| X_{l_2(s)} = false \right\}.$$

Next, we define a multi-index matrix of variables $x^* = \|x_{ijk}^*\|$:

$$x_{ijk}^* = \begin{cases} 1, & \text{if } (i, j, k) \in P(X) \\ 0, & \text{otherwise} \end{cases}, i \in I, j \in J, k \in K.$$

In step 2 there are $NK + (N-3)K$ elements included into the set $P(X)$. Since the 3-CNF takes true value on X, in step 3 there are $3K$ elements included into $P(X)$. Hence, $|P(X)| = 2NK$. For any pair $p_1, p_2 \in P(x)$, that $p_1 \neq p_2$, the following condition holds

$$p_1 = (i_1, j_1, k_1), p_2 = (i_2, j_2, k_2), i_1 \neq i_2, j_1 \neq j_2, k_1 \neq k_2.$$

Therefore, x^* satisfies the system of constraints (1)–(4).

By construction, $P(X) \subseteq P$, since in step 2 only elements from the sets P_1, P_2 may be included into $P(X)$, then in step 3 only elements from P_1, P_2, P_3, P_4 may be included into $P(X)$. Hence, x^* is a feasible solution of the combination problem $Z(W(x^1, x^2, x^3, x^4))$. Further, by construction, $P(X) \subseteq R$, since in step 2 only elements from R_1, R_5 may be included into set $P(X)$, then in step 3 only elements from R_2, R_3, R_4 may be included into $P(X)$. From this it follows that $C(x^*) = 0$. And hence, x^* is the optimal solution to problem $Z(W(x^1, x^2, x^3, x^4))$, and the optimal criterion value for this problem is 0.

Thus, the optimal criterion value of the constructed problem $Z(W(x^1, x^2, x^3, x^4))$ is equal to 0 if and only if the 3-CNF is satisfiable. The above procedure of constructing the problem $Z(W(x^1, x^2, x^3, x^4))$ requires a polynomial time in the size of the initial 3-CNF. Therefore, the class of problems of optimal combination of four feasible solutions is NP-hard. The theorem is proved.

5. Conclusions

Approximate and heuristic algorithms for solving an NP-hard axial assignment problem are well known in literature. Usually, such algorithms construct a series of feasible solutions to the problem and, in the final step, select the best solution among those constructed. As an improvement of this commonly used approach of selecting the best solution in the final step of the algorithm we propose solving the problem of optimal combination of constructed m solutions. The case $m = 2$ (i.e., optimal combination of a pair of feasible solutions) can be handled using a linear complexity algorithm. For $m \geq 3$ it is impossible to find an optimal solution to the combining problem via successive combination of pairs. Nevertheless, in practice the strategy of sequential combination of pairs proves to produce better results than are obtainable with the conventional technique of selecting the best solution. In this paper we demonstrated that the solutions combination problem turns out to already be NP-hard when $m = 4$. The combination complexity in the case $m = 3$ remains an open problem.

Author Contributions: Conceptualization and methodology L.G.A., formal analysis and investigation M.D.E. All authors have read and agreed to the published version of the manuscript.

Funding: This research received no external funding.

Informed Consent Statement: Not applicable.

Data Availability Statement: Not applicable.

Acknowledgments: The authors would like to thank anonymous reviewers for their suggestions and comments.

Conflicts of Interest: The authors declare no conflict of interest.

References

1. Spieksma, F.C.R. Multi Index Assignment Problems. Complexity, Approximation, Applications. In *Nonlinear Assignment Problems: Algorithms and Applications*; Pardalos, P.M., Pitsoulis, L.S., Eds.; Kluwer Acad. Publishers: Dordrecht, The Netherlands, 2000; pp. 1–11.
2. Afraimovich, L.G. A Heuristic Method for Solving Integer-Valued Decompositional Multiindex Problems. *Autom. Remote Control* **2014**, *75*, 1357–1368. [CrossRef]
3. Afraimovich, L.G.; Prilutskii, M.K. Multiindex Optimal Production Planning Problems. *Autom. Remote Control* **2010**, *71*, 2145–2151. [CrossRef]
4. Garey, M.R.; Johnson, D.S. *Computers and Intractability: A Guide to the Theory of NP-Completeness*; Freeman: San Francisco, CA, USA, 1979.
5. Crama, Y.; Spieksma, F.C.R. Approximation Algorithms for Three-Dimensional Assignment Problems with Triangle Inequalities. *Eur. J. Oper. Res.* **1992**, *60*, 273–279. [CrossRef]
6. Huang, G.; Lim, A. A Hybrid Genetic Algorithm for the Three-Index Assignment Problem. *Eur. J. Oper. Res.* **2006**, *172*, 249–257. [CrossRef]
7. Karapetyan, D.; Gutin, D. A New Approach to Population Sizing for Memetic Algorithms: A Case Study for the Multidimensional Assignment Problem. *Evol. Comput.* **2011**, *19*, 345–371. [CrossRef] [PubMed]
8. Medvedev, S.N.; Medvedeva, O.A. An Adaptive Algorithm for Solving the Axial Three-Index Assignment Problem. *Autom. Remote Control* **2019**, *80*, 718–732. [CrossRef]
9. Gabrovšek, B.; Novak, T.; Povh, J.; Rupnik, P.D.; Žerovnik, J. Multiple Hungarian Method for k-Assignment Problem. *Mathematics* **2020**, *8*, 2050. [CrossRef]
10. Gimadi, E.K.; Korkishko, N.M. An Algorithm For Solving the Three-Index Axial Assignment Problem on One-Cycle Permutations. *Diskretnyi Anal. Issled. Oper. Ser. 1* **2003**, *10*, 56–65.
11. Balas, E.; Saltzman, M.J. An Algorithm for the Three-Index Assignment Problem. *Oper. Res.* **1991**, *39*, 150–161. [CrossRef]
12. Afraimovich, L.G.; Emelin, M.D. Combining solutions of the axial assignment problem. *Autom. Remote Control* **2021**, *82*, 1418–1425. [CrossRef]
13. Afraimovich, L.G.; Emelin, M.D. Heuristic Strategies for Combining Solutions of the Three-Index Axial Assignment Problem. *Autom. Remote Control* **2021**, *82*, 1635–1640. [CrossRef]

Autonomous Digital Twin of Enterprise: Method and Toolset for Knowledge-Based Multi-Agent Adaptive Management of Tasks and Resources in Real Time

Vladimir Galuzin [1,2], Anastasia Galitskaya [2], Sergey Grachev [1,2], Vladimir Larukhin [1,2,3], Dmitry Novichkov [1], Petr Skobelev [3,*] and Alexey Zhilyaev [2]

1. Information Technology Faculty, Samara State Technical University, Molodogvardeyskaya Str. 244, 443100 Samara, Russia; vladimir.galuzin@gmail.com (V.G.); sergey.grachev@gmail.com (S.G.); larukhin@gmail.com (V.L.); d.novichkov@kg.ru (D.N.)
2. Knowledge Genesis Group, Skolkovo, Bolshoy Bulv. 42, 121205 Moscow, Russia; galitckaya@smartsolutions-123.ru (A.G.); zhilyaev.alexey@gmail.com (A.Z.)
3. Samara Federal Center of Russian Academy of Science, Studenchesky Str., 3A, 443001 Samara, Russia
* Correspondence: petr.skobelev@gmail.com; Tel.: +7-902-372-3202

Abstract: Digital twins of complex technical objects are widely applied for various domains, rapidly becoming smart, cognitive and autonomous. However, the problem of digital twins for autonomous management of enterprise resources is still not fully researched. In this paper, an autonomous digital twin of enterprise is introduced to provide knowledge-based multi-agent adaptive allocation, scheduling, optimization, monitoring and control of tasks and resources in real time, synchronized with employees' plans, preferences and competencies via mobile devices. The main requirements for adaptive resource management are analyzed. The authors propose formalized ontological and multi-agent models for developing the autonomous digital twin of enterprise. A method and software toolset for designing the autonomous digital twin of enterprise, applicable for both operational management of tasks and resources and what-if simulations, are developed. The validation of developed methods and toolsets for IT service desk has proved increase in efficiency, as well as savings in time and costs of deliveries for various applications. The paper also outlines a plan for future research, as well as a number of new potential business applications.

Keywords: autonomy; digital twin; enterprise; resource management; ontology; multi-agent technology; adaptability; real time

MSC: 68T20; 68T30

1. Introduction

The concept of "digital twin" [1,2] was introduced not long ago, but it is already expanding very quickly in many directions. Starting with digital shadows and computer models, they have evolved to more complex, adaptive, smart and cognitive digital twins. The future holds intelligent digital twins, which will integrate cyber-physical systems with knowledge bases, machine learning and collective decision-making.

However, in spite of this progress, digital twins have been mainly applied for complex technical objects. The problem of designing digital twins for autonomous management of enterprise resources is still not fully researched.

In this paper, we will introduce digital twins for autonomous enterprise resource management, applying mobile devices for synchronization of orders, tasks and resources of an enterprise with its computer knowledge-based multi-agent model. The proposed autonomous digital twin of enterprise is aimed at implementation of fully autonomous Deming cycle of adaptive allocation, scheduling, optimization, monitoring and control of tasks and resources in real time. This solution must make this routine work with minimum involvement of humans or, in the future, without them at all.

The autonomous digital twin of enterprise is designed as an intelligent cyber-physical decision-making system which provides convergence of cyber-physical and AI technologies, including ontologies and multi-agent technology. The knowledge-based resource management means that the focus is given on semantic specification of tasks and use of decision-making rules for their matching with required resources. Application of ontologies and knowledge-based reasoning makes it possible to formalize the enterprise domain and create its ontological models, which specify classes of orders, processes and tasks, resources, products and tools, competencies of employees, etc. Application of multi-agent technology makes it possible to provide initial multi-objective planning and adaptive re-planning of tasks to resources by processing events in real time using mobile devices. Multi-agent resource management also means that the system takes into consideration the balance of interests, preferences and constraints of all parties involved in decision making, including not only humans, managers and employees, but also orders, machines, products, equipment, etc.

As a result, an autonomous digital twin of enterprise could be considered as the next step of smart cyber-physical enterprise resource planning (Smart ERP) or, more specifically, advanced planning and scheduling (Smart APS) systems.

The paper formalizes ontology-based multi-agent models and methods for scheduling and optimization of resources, as well as proposing a method and toolset for creating autonomous digital twins of enterprise. The developed models, methods and toolset are applied to different domains, including aircraft and electric cars manufacturing, gas and oil drilling, IT help desk service, etc.

The paper is organized as follows. The second section discusses modern trends in resource management. The third section introduces the concept of the autonomous digital twin of enterprise. The fourth section presents more formally developed ontological and multi-agent models and methods for resource management in the autonomous digital twins of enterprises, which can be customized for a specific enterprise. The fifth section is focused on the method for developing autonomous digital twins of enterprises. The sixth section presents functionality and architecture of the software toolset for developing autonomous digital twins of enterprises. It fully automates business processes of resource allocation, scheduling, optimization, monitoring and control of tasks and resources in real time. The seventh section contains applications of developed method and toolbox for implementing autonomous digital twins of enterprise for different domains, including manufacturing of airplanes, electric cars, gas-oil drilling, etc. The eighth section demonstrates an example of application for IT help desk service and shows the effect and value for business. The ninth section gives an outlook on future research and potential applications.

Application of the developed models, methods and tools is intended to solve complex problems of resource management in real time, reduce peaks, idle-runs and lack of resources, increase business efficiency and decrease man-efforts, time and costs for development and maintenance of autonomous digital twins of enterprise.

2. The Modern View on the Resource Management Problem

Modern enterprise resource management requires high adaptability of scheduling and optimization because of high uncertainty and turbulence on global and local markets, when a number of unpredictable events take place very often and constantly ruin the previously agreed plans. Some examples of such unforeseen events include a new order, broken equipment, an unavailable worker, delay in supply, etc.

The discussed complexity and high turbulent dynamics lead to the fact that traditional, centralized, hierarchically organized, sequential methods and algorithms of combinatorial search or heuristics cannot effectively solve the problem of adaptive resource management with acceptable quality and within the available time.

According to [3], many existing software solutions for resource management (for example, IBM i-Log, SAP, i2, j-Log, Quintiq, Maximal Software, FICO, etc.) are still primarily based on traditional linear, dynamic or constraint programming methods with high computational complexity and a number of restrictions.

To reduce the complexity and provide more efficient search of options in decision making space, a number of new methods are based on heuristics and meta-heuristics providing near-to-optimal (not fully optimal) solutions of the problem:

- Greedy local search algorithms based on rules of the problem domain;
- Neural networks and fuzzy logic;
- Bio-inspired methods: genetic algorithms, ant colony and particle swarm optimization, etc.;
- Tabu search;
- Simulated annealing;
- Stochastic methods (such as the Monte Carlo method);
- Metaheuristics: combination of heuristic algorithms of optimization, etc.

Unfortunately, these methods and tools also become not fully applicable for modern enterprises. The developed methods and tools work very well in centralized and hierarchic environment, assuming that all orders and resources are given in advance, have the same objectives and do not change during execution of plans. They ignore individual preferences and constraints and do not support real-time networking, including communication, coordination and negotiations for conflict resolving between all participants. However, the progress of cyber-physical systems and mobile devices already made all assets and participants visible in real time and able to participate in decision making.

As a result, in case of unpredictable events, modern enterprises usually involve additional staff, delay their reaction, freeze a bigger number of products in storages, etc. Such extensive and slow reaction further requires the enterprises to cover costs and increase prices for clients. As a result, enterprises end up losing orders and wasting resources, which leads to a decrease of quality, efficiency of services and competitive advantages.

The objective of this paper is to develop new models, methods and toolsets of tasks and resource management for modern enterprises with the main focus on adaptive resource allocation, scheduling, optimization, monitoring and control in real time, when all orders and resources are not given in advance and can change at any time.

3. The Concept of the Autonomous Digital Twin of Enterprise

The concept of digital twin was introduced about 20 years ago in the context of cyber-physical systems and Industry 4.0 [4,5].

At the moment, it is still not fully defined and formalized (the new standard ISO 23247 "Digital Twin framework for manufacturing" is on the way), but in practice, one can define [2] the following three main properties of digital twins:

(1) Being a virtual representative of the physical object, which can be applied for planning and simulations;
(2) Providing ongoing self-synchronization between the model and real object;
(3) Supporting the autonomy of a virtual object compared to the real object.

This vision of digital twin reflects the fast-going convergence of modern information technologies to create holistic virtual model of object, which can operate autonomously, in parallel with the real object.

The number of applications of digital twins is also growing promptly and Gartner includes digital twins in the most perspective technologies [6]. The key software providers, including Siemens, IBM, Oracle, SAP, Autodesk, ANSYS and many others, are currently developing IoT platforms and solutions for creating digital twins of various objects.

The market of digital twin solutions already has an increase of 20% annually [7] and, as expected, it will continue to grow from 3.1 billion USD in 2020 to 48.2 billion USD in 2025 (an approximate 15-fold increase). The number of research papers (according to Web of Science) has increased 10 times in the last 5 years [7].

At the current stage of research and development, digital twins are mainly associated with models of technical objects [1,2,4,5]. However, recently, digital twins have also been applied for enterprise modeling [8–14]. For example, one paper [14] focused on designing digital twins of new post offices in France based on the cooperation of humans and robots. The developed models and methods of digital twins for enterprise modeling include machine learning, simulations, surrogate models, etc.

As a result, digital twins are now considered as a new paradigm of digitalization and automation of enterprises which integrate virtual models of objects (including enterprises) with partially or fully autonomous decision making.

In this paper, we introduce the autonomous digital twin of enterprise as a hybrid knowledge-based multi-agent cyber-physical system which can contain a cyber-physical subsystem, including sensors, computers, communication units and executors, and an intelligent decision-making subsystem, which contains a knowledge base and a multi-agent decision making system, synchronized with enterprise equipment via sensors and with employees via mobile devices.

Autonomous systems are considered goal-driven knowledge-based systems which are able to analyze problems, use knowledge base and plan their activities to solve problems and control results. In the domain of resource management, autonomous systems can provide planning, optimization and control of trucks, factories or supply chains, all without the involvement of people. In the future, autonomous systems will provide unmanned management not only for humans as employees, but also for driverless trucks, fully robotic factories or supply chains, fully working without humans. Autonomous systems integrate many modern information technologies such as cyber-physical systems [15,16], classical planning and optimization [17], multi-agent technologies [18–20], model-driven simulations [21–24], knowledge-based decision making and reasoning [25], etc.

The fast-going convergence of these technologies has resulted in the different concepts and archetypes of autonomous digital twins of things [26,27].

The functionality of the autonomous digital twin of enterprise (autonomous enterprise) for task and resource management will include:

- Ontological specification of enterprise structure, products, business processes and resources in a knowledge base;
- Loading of enterprise model specifications from knowledge base to take into account its characteristic aspects;
- Reaction to events, decomposition of processes to the level of tasks, allocation of tasks to resources, planning and optimization of resources;
- Communication of plans and results with employees;
- Approve and coordinate plans for employees;
- Monitoring and control of plan execution;
- In case of growing gap between plan and reality, adaptive re-scheduling is triggered automatically;
- Evaluation of enterprise productivity and efficiency.

The main steps in synchronization procedure between real and autonomous enterprises are illustrated in Figure 1, where real enterprise is shown on the left side and its autonomous digital twin, which is mirroring its current state, is on the right side.

Processes of synchronization of real and virtual enterprises presuppose the following kinds of communication:

- The flow of new unpredictable events is coming from the real enterprise to the autonomous digital twin of enterprise and each event triggers an adaptation of the plans;
- New allocation, scheduling and optimization of resources take place and new dynamic schedules become available for employees, i.e., managers and workers;
- Managers and workers approve schedules or change them according to their own preferences and constrains;
- The resulting collectively formed schedules are sent to all affected employees as instructions;

- The execution of each task is confirmed by employees via their mobile devices or using factory sensors;
- In case the task is not confirmed in time, the autonomous digital twin of enterprise checks the availability of the employees and starts adaptive re-scheduling of resources or escalates the issue onto the next level for managers.

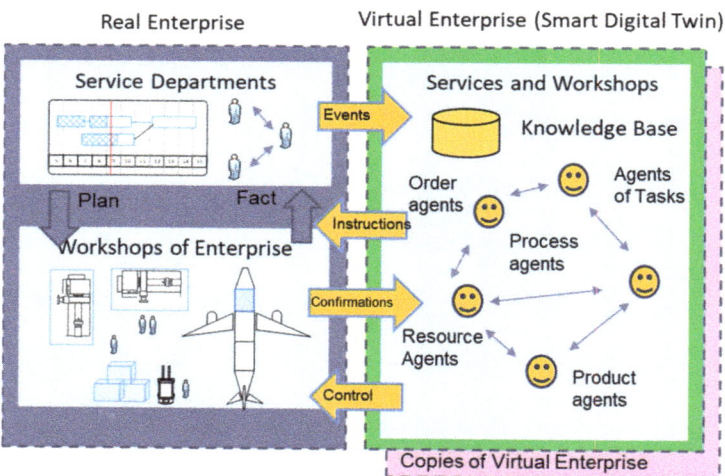

Figure 1. Synchronization between real and virtual enterprises.

Let us define $S_{twin} = \{s_I\}$, where $s_i = (model_i, plan_i, kpi_i)$, where S_{twin} is the state of a digital twin of the actual enterprise, $model_i$ is an ontological model of the enterprise, $plan_i$ is the schedule of orders and resources, kpi_i is a key performance indicators (for example, service level, profit, time of delivery, etc.) and $I = 1, \ldots, n$ is the number of states.

Whenever a disruptive event $\left(Event^{(k)}\right)$ occurs in the actual enterprise, the schedule of the virtual enterprise must change as quickly as possible to a new state in order to achieve adaptation:

$$S_{twin}^{(k+1)} = F\left(S_{twin}^{(k)}, Event^{(k)}\right)$$

This means that a new $k + 1$ state $S_{twin}^{(k+1)}$ of a virtual enterprise is formed by processing of the new coming event $Event^{(k)}$ by the functionality of the virtual enterprise, which has at the moment the current state $S_{twin}^{(k)}$; F is the functionality of adapting the enterprise schedule in case of event $Event$.

Let us define D as a function describing the difference between the actual and virtual enterprise schedules. It is essential that the state of the actual enterprise S_{real} and the state of its digital twin (virtual enterprise) S_{twin} are always as close as possible.

Then the key objective of the autonomous digital twin of enterprise is to minimize difference in KPIs between real and virtual enterprises at every moment of time k:

$$D\left(S_{real}^{(k)}, S_{twin}^{(k)}\right) \to 0$$

where D is the difference in KPI between real and virtual enterprises, $S_{twin}^{(k)}$ is the state of the virtual enterprise and $S_{real}^{(k)}$ is the state of the real enterprise.

The same description can be granulated to the states of each department, employee, process, task, machine, product, equipment or other resource of the enterprise: let us define $s(O)$ as a state of the object O in the business process of the enterprise.

We assume that all objects in the developed approach will have their own dynamic personal schedules and KPIs. These schedules are not pre-defined and can change depending on events, at any time. For example, the task can be unsatisfied with its KPI, leave the plan of a certain worker or equipment and find a more suitable one for its execution.

The autonomous digital twin of enterprise must be also applicable for real-time simulations of enterprise for modeling such events as modernization of equipment, changing the number of workers, reorganization of daily shifts, etc.

4. Formal Model of Domain Knowledge and Multi-Agent Decision Making in the Autonomous Digital Twin of Enterprise

4.1. Basic and Extended Domain Ontology of Resource Management and Ontological Model of Enterprise

Formalization of collective decision making in the autonomous digital twin of enterprise is based on the application of ontologies and multi-agent technology.

Ontology is defined as conceptualization and formal specification of the domain knowledge [28–30]. Usually, ontology consists of the most generic and abstract classes of concepts and relations which form semantic networks. Instances of concepts and relations form a knowledge base, which can additionally contain rules of reasoning.

One of the first applications of ontologies is Semantic Web, used for the annotation of Internet pages, but it is also applied for various smart services, data management, etc. [31,32]. Recently, ontologies have been applied for specifying manufacturing capacities [33] and digital twins in manufacturing [34], but they were not granulated to the task level of operations.

The idea of using ontologies in this paper is to automate the development of the autonomous digital twin of enterprise by creating and customizing ontological models of enterprises at the level of tasks and resources, which can be loaded into a unified multi-agent system for autonomous task and resource management.

This process requires basic ontology of resource management, which was not available in the literature. As a result of interviews with experts, a review of a number of publications and a systematic analysis of a number of software solutions for resource management, the following basic classes of concepts were extracted: "order", "business process", "product" or "service", "resource", "tool", "part" or "material" and some others. Besides such concepts, it will also require basic classes of relations, such as that an order "requires" a business process, a business process "consists" of "tasks", a task "requires" an employee, an employee "has" competencies, etc. The idea was to select such concepts and relations which can help to specify wide spectrum of situations with resources in real enterprises.

Using these concepts and relations, it becomes possible to create ontological specification of different enterprises in one language ("dictionary"), which is "understandable" for the unified multi-agent system for adaptive resource management.

Let us define ontology as the following set:

$$O = (C, R, F),$$

where C is a subset of object classes or concepts, R is a subset of properties and relations and F is a subset of procedures to operate with concepts and relations, including:

1. Concepts = $\phi_1(c)$—get a set of all concepts Concepts $\subseteq$ C, which are produced from c$\in$C;
2. Relations = $\phi_2(c)$—get a set of all relations Relations $\subseteq$ R, which are produced from r$\in$R;
3. Instances = $\phi_3(c)$—get a set of all Instances of Class c $\in$ C (including instances);
4. AreRelated = $\phi_4(c_1, c_2)$—check if concept c_1 $\in$ C is produced from c_2 $\in$ C;
5. AreRelated = $\phi_5(r_1, r_2)$—check if relation r_1 $\in$ R is produced from r_2 $\in$ R;
6. IsPart = $\phi_6(i, set)$—find out if instance i belongs to the given set, by comparing attributes and relations of instance with the given set;
7. Tasks = $\phi_7(p)$—find all tasks, which produce the given product p $\in$ ProducedProduct;

8. Resources = $\phi_8(t)$—find all resources which are required for the given task t ∈ Task;
9. Products = $\phi_9(t)$—find all products for the given task t ∈ Task.

The developed interpretation Φ provides possibility for more complex requests, for example, Resources = $\phi_8(\phi_7(p))$, to find a set or resources which are required for manufacturing product p.

These components are implemented as Java services and are available for decision making and reasoning of agents.

Let us define an ontology for adaptive resource management as basic ontology, Ob which contains objects (see Table 1), and its extension, domain ontology, Od, which will contain concepts and relations specific to enterprises, operating in the following domain:

$$Od \supseteq Ob.$$

Table 1. Basic ontology concepts for managing resources.

Order	Specification of the required product, quantity of these products and the time interval of order execution
Product	Specification of products which can be consumed or produced
Task	Specification of input and output objects, next and previous tasks, composition of tasks and required resources for the action
Resource	Specification of human, physical or financial resources required

Ob, the basic ontology, will be supported by unified multi-agent system for adaptive resource management, which will have hardcoded basic classes of agents, providing access to ontology through an interpretation function F.

Extensions of the concepts and relations of domain ontology, Od, are inherited from concepts and relations of the basic ontology, Ob, to establish a link between the two parts of ontology and, thus, enable agents to manage enterprise specifics. If some of the concepts and relations in Od, required for solving domain problems, are not inherited from Ob, it will require introduction of new specific agents in unified multi-agent system for adaptive resource management.

The main idea of the developed ontological models of enterprises can be described in a following way. The designed basic classes of agents (will be described below) are pre-programmed and hardcoded for processing concepts and relations of basic ontology only (order, object, task, resource, etc.). These concepts do not represent any specific domain knowledge, which is always required for enterprises' planning and scheduling. The specifics are given in domain ontology, which is designed as an extension of basic ontology. In the domain ontology, one can specify concrete types of orders, structure of manufactured products, equipment or competencies of workers which are required for scheduling specific objects, for example, to assemble the airplane. Agents read this domain knowledge from the knowledge base, when new order arrives, and apply this knowledge for reasoning and decision-making. For example, the agent of each task can find all types of resources using the "require" relation: equipment, workers, etc. Then, the agent of the task, using the types of required resources, can find concrete equipment and concrete workers, which are in full or partial match with these requirements. As a result, new types of requirements can be added to the knowledge base "on the fly" during computations and do not require system stop and re-programming of the system.

Concepts of the basic ontology described in Table 1 can be formally specified as:

$$Ob = \{Order, Product, Task, Resource\}.$$

Each order creates a product connected to an appropriate task:

$$\forall_x \exists_y \, (Order(x) \rightarrow Product(y) \wedge create(x,y)).$$

The products are separated into produced products and utilized ones. The relation between a task and these two types is given by the following formulas:

$$\forall_x \exists_y (ProducedProduct(x) \rightarrow Product(x) \land Task(y) \land produce(y,x)),$$

$$\forall_x \exists_y (ConsumedProduct(x) \rightarrow Product(x) \land Task(y) \land consume(y,x)).$$

Each task can be specified as subsets of the atomic tasks or the group tasks.

The main classes of relations between tasks are "to be part of" and one task "is followed" by another task. The discussed relations help agents find the previous and the next task whenever a need occurs to change the sequence of tasks due to occurrence of a disruptive event:

$$\forall_{x,y} (partof(x,y) \rightarrow Task(x) \land Task(y)),$$

$$\forall_{x,y} (follow(x,y) \rightarrow Task(x) \land Task(y)),$$

$$\forall_x \exists_y (GroupTask(x) \leftrightarrow Task(x) \land Task(y) \land partof(y,x)),$$

$$\forall_x (AtomicTask(x) \leftrightarrow \neg GroupTask(x)).$$

The basic classes of tasks are given in Table 2 and classes of resources-in Table 3.

Table 2. Types of basic tasks.

Atomic task with fixed task duration	Specification of the task which must be completed within a specified interval of time
Atomic task with fixed work volume	Specification of the task, the duration of which depends on resources and/or product volume
Atomic task (hammock)	Specification of the task, which must be accomplished in a correct sequence
Composite task	Specification of the task, the duration of which equals the sum duration of sub-tasks

Table 3. Types of basic resources.

Consumable resource	Specification of the resource, which is consumed during the task fulfilment
Reusable resource	Specification of the resource, which is available for the next task immediately after completion of its use

The key class of relations is "require", which describes the type of resources required for fulfillment of a task; for example, it could be a human with competencies and experience, some equipment or tools and materials.

One task can require many different types of resources of different kinds.

$$\forall_{(x,y)} (require(x,y) \rightarrow Task(x) \land (ResourceRequirenment(y) \lor Resource(y)))$$

Products may need to be "stored":

$$\forall_{(x,y)} (stored(x,y) \rightarrow Product(x) \land ReusableResource(y))$$

A set of basic relations can be formally described as the following:

$$R\_b = \{create, consume, produce, partof, follow, require, stored\}$$

Note that it is possible to introduce new concepts and relations in the domain ontology O_d, which are linked to the basic ontology, O_b, whenever required, and it will not change the agents' logic and behavior.

This essential feature is enabled through appropriate F interpretations of concepts and relations. For example, in the manufacturing domain, new types of products could be introduced, for example, "*components*", "*assembly elements*" and "*final products*". Tasks could be specified as a "*process*" and "*operation*", and resources as "*equipment*", "*tool*" or "*employee*", and it will not require changes in agents logic if F provides an opportunity to make the required reasoning:

$$\forall_x \; (Product(x) \rightarrow Component(x) \vee AssemblyElement(x) \vee FinalProduct(x)),$$

$$\forall_x \; (Task(x) \rightarrow Process(x) \vee Operation(x)),$$

$$\forall_x \; (Resource(x) \rightarrow Equipment(x) \vee Tool(x) \vee Employee(x)).$$

The enterprise ontological model, M, is built from the basic ontology, O_b, and domain ontology, O_d, as follows:

$$M = \{O_d(O_b), I\},$$

where I is a subset of instances of the previously entered concepts, such as "equipment units" with inventory numbers.

The enterprise scene, S, which represents an instantaneous state of the enterprise and contains values of attributes of all instances of enterprise concepts and relations at time t, is built in the following way:

$$S = M(t). \tag{1}$$

The enterprise scene is implemented as a database of interconnected instances of concepts and relations that enable agents to easily find a task specification and use the topology of complex schedules to rapidly select an appropriate group of agents for every collective decision making, substantially reducing the time required for considering decision options and performing calculations.

Figures 2 and 3 illustrate the basic and domain ontologies, respectively, for a manufacturing enterprise.

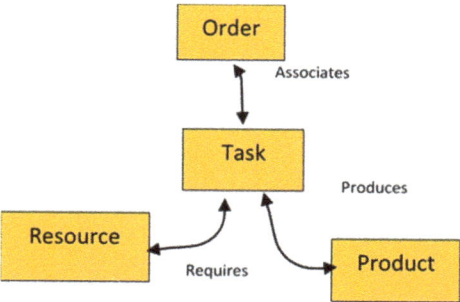

Figure 2. The basic ontology: key concepts and relations.

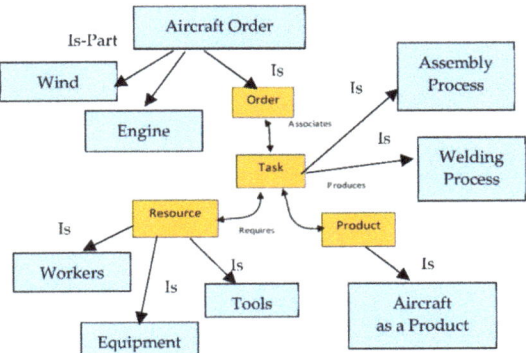

Figure 3. Domain ontology for manufacturing: concepts and relations (in blue) which provide extension to basic ontology (in yellow).

As was already mentioned, the main element of ontologies for any adaptive scheduler is the concept of "task", which defines what resources are required, which is the previous and next "task" and some other relations.

An example of a concrete task for assembling aircraft MC-21 in the Irkut factory is presented in Figure 4.

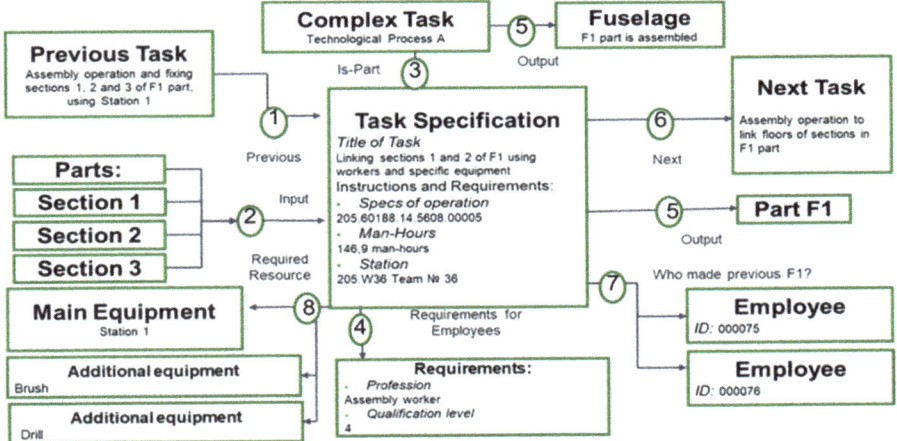

Figure 4. An example of one concrete task for assembling of aircraft MC-21 in the Irkut factory.

The highlighted relations (in circles) play the following roles for task specification:

1. Previous Task—specifies the link to the previous task;
2. Input Objects—specifies the set of objects that can trigger the task in case they all are available;
3. Upper Technology Process—specifies the Technology Process, which must receive the information about successful implementation of planning or execution or to which some issues may be escalated;
4. Required Resources—specifies all human, equipment or other resources required for task planning or execution;
5. Next Task—specifies the link to the next task;
6. Output Objects—specifies the set of resulting objects;

7. Who performed this task in the past?—specifies the person who is an expert in this task implementation and can provide consultation in case of any issues.

The basic agent of the "task" class can read this information and create instances of this agent for this specific task, which will represent interests of this task and work on its behalf. For example, if a delay is identified in the current task, then the agent will find the next task and send a message to it with a warning. This message may trigger re-planning of the next task in case of shortage of time and its re-allocation to some other resources.

The last relation is not implemented in the core part of this basic agent of task and may need additional work for supporting this relation in the unified multi-agent system for adaptive resource management.

The number of such kind of relations for each and every task, hundreds and thousands of which are usually required, helps formalize and utilize domain- and enterprise-specific semantics of tasks for better quality and efficiency of scheduling and optimization.

In this case, the ontology and ontological models specify the directions for agents negotiations, significantly reducing the number of options in the decision-making space and the number of computations in the process of conflict resolving.

4.2. Multi-Agent Model and Method of Adaptive Allocation, Scheduling, Optimization, Monitoring and Control of Tasks and Resources

Multi-agent technology is a new paradigm for developing autonomous, distributed and self-organized systems [35]. Multi-agent technology complements digital twin concept by decision making mechanisms and applied for BIM modeling [36], control of quality of manufacturing [37], process optimization [38], collaborative decision making in maintenance [39], etc.

An agent is defined as an autonomic software object which is able to react to events, make decisions and communicate and coordinate these decisions with other agents. However, despite the fact that multi-agent technology is a very attractive paradigm for software engineering, up until recently, it was mainly well known in the academic community. The main reason for this is that multi-agent systems are hard to develop and are lacking adequate models, methods and tools for collective decision-making, particularly in the domain of complex resource scheduling and optimization problems.

The hypothesis of this paper is a new research and development paradigm, in which the solution to any complex problem can be formed by self-organization of goal-driven autonomous agents, which have conflicting objectives but are able to continuously negotiate and solve conflicts by finding trade-offs.

In our previous research, we have already developed multi-agent models, methods and tools for solving various complex problems in industry, including resource management, text understanding, clustering, etc. [40,41]. It was experimentally proved that the developed multi-agent methods for collective decision making provide benefits for adaptive scheduling of resources for transportation, factories, supply chains and logistics.

In this paper, we will make the next step and develop new multi-agent models and methods to cover a full Deming cycle by combining resource allocation, scheduling and optimization with monitoring and control of the states of tasks and resources in real time. The problem is complex enough and requires taking into consideration a lot of domain-specific semantics, which will be represented by ontology-based models of enterprises.

For solving resource management problems, we are proposing the Order-Technology-Process-Task-Product-Resource-Staff agent model (OTPTPRSA-model), which will extend the Product-Resource-Order-Staff-Agent model (PROSA-model) developed in [42]. In the proposed approach, each type of agent has its individual goal, preferences and constraints and is constantly trying to achieve better results. Instances (clones) of basic agents can also have individually defined settings of goals, for example, as a liner combination of service level, time, cost and risk functions [43].

The process of forming plans of resources in the developed approach is based on the Virtual Market (VM) concept, in which agents can buy and sell time slots in the enterprise schedule. The origins of VM concept can be found in works on electronic auctions, but the most fundamental results are presented in [44,45]. It was proved that VM methods and algorithms in some cases are equal to linear programming, for example, in solving the assigning problem, and many good properties of these methods were identified: flexible, efficient, well parallelized, easy to understand, stable to specification changes, etc.

In the developed VM approach, the main agents are task agents, which are looking for the required time slots of resources and book these time slots, whereas resource agents are looking for the most suitable orders and tasks to cover their costs. Agents of tasks and resources compete and cooperate not only for free time slots, but also for already booked ones. If a conflict is detected, for example, a resource is already occupied by a task, an agent of the task that brings less value to the system gives way, but may receive compensation from the resource or from the system as a whole. This compensation is calculated during new allocation of this task with the use of individual satisfaction and bonus penalty functions. As a result, the problem solution is self-organized in a step-by-step way by collective, parallel and asynchronous processes of detecting and solving conflicts between orders, products, processes, tasks and resources. Developed protocols of solving conflicts among agents implement methods of negotiations for finding elastic trade-offs using penalties and bonuses in very concrete situations. The solution is found when a "competitive equilibrium" ("consensus") is reached and no agent can improve its KPIs in the given situation. Due to self-organization by autonomous collective decision-making principle, the whole schedule can flexibly adapt itself in case of unforeseen events.

Let us assume that VM is triggered by disruptive events coming from the real enterprise. The purpose of the multi-agent system for adaptive resource management will be to minimize the negative consequences of this disruption and achieve this goal by initiating a wave of changes in the self-organized schedule. This wave triggered by the first affected agent that received information on disruption. Decisions on the change are made through negotiation of affected agents to resolve conflicts and achieve a new consensus.

As was stated above, the enterprise state is defined as a sum of states of all objects and agents participating in the enterprise technology or business processes, including orders, technology or business processes, tasks, products, human resources, equipment and materials. Whenever a disruptive event occurs in the actual enterprise, the schedule of the virtual enterprise must change as quickly as possible to a new state.

For every basic ontological object, s_i, a corresponding digital agent, a_i, exhibits the object's behavior, as shown in Table 4.

An instantiation of the developed agent classes for the example of the factory workshop is presented in Figure 5.

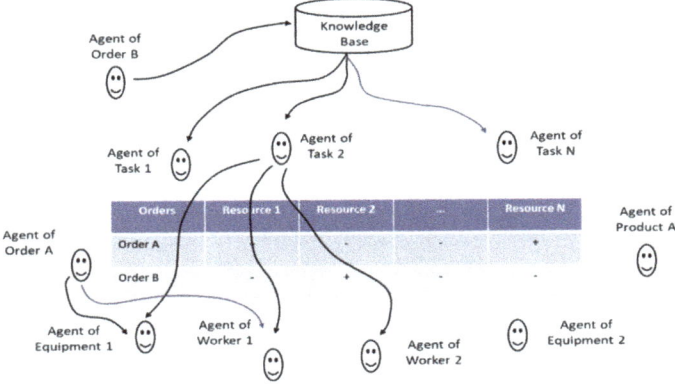

Figure 5. An instantiation of the agent classes for the example of the factory workshop.

Table 4. Objectives, preferences and constraints of the agents.

Agent Type	Objectives, Preferences and Constraints	Attributes
Order agent	To be realized with minimum delay, c, and cost, p, $$Y_i = w_1\left(1 - \frac{c}{c_{\text{кр}}}\right) + w_2\left(1 - \frac{p}{p_{\text{кр}}}\right)$$	Deadlines, volume, unit costs
Technology/Task agent (atomic, composite)	To be realized using appropriate resource, before deadline, in time ($\tau_i = finish_i - start_i$) $$Y_i = \begin{cases} 1, & \tau_i < \tau_{\text{опт}} \\ \frac{\tau_i - \tau_{\text{кр}}}{\tau_{\text{опт}} - \tau_{\text{кр}}}, & otherwise \end{cases}$$	Features of resources, products; Deadlines for beginning and ending; connections with other tasks
Resource agent (humans, equipment, etc.)	To be engaged to its max capacity To minimize idle and readjustment times $$Y_i = \begin{cases} 0, & u_i < u_{\text{кр}} \\ \frac{u_i - u_{\text{кр}}}{u_{\text{опт}} - u_{\text{кр}}}, & otherwise \end{cases}$$	Schedule, periods of unavailability, rules for servicing and readjustments, productivity
Product agent	To arrange its own storage To minimize intervals between production and consumption, e $$Y_i = 1 - \frac{e_i}{e_{\text{кр}}}$$	Storage specifications, the time required for delivery, production or consumption
Enterprise (staff) agent	Coordination of agent activities	Planning time, depth of modification chains

Figure 5 shows that new Order B is arriving when Order A has already successfully been scheduled. Order B reads the technological process from the Knowledge Base and created agents of Tasks 1, 2, ..., N. Agents of the tasks start looking for required resources and a new process of agent collective negotiations is triggered. As a result, two conflicts between Order A and Order B are discovered on workers and equipment. The conflicts can be solved by shifts, swaps and drops of tasks with the view on objectives of these and other agents.

Objectives for every software agent are defined using an agent satisfaction function, $Y_i(plan_i)$, which is specified as a linear combination (weighted sum) of M elements belonging to kpi_i and calculated based on the current schedule, $plan_i$, related to the object agent as the following:

$$Y_i = \sum_{j=1}^{M} w_{ij} y_{ij},$$

where y_{ij}, is an element of satisfaction function defined by criterion $j = \overline{1, M}$ and w_{ij} is weighting coefficient $0 \leq w_{ij} \leq 1$ and $\sum_{j=1}^{M} w_{ij} = 1\ \forall_i$.

As discussed, the task agents on the VM can purchase time slot from resource agents and resolve conflicts in case several task agents request the same usage time from a resource agent by paying compensation to agents giving up their requests. For this reason, agents can use bonuses awarded for good performance or provide fines for underperforming. Performance is measured by its satisfaction function defined above. For this purpose, each agent has a bonus (fine) function, Bi (Yi). Virtual money received or expected can be used to compensate to those agents that are losing in negotiations.

VM can have diverse agents with different satisfaction and bonus/fines functions and a facility that allows for an agent instance assigned to every enterprise ontology object instance. Functions of satisfaction and bonuses/fines are introduced to motivate agents to perform as close as possible to their specified KPIs. Resource agents have an additional feature, a cost function, related to the cost of tasks.

Allocation of resources to orders is done in the following way:

1. Following the current state of the abstract world, S_{twin}, instances of order agents, resource agents and product agents are created and receive permission from the enterprise agent to act and take decisions.
2. Agent of an active order, A_k, picks up from the knowledge base the business process for the appropriate product and triggers the required task agents that are connected by nesting or sequencing relations.
3. A high-level task agent checks that relevant products and resources are available and ensures task performance in the specified time.
4. The task solution process starts from generating options by analyzing required resources, comparing task requirements and resource capabilities, resolving resource access timing issues and selecting by the branch and bound method.
5. The computation is based on identification of the set of conflicting orders which substantially reduce the number of solution options:

$$\{a_i \mid i \neq k,\ plan'_k \cap plan_i \neq \varnothing\},$$

6. The next step is to allocate resources to tasks. Constituent agents allocate resources following the procedure described above. The results are delivered to the relevant group agents, which may accept or reject them and, in the latter case, request a new solution.
7. The group reports to the order agent on the proposed allocation of resources.
8. The order agent negotiates with conflicting orders to resolve conflicts.

The resulting chain of schedule modifications produces losses suffered by agents who agreed to change their requirements to resolve the conflict ΔB_i.

9. This chain of modifications is successfully dimmed if the corresponding order agent can compensate losses of conflicting agents from the gains earned by its bonuses, ΔB_k:

$$\Delta B_k \geq \sum_{i \neq k}^{n} \Delta B_i$$

10. If this is the case, the schedule is accepted; if not, a new round of negotiations is performed.
11. The order agent then identifies all products linked to it by the "produces" relation and informs their agents when they must be delivered to appropriate stores.
12. The activity ends when a consensus is reached; in other words, when every agent a_k reaches a state in which no further adjustment of the schedule $plan'_k$ can improve their satisfaction function ΔY_k, and consequently, increase their bonus function ΔB_k or when the time available for negotiations runs out:

$$\Delta B_k + \sum_{i \neq k}^{n} \Delta B_i < 0\ \forall k.$$

13. Once a consensus is reached, the VM stops working and is switched to a standby mode, awaiting the next disruptive event.

The fragment of the discussed scheme is illustrated in Figure 6, where it is shown how agents adaptively change the schedule.

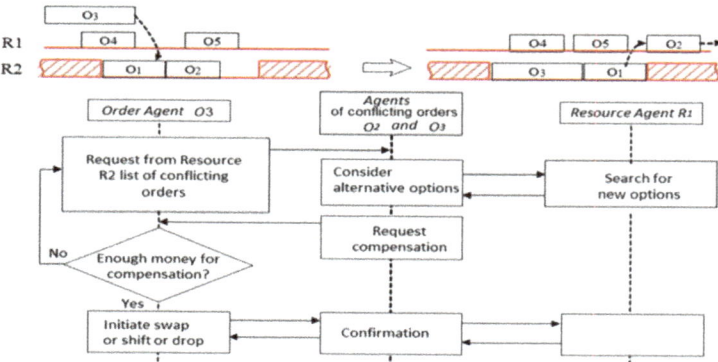

Figure 6. A fragment of agent negotiations for resolving 'task-resource' conflicts.

The time required to find the optimal schedule is substantially reduced if the order agents only resolve conflicts in an adaptive manner without full combinatorial search.

If changes in the basic ontology are required, the VM must be re-developed. In contrast no re-developing is needed if only domain ontology is expanded.

5. The Method of Designing Autonomous Digital Twins of Enterprises for Adaptive Task and Resource Management

The developed method for designing Autonomous Digital Twins of Enterprises for adaptive task and resource management has the following procedure.

1. In the first step, the basic ontology is formalized with the help of experts in ontology editor and basic functionality is implemented in a unified multi-agent system for adaptive resource management covering the Deming cycle.
2. In the second step, the basic ontology is extended by domain-specific concepts and relations for different domains of applications. For example, for the aviation industry, one can introduce aviation ontology, which will specify typical parts of an aircraft, basic assembly processes and tasks, competencies of workers, etc. For the gas and oil drilling industry, the domain ontology will specify typical oil equipment, technological processes, etc.
3. In the third step, the domain ontology can be applied for building ontological models of concrete enterprises specifying its departments, business processes, persons and their roles and competencies, etc. Two different enterprises, working in one domain, can have the same domain ontology or can expand and modify their copies of common domain ontology to make it more suitable for their business aspects.
4. Ontological models of enterprise can be loaded into the unified multi-agent system for resource management. A set of such models can form a collection in the knowledge base for the domain of enterprises and play a role of standards in future.
5. To launch the Autonomous Digital Twins of Enterprises, users only need to load the selected ontological model of enterprise and to specify the initial scene or state of the enterprise, including the values of object attributes.

As a result, the proposed method provides the opportunity to formalize domain-specific knowledge of enterprises, which is usually "out of consideration" in traditional methods and tools of planning and optimization. For example, ontological specifications of the domain can help take into consideration what kind of resources is required for this particular task (operation), what input objects can trigger this task, what is the previous and the next task, etc.

The structure of ontological specifications of the method is given in Figure 7.

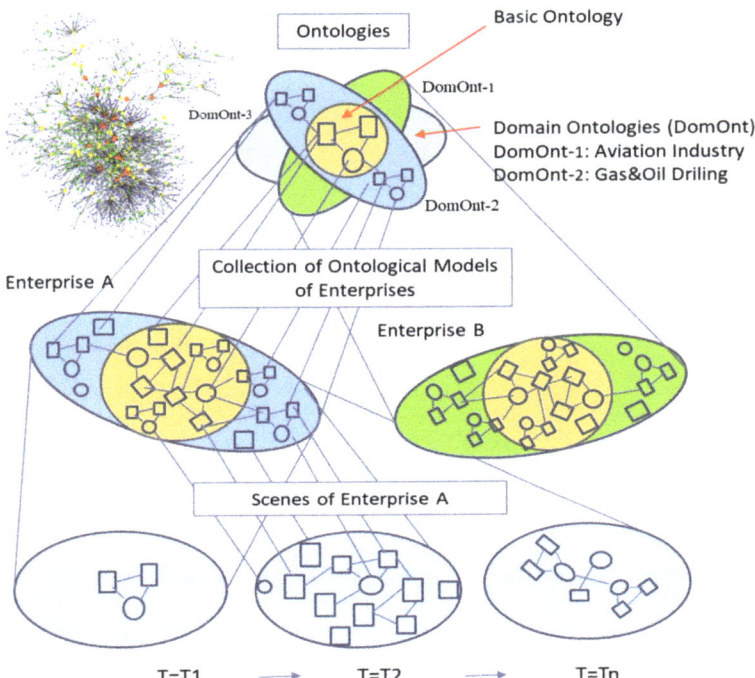

Figure 7. Structure of the ontological specifications of the enterprises.

In this case, this domain-specific knowledge and logic can be separated from the source code of the system, which will become more generic and unified for various applications.

There is a number of ontologies developed for many different domains, including manufacturing, transport or agriculture.

However, applications for task-centric resource management and customization of multi-agent systems are not yet known and researched.

When the ontological enterprise model is loaded, agents make copies (clones) of their basic classes and use the formalized knowledge from ontology to specify behavior of agents of each task; for example, under what conditions can each task be launched, what are the previous and next tasks, what kind of resources this task requires, etc.

The design of a typical agent, is presented in Figure 8, including the components:

- State machine of agent—the set of states and transition rules which are connected and triggered by scene events or messages from other agents;
- Agent services—a number of software components to get input data, make computations, store data, etc.;
- Communication tools—software components to send/receive messages;
- Access to Knowledge Base—software components for accessing the Knowledge Base, reasoning and navigation through semantic networks.

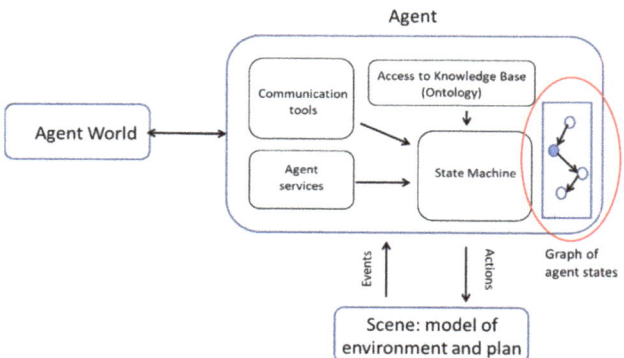

Figure 8. Typical agent structure.

Agent World is a software component for running and dispatching instances of agent classes, for example, the schedule of middle-size workshop with 300 equipment units and 150 workers for the 3–6-month horizon may require more than 5 thousand interconnected instances of Task Agents, and all these instances of agents will be individually customized by the ontological model of enterprise.

The other core part of the autonomous digital twin of enterprise is the ontology-driven knowledge base, which will provide knowledge graph methods and tools to collect, digitalize, formalize and systemize domain-specific knowledge of enterprise, including detailed specifications of orders, business or technology processes, tasks and required resources, humans, machines and equipment, competencies of employees, etc. The granularity of formal specifications of business or technology processes will provide possibility to specify each task in enterprise operation and automatically find the required resources more semantically, individually, adaptively and dynamically.

The discussed concept of the autonomous digital twin of enterprise requires modification of the previously developed methods and tools and integration of ontologies to support the full cycle of resource management, with detailed granulation of specifications to each and every task in business or technology processes.

6. Architecture of Knowledge-Based Multi-Agent Toolset for Designing the Autonomous Digital Twin of Enterprise

The described method was implemented in a Knowledge-Based Multi-Agent Toolset for developing the Autonomous Digital Twins of Enterprise.

The architecture of the Knowledge-Based Multi-Agent Toolset includes the following main components (Figure 9):

- Basic Ontology of Resource Management—contains basic classes of concepts and relations for resource management;
- Domain Ontology of Enterprise—contains domain-specific classes of concepts and relations for the concrete enterprise;
- Ontological Models of Enterprises 1, 2, ... , N—fully specified enterprise, including types of orders, technology or business processes, employees and other resources;
- Scenes of Enterprise, synchronized with the state of real enterprise 1, 2, ... , N—ontological models of enterprises with concretization of attributes of properties and relations in the initial moment of time;
- Ontology, Knowledge Base and Scene Editors—software components for modifying ontologies, knowledge bases and scenes;
- Events—event queue for registering input events and sending them for processing in multi-agent system;

- Ontology-Based Multi-Agent System for Adaptive Resource Management—the unified software component for loading ontological models of enterprises;
- User Interface—web interface and mobile application for communication with users and coordinating decisions.

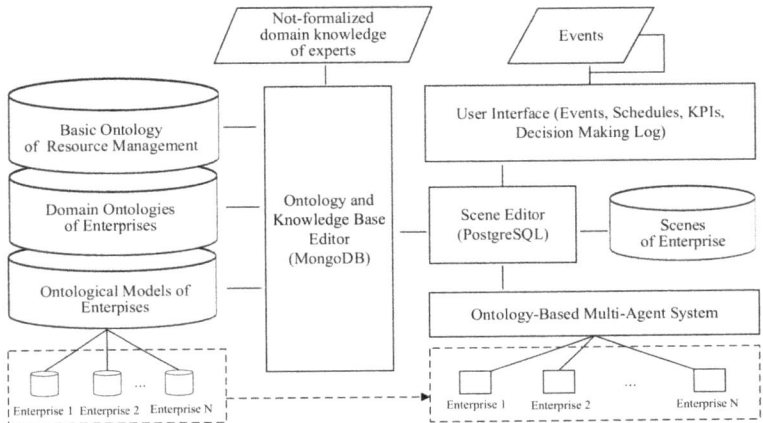

Figure 9. Architecture of a Toolset for Developing Autonomous Digital Twins of Enterprises.

The core parts of Autonomous Digital Twins of Enterprises are the Knowledge Base and Ontology-Based Multi-Agent System for Adaptive Resource Management.

The loading of the Ontological Model of Enterprise in the Ontology-Based Multi-Agent System triggers the creation of a new virtual world, which represents and mirrors tasks and resources of the real enterprise. In this sense, the developed Multi-Agent System is unified for a wide range of enterprises and it significantly reduces the time and cost of the developments.

At any moment of time, the Ontology-Based Multi-Agent System can be copied and the separate scene can be used for real-time simulations and what-if games; for example, entering new potential order, changing technological processes or shifts of workers, modernization of equipment, etc.

The Autonomous Digital Twins of Enterprises can be delivered to client as a stand-alone software solution or it can be integrated as a service with any other digital platforms or the cyber-physical system.

The developed tools can speed up development and save human effort, time and costs of developments and maintenance of the solution.

7. Evaluation of the Efficiency of the Method and Toolset for the Autonomous Digital Twins of Enterprises Development Process

To evaluate efficiency of the discussed method and toolset for developing Autonomous Digital Twins of Enterprises, the following resource management applications were considered:

- Aircraft assembly process for MC-21 for the Irkut Corporation (Irkutsk, Russia);
- Assembly of electric cars using robotic line for the TPA Company (Saint Petersburg, Russia);
- Oil drilling process for the Gaspromneft-Yamal enterprise (Saint Petersburg, Russia);
- Wheat crowing for the Rassvet agrofarm (Rostov region, Russia);
- Group of satellites for Earth remote sensing for the Rocket and Space Corporation "Progress" (Samara, Russia).

The Autonomous Digital Twins of Enterprises were prototyped independently for each of these domains, including collecting and formalizing domain knowledge, creating an ontological model of enterprise and implementing modifications of basic ontology and a unified multi-agent system.

The idea of experiment was to measure the scope and total amount of development work (man-hours), including ontological and multi-agent features only:

- Changes in basic ontology (if needed);
- Extension of domain ontology;
- Changes in agent class logic;
- Addition of new agent classes.

During the experiment, the number of agents and size of ontologies was measured.

Aircraft assembly process for MC-21 for the Irkut Corporation

Input data: set of orders and list of events, in real time, storage of products.

Knowledge Base: product structure breakdown, technological processes with specification of each task, matching rules between tasks and resources, equipment, materials number of workers and their competencies.

Criteria: just-in-time order production, minimization of order execution time and usage of resources, balanced load of workers.

Assembly of electric cars using robotic line for the TPA Company

Input data: set of orders and list of events, coming in real time, storage of products plan and tariff of DHL deliveries of car parts.

Knowledge Base: product structure breakdown, technological processes with specification of each task, matching rules between tasks and resources, equipment, materials number of robots and their functionality.

Criteria: just-in-time order production, minimization of order execution time and usage of resources, balanced load of robots.

Oil drilling process for the Gaspromneft-Yamal enterprise

Input data: requirements for oil drilling, storage of required materials.

Knowledge Base: best practices and technological processes of oil drilling with specification of each task, matching rules between tasks and resources, equipment, materials, number of workers and their competencies.

Criteria: minimization of oil drilling time and usage of resources.

Wheat crowing for the Rassvet agrofarm

Input data: wheat variety, the number of fields and days of wheat seeding, weather forecast and actual data.

Knowledge Base: stages of plant growth with specification of each phase, matching rules between stages, weather conditions and available resources.

Criteria: minimization of time for stages and maximization of harvest forecast.

Group of satellites for Earth remote sensing for the Rocket and Space Corporation "Progress"

Input data: the state of satellites and ground stations, set of orders for remote Earth observation.

Knowledge Base: satellites break-down structure, ballistics, technological processes of data imaging with specification of each task, matching rules between tasks and resources of satellites and their equipment functionality.

Criteria: minimization of reaction time and maximization of image resolution.

The results of discussed developments are shown in Table 5.

Table 5. Results of using the developed method and toolset for developing prototypes of Autonomous Digital Twins of Enterprises in different domains (KB—Knowledge Base and MAS—Multi-Agent System).

Domain of Enterprise	Size of Basic Ontology	Size of Domain Ontology	Size of Ontological Model of Enterprise	Number of Agents	Development Time (Man * Months)	
					KB	MAS
Aircraft Assembly		152	925	>350	3	3.5
Electro-Cars Assembly		89	382	>520	1	2
Oil Drilling	61	85	441	>5000	2	3
Digital Twin of Plant		42	236	>100	1	1
Swarm of Satellites		112	304	>450	1	4

The basic ontology O_b was stabilized with about 60 main concepts and relations. Domain ontologies expand this basic ontology up to 2–3 times. Ontological models of enterprises, which include instances of concepts and relations, may differ very much and include from 236 to 925 instances. These ontological moles were loaded into the unified multi-agent system and automatically created instances of basic classes of agents. The required development and customization of the unified multi-agent system for these new applications took about 2–4 months.

Compared with the traditional approach for developing smart solutions, when the process of development takes 9–12 months [35], the application of the developed method and toolset makes it possible to significantly (up to 3–4 times) reduce complexity, cost and time of development process.

More detailed results and examples of applications can be found in [46].

8. Example of the Method and Toolset Application

Let us consider an example of the application of the presented method and toolset for the development of the autonomous digital twin of enterprise for the Service Desk Center of the Russian National Railways.

The Service Desk Center serves about 2500 information systems by 4500 employees, which have competencies in different software solutions.

At the moment, the Service Desk Center of the Russian National Railways has an old-fashioned IT system which is planned to be replaced by a more advanced and intelligent decision-making system for scheduling employees and chat bots for users.

The existing system has a module of auto-allocation of new orders to employees in an empiric manner "First In—First Out" and up to 10 orders per employee (other orders are staying in the queue and can lose their service level). This module has no adaptability, so new orders cannot change allocation of the previously allocated resources. Moreover, this module serves orders without any knowledge about semantics of the detected problem, service level for specific system, time zones, competencies of employees and their planned load and other preferences and constraints.

The autonomous digital twin of enterprise for the Service Desk Center was proposed as a solution of the problem and the pilot project was started in the summer of 2021.

The developed new system reads orders and creates their semantic descriptors, analyzes its content and adaptively schedules and optimizes tasks more individually, taking into consideration all the above parameters, including employee competencies. However, it also combines scheduling and optimization with monitoring and control of task execution. For example, if one task is significantly delayed by an employee and has a risk to break services, the next tasks in the schedule of this employee will automatically become active and start searching for other options. As a result of such negotiations for solving conflicts, these tasks can be reallocated and re-scheduled to other employees, for example, who fulfilled the planned tasks faster than expected, and have the needed spare time and competencies.

The difference between two systems is shown in Figure 10: in the existing system (left), new orders are staying in the queue waiting for allocation. In the new system (right), new orders are immediately adaptively allocated and scheduled by solving conflicts in the schedules of employees. Red circles here identify the detected conflicts and re-scheduling of the previously scheduled orders.

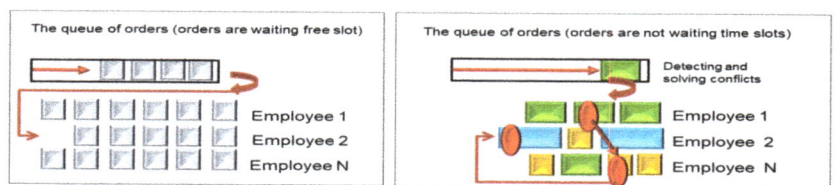

Figure 10. The difference between the existing (**left**) and developed (**right**) systems.

The prototype of the autonomous digital twin of the Service Desk Center was developed in 3 months and researched for one group of 34 employees working with 25 software systems in the domain of logistics.

To evaluate the efficiency of the solution, the data records from Service Desk Center for Q1 2021 were collected and analyzed.

The basic ontology was applied and domain ontology and ontological model of the selected logistics group of employees were created, which includes about 100 technological processes (Figure 11) and the matrix of employees' competencies (Figure 12).

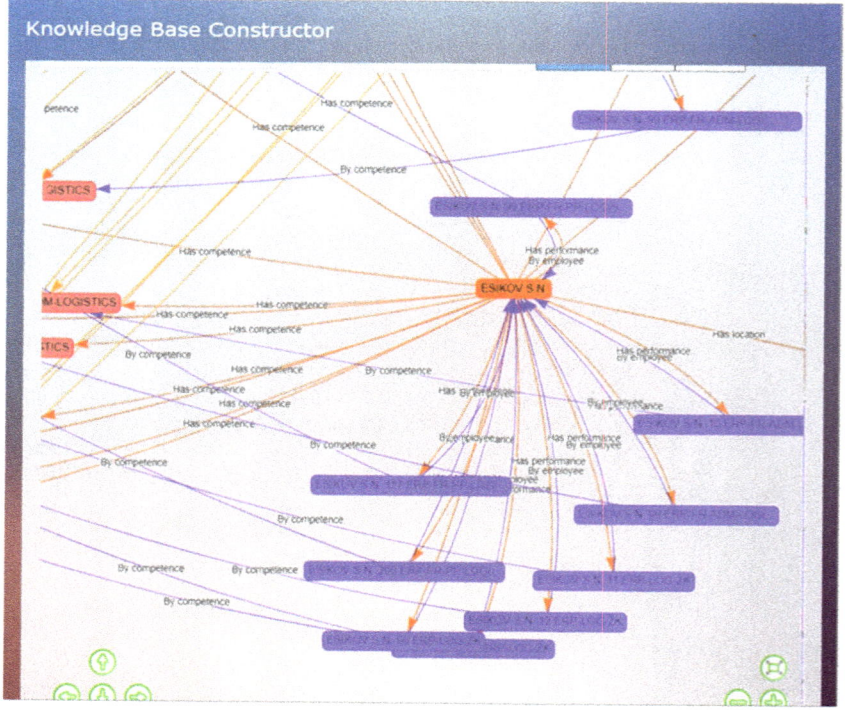

Figure 11. A fragment of domain ontology and ontological model of logistics group of employees (yellow—issues of IT systems, green—technological processes, red—tasks).

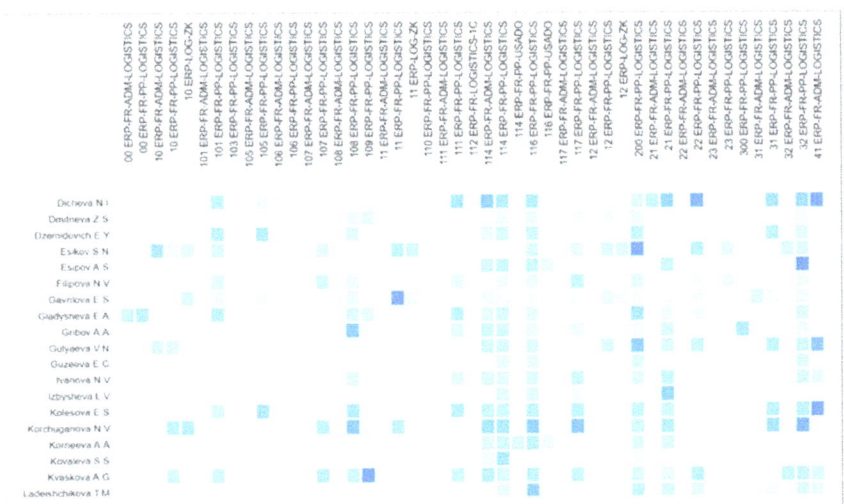

Figure 12. The fragment of competencies matrix (darker blue color—better employee competencies and faster task implementation).

The validation of the developed solution was made with the use of pre-selected real data on 1 September 2021. The test run included 34 employees from the selected team, which processed 304 orders in about 5 h.

The adaptive schedule of employees of the logistics group is presented in Figure 13. One can see here that every employee has tasks with the same color. It means that the system schedules only those tasks that match with the competencies of this employee.

Figure 13. Adaptive schedule of employees of the logistics group.

Figure 14 shows how multi-agent technology works by presenting the satisfaction function and bonus-penalty functions of the system (as a whole), the number of agents involved and the number of changes in the schedule.

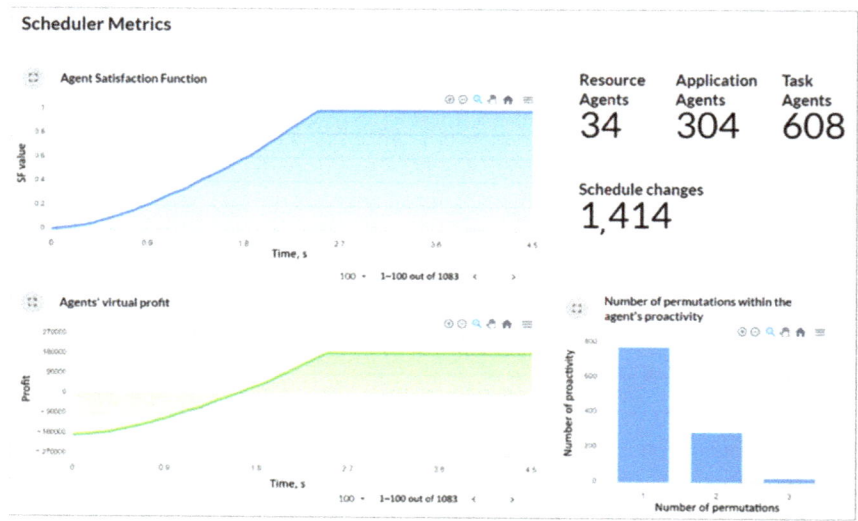

Figure 14. Characteristics of the multi-agent decision-making process.

Here, 304 agents of tasks were allocated to 34 agents of employees. During the negotiation process, the schedule was changed 1429 times and some tasks were allocated at the first attempt, while other tasks changed their positions a few times.

Figure 15 presents results of work of the existing system versus the new one and helps compare these results and evaluate the advantages of the new system.

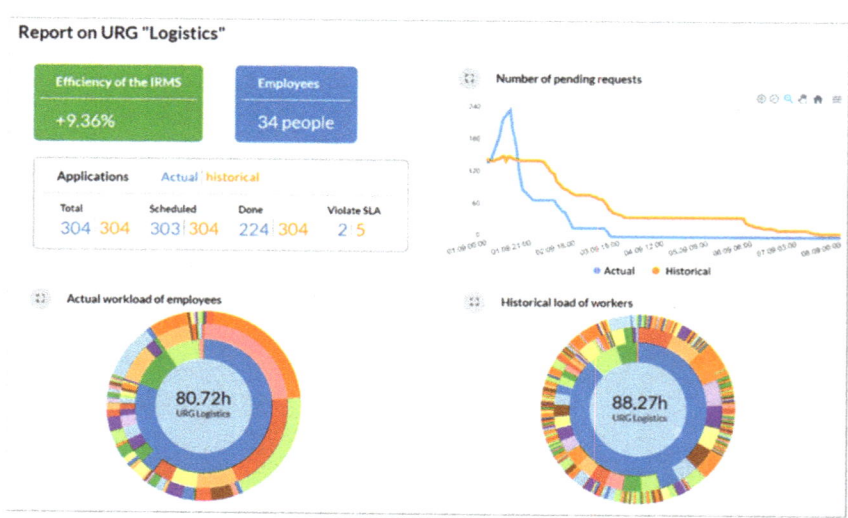

Figure 15. Comparison of results of the existing system and the new one.

The left diagram shows that the developed solution provides an increase of 9.36% compared to the existing solution for resource allocation: the new solution requires 80.72 h of work to process requests and the old solution requires 88.27 h for the same requests. The right diagram shows that the new solution (blue) processes many more orders in the beginning compared to the existing one (yellow). One can see that the new solution has a bigger number of pending requests in the beginning of a day, i.e., the 1st of September (blue line on diagram), compared with the existing scheduler (yellow line). This means that the scheduler found and scheduled employees with required competencies for solving the problem. Moreover, at the end of the day, the biggest part of all requests was successfully executed and the rest of the scheduled (pending) requests was much lower. This means that the found employees have a bigger productivity and efficiency and are able to process the number of requests much faster than in the existing solution.

The external radiuses of circle diagrams show what tasks are scheduled (in different colors) and their allocation to employees, teams and departments accordingly (internal radiuses). The achieved resource allocation now (on the left) is not so random and fragmented (on the right)—the new solution performs allocation and scheduling of orders more smoothly, using the semantics of the requests and the competencies of employees.

The results of the prototype were analyzed and a number of new opportunities were identified, specifically how to provide a better service for customers, increase the productivity and efficiency of staff, motivate employees to acquire new competencies and reduce risks and penalties.

9. The Discussion and Outlook of Future Developments

The main contribution of this paper is to propose the autonomous digital twin of enterprise based on ontology and multi-agent technology for implementing a full Deming cycle of adaptive resource management, including real-time resource allocations, planning and optimization, monitoring and control of plan execution.

The developed ontology-driven multi-agent approach and software toolset for designing autonomous digital twins of enterprises provides high adaptability for businesses and increases the efficiency of resources under conditions of high uncertainty and turbulent dynamics of demand and supply. The implementation of domain ontology can be done by knowledge engineers for customization of the solution for different enterprises, and this process does not require re-programming of the unified multi-agent system. In case of new types of enterprises, the multi-agent system needs to be modified by new classes of agents and protocols of their communications.

The limitations of the approach are related to egoistic behavior of agents (myopia), which can block the system in local optimums, but this is mitigated by mutual compensations. As a next step, the following modifications can be made: advanced virtual market models, non-deterministic collective decision making with dynamically balanced positive and negative feedback mechanisms, proactivity of both demand and resource agents, etc.

Machine learning/data-driven methods could also be applied for digital twins of enterprises when big data are available and in a situation where orders and resources are not changing during the time period. However, if an enterprise does not have big data or the if situation with orders and resources is continuously changing, these methods cannot be fully applied. However, in the future, these methods could be efficiently combined in a new hybrid method.

Another issue of the developed approach is the scalability for large enterprises and supply chains. The solution could be based on holonic and network-centric architectures for cooperation and competition of autonomous digital twins of enterprises. For example, the autonomous digital twin of one workshop can interact with the autonomous digital twin of another workshops. Autonomous digital twins of workshops can populate autonomous digital twins of factory, etc.

The plans for future research and developments include the following:

- Analysis of non-deterministic decision making in self-organized multi-agent systems and phenomena of emergent intelligence;
- Collection of pre-built ontologies and ontological models of enterprises and basic classes of agents for a wide range of different domains;
- Distributed knowledge base for supporting automatic decision making in specific teams of employees;

- Digital platform and digital ecosystems for p2p competition and cooperation between Autonomous Digital Twins of Enterprises;
- Integration with chat bots and software robots for business processes;
- Integration with Internet of Things (IoT) platforms.

The autonomous digital twin of enterprise can be applied for automatic resource management synchronized with real enterprise or as a real-time simulation tool.

The results could be used for academic research and industry, including potential business applications for project management, agile programming, remote work from home in pandemic times and other cases.

Author Contributions: Conceptualization, P.S.; Formal analysis, V.L.; Investigation, D.N.; Methodology, S.G.; Software, A.G.; Writing—original draft, V.G. and A.Z. All authors have read and agreed to the published version of the manuscript.

Funding: This research is funded by a grant of the Russian Science Foundation No. 22-41-08003, https://rscf.ru/project/22-41-08003/.

Informed Consent Statement: Informed consent was obtained from all subjects involved in the study

Data Availability Statement: Not applicable.

Conflicts of Interest: The authors declare no conflict of interest.

References

1. Grieves, M.; Vickers, J. Digital Twin: Mitigating Unpredictable, Undesirable Emergent Behavior in Complex Systems. In *Transdisciplinary Perspectives on Complex Systems: New Findings and Approaches*; Kahlen, F.-J., Flumerfelt, S., Alvesm, A., Eds.; Springer: Berlin/Heidelberg, Germany, 2017; pp. 85–113.
2. Barricelli, B.; Casiraghi, E.; Fogli, D. A Survey on Digital Twin: Definitions, Characteristics, Applications, and Design Implications. *IEEE Access* **2019**, *7*, 167653–167671. [CrossRef]
3. Proceedings of the 31st European International Conference on Operational Research, Athens, 11–14 July 2021. Available online: https://euro2021athens.com/ (accessed on 5 March 2022).
4. Qi, Q.; Tao, F. Digital Twin and Big Data Towards Smart Manufacturing and Industry 4.0: 360 Degree Comparison. *IEEE Access* **2018**, *6*, 3585–3593. [CrossRef]
5. Tao, F.; Cheng, J.; Qi, Q.; Zhang, M.; Zhang, H.; Sui, F. Digital twin-driven product design, manufacturing and service with big data. *Int. J. Adv. Manuf. Technol.* **2018**, *94*, 3563–3576. [CrossRef]
6. Panetta, K. Gartner Top 10 Strategic Technology Trends for 2019. Available online: https://www.gartner.com/smarterwithgartner/gartner-top-10-strategic-technology-trends-for-2019/ (accessed on 5 March 2022).
7. Shen, Z.; Wang, L.; Deng, T. Digital Twin: What It Is, Why Do It, Related Challenges and Research Opportunities for Operations Research. 2 February 2021, p. 53. Available online: https://papers.ssrn.com/sol3/papers.cfm?abstract_id=3777695 (accessed on 6 March 2022).
8. Kuehn, W. Digital twins for decision making in complex production and logistic enterprises. *Int. J. Des. Nat. Ecodynamics* **2018**, *13*, 260–271. [CrossRef]
9. Kuliaev, V.; Atmojo, U.D.; Erla, S.S.; Blech, J.O.; Vyatkin, V. Towards Product Centric Manufacturing: From Digital Twins to Product Assembly. In Proceedings of the 2019 IEEE 17th International Conference on Industrial Informatics (INDIN), Espoo, Finland, 22–25 July 2019; pp. 164–171. [CrossRef]
10. Bao, J.; Guo, D.; Li, J.; Zhang, J. The modelling and operations for the digital twin in the context of manufacturing. *Enterp. Inf. Syst.* **2018**, *13*, 534–556. [CrossRef]
11. Kulkarni, V.; Barat, S.; Clark, T. Towards Adaptive Enterprises Using Digital Twins. In Proceedings of the 2019 Winter Simulation Conference (WSC), National Harbor, MD, USA, 8–11 December 2019; pp. 60–74. [CrossRef]
12. Bárkányi, Á.; Chován, T.; Németh, S.; Abonyi, J. Modelling for Digital Twins—Potential Role of Surrogate Models. *Processes* **2021**, *9*, 476. [CrossRef]
13. Yildiz, E.; Møller, C.; Bilberg, A. Demonstration and evaluation of a digital twin-based virtual factory. *Int. J. Adv. Manuf. Technol.* **2021**, *114*, 185–203. [CrossRef]
14. Niati, A.; Selma, C.; Tamzalit, D.; Bruneliere, H.; Mebarki, N.; Cardin, O. Towards a Digital Twin for Cyber-Physical Production Systems: A Multi-Paradigm Modeling Approach in the Postal Industry. In Proceedings of the 23rd ACM/IEEE International Conference on Model Driven Engineering Languages and Systems: Companion Proceedings (MODELS '20 Companion), Virtual Conference, Canada, 12–23 October 2020; pp. 1–7.
15. Leitão, P.; Colombo, A.W.D.; Karnouskos, S. Industrial automation based on cyber-physical systems technologies: Prototype implementations and challenges. *Comput. Ind.* **2016**, *81*, 11–25. [CrossRef]

26. Karnouskos, S.; Leitao, P.; Ribeiro, L.; Colombo, A.W. Industrial Agents as a Key Enabler for Realizing Industrial Cyber-Physical Systems: Multiagent Systems Entering Industry 4.0. *IEEE Ind. Electron. Mag.* **2020**, *14*, 18–32. [CrossRef]
27. Lazarev, A.; Pravdivets, N.; Werner, F. On the Dual and Inverse Problems of Scheduling Jobs to Minimize the Maximum Penalty. *Mathematics* **2020**, *8*, 1131. [CrossRef]
28. Alkhabbas, F.; Spalazzese, R.; Davidsson, P. An Agent-Based Approach to Realize Emergent Configurations in the Internet of Things. *Electronics* **2020**, *9*, 1347. [CrossRef]
29. Hrabia, C.-E.; Lützenberger, M.; Albayrak, S. Towards adaptive multi-robot systems: Self-organization and self-adaptation. *Knowl. Eng. Rev.* **2018**, *33*, e16. [CrossRef]
30. Chopra, A.K.; Singh, M.P. An Evaluation of Communication Protocol Languages for Engineering Multiagent Systems. *J. Artif. Intell. Res.* **2020**, *69*, 1351–1393. [CrossRef]
31. Dalpiaz, F.; Chopra, A.K.; Giorgini, P.; Mylopoulos, J. Adaptation in Open Systems: Giving Interaction Its Rightful Place. In *Conceptual Modeling—ER 2010*; LNCS 6412; Springer: Berlin/Heidelberg, Germany, 2010; pp. 31–45.
32. Dalpiaz, F.; Giorgini, P.; Mylopoulos, J. Adaptive socio-technical systems: A requirements-based approach. *Requir. Eng.* **2013**, *18*, 1–24. [CrossRef]
33. Bures, T.; Gerostathopoulos, I.; Hnetynka, P.; Keznikl, J.; Kit, M.; Plasil, F. DEECO: An ensemble-based component system. In Proceedings of the 16th International ACM Sigsoft Symposium on Component-Based Software Engineering, Vancouver, BC, Canada, 17–21 June 2013; ACM: New York, NY, USA, 2013; pp. 81–90.
34. Gascueña, J.M.; Navarro, E.; Fernández-Caballero, A. Model-driven engineering techniques for the development of multi-agent systems. *Eng. Appl. Artif. Intell.* **2012**, *25*, 159–173. [CrossRef]
35. García-Sánchez, F.; Valencia-García, R.; Martínez-Béjar, R.; Breis, J.T.F. An ontology, intelligent agent-based framework for the provision of semantic web services. *Expert Syst. Appl.* **2009**, *36*, 3167–3187. [CrossRef]
36. Van der Valk, H.; Haße, H.; Möller, F.; Otto, B. Archetypes of Digital Twins. *Bus. Inf. Syst. Eng.* **2021**. [CrossRef]
37. Eramo, R.; Bordeleau, F.; Combemale, B.; van Den Brand, M.; Wimmer, M.; Wortmann, A. *Conceptualizing Digital Twins*, hal-03466396, Version 1; IEEE Software; Institute of Electrical and Electronics Engineers: Piscataway, NJ, USA, 2021; pp. 1–7. Available online: https://hal.inria.fr/hal-03466396 (accessed on 3 March 2022).
38. Gruber, T. Toward principles for the design of ontologies used for knowledge sharing? *Int. J. Hum. Comput. Stud.* **1995**, *43*, 907–928. [CrossRef]
39. Lemaignan, S.; Siadat, A.; Dantan, J.Y.; Semenenko, A. MASON: A proposal for an ontology of manufacturing domain. In Proceedings of the IEEE Workshop on Distributed Intelligent Systems—Collective Intelligence and Its Applications (DIS 2006), Prague, Czech Republic, 15–16 June 2006; pp. 195–200.
40. Usman, Z.; Young, R.I.M.; Chungoora, N.; Palmer, C.; Case, K.; Harding, J. A Manufacturing Core Concepts Ontology for Product Lifecycle Interoperability. In Proceedings of the International IFIP Working Conference on Enterprise Interoperability IWEI 2011, Stockholm, Sweden, 22–23 March 2011; Springer: Berlin/Heidelberg, Germany, 2011; pp. 5–18.
41. Minhas, S.U.H.; Berger, U. Ontology Based Environmental Knowledge Management—A System to Support Decisions in Manufacturing Planning. In Proceedings of the 6th International Conference on Knowledge Engineering and Ontology Development (KEOD), Rome, Italy, 21–24 October 2014; pp. 397–404.
42. Sormaz, D.; Sarkar, A. SIMPM—Upper-level ontology for manufacturing process plan net-work generation. *Robot. Comput. Integr. Manuf.* **2019**, *55*, 183–198. [CrossRef]
43. Järvenpää, E.; Siltala, N.; Hylli, O.; Lanz, M. The development of an ontology for describing the capabilities of manufacturing resources. *J. Intell. Manuf.* **2018**, *30*, 959–978. [CrossRef]
44. Bao, Q.; Zhao, G.; Yu, Y.; Dai, S.; Wang, W. Ontology-based modeling of part digital twin oriented to assembly. *Proc. Inst. Mech. Eng. Part B J. Eng. Manuf.* **2020**, *236*, 16–28. [CrossRef]
45. Marik, V.; Gorodetsky, V.; Skobelev, P. Multi-Agent Technology for Industrial Applications: Barriers and Trends. In Proceedings of the 2020 IEEE International Conference on Systems, Man, and Cybernetics (SMC 2020), Toronto, ON, Canada, 11–14 October 2020; pp. 1980–1987.
46. Lu, Q.; Xie, X.; Heaton, J.; Parlikad, A.K.; Schooling, J. From BIM towards digital twin: Strategy and future development for smart asset management. In Proceedings of the International Workshop on Service Orientation in Holonic and Multi-Agent Manufacturing, Valencia, Spain, 3–4 October 2019; Springer: Cham, Switzerland, 2019; pp. 392–404.
47. Zheng, X.; Psarommatis, F.; Petrali, P.; Turrin, C.; Lu, J.; Kiritsis, D. A quality-oriented digital twin modelling method for manufacturing processes based on a multi-agent architecture. *Procedia Manuf.* **2020**, *51*, 309–315. [CrossRef]
48. Nie, Q.; Tang, D.; Zhu, H.; Sun, H. A multi-agent and internet of things framework of digital twin for optimized manufacturing control. *Int. J. Comput. Integr. Manuf.* **2021**, 1–22. [CrossRef]
49. Lorente, Q.; Villeneuve, E.; Merlo, C.; Boy, G.A.; Thermy, F. Development of a digital twin for collaborative decision-making, based on a multi-agent system: Application to prescriptive maintenance. *INCOSE Int. Symp.* **2022**, *32*, 109–117. [CrossRef]
50. Rzevski, G.; Skobelev, P. *Managing Complexity*, 1st ed.; WIT Press: London, UK; Boston, MA, USA, 2014; p. 216.
51. Skobelev, P. Towards Autonomous AI Systems for Resource Management: Applications in Industry and Lessons Learned. In Proceedings of the 16th International Conference on Practical Applications of Agents and Multiagent Systems (PAAMS 2018), Toledo, Spain, 20–22 June 2018; LNAI 10978. pp. 12–25.

42. Van Brussel, H.; Wyns, J.; Valckenaers, P.; Bongaerts, L.; Peeters, P. Reference Architecture for Holonic Manufacturing Systems PROSA. *Comput. Ind.* **1998**, *37*, 255–274. [CrossRef]
43. Skobelev, P.; Zhilyaev, A.; Larukhin, V.B.; Grachev, S.; Simonova, E.V. Ontology-based open multi-agent systems for adaptive resource management. In Proceedings of the 12th International Conference on Agents and Artificial Intelligence (ICAART 2020), Valetta, Malta, 22–24 February 2020; SciTePress: Setúbal, Portugal, 2020; Volume 1, pp. 127–135.
44. Shoham, Y.; Leyton-Brown, K. *Multi-Agent Systems: Alghoritmic, Game Theoretic and Logical Foundations*; Cambridge University Press: Cambridge, UK, 2009. Available online: http://www.masfoundations.org (accessed on 8 March 2022).
45. Easley, D.; Kleinberg, J. *Networks, Crowds, and Markets: Reasoning about a Highly Connected World*; Cambridge University Press: Cambridge, UK, 2010. Available online: http://www.cs.cornell.edu/home/kleinber/networks-book/ (accessed on 8 March 2020).
46. Grachev, S.P.; Zhilyaev, A.A.; Laryukhin, V.B.; Novichkov, D.E.; Galuzin, V.A.; Simonova, E.V.; Maiyorov, I.V.; Skobelev, P.O. Methods and Tools for Developing Intelligent Systems for Solving Complex Real-Time Adaptive Resource Management Problems. *Autom. Remote Control* **2021**, *82*, 1857–1885. [CrossRef]

Mathematical Circuit Root Simplification Using an Ensemble Heuristic–Metaheuristic Algorithm

Navid Behmanesh-Fard [1], Hossein Yazdanjouei [2], Mohammad Shokouhifar [3,*] and Frank Werner [4,*]

1. Department of Electrical Engineering, Technical and Vocational University (TVU), Tehran 1435661137, Iran
2. Microelectronics Research Laboratory, Urmia University, Urmia 5756151818, Iran
3. Department of Electrical and Computer Engineering, Shahid Beheshti University, Tehran 1983969411, Iran
4. Faculty of Mathematics, Otto-Von-Guericke-University, 39016 Magdeburg, Germany
* Correspondence: m_shokouhifar@sbu.ac.ir (M.S.); frank.werner@ovgu.de (F.W.)

Abstract: Symbolic pole/zero analysis is a crucial step in designing an analog operational amplifier. Generally, a simplified symbolic analysis of analog circuits suffers from NP-hardness, i.e., an exponential growth of the number of symbolic terms of the transfer function with the circuit size. This study presents a mathematical model combined with a heuristic–metaheuristic solution method for symbolic pole/zero simplification in operational transconductance amplifiers. First, the circuit is symbolically solved and an improved root splitting method is applied to extract symbolic poles/zeroes from the exact expanded transfer function. Then, a hybrid algorithm based on heuristic information and a metaheuristic technique using simulated annealing is used for the simplification of the derived symbolic roots. The developed method is tested on three operational transconductance amplifiers. The obtained results show the effectiveness of the proposed method in achieving accurate simplified symbolic pole/zero expressions with the least complexity.

Keywords: operational transconductance amplifiers; symbolic circuit analysis; pole/zero extraction; root splitting; simplification; simulated annealing

MSC: 90-08; 90C59

1. Introduction

Symbolic analysis is a method of analyzing analog circuits in which the circuit equations are expressed in terms of symbolic variables. This technique is useful for designing and analyzing complex analog circuits (especially those with nonlinear components) as it provides engineers with a deep insight into the relations between the circuit variables rather than simply relying on numerical methods. Therefore, this method can help circuit designers to quickly evaluate different design alternatives by allowing them to manipulate circuit equations algebraically, enabling the study of the effects of different component values on the circuit performance. One of the major applications of symbolic analysis is to determine the location and characteristics of circuits' poles and zeroes, which is needed to analyze the stability and frequency response of the circuit [1].

Recently, multi-stage operational transconductance amplifiers (OTAs) have become widely applied in modern microelectronics, as OTAs can provide a large output swing and high gain with very low overdrive voltage [2]. However, as each stage has its own poles and zeroes, the bandwidth may be reduced. In addition to the poles and zeroes of each additional stage, the compensated capacitors may add some extra poles and zeroes [3]. One of the main challenges in the design of multi-stage OTAs is to devise a frequency compensation procedure capable of providing wide bandwidth and high gain with appropriate stability margins [4]. In this regard, a simplified extraction of symbolic poles and zeroes can give better analytical expressions and assist designers in making a straight decision when designing an OTA and a frequency compensation circuit [5].

Generally, an exact symbolic analysis of OTAs is error-prone and time-consuming if performed by hand, even for circuits with a small number of components [6]. In this regard, a computer-aided automatic symbolic analysis can be helpful by solving the circuit equations with mathematical solvers such as Cramer's rule [7]. It can be performed by exploiting symbolic analysis solvers using software tools such as MATLAB, GNU Octave and MAPLE [8]. The main drawbacks of a symbolic analysis are that the derived symbolic equations are very complex and cannot effectively guide the circuit designer [9]. Although various symbolic simplification techniques have been introduced, simplified expressions are not provided in a factorization form. Thus, it is difficult to evaluate the effects of roots on the behavior of the circuit.

Although the existing symbolic pole/zero analysis methods incorporate some types of approximations during the calculation of the transfer function, they suffer from some drawbacks which limit their effectiveness for use in real-world OTAs. First, these methods are inefficient in the case of overall generated error rates in terms of magnitude, phase, poles and zeroes [10]. Second, the correlation between eliminated terms in different polynomials is not effectively considered in polynomial-oriented methods. Third, pole/zero displacements due to approximations are not under control [7]. Fourth, those closely spaced pole/zero pairs may disappear due to a magnitude-/phase-oriented approximation, which can generate high error rates at points other than the nominal ones [8].

Over the past years, metaheuristics have also been presented for use in the parameter selection and symbolic simplification in electrical circuits. Shokouhifar and Jalali [10] presented a combined algorithm based on the genetic algorithm (GA) and simulated annealing (SA) as a metaheuristic-based optimization technique for symbolic term selection in the symbolic voltage gain of analog circuits containing transistors. Akbari et al. [3] proposed a symbolic analysis for the design of analog integrated circuits using an ant colony optimization (ACO) algorithm which takes noise optimization into account. Another technique, outlined in [11], involved performing GA, SA, and particle swarm optimization (PSO) to simplify the symbolic expressions for the common-mode rejection ratio (CMRR) and power supply rejection ratio (PSRR) of the analog amplifier. Sathasivam et al. [12] presented a combined metaheuristic algorithm based on GA and tabu search (TS) with restricted neural symbolic integration for solving the maximum k-satisfiability problem. Ali et al. [13] proposed a new hybrid metaheuristic algorithm based on the marine predator algorithm and sine cosine algorithm for selecting the best parameters for hybrid active power filters.

Although various metaheuristics have been presented for circuit simplification, they mostly present symbolic expressions in expanded forms. The existing symbolic root simplification techniques typically use simple criteria which are separately applied to each polynomial of the exact symbolic roots. Thus, these techniques do not guarantee a good match of the simplified root expressions compared to the exact ones. Although the maximum error of each simplified polynomial is limited, the displacement of poles and zeroes is not under control [7]. Therefore, despite the simplicity of the traditional methods, they may generate large errors in the simplified root expressions.

In this study, a simplified symbolic pole/zero extraction technique is presented based on an extension of the root splitting technique [14] and SA [15]. In this regard, we first introduce an enhanced root splitting (named ERS) for the symbolic pole/zero extraction from the exact transfer function. In this method, pole/zero displacements cannot exceed a pre-specified threshold. Then, we apply a metaheuristic-driven simplification method based on SA (named PZSA) to simplify the derived pole/zero expressions. Our main motivation is to mathematically formulate the pole/zero simplification problem in analog circuits as a multi-objective constrained optimization problem. The established problem can be solved by the use of optimization algorithms such as heuristics, single-solution metaheuristics, or population-based evolutionary and swarm intelligence algorithms. Thus, this paper applies a combined heuristic–metaheuristic algorithm based on the heuristic information available in the circuit model and SA to solve the symbolic root simplification problem. The key contributions outlined in this study can be characterized as follows:

- Introducing a combined mathematical modeling and optimization technique for the extraction and simplification of symbolic poles and zeros in OTAs.
- Proposing an enhanced root splitting technique, named ERS, to accurately extract the exact pole/zero expressions.
- Applying a combined heuristic–metaheuristic optimization algorithm to solve the proposed symbolic root simplification problem, utilizing the heuristic knowledge available in the circuit model and SA.
- Programming the proposed method in a MATLAB m-file, wherein simplified root equations are automatically generated from the circuit netlist.
- Successfully driving symbolic pole/zero expressions for three OTAs.

The rest of this study is organized as follows: In Section 2, the existing literature for a symbolic simplification and symbolic pole/zero extraction is reviewed. In Section 3, the proposed methodology is presented with details, and then the developed method in MATLAB is evaluated in Section 4. Finally, in Section 5, some concluding remarks are made and future directions are addressed.

2. Literature Review

Over recent years, along with the increasing advancement and development in analog circuit design, various symbolic simplification techniques and symbolic pole/zero extraction methods have been proposed. According to the existing literature, these methods can be described in the following manners outlined below.

2.1. Symbolic Simplification Techniques

The symbolic analysis of OTAs suffers from NP-hardness [7]. For instance, the μA741 amplifier has approximately 10^{34} terms within its voltage transfer function [16]. Therefore, symbolic analysis tools must rely on simplification techniques to tackle the complexity and hardness of real-world circuits. Based on the steps taken in the simplification process, simplification algorithms can be categorized into SAG (simplification-after-generation), SDG (simplification-during-generation), and SBG (simplification-before-generation) [17]. It is worth noting that the proposed PZSA algorithm in this study is an SAG technique. An SAG is performed once the symbolic circuit analysis is done and, as a result, the exact symbolic expressions have been obtained. Therefore, simplified functions can be constructed from some terms of the exact expressions. In the following section, we discuss the details of the SAG technique used in the proposed method.

The small-signal transfer function of a linear or linearized circuit can be represented as a function of the frequency s and the circuit parameters $\mathbf{x}$, according to Equation (1) [8], where each polynomial $f'_i(\mathbf{x})$ or $f_i(\mathbf{x})$ is a sum-of-product (SOP) of $\mathbf{x}$. This is expressed as $h_k(\mathbf{x}) = h_{k1}(\mathbf{x}) + h_{k2}(\mathbf{x}) + \ldots + h_{kT}(\mathbf{x})$, where $h_k(\mathbf{x})$ is the k-th polynomial within the circuit transfer function $H(s, \mathbf{x})$, comprising T terms.

$$H(s, \mathbf{x}) = \frac{N(s, \mathbf{x})}{D(s, \mathbf{x})} = \frac{f'_0(\mathbf{x}) + f'_1(\mathbf{x})s + f'_2(\mathbf{x})s^2 + \ldots + f'_{n'}(\mathbf{x})s^{n'}}{f_0(\mathbf{x}) + f_1(\mathbf{x})s + f_2(\mathbf{x})s^2 + \ldots + f_n(\mathbf{x})s^n} \quad (1)$$

The simplification method in [18] finds the largest term in terms of the magnitude, $h_{km}(\mathbf{x})$, for the polynomial $h_k(\mathbf{x})$. Then, all other terms within the polynomial $h_k(\mathbf{x})$ are considered one by one. The condition for which the term $h_{kl}(\mathbf{x})$ can be discarded from the polynomial $h_k(\mathbf{x})$ is $|h_{kl}(\mathbf{x})| \leq \varepsilon \times |h_{km}(\mathbf{x})|$. Here, ε ($0 < \varepsilon < 1$) is a user-specified threshold to limit the maximum error. The main drawback of this method is that the error may be accumulated. To overcome this drawback, the reported criterion in [19] sorts the terms within $h_k(\mathbf{x})$ based on their magnitude obtained in the nominal point. Afterwards, P terms with the least accumulated magnitude are discarded from the polynomial if the error is below ε. The condition on the P terms for which they could be discarded can be expressed as Equation (2):

$$\left|\sum_{l=1}^{P} h_{kl}(\mathbf{x})\right| < \varepsilon \times \left|\sum_{l=1}^{T} h_{kl}(\mathbf{x})\right| \qquad (2)$$

Although this method achieves more accurate expressions at the nominal point, it may cause significant errors for other values of the parameters. To avoid the elimination of the mutually canceling terms, the method in [20] presented an enhanced condition for which the P terms with the lowest magnitude can be discarded if:

$$\sum_{l=1}^{P} |h_{kl}(\mathbf{x})| < \varepsilon \times \sum_{l=1}^{T} |h_{kl}(\mathbf{x})| \qquad (3)$$

In the above-mentioned techniques, the maximum error is limited for each polynomial. However, the obtained error in the poles and zeroes is not under consideration. If the same error (ε_M) occurs in all polynomials, no pole and/or zero displacement can be observed [21]. To overcome this drawback, an adaptive ε can be used, in which the term elimination process is performed step by step while displacements in poles and zeroes are monitored at every step. Thus, the term pruning procedure can be finished if the obtained displacements are beyond a pre-determined threshold [19].

Recently, various swarm and evolutionary metaheuristic algorithms in [7,10,22–26] have been applied for the simplified symbolic analysis of OTAs. In these techniques different criteria (such as the magnitude error, phase error, and pole/zero displacements) have been used to evaluate feasible solutions generated by the metaheuristic algorithm. Although these methods achieve a low mean error rate, the worst cases of the displacements in the poles and zeroes are not accurately under consideration. The common drawback of the existing techniques is that the simplified function is achieved in either expanded or nested form. In other words, the transfer function is not derived in a factorization form, which makes it difficult to evaluate the contribution of roots.

2.2. Symbolic Pole/Zero Extraction Techniques

The symbolic pole/zero analysis also suffers from NP-hardness as some operations have to be performed between the polynomials. Generally, a direct calculation of the roots from the expanded transfer functions yields very complex results in the form of polynomials with degrees larger than two [7]. Since the numerator and denominator of a transfer function in practical OTAs generally have degrees much larger than 2, it is rarely possible to mathematically find the exact symbolic pole/zero expressions [27].

In the following section, the existing pole/zero extraction methods are discussed, including root spitting, time-constant analysis, and eigenvalue analysis. Root splitting [14] is one of the well-known root extraction techniques. It extracts poles, assuming them to be reciprocally dominant. By factorization, the denominator of the exact function in Equation (1) can be re-written as a function of the poles p_i as follows:

$$D(s,\mathbf{x}) = f_0 \cdot \left(1 - \frac{s}{p_1}\right) \cdot \left(1 - \frac{s}{p_2}\right) \cdots \left(1 - \frac{s}{p_n}\right) \qquad (4)$$

It follows from Equation (1) that

$$f_1 = f_0 \cdot \sum_{i=1}^{n} \left(-\frac{1}{p_i}\right) \qquad (5)$$

Therefore, assuming p_1 is the dominant pole within the denominator, the first pole can be approximately expressed as:

$$p_1 \approx -\frac{f_0}{f_1} \qquad (6)$$

Consequently, with a similar approach, considering p_i to dominate the other poles, p_i can be given by the negative quotient of the two consecutive coefficients f_{i-1} and f_i [8]. Similar argumentations can be performed to calculate simplified zeroes in the numerator of the transfer function. The root splitting method is not appropriate for manual pole/zero calculations (hand-and-paper analysis), as some estimations and simplifications should be developed to allow the circuit designer to extract approximate the dominant poles and zeroes manually. The most popular approach in such techniques is the time-constant method [27–30], which is expressed in Equation (7), where τ_k can be achieved by multiplying the resistance R_k by the capacitance C_k.

$$p_1 \approx -\left(\sum_k \tau_k\right)^{-1} \qquad (7)$$

This technique is error-prone, as there is no information about the accuracy of the obtained symbolic results. Moreover, zeroes and higher-order poles cannot be determined by this approach at all. A more general approach in this context was reported in [29], one which also has the ability to extract the higher-order poles. This method is based on the use of open-circuits and short-circuits analysis to calculate the time constants of the circuit.

There are also some pole/zero extraction methods, which operate on the basis of the solution derived from the eigenvalue problem. A positive feature of these methods is that the simplification is no longer driven by the magnitude and the phase errors but by the pole/zero position, allowing improved error control. For example, a modified signal flow graph (MSFG) was recently developed to represent the equivalences between the system and SPICE outcomes of static nonlinear OTAs [31]. In this method, the circuit is firstly converted into an MSFG. Then, the graph is simplified in particular polynomials by minimizing the MSFGs. In [32], the implementation of some simplification procedures during the eigenvalue computation via a symbolic LR algorithm was addressed, in which the LR method is applied to compute the reduced matrix corresponding to the eigenvalue cluster. This technique is followed in [33] by the use of an algorithm to reduce the circuit matrix into a row echelon format. After determining the symbolic state matrix, the approximated poles and zeroes are achieved using the LR algorithm.

The main drawback of the existing symbolic pole/zero analysis methods is that the simplified expressions of poles and zeroes are not so compact that no SAG is applied to the final expressions. Thus, in this study, we utilize a combined heuristic–metaheuristic SAG algorithm to ensure the obtention of simplified symbolic pole/zero expressions with the least achievable complexity.

3. Proposed Method

The overall flowchart of the proposed symbolic pole/zero analysis can be seen in Figure 1. The list of indices, sets, parameters, and decision variables used in the following equations of this section are provided in Table 1. To sum up, the main steps of the proposed methodology can be summarized as follows:

- The input circuit netlist is loaded as a text file (in .txt format).
- All transistors are replaced via proper small-signal modeling.
- The symbolic circuit is solved via a modified nodal analysis (MNA).
- The exact transfer function (TF) is achieved in the expanded symbolic form.
- The exact expressions of poles and zeroes are derived using ERS.
- The numerical results of the exact symbolic pole/zero expressions are stored.
- A heuristic algorithm is performed to generate a near-optimal solution, utilizing the circuit-based knowledge available in the exact poles and zeroes.
- SA is performed to improve further the quality of the heuristic solution in order to generate the final simplified symbolic pole/zero expressions.
- The numerical results of the obtained simplified symbolic pole/zero expressions are calculated.

- The numerical results of the exact and simplified poles/zeroes are compared against HSPICE and other simplification algorithms.

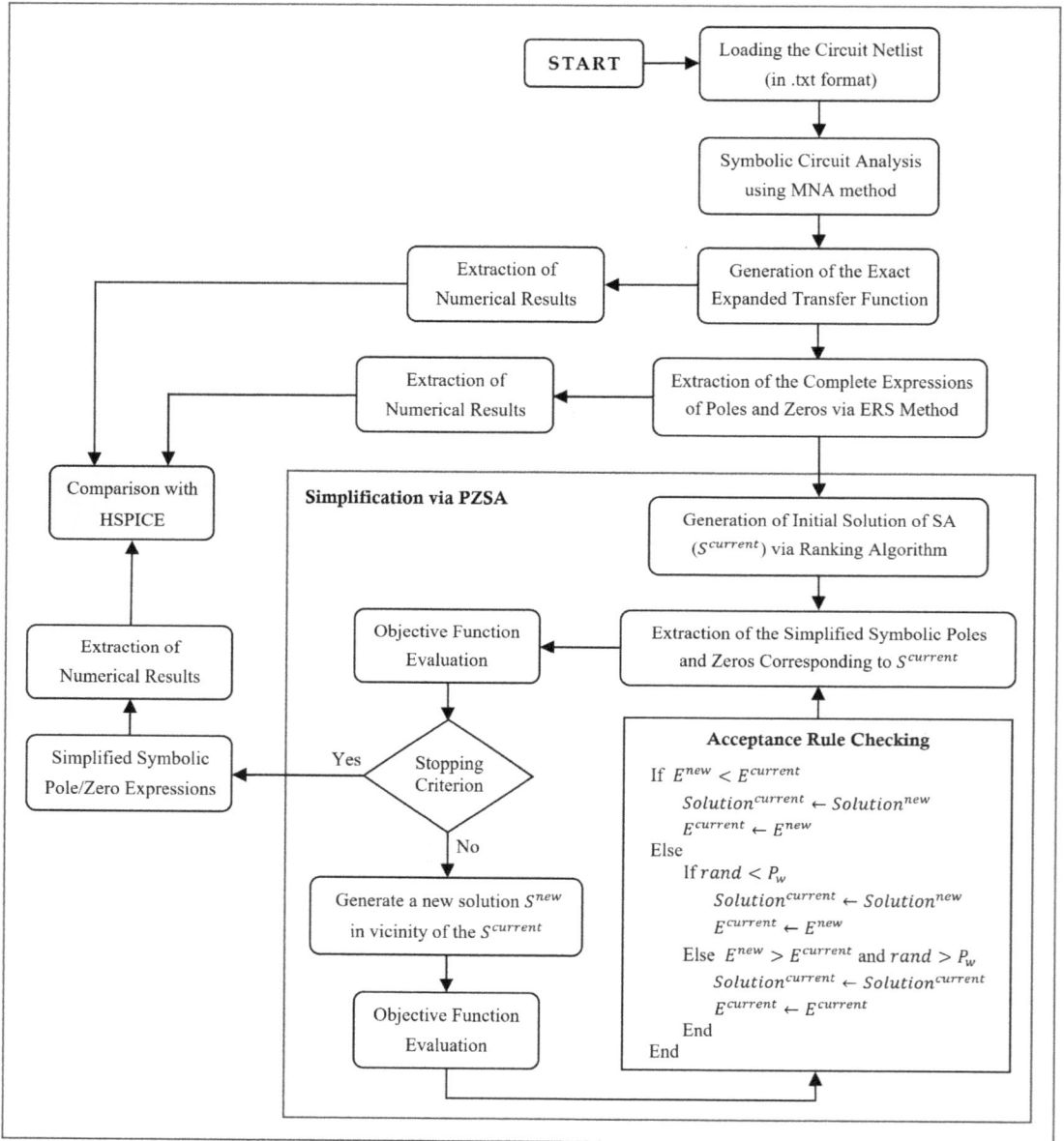

Figure 1. Overall flowchart of the proposed methodology.

Table 1. Notations.

Sets/Parameters	Definition
i	Index of poles, $i = 1, 2, \ldots, n$
j	Index of zeroes, $j = 1, 2, \ldots, \acute{n}$
n	Degree of the denominator within the exact expanded TF
$\acute{n}$	Degree of the numerator within the exact expanded TF
k	Index of the symbolic terms, $k = 1, 2, \ldots, L$
L	Number of symbolic terms within all pole/zero expressions
$[f_{min}, f_{max}]$	Defined frequency bound range for the pole/zero extraction
S_k	A binary parameter: 1 if the k-th term is presented; 0 otherwise
E_n	Percentage of the selected symbolic terms
PoleSet	Set of poles in the frequency range of $[f_{min}, f_{max}]$
ZeroSet	Set of zeroes in the frequency range of $[f_{min}, f_{max}]$
$p_{E,i}$	i-th pole within the exact expanded TF
$p_{ERS,i}$	i-th extracted pole via ERS
$p_{SA,i}$	i-th simplified pole via SA
E_p	Mean pole displacements
$z_{E,j}$	j-the zero of the exact expanded TF
$z_{ERS,j}$	j-th extracted zero via ERS
$z_{SA,j}$	j-th simplified zero via SA
E_z	Mean zero displacements
T_{ERS}	Maximum allowable pole/zero extraction error via ERS
T_{SA}	Maximum allowable pole/zero simplification error via SA

3.1. Symbolic Pole/Zero Extraction via ERS

After the netlist pre-processing, the circuit is solved using MNA [1], and consequently, the exact symbolic TF is achieved in expanded form. Then, the obtained exact pole/zero expressions are approximately calculated using the proposed ERS method, which is an enhanced version of the traditional root splitting algorithm. Generally, an expanded TF could be converted into the factorized form according to Equation (8), where $Z(s, \mathbf{x})$ is a function of $\acute{n}$ (real or complex conjugate) zeroes $z_1, z_2, \ldots, z_{\acute{n}}$, and $P(s, \mathbf{x})$ is a function of n (real or complex conjugate) poles $p_1, p_2, \ldots, p_n$.

$$(s, \mathbf{x}) \approx \frac{f'_0 \cdot Z(s, \mathbf{x})}{f_0 \cdot P(s, \mathbf{x})} \tag{8}$$

In the ERS algorithm, only poles and zeroes located in the interval $[f_{min}, f_{max}]$ are extracted, where f_{min} and f_{max} are the minimum and maximum user-specified frequencies for the pole/zero extraction, respectively. If the user does not specify the frequency range, it is considered as the default range of $[0, 10f_T]$, where f_T is the unity gain frequency of the exact expression in the nominal point. In the following section, the pole extraction procedure for $P(s, \mathbf{x})$ is described. By comparing Equations (1) and (8), $P(s, \mathbf{x})$ can be calculated as:

$$P(s, \mathbf{x}) = \frac{D(s, \mathbf{x})}{f_0} = 1 + \left(\frac{f_1}{f_0}\right)s + \left(\frac{f_2}{f_0}\right)s^2 + \left(\frac{f_3}{f_0}\right)s^3 + \cdots + \left(\frac{f_n}{f_0}\right)s^n \tag{9}$$

Assuming p_1 to be dominant and all other poles (typically occurred in OTAs) to be located at much higher frequencies, i.e., $\|p_1\| \ll \|p_2\|, \|p_3\|, \ldots, \|p_n\|$, the first pole can be split, and thus, $P(s, \mathbf{x})$ can be approximately written as:

$$\begin{aligned} P(s, \mathbf{x}) &= \left(1 - \tfrac{s}{p_1}\right) \cdot \left(1 + g_1 s + g_2 s^2 + \cdots + g_{n-1} s^{n-1}\right) \\ &= 1 + \left(-\tfrac{1}{p_1} + g_1\right)s + \left(-\tfrac{g_1}{p_1} + g_2\right)s^2 + \left(-\tfrac{g_2}{p_1} + g_3\right)s^3 + \cdots + \left(-\tfrac{g_{n-2}}{p_1} + g_{n-1}\right)s^{n-1} + \left(-\tfrac{g_{n-1}}{p_1}\right)s^n \end{aligned} \tag{10}$$

By equating the s coefficients of $P(s, \mathbf{x})$ in Equation (10) to those in Equation (9), the dominant real pole p_1 can be approximated given as:

$$p_1 \approx -\frac{f_0}{f_1} \tag{11}$$

Consequently, by assuming the condition in Equation (12), we can simplify the rightmost expression of Equation (10) as Equation (13). By equating the s coefficients of Equation (13) to the same s coefficients in Equation (9), the parameters g_i can be calculated as Equation (14).

$$\left|\frac{1}{p_1}\right| \gg |g_1|, \quad \left|\frac{g_{i-1}}{p_1}\right| \gg |g_i| \quad \forall i \in \{2, 3, \ldots, n-1\} \tag{12}$$

$$P(s, \mathbf{x}) \approx 1 + \left(-\frac{1}{p_1}\right)s + \left(-\frac{g_1}{p_1}\right)s^2 + \left(-\frac{g_2}{p_1}\right)s^3 + \cdots + \left(-\frac{g_{n-1}}{p_1}\right)s^n \tag{13}$$

$$g_i = \frac{f_{i+1}}{f_1} \quad \forall i \in \{1, 2, \ldots, n-1\} \tag{14}$$

and thus, the leftmost expression in Equation (10) can be expressed as:

$$P(s, \mathbf{x}) \approx \left(1 + \frac{f_1}{f_0}s\right) \cdot \left(1 + \frac{f_2}{f_1}s + \frac{f_3}{f_1}s^2 + \cdots + \frac{f_n}{f_1}s^{n-1}\right) \tag{15}$$

The circumstances of s coefficients in the original denominator $D(s, \mathbf{x})$, for which Equation (15) is valid, are:

$$\left|\frac{f_1}{f_0}\right| \gg \left|\frac{f_i}{f_{i-1}}\right| \quad \forall i \in \{2, 3, \ldots, n\} \tag{16}$$

Equation (15) shows that $P(s, \mathbf{x})$ can be simplified into a product of a first-order polynomial (i.e., first dominant pole) and a high-order polynomial corresponding to other high-frequency poles. In a more general case, assuming the first m poles ($1 < m < n$) to be successively dominant in pairs (i.e., p_1 dominates p_2, p_2 dominates p_3, and so on, p_{m-1} dominates p_m), $P(s, \mathbf{x})$ can be approximated as follows:

$$\begin{aligned}
P(s, \mathbf{x}) &= \left(1 - \frac{s}{p_1}\right) \cdot \left(1 - \frac{s}{p_2}\right) \cdots \left(1 - \frac{s}{p_m}\right) \cdot (1 + g_1 s + g_2 s^2 + \cdots + g_{n-m} s^{n-m}) \\
&= 1 + \left(-\sum_{i=1}^{m} \frac{1}{p_i} + g_1\right)s + \left(\sum_{i=1}^{m-1}\sum_{j=i+1}^{m} \frac{1}{p_i p_j} - g_1 \sum_{i=1}^{m} \frac{1}{p_i} + g_2\right)s^2 \\
&+ \left(-\sum_{i=1}^{m-2}\sum_{j=i+1}^{m-1}\sum_{k=j+1}^{m} \frac{1}{p_i p_j p_k} + g_1 \sum_{i=1}^{m-1}\sum_{j=i+1}^{m} \frac{1}{p_i p_j} - g_2 \sum_{i=1}^{m} \frac{1}{p_i} + g_3\right)s^3 + \cdots \\
&+ \left((-1)^m g_{n-m-1} \prod_{i=1}^{m} \frac{1}{p_i} + (-1)^{m-1} g_{n-m} \sum_{i_1=1}^{2}\sum_{i_2=i_1+1}^{3}\cdots\sum_{i_{m-1}=i_{m-2}+1}^{m} \frac{1}{p_{i_1} p_{i_2} p_{i_{m-1}}}\right)s^{n-1} + \left((-1)^m g_{n-m} \prod_{i=1}^{m} \frac{1}{p_i}\right)s^n
\end{aligned} \tag{17}$$

By similar approximations as performed in the previous case, $P(s, \mathbf{x})$ can be simplified according to:

$$\begin{aligned}
P(s, \mathbf{x}) &\approx 1 + \left(-\frac{1}{p_1}\right)s + \left(\frac{1}{p_1 p_2}\right)s^2 + \left(-\frac{1}{p_1 p_2 p_3}\right)s^3 + \cdots + \left((-1)^m \prod_{i=1}^{m} \frac{1}{p_i}\right)s^m + \cdots \\
&+ \left((-1)^m g_1 \prod_{i=1}^{m} \frac{1}{p_i}\right)s^{m+1} + \cdots + \left((-1)^m g_{n-m-1} \prod_{i=1}^{m} \frac{1}{p_i}\right)s^{n-1} + \left((-1)^m g_{n-m} \prod_{i=1}^{m} \frac{1}{p_i}\right)s^n
\end{aligned} \tag{18}$$

By equating the s coefficients of Equations (18) and (9), the m first poles are derived as Equation (19). Additionally, the parameters g_i can be expressed as Equation (20). Thus, $P(s, \mathbf{x})$ can be simplified into the multiplication of $m+1$ polynomials: m first-order polynomials (representing the m first poles) and a high-order polynomial, as Equation (21). The conditions on s coefficients of $D(s, \mathbf{x})$, for which Equation (21) is valid, can be expressed as Equations (22) and (23).

$$p_i = -\frac{f_{i-1}}{f_i} \quad \forall i \in \{1, 2, \ldots, m\} \tag{19}$$

$$g_i = \frac{f_{m+i}}{f_m} \quad \forall i \in \{1, 2, \ldots, n-m\} \tag{20}$$

$$P(s, \mathbf{x}) = \left(1 + \frac{f_1}{f_0}s\right) \cdot \left(1 + \frac{f_2}{f_1}s\right) \cdots \left(1 + \frac{f_m}{f_{m-1}}s\right) \cdot \left(1 + \frac{f_{m+1}}{f_m}s + \frac{f_{m+2}}{f_m}s^2 + \cdots + \frac{f_n}{f_m}s^{n-m}\right) \tag{21}$$

$$\left|\frac{f_i}{f_{i-1}}\right| \gg \left|\frac{f_{i+1}}{f_i}\right| \quad \forall i \in \{1, 2, \ldots, m-1\} \tag{22}$$

$$\left|\frac{f_i}{f_{i-1}}\right| \gg \left|\frac{f_j}{f_{j-1}}\right| \quad \forall i \in \{1, 2, \ldots, m\}, j \in \{m+1, m+2, \ldots, n\} \tag{23}$$

In the general case, let us extend the above formulations to the case that all the n poles are dominant reciprocally, in which $P(s, \mathbf{x})$ can be approximated as follows:

$$\begin{aligned} P(s, \mathbf{x}) &= \left(1 - \frac{s}{p_1}\right) \cdot \left(1 - \frac{s}{p_2}\right) \cdot \left(1 - \frac{s}{p_3}\right) \cdots \left(1 - \frac{s}{p_n}\right) \\ &= 1 + \left(-\sum_{i=1}^{n}\frac{1}{p_i}\right)s + \left(\sum_{i=1}^{n-1}\sum_{j=i+1}^{n}\frac{1}{p_i p_j}\right)s^2 + \left(-\sum_{i=1}^{n-2}\sum_{j=i+1}^{n-1}\sum_{k=j+1}^{n}\frac{1}{p_i p_j p_k}\right)s^3 \\ &+ \cdots + \left((-1)^{n-1}\sum_{i_1=1}^{2}\sum_{i_2=i_1+1}^{3}\cdots\sum_{i_{n-1}=i_{n-2}+1}^{n}\frac{1}{p_{i_1} p_{i_2} \cdots p_{i_{n-1}}}\right)s^{n-1} + \left((-1)^n \prod_{i=1}^{n}\frac{1}{p_i}\right)s^n \end{aligned} \tag{24}$$

Under the assumption that all poles are dominant in pairs (i.e., p_1 dominates p_2, p_2 dominates p_3, and so on), the following conditions are satisfied:

$$\left|\frac{f_i}{f_{i-1}}\right| \gg \left|\frac{f_{i+1}}{f_i}\right| \quad \forall i \in \{1, 2, 3, \ldots, n-1\} \tag{25}$$

Therefore, the rightmost expression in Equation (24) can be approximated as Equation (26). By equating s coefficients of Equation (26) and Equation (9), $P(s, \mathbf{x})$ can be approximately expressed as Equation (27), where each pole p_i can be calculated according to Equation (28).

$$P(s, \mathbf{x}) \approx 1 + \left(-\frac{1}{p_1}\right)s + \left(\frac{1}{p_1 p_2}\right)s^2 + \cdots + \left((-1)^{n-1}\prod_{i=1}^{n-1}\frac{1}{p_i}\right)s^{n-1} + \left((-1)^n \prod_{i=1}^{n}\frac{1}{p_i}\right)s^n \tag{26}$$

$$P(s, \mathbf{x}) \approx \left(1 + \frac{f_1}{f_0}s\right) \cdot \left(1 + \frac{f_2}{f_1}s\right) \cdot \left(1 + \frac{f_3}{f_2}s\right) \cdots \left(1 + \frac{f_n}{f_{n-1}}s\right) \tag{27}$$

$$p_i = -\frac{f_{i-1}}{f_i} \quad \forall i \in \{1, 2, \ldots, n\} \tag{28}$$

The interesting point is that all poles are derived from s coefficients of the denominator of the transfer function. The above formulations operate under the assumption that all poles are real. In other words, the approach fails for closely spaced or complex conjugate poles. Therefore, the method should be extended to cases where two consecutive poles are located in a cluster. Assuming that p_i and p_{i+1} constitute a pair of poles (real or conjugate), they remain split off in the expression $P(s, \mathbf{x})$ and can be expressed via a second-order polynomial $(1 + as + bs^2)$, where a and b can be calculated as follows:

$$a = \frac{f_i}{f_{i-1}} + \frac{f_{i+1}}{f_i}, b = \frac{f_{i+1}}{f_{i-1}} \tag{29}$$

The condition for which the poles p_i and p_{i+1} are real is $a^2 \geq 4b$. If the condition has been satisfied, the real poles p_i and p_{i+1} can be expressed as Equation (30). Otherwise these poles can be represented as complex conjugate poles according to Equation (31).

$$p_i = -a + \frac{\sqrt{a^2 - 4b}}{2b}, \quad p_{i+1} = -a - \frac{\sqrt{a^2 - 4b}}{2b} \tag{30}$$

$$p_{i,i+1} = -a \pm j\frac{\sqrt{4b - a^2}}{2b} \tag{31}$$

It should be emphasized that all the above formulations could be used to extract simplified zeroes $Z(s, \mathbf{x})$ from the numerator $N(s, \mathbf{x})$ of the expanded TF. In ERS, the pole p_i (or zero z_j) can be separated using Equation (27) if the conditions in Equations (32) and (33) are met, where $p_{ERS,i}$ ($z_{ERS,j}$) is the absolute of the numerical value of i-th pole (j-th zero) extracted via the ERS method and $p_{E,i}$ ($z_{E,j}$) is the absolute of the i-th pole (j-th zero) of the exact function of Equation (1). These are numerically achieved by the calculation of the roots of the transfer function. *PoleSet* (*ZeroSet*) refers to the set of poles (zeroes) which are in the range of the interval $[f_{min}, f_{max}]$. Additionally, T_{ERS} is a pre-determined constant parameter used to specify the maximum allowable root displacement for each ERS root compared with the exact one.

$$\left|\frac{p_{ERS,i} - p_{E,i}}{p_{E,i}}\right| \leq T_{ERS} \quad \forall p_{E,i} \in PoleSet \tag{32}$$

$$\left|\frac{z_{ERS,j} - z_{E,j}}{z_{E,j}}\right| \leq T_{ERS} \quad \forall z_{E,j} \in ZeroSet \tag{33}$$

The ERS pole/zero extraction method comprises evaluation and extraction steps. In the evaluation step, all poles and zeroes within the interval $[f_{min}, f_{max}]$ are assumed to be reciprocally dominant. Thus, their ERS values are numerically obtained according to Equation (27). In the extraction step, the conditions of Equations (32) and (33) are checked for all extracted poles and zeroes. Then, each pole (zero) that has satisfied the mentioned condition can be symbolically extracted according to Equation (27). Otherwise, a pair of real or complex conjugate poles (zeroes) remains split off, and the condition $a^2 \geq 4b$ is checked for them. If the condition has been satisfied, the poles (zeroes) are a pair of real poles (zeroes) and can be calculated by Equation (30); otherwise, they are considered as complex conjugate poles (zeroes) which are extracted by means of Equation (31). To gain further insight into the details of the ERS method, the pseudo-code of the symbolic pole/zero extraction method is provided in Algorithm 1.

3.2. Symbolic Pole/Zero Simplification via PZSA

The extracted symbolic pole/zero expressions cannot provide analytical information about the circuit behavior due to their high complexity. Thus, a pole/zero simplification based on PZSA is used to simplify the exact pole/zero expressions. SA is a single-solution metaheuristic method inspired by metallurgy annealing, which involves heating and then slowly cooling a material to reduce its defects [15]. Generally, SA starts its search from a fully random solution and then iteratively updates the solution until arriving at the stopping criterion [34]. However, to improve the quality and speed of the search process in SA, we utilize the knowledge from the exact circuit expressions as heuristic information to guide the SA algorithm by starting from a near-optimal solution. After generating the initial solution using the heuristic algorithm, SA is performed to further improve the solution's quality using local search operators in an iterative procedure. In the following section, the main steps of the PZSA algorithm are described.

Algorithm 1. Symbolic Pole/Zero Extraction using ERS

Inputs:
  Symbolic exact expanded transfer function
  Numerical values of the circuit parameters in the nominal point
  Maximum allowable root displacement (T_{ERS})
Output:
  Symbolic expressions of poles and zeros
Numerical Analysis:
1. Extract coefficients of the numerator $(\acute{f}_0, \acute{f}_1, \ldots, \acute{f}_\acute{n})$ and the denominator $(f_0, f_1, \ldots, f_n)$
2. Numerically evaluate the exact expanded transfer function in the nominal point
3. Numerically find roots of the numerator and the denominator in $[f_{min}, f_{max}]$
4. Sort the exact numerical zeroes $(z_{E,j})$ and poles $(p_{E,i})$ by their magnitude

Extraction of Symbolic Zeros:
5.   **for** $j \in ZeroSet$
6.   Numerically estimate the position of zero j as $z_{ERS,j} = -\acute{f}_{j-1}/\acute{f}_j$
7.   **if** $\left| (z_{ERS,j} - z_{E,j})/z_{E,j} \right| \leq T_{ERS}$
8.   Extract the real zero j as $z_j = \acute{f}_{j-1}/\acute{f}_j$
9.   **else**
10.   Consider z_j and z_{j+1} in one cluster
11.   Calculate $a = (\acute{f}_j/\acute{f}_{j-1}) + (\acute{f}_{j+1}/\acute{f}_j)$ and $b = \acute{f}_{j+1}/\acute{f}_{j-1}$
12.   **if** $a^2 \geq 4b$
13.   Extract the real zero j as $z_j = -a + \left(\sqrt{a^2 - 4b}/2b\right)$
14.   Extract the real zero $j+1$ as $z_{j+1} = -a - \left(\sqrt{a^2 - 4b}/2b\right)$
15.   **else**
16.   Extract the complex conjugate zeroes j and $j+1$ as $z_{j,j+1} = -a \pm j\left(\sqrt{a^2 - 4b}/2b\right)$
17.   **end if**
18.   **end if**
19.   **end for**

Extraction of Symbolic Poles:
20.   **for** $i \in PoleSet$
21.   Numerically estimate the position of pole i as $p_{ERS,i} = -f_{i-1}/f_i$
22.   **if** $\left| (p_{ERS,i} - p_{E,i})/p_{E,i} \right| \leq T_{ERS}$
23.   Extract the real pole i as $p_i = f_{i-1}/f_i$
24.   **else**
25.   Consider p_i and p_{i+1} in one cluster
26.   Calculate $a = (f_i/f_{i-1}) + (f_{i+1}/f_i)$ and $b = f_{i+1}/f_{i-1}$
27.   **if** $a^2 \geq 4b$
28.   Extract the real pole i as $p_i = -a + \left(\sqrt{a^2 - 4b}/2b\right)$
29.   Extract the real pole $i+1$ as $p_{i+1} = -a - \left(\sqrt{a^2 - 4b}/2b\right)$
30.   **else**
31.   Extract the complex conjugate poles i and $i+1$ as $p_{i,i+1} = -a \pm j\left(\sqrt{a^2 - 4b}/2b\right)$
32.   **end if**
34.   **end if**
35.   **end for**

3.2.1. Solution Encoding/Decoding

A possible solution to the pole/zero simplification problem, as shown in Figure 2, is a binary vector of length L, where L is the number of original terms, which can be calculated as follows:

$$L = (L_{z_1} + L_{z_2} + \cdots + L_{z_{n'}}) + (L_{p_1} + L_{p_2} + \cdots + L_{p_n}) = \sum_{j=1}^{n'} L_{z_j} + \sum_{i=1}^{n} L_{p_i} \quad (34)$$

where L_K, L_{z_j}, and L_{p_i} are the number of symbolic terms within the DC-gain K, j-th zero and i-th pole, respectively.

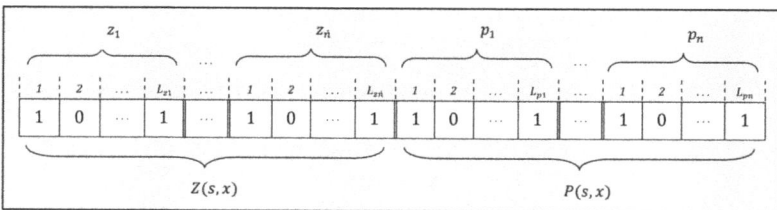

Figure 2. Encoding of a solution: If $S_i = 1$, the i-th symbolic term is present in the solution; otherwise if $S_i = 0$, the i-th term has been discarded from the solution.

3.2.2. Generation of the Initial Solution

To construct the initial solution of SA, we utilize heuristic information available in the circuit via a ranking algorithm (RA). This not only improves the convergence speed of SA as it utilizes a near-optimal solution but can also effectively enhance the quality of the final solution. An RA comprises an evaluation step and a selection step. In the first step, each term is eliminated, and accordingly, the generated error rate is measured and stored. After the evaluation of all terms, they are sorted into a list from the best to the worst. In the selection phase, an empty solution is considered, after which the terms within the list are added one by one until all constraints have been satisfied.

3.2.3. Objective Function Evaluation

To evaluate the performance of each solution, an objective function is formulated which compares the simplified pole/zero expressions with the exact ones in terms of the number of terms and mean pole/zero displacements. Moreover, each pole/zero displacement should not exceed the user-specified margin T_{SA}. In this direction, the objective function is expressed as a weighted average of three sub-objectives. The first sub-objective (E_n) demonstrates the proportion of the selected symbolic terms to the total number of exact terms extracted by the ERS method. Additionally, the second and third sub-objectives (E_p and E_z) express the mean displacements of the simplified poles and zeroes, respectively. According to Equation (35), these three sub-objectives are merged into a single objective function (OF) to be minimized by the PZSA method, where the sub-objectives E_n, E_p, and E_z are calculated via Equations (36)–(38), respectively.

$$\text{minimize } OF = \{w_n E_n + w_p E_p + w_z E_z\} \quad (35)$$

$$E_n = \frac{1}{L} \sum_{k=1}^{L} S_k \quad (36)$$

$$E_p = \frac{1}{n} \sum_{i=1}^{n} \left(\left| \frac{p_{SA,i} - p_{E,i}}{p_{E,i}} \right| \right) \quad (37)$$

$$E_z = \frac{1}{n'} \sum_{j=1}^{n'} \left(\left| \frac{z_{SA,j} - z_{E,j}}{z_{E,j}} \right| \right) \qquad (38)$$

subject to:

$$\left| \frac{p_{SA,i} - p_{E,i}}{p_{E,i}} \right| \leq T_{SA} \quad \forall p_{E,i} \in PoleSet \qquad (39)$$

$$\left| \frac{z_{SA,j} - z_{E,j}}{z_{E,j}} \right| \leq T_{SA} \quad \forall z_{E,j} \in ZeroSet \qquad (40)$$

In Equation (35), w_n, w_p, and w_z, are constant parameters ($w_n + w_z + w_z = 1$) that specify the relative impacts of the three objectives. As the worst-case pole/zero displacements are limited by Equations (39) and (40), w_n is set as being much larger than w_p and w_z to ensure achieving the simplest expressions.

3.2.4. Generation of a New Solution

In each iteration, a neighbor solution, S^{new}, is constructed in the vicinity of the current solution, $S^{current}$. We adopt swap (Figure 3) and an exchange (Figure 4) operators as neighborhood search strategies in SA. The reason behind using these operators is to introduce randomness into the optimization process, allowing it to escape from local optima and search for better solutions in the search space. The swap operator adds or removes a term in the exact pole/zero expression, and the exchange operator selects from the available terms while preserving the total number of terms constant. To generate a new solution, an operator is randomly selected with a probability of 50%, and then it operates on the solution $S^{current}$.

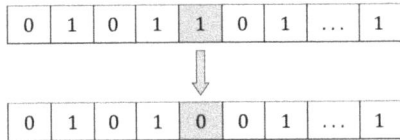

Figure 3. Swap: a symbolic term is randomly selected and inverted.

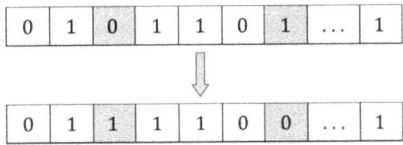

Figure 4. Exchange: a term "0" and a term "1" are randomly selected and exchanged.

3.2.5. Acceptance Rule Checking

In each iteration, if $OF^{new} < OF^{current}$, the new solution is accepted. Otherwise, if $OF^{new} \geq OF^{current}$, the new solution (worse solution) has a chance to be accepted with the probability of P_w, which can be calculated according to the current temperature T and the differences between the objective function values of the two solutions as follows:

$$P_w = \exp\left(-\frac{E^{new} - E^{current}}{T} \right) \qquad (41)$$

where T is considered to be linearly decreasing during the execution of SA from $T_{initial}$ (initial temperature) to T_{final} (final temperature), as follows:

$$T = T_{initial} + \frac{t}{iter}\left(T_{final} - T_{initial} \right) \qquad (42)$$

4. Performance Evaluation

All simulations are conducted on a PC with a 2.6 GHz CPU and 6 GB RAM. The presented tool has been successfully coded in an MATLAB R2020b m-file running on Windows 10. In order to analyze the performance of the proposed method, we have applied it to three different circuits. All MOS transistors in these circuits are modeled via a small-signal model, as shown in Figure 5. The parameters of the proposed tool have been divided into two categories: Model parameters and SA parameters.

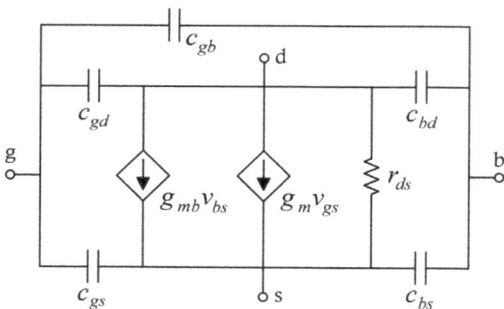

Figure 5. Small signal representation of MOS transistors.

Table 2 provides the selected values for the model parameters. As shown in this table, the model parameters include f_{min}, f_{max}, T_{SA}, T_{ERS}, w_n, and w_{pz}, which engineers should determine based on the desired specifications of the circuit's application. To perform the experiments in this study, we deploy the typical values for the model parameters which are generally used in the circuit design process. In this regard, the frequency range in which the poles/zeroes are analyzed equals 1 Hz to 10 times the unity gain bandwidth of the active components ($10 \times f_T$). The reason for choosing a final frequency of $10 \times f_T$ is to ensure that the circuit response is analyzed up to a frequency where the active components, such as transistors or amplifiers, are still able to provide reasonable gain. At frequencies beyond $10 \times f_T$, the gain of the active components typically drops significantly, and the circuit response may be dominated by the passive components [35]. Additionally, T_{ERS} has been set to 10%, and thus, the poles and zeroes with no more than 10% displacement can be simplified via first-order polynomials, while the other poles and zeroes are expressed via second-order polynomials. Moreover, T_{SA} is selected so that the displacements of the poles/zeroes in the simplified expressions derived by SA are confined to 20%. Eventually, since the maximum displacements of the poles/zeroes are limited by T_{SA}, the weight of the term related to the compactness of the symbolic expressions in OF (w_n) is set to be much larger than the weight of the average pole/zero displacement (w_{pz}). Therefore, the values w_n and w_{pz} are set as 0.99 and 0.01, respectively. As mentioned above, it should be emphasized that the choice of the model parameters depends on the specific circuit and should be modified by the circuit designers according to the application requirements.

Table 2. Model parameter settings.

Phase	Parameter	Value/Description
Model Parameters	f_{min}	1 Hz
	f_{max}	$10 \times f_T$
	T_{ERS} in Equations (32) and (33)	10%
	T_{SA} in Equations (39) and (40)	20%
	w_n in Equation (35)	0.99
	w_p in Equation (35)	0.005
	w_z in Equation (35)	0.005

Additionally, in the case of the SA parameters, the Taguchi method is utilized to adjust the controllable parameters of SA, comprising maximum iterations, local search operators, $T_{initial}$, and T_{final}. In this study, the value of the objective function (OF) is used to evaluate the effectiveness of the algorithm. In order to implement the Taguchi method, we have conducted each experiment 10 times, and the mean and standard deviation values of the objective function are considered as signal and noise values in the Taguchi method, respectively. Table 3 presents the analyzed levels for each SA parameter and the optimal level obtained by the Taguchi method.

Table 3. SA parameter settings using the Taguchi method.

Phase	Parameter		Parameter Levels			Selected Value
SA Parameters	Maximum iterations	L	$5 \times L$	$10 \times L$		$5 \times L$
	Local search operators	Swap	Exchange	Swap/Exchange		Swap/Exchange
	$T_{initial}$ in Equation (42)	10^{-5}	10^{-4}	10^{-3}		10^{-5}
	T_{final} in Equation (42)	0	10^{-8}	10^{-10}		0

To justify the proposed methodology, we compare it against a time-constant approach [29], an eigenvalue technique [31], and an evolutionary-based algorithm using a genetic algorithm [26].

4.1. Results for a Three-Stage Amplifier in the RCg_m Model (Circuit 1)

The block diagram of a three-stage compensation OTA is shown in Figure 6. The circuit is described by the RCg_m model. First, the exact expanded TF is derived according to Equation (43) using the MNA technique. Next, by applying the simplification algorithm in [26], the simplified expanded TF is obtained according to Equation (44). By performing PZSA, 3 poles and 2 zeroes can be achieved as Equations (45)–(49).

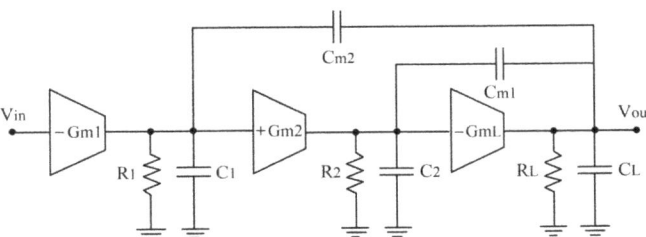

Figure 6. A three-stage amplifier in the RCg_m model.

The comparison of the different methods is summarized in Table 4. According to the obtained results, the exact expanded TF has a total of 40 symbolic terms. The simplification method in [26] obtained an expanded TF according to Equation (44) containing 10 terms. However, even in the simplified form, it cannot give effective insights for the circuit designer to evaluate the positions of the poles and zeroes. By performing the proposed ERS method, 3 poles and 2 zeroes with 10, 26, 25, 3, and 4 terms, resulting in a total of 68 terms, have been extracted. Finally, the proposed PZSA algorithm has reduced the number of terms within these roots to 1, 3, 3, 2, and 2 terms, i.e., totaling 11 terms. Moreover, the numerical results of the different methods are provided in Table 5, where the last four rows illustrate the error of the simplified equations in terms of the pole and zero displacements when compared to the exact expressions. According to the obtained results, all pole/zero displacements in the derived simplified expressions by the proposed method are less than $T_{SA} = 20\%$. Although in some cases the existing methods have achieved less pole/zero displacements, the resulting expressions are not as compact as the proposed method. This occurs due to the selection of a much larger value for w_n compared to the values w_p and w_z

in the defined objective function. However, as previously mentioned, these values can be modified by the circuit designer based on the desired application requirements.

$$H_E(s) = \frac{-R_L R_1 Gm_1 \left((C_2 R_2 C_{m2} + C_{m1} R_2 C_{m2}) s^2 - (Gm_2 R_2 C_{m1} + C_{m2}) s - Gm_2 R_2 Gm_L \right)}{\begin{pmatrix} C_{m1} R_2 C_L R_L C_1 R_1 + C_{m1} R_2 C_L R_L C_{m2} R_1 + C_2 R_2 C_{m1} R_L C_{m2} R_1 + C_2 R_2 C_L R_L C_{m2} R_1 \\ + C_2 R_2 C_{m1} R_L C_1 R_1 + C_2 R_2 C_{m2} R_L C_1 R_1 + C_{m1} R_2 C_{m2} R_L C_1 R_1 + C_2 R_2 C_L R_L C_1 R_1 \end{pmatrix} s^3} \tag{43}$$

$$+ \begin{pmatrix} C_2 R_2 C_{m1} R_L + C_{m1} R_L C_{m2} R_1 + C_{m1} R_2 R_L Gm_L C_1 R_1 - C_{m1} R_1 R_L Gm_2 C_{m2} R_2 \\ + C_L R_L C_1 R_1 + C_2 R_2 C_{m2} R_1 + C_{m1} R_L C_{m2} R_1 + C_2 R_2 C_1 R_1 + C_{m2} R_2 C_{m1} R_1 \\ + C_2 R_2 R_L C_{m2} + C_2 R_2 R_L C_L + C_{m1} R_2 R_L C_{m2} + C_{m1} R_2 R_L C_L + C_{m2} R_L C_1 R_1 \\ + C_{m1} R_2 C_1 R_1 + C_{m1} R_2 R_L Gm_L C_{m2} R_1 + C_L R_L C_{m2} R_1 + C_{m1} R_L C_1 R_1 \end{pmatrix} s^2$$

$$+ \begin{pmatrix} R_L C_L + R_L C_{m2} + R_L C_{m1} + R_2 C_{m1} + R_2 C_2 + R_1 C_1 \\ + R_1 C_{m2} + R_1 C_{m2} R_L Gm_2 R_2 Gm_L + C_{m2} R_L R_2 Gm_L \end{pmatrix} s + 1$$

$$H_{S,E}(s) = \frac{-(C_2 R_1 R_2 R_L C_{m1} C_{m2} + Gm_1 R_1 R_2 R_L C_{m1} C_{m2}) s^2 + (Gm_1 Gm_2 R_1 R_2 R_L C_{m1}) s + Gm_1 Gm_2 Gm_L R_1 R_2 R_L}{(C_{m1} R_2 C_L R_L C_{m2} R_1) s^3 + (C_{m1} R_2 R_L Gm_L C_1 R_1 + C_{m1} R_1 R_2 R_L Gm_L C_{m2} - C_{m1} C_{m2} R_1 R_2 R_L Gm_2) s^2 + (R_1 C_{m2} R_L Gm_2 R_2 Gm_L) s + 1} \tag{44}$$

$$P_1 = -\frac{1}{R_1 Gm_2 R_2 Gm_L R_L C_{m2}} \tag{45}$$

$$P_2 = -\frac{Gm_2 Gm_L}{C_{m1}(Gm_L - Gm_2)} \tag{46}$$

$$P_3 = -\frac{(Gm_L - Gm_2)}{C_L} \tag{47}$$

$$Z_1 = \frac{Gm_L}{C_{m1}} \tag{48}$$

$$Z_2 = -\frac{Gm_2}{C_{m2}} \tag{49}$$

Table 4. Number of terms within simplified symbolic poles/zeroes in Circuit 1.

Expression	Expanded TF (Exact)	Ref. [26]	Ref. [29]	Ref. [31]	Proposed Exact (ERS)	Proposed Simplified (SA)
P1	-	-	1	10	10	1
P2	-	-	4	26	26	3
P3	-	-	5	25	25	3
Z1	-	-	2	9	3	2
Z2	-	-	2	9	4	2
Overall TF	40	10	-	-	-	-

Table 5. Numerical results for Circuit 1.

Parameter	HSPICE	Expanded TF (Exact)	Ref. [26]	Ref. [29]	Ref. [31]	Proposed Exact	Proposed Simplified
P1 (Hz)	−12.8	−12.8	−13.3	−13.2	−12.8	−12.8	−13.2
P2 (MHz)	−3.19	−3.19	−3.49	−3.19	−2.96	−2.96	−3.18
P3 (MHz)	−40.6	−40.6	−36.3	−43.9	−43.8	−43.8	−39.8
Z1 (MHz)	2.72	2.72	2.72	3.18	3.36	3.18	3.18
Z2 (MHz)	−18.6	−18.6	−18.6	−15.9	−17.5	−15.9	−15.9
Mean pole displacement (%)	-	-	7.8	3.8	5	5	1.9
Max pole displacement (%)	-	-	10.6	8.36	7.9	7.9	3.5
Mean zero displacement (%)	-	-	0.03	15.9	14.7	15.8	15.9
Max zero displacement (%)	-	-	0.04	17.1	23.6	17.1	17.1

4.2. Results for a Two-Stage Miller Compensated Amplifier (Circuit 2)

The second circuit is a folded cascode two-stage OTA with compensation, as shown in Figure 7. The exact expanded TF obtained by MNA contains 134 symbolic terms. By performing the simplification method outlined in [26], the simplified TF has been obtained according to Equation (50). As shown in Table 6, the proposed ERS method has extracted 2 poles and 1 zero with 104, 82, and 18 terms, respectively. Subsequently, the proposed PZSA method has simplified these roots based on Equations (51)–(53), resulting in 5, 2, and 2 terms, respectively. Additionally, a comparison of the numerical results is shown in Table 7, which shows that all pole/zero displacements do not exceed $T_{SA} = 20\%$.

$$H(s) = \frac{-g_{m1}(g_{m1}ro_1ro_3ro_6ro_7C_c + g_{mb1}ro_1ro_3ro_6ro_7C_c)s + (g_{m1}g_{m6}ro_1ro_3ro_6ro_7 + g_{m6}g_{mb1}ro_1ro_3ro_6ro_7)}{ro_1(g_{m1}ro_3ro_6ro_7C_cC_L + g_{mb1}ro_3ro_6ro_7C_cC_L)s^2 + (g_{m1}g_{m6}ro_3ro_6ro_7C_c + g_{mb1}g_{m6}ro_3ro_6ro_7C_c)s + (g_{m1}ro_6 + g_{m1}ro_7 + g_{m1}ro_3ro_7/ro_1)} \quad (50)$$

$$P_1 = -\frac{(ro_1ro_6 + ro_1ro_7 + ro_3ro_6 + ro_3ro_7)}{g_{m6}ro_1ro_3ro_6ro_7C_c} = -\frac{1}{g_{m6}(ro_1\|ro_3)(ro_6\|ro_7)C_c} \quad (51)$$

$$P_2 = -\frac{g_{m6}}{C_L} \quad (52)$$

$$Z = \frac{g_{m6}}{C_c} \quad (53)$$

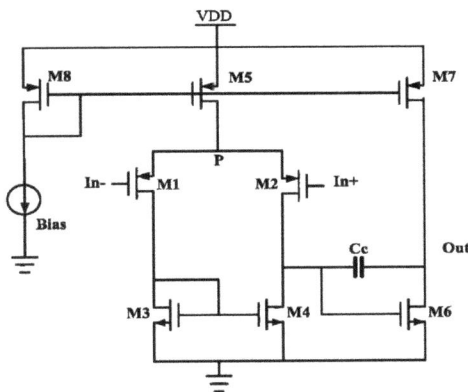

Figure 7. Two-stage compensation amplifier.

Table 6. Number of terms within the simplified symbolic poles/zeroes in Circuit 2.

Expression	Expanded TF (Exact)	Ref. [26]	Ref. [29]	Ref. [31]	Proposed Exact (ERS)	Proposed Simplified (SA)
P1	-	-	5	104	104	5
P2	-	-	7	82	82	2
Z	-	-	4	18	18	2
Overall TF	134	11	-	-	-	-

Table 7. Numerical results for Circuit 2.

Parameter	HSPICE	Expanded TF (Exact)	Ref. [26]	Ref. [29]	Ref. [31]	Proposed Exact	Proposed Simplified
P1 (KHz)	−177.1	−178.5	−192	−152.8	−178.4	−178.4	−152.8
P2 (MHz)	−377.4	−435.4	−409.1	−341	−435.6	−435.6	−409.3
Z (MHz)	407.2	409.3	409.3	409.3	409.3	409.3	409.3
Mean pole displacement (%)	-	-	6.8	18	0.04	0.04	10.2
Max pole displacement (%)	-	-	7.5	21.7	0.04	0.04	14.4
Zero displacement (%)	-	-	0.01	0.01	0	0	0.01

4.3. Results for a Three-Stage Amplifier in Transistor Model (Circuit 3)

The last circuit is a transistor-level three-stage amplifier with miller compensation, as shown in Figure 8. The exact expanded TF of this circuit contains 1320 symbolic terms. Considering the approximation algorithm in [26], the simplified expanded TF with 18 symbolic terms is shown in Equation (54). The ERS method extracted 3 poles and 2 zeroes with a total of 2061 terms. As shown in Equations (55)–(59), applying PZSA to the exact extracted roots reduced them to only a total of 19 terms. The number of simplified terms and numerical results of the different algorithms are summarized in Tables 8 and 9, respectively.

$$H(s) = \frac{\begin{array}{c}-(g_{m1}g_{m8}r o_1 r o_3 r o_6 r o_7 r o_8 r o_9 r o_{10} r o_{11} C_{m1} C_{m2}) s^2 - (g_{m1}g_{m6}g_{m9} r o_1 r o_3 r o_6 r o_7 r o_8 r o_9 r o_{10} r o_{11} C_{m2}) s \\ + g_{m1}g_{m6}g_{m9}g_{m11} r o_1 r o_3 r o_6 r o_7 r o_8 r o_9 r o_{10} r o_{11}\end{array}}{\begin{array}{c}\left(\begin{array}{c}g_{m8} r o_1 r o_6 r o_7 r o_8 r o_{10} + g_{m8} r o_3 r o_6 r o_8 r o_9 r o_{10} + g_{m8} r o_1 r o_6 r o_8 r o_9 r o_{10} + g_{m8} r o_3 r o_6 r o_8 r o_9 r o_{11} \\ + g_{m8} r o_3 r o_6 r o_7 r o_8 r o_{10} + g_{m8} r o_1 r o_6 r o_7 r o_8 r o_{11} + g_{m8} r o_3 r o_6 r o_7 r o_8 r o_{11} + g_{m8} r o_1 r o_6 r o_8 r o_9 r o_{11}\end{array}\right) \\ + (g_{m8} r o_1 r o_3 r o_6 r o_7 r o_8 r o_9 r o_{10} r o_{11} C_{m1} C_{m2} C_L) s^3 + (g_{m6}g_{m9}g_{m11} r o_1 r o_3 r o_6 r o_7 r o_8 r o_9 r o_{10} r o_{11} C_{m1}) s \\ + \left(\begin{array}{c}g_{m8} r o_1 r o_3 r o_6 r o_7 r o_8 r o_9 r o_{10} C_{m1} C_{m2} - g_{m6}g_{m9} r o_1 r o_3 r o_6 r o_7 r o_8 r o_9 r o_{10} r o_{11} C_{m1} C_{m2} \\ + g_{m11} r o_1 r o_3 r o_7 r o_8 r o_9 r o_{10} r o_{11} C_{m1} C_{m2} + g_{m11} r o_1 r o_3 r o_6 r o_7 r o_9 r o_{10} r o_{11} C_{m1} C_{m2} \\ + g_{m8} g_{m11} r o_1 r o_3 r o_6 r o_7 r o_8 r o_9 r o_{10} r o_{11} C_{m1} C_{m2}\end{array}\right) s^2\end{array}} \quad (54)$$

$$P_1 = -\frac{g_{m8}(r o_1 + r o_3)(r o_7 + r o_9)(r o_{10} + r o_{11})}{g_{m6}g_{m9}g_{m11} r o_1 r o_3 r o_7 r o_9 r o_{10} r o_{11} C_{m1}} = -\frac{g_{m8}}{g_{m6}g_{m9}g_{m11} C_{m1}(r o_1 \| r o_3)(r o_7 \| r o_9)(r o_{10} \| r o_{11})} \quad (55)$$

$$P_2 = -\frac{g_{m6}g_{m9}g_{m11}}{(g_{m8}g_{m11} - g_{m6}g_{m9}) C_{m2}} \quad (56)$$

$$P_3 = -\frac{(g_{m8}g_{m11} - g_{m6}g_{m9})}{g_{m8} C_L} \quad (57)$$

$$Z_1 = \frac{g_{m11}}{C_{m2}} \quad (58)$$

$$Z_2 = -\frac{g_{m6}g_{m9}}{g_{m8} C_{m1}} \quad (59)$$

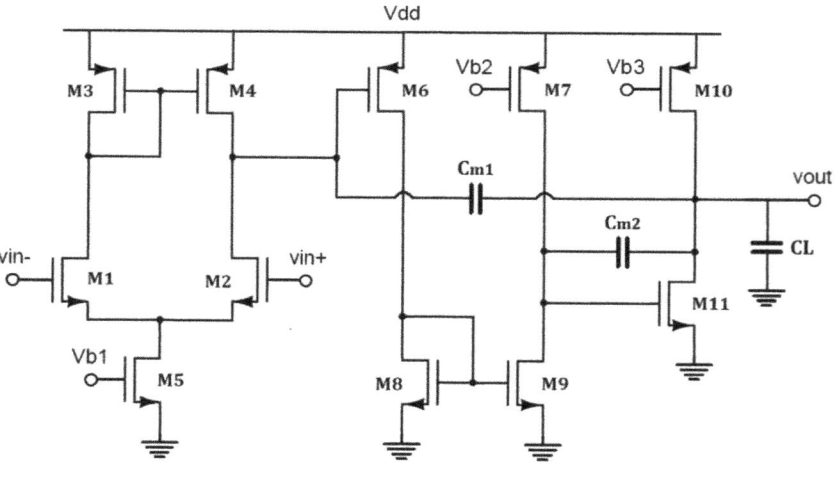

Figure 8. A three-stage amplifier in the transistor model.

Table 8. Number of terms within the simplified symbolic poles/zeroes in Circuit 3.

Expression	Expanded TF (Exact)	Ref. [26]	Ref. [29]	Ref. [31]	Proposed Exact (ERS)	Proposed Simplified (SA)
P1	-	-	29	714	714	9
P2	-	-	21	837	837	3
P3	-	-	23	330	330	3
Z1	-	-	15	75	75	2
Z2	-	-	13	105	105	2
Overall TF	1320	18	-	-	-	-

Table 9. Numerical results for Circuit 3.

Parameter	HSPICE	Expanded TF (Exact)	Ref. [26]	Ref. [29]	Ref. [31]	Proposed Exact	Proposed Simplified
P1 (Hz)	−27.7	−27.9	−20.6	−20.5	−27.9	−27.9	−22.8
P2 (MHz)	−1.84	−1.84	−2.03	−2.16	−1.76	−1.76	−2.07
P3 (MHz)	−36.6	−40.2	−36.3	−36.1	−42.1	−42.1	−35.7
Z1 (MHz)	1.4	1.4	1.4	2.23	1.62	1.62	1.62
Z2 (MHz)	−10.3	−10.2	−10.5	−7.37	−8.81	−8.81	−9.1
Mean pole displacement (%)	-	-	15.6	18	3	3	14.2
Max pole displacement (%)	-	-	26.4	26.5	4.6	4.6	18.4
Mean zero displacement (%)	-	-	1.7	43.5	14.8	14.8	13.5
Max zero displacement (%)	-	-	2.9	59.3	15.9	15.9	16.1

4.4. Discussion

Generally, in the reported simplified symbolic pole/zero expressions, three types of errors can be observed:

Error-1: the first type of error may occur by comparing HSPICE with the exact expanded TF achieved by MNA. This error may be observed for OTAs described at the transistor level, as HSPICE considers a more accurate small-signal transistor model than the simple model in our program.

Error-2: the second type of error may be observed when comparing the exact TF with the exact extracted poles/zeroes because of the simplifications induced by the root extraction process in the ERS method.

Error-3: the third error may occur between exact pole/zero expressions and the simplified ones due to the simplifications done by PZSA.

As mentioned above, Error-1 is inevitable in symbolic analysis, which is observed in all symbolic tools. However, Error-2 and Error-3 may occur because of our pole/zero extraction and simplification methods, respectively. Therefore, in the results shown in Tables 5, 7 and 9, we have reported these errors for each algorithm by comparing them with the exact expanded TF. Thus, the numerical results of the poles and zeroes in the exact TF were considered as references to justify the performance of the different techniques.

Table 10 reports the obtained values of the three sub-objectives (E_n, E_p, and E_z) for the different circuits. As previously mentioned, the total number of terms in the exact poles/zero expressions extracted by the ERS method are 68, 204, and 2061 for circuits 1, 2, and 3, respectively. Subsequently, these expressions are then simplified by the PZSA method resulting in a total of 11, 9, and 19 terms. As a result, the first sub-objective (E_n) equals the proportion of the number of simplified terms to the exact terms for each circuit. Additionally, the obtained results for the sub-objectives E_p and E_z demonstrate that all pole/zero displacements do not exceed the pre-specified threshold of $T_{SA} = 20\%$.

Table 10. Sub-objective values for different circuits.

Circuit/Objective	E_n	E_p	E_z
Circuit 1	0.1617	0.019	0.159
Circuit 2	0.0441	0.102	0.0001
Circuit 3	0.0092	0.142	0.135

In addition, since SA is a non-deterministic algorithm that produces different results in each run, its performance was assessed by running it on each circuit 10 times. The resulting objective function values and their average and standard deviation are summarized in Table 11. According to the obtained results, the proportion of the standard deviation to the average values equals 5.1%, 3.6%, and 4.7% for circuits 1, 2, and 3, respectively, which demonstrates the robustness of the proposed PZSA.

Table 11. Overall objective function values in 10 successive runs for different circuits.

Circuit/Objective	Circuit 1	Circuit 2	Circuit 3
Run 1	0.1619	0.0447	0.0119
Run 2	0.162	0.0451	0.013
Run 3	0.1618	0.0448	0.0128
Run 4	0.1766	0.045	0.0123
Run 5	0.162	0.0447	0.0114
Run 6	0.1767	0.0445	0.0115
Run 7	0.1617	0.0446	0.012
Run 8	0.1616	0.0449	0.0129
Run 9	0.1473	0.0398	0.0117
Run 10	0.1621	0.0447	0.0121
Average	0.1634	0.0443	0.0122
Standard Deviation	0.0083	0.0016	0.0006

5. Conclusions

This paper presented a mathematical technique for symbolic circuit pole/zero extraction, followed by a combined heuristic–metaheuristic algorithm to simplify the extracted expressions. In the proposed method, a mathematical model was presented for extracting the exact poles and zeroes from the original expanded expression of OTA. Then, an ensemble heuristic–metaheuristic approach was proposed to obtain the simplest symbolic pole/zero equations from the exact ones. In the proposed ensemble method, a near-optimal solution was constructed using the knowledge-based heuristic information available in the circuit model. Subsequently, a metaheuristic algorithm based on simulated annealing was used to obtain the simplest pole/zero expressions with the best achievable quality. The proposed tool has been coded in an m-file of MATLAB to extract simplified pole/zero equations directly from the circuit netlist. Simulations on three OTAs demonstrated the effectiveness and superiority of the proposed technique against the existing algorithms in the literature.

Besides the advantages mentioned above, the proposed method has some limitations that can be addressed in future studies. The proposed methodology relies on a single nominal point for the circuit parameters, and thus, the simplified root expressions are valid around the nominal point. As a future work, the proposed method can be extended to deal with the uncertainties of the circuit parameters using robust optimization techniques, Monte Carlo simulation, fuzzy arithmetic, etc. Another limitation of this study is that the suggested method is a simplification-after-generation technique, in which the symbolic expressions should be generated exactly before the simplification process. Since circuit simplification is an NP-hard problem, the computational complexity of the exact expressions increases exponentially with the circuit size. Thus, the use of metaheuristic algorithms is challenging for large-size circuits from the time complexity point of view. As an interesting future research direction, the proposed method can be hybridized with simplification-before-generation approaches to deal with larger circuits. Moreover, we suggest performing other metaheuristics and their hybridizations with other soft computing techniques [36,37] in order to solve the root simplification problem.

Author Contributions: Conceptualization, N.B.-F., H.Y. and M.S.; methodology, M.S.; software, M.S.; validation, M.S. and F.W.; investigation, M.S.; data curation, N.B.-F., H.Y. and M.S.; resources, N.B.-F. and H.Y.; writing—original draft preparation, N.B.-F. and M.S.; writing—review and editing, M.S., H.Y. and F.W.; visualization, N.B.-F.; formal analysis, F.W.; supervision, M.S. and F.W. All authors have read and agreed to the published version of the manuscript.

Funding: This research received no external funding.

Institutional Review Board Statement: Not applicable.

Informed Consent Statement: Not applicable.

Data Availability Statement: The data used in the study is available with the authors and can be shared upon reasonable requests.

Conflicts of Interest: The authors declare no conflict of interest.

References

1. Gielen, G.; Sansen, W.M. *Symbolic Analysis for Automated Design of Analog Integrated Circuits*; Springer Science + Business Media: Berlin, Germany, 2012; Volume 137.
2. Riad, J.; Soto-Aguilar, S.; Estrada-López, J.J.; Moreira-Tamayo, O.; Sánchez-Sinencio, E. Design Trade-Offs in Common-Mode Feedback Implementations for Highly Linear Three-Stage Operational Transconductance Amplifiers. *Electronics* **2021**, *10*, 991. [CrossRef]
3. Akbari, M.; Shokouhifar, M.; Hashemipour, O.; Jalali, A.; Hassanzadeh, A. Systematic design of analog integrated circuits using ant colony algorithm based on noise optimization. *Analog. Integr. Circuits Signal Process.* **2016**, *86*, 327–339. [CrossRef]
4. Rodovalho, L.H.; Toledo, P.; Mir, F.; Ebrahimi, F. Hybrid Inverter-Based Fully Differential Operational Transconductance Amplifiers. *Chips* **2023**, *2*, 1–19. [CrossRef]
5. Akbari, M.; Hussein, S.M.; Hashim, Y.; Khateb, F.; Kulej, T.; Tang, K.T. Implementation of a Multipath Fully Differential OTA in 0.18-μm CMOS Process. *IEEE Trans. Very Large Scale Integr. (VLSI) Syst.* **2022**, *31*, 147–151. [CrossRef]
6. Aminzadeh, H.; Grasso, A.D.; Palumbo, G. A methodology to derive a symbolic transfer function for multistage amplifiers. *IEEE Access* **2022**, *10*, 14062–14075. [CrossRef]
7. Shokouhifar, M.; Jalali, A. Simplified symbolic transfer function factorization using combined artificial bee colony and simulated annealing. *Appl. Soft Comput.* **2017**, *55*, 436–451. [CrossRef]
8. Grasso, A.D.; Marano, D.; Pennisi, S.; Vazzana, G. Symbolic factorization methodology for multistage amplifier transfer functions. *Int. J. Circuit Theory Appl.* **2015**, *44*, 38–59. [CrossRef]
9. Shi, G.; Tan, S.X.D.; Tlelo-Cuautle, E. *Advanced Symbolic Analysis for VLSI Systems*; Springer: Berlin, Germany, 2014.
10. Shokouhifar, M.; Jalali, A. An evolutionary-based methodology for symbolic simplification of analog circuits using genetic algorithm and simulated annealing. *Expert Syst. Appl.* **2015**, *42*, 1189–1201. [CrossRef]
11. Shokouhifar, M.; Jalali, A. Simplified symbolic gain, CMRR and PSRR analysis of analog amplifiers using simulated annealing. *J. Circuits Syst. Comput.* **2016**, *25*, 1650082. [CrossRef]
12. Sathasivam, S.; Mamat, M.; Kasihmuddin, M.S.M.; Mansor, M.A. Metaheuristics approach for maximum k satisfiability in restricted neural symbolic integration. *Pertanika J. Sci. Technol.* **2020**, *28*, 545–564.
13. Ali, S.; Bhargava, A.; Saxena, A.; Kumar, P. A Hybrid Marine Predator Sine Cosine Algorithm for Parameter Selection of Hybrid Active Power Filter. *Mathematics* **2023**, *11*, 598. [CrossRef]
14. Dziedziewicz, S.; Warecka, M.; Lech, R.; Kowalczyk, P. Self-Adaptive Mesh Generator for Global Complex Roots and Poles Finding Algorithm. *IEEE Trans. Microw. Theory Tech.* **2023**, *66*, 7198–7205. [CrossRef]
15. Kirkpatrick, S.; Gelatt, C.D.; Vecchi, M.P. Optimization by Simulated Annealing. *Science* **1983**, *220*, 671–680. [CrossRef] [PubMed]
16. Hennig, E. *Symbolic Approximation and Modeling Techniques for Analysis and Design of Analog Circuits*; Shaker Verlag: Herzogenrath, Germany, 2000.
17. Toumazou, C.; Moschytz, G.S.; Gilbert, B. *Trade-Offs in Analog Circuit Design: The Designer's Companion*; Kluwer Academic Publishers: New York, NY, USA, 2014.
18. Wierzba, G.; Srivastava, A.; Joshi, V.; Noren, K.; Svoboda, J. SSPICE-A symbolic SPICE program for linear active circuits. *Midwest Symp. Circuits Syst.* **1989**, *2*, 1197–1201.
19. Fernández, F.V.; Rodríguez-Vázquez, A.; Huertas, J.L. Interactive AC modeling and characterization of analog circuits via symbolic analysis. *Kluwer J. Analog. Integr. Circuits Signal Process.* **1991**, *1*, 183–208.
20. Gielen, G.; Walscharts, H.; Sansen, W. ISAAC: A symbolic simulator for analog integrated circuits. *IEEE J. Solid-State Circuits* **1989**, *24*, 1587–1597. [CrossRef]
21. Fakhfakh, M.; Cuautle, E.T.; Fernandez, F.V. *Design of Analog Circuits through Symbolic Analysis*; Bentham Science Publishers: Sharjah, United Arab Emirates, 2012.
22. Shokouhifar, M.; Jalali, A. Automatic Simplified Symbolic Analysis of Analog Circuits Using Modified Nodal Analysis and Genetic Algorithm. *J. Circuits Syst. Comput.* **2015**, *24*, 1–20. [CrossRef]

23. Shokouhifar, M.; Jalali, A. Evolutionary based simplified symbolic PSRR analysis of analog integrated circuits. *Analog. Integr Circuits Signal Process.* **2016**, *86*, 189–205. [CrossRef]
24. Panda, M.; Kumar Patnaik, S.; Kumar Mal, A.; Ghosh, S. Fast and optimised design of a differential VCO using symbolic technique and multi objective algorithms. *IET Circuits Devices Syst.* **2019**, *13*, 1187–1195. [CrossRef]
25. Panda, M.; Patnaik, S.K.; Mal, A.K. An efficient method to compute simplified noise parameters of analog amplifiers using symbolic and evolutionary approach. *Int. J. Numer. Model. Electron. Netw. Devices Fields* **2021**, *34*, e2790. [CrossRef]
26. Zhou, R.; Poechmueller, P.; Wang, Y. An Analog Circuit Design and Optimization System with Rule-Guided Genetic Algorithm. *IEEE Trans. Comput.-Aided Des. Integr. Circuits Syst.* **2022**, *41*, 5182–5192. [CrossRef]
27. Hayes, M. Lcapy: Symbolic linear circuit analysis with Python. *PeerJ Comput. Sci.* **2022**, *8*, e875. [CrossRef] [PubMed]
28. Guerra, O.; Rodriguez-Garcia, J.D.; Fernandez, F.V.; Rodríguez-Vázquez, A. A symbolic pole/zero extraction methodology based on analysis of circuit time-constants. *Analog. Integr. Circuits Signal Process.* **2002**, *31*, 101–118. [CrossRef]
29. Gomes, J.L.; Nunes, L.C.; Gonçalves, C.F.; Pedro, J.C. An accurate characterization of capture time constants in GaN HEMTs. *IEEE Trans. Microw. Theory Tech.* **2019**, *67*, 2465–2474. [CrossRef]
30. Cao, H.; Zhang, Y.; Han, Z.; Shao, X.; Gao, J.; Huang, K.; Shi, Y.; Tang, J.; Shen, C.; Liu, J. Temperature compensation circuit design and experiment for dual-mass MEMS gyroscope bandwidth expansion. *IEEE/ASME Trans. Mechatron.* **2019**, *24*, 677–688. [CrossRef]
31. Coşkun, K.Ç.; Hassan, M.; Drechsler, R. Equivalence Checking of System-Level and SPICE-Level Models of Linear Circuits. *Chips* **2022**, *1*, 54–71. [CrossRef]
32. Evnin, O. Melonic dominance and the largest eigenvalue of a large random tensor. *Lett. Math. Phys.* **2021**, *111*, 66. [CrossRef]
33. Gheorghe, A.G.; Constantinescu, F. Pole/Zero Computation for Linear Circuits. In Proceedings of the 2012 Sixth UKSim/AMSS European Symposium on Computer Modeling and Simulation, Valletta, Malt, 14–16 November 2012; pp. 477–480.
34. Sohrabi, M.; Zandieh, M.; Shokouhifar, M. Sustainable inventory management in blood banks considering health equity using a combined metaheuristic-based robust fuzzy stochastic programming. *Socio-Econ. Plan. Sci.* **2022**, *86*, 101462. [CrossRef]
35. Razavi, B. *Fundamentals of Microelectronics*; John Wiley & Sons: New York, NY, USA, 2021.
36. Ghasemi Darehnaei, Z.; Shokouhifar, M.; Yazdanjouei, H.; Rastegar Fatemi, S.M.J. SI-EDTL: Swarm intelligence ensemble deep transfer learning for multiple vehicle detection in UAV images. *Concurr. Comput. Pract. Exp.* **2022**, *34*, e6726. [CrossRef]
37. Aziz, R.M.; Mahto, R.; Goel, K.; Das, A.; Kumar, P.; Saxena, A. Modified Genetic Algorithm with Deep Learning for Fraud Transactions of Ethereum Smart Contract. *Appl. Sci.* **2023**, *13*, 697. [CrossRef]

Disclaimer/Publisher's Note: The statements, opinions and data contained in all publications are solely those of the individual author(s) and contributor(s) and not of MDPI and/or the editor(s). MDPI and/or the editor(s) disclaim responsibility for any injury to people or property resulting from any ideas, methods, instructions or products referred to in the content.

Scheduling of Software Test to Minimize the Total Completion Time [†]

Man-Ting Chao and Bertrand M. T. Lin *

Institute of Information Management, National Yang Ming Chiao Tung University, Hsinchu 300, Taiwan; manting417@gmail.com
* Correspondence: bmtlin@nycu.edu.tw
[†] This document is based upon the thesis of Man-Ting Chao submitted for her master degree.

Abstract: This paper investigates a single-machine scheduling problem of a software test with shared common setup operations. Each job has a corresponding set of setup operations, and the job cannot be executed unless its setups are completed. If two jobs have the same supporting setups, the common setups are performed only once. No preemption of any processing is allowed. This problem is known to be computationally intractable. In this study, we propose sequence-based and position-based integer programming models and a branch-and-bound algorithm for finding optimal solutions. We also propose an ant colony optimization algorithm for finding approximate solutions, which will be used as the initial upper bound of the branch-and-bound algorithm. The computational experiments are designed and conducted to numerically appraise all of the proposed methods.

Keywords: single-machine scheduling; shared common setups; total completion time; integer programming; branch-and-bound; ant colony optimization

MSC: 68M20; 90B35; 90C57

Citation: Chao, M.-T.; Lin, B.M.T. Scheduling of Software Test to Minimize the Total Completion Time. *Mathematics* **2023**, *11*, 4705. https://doi.org/10.3390/math11224705

Academic Editor: Ripon Kumar Chakrabortty

Received: 9 October 2023
Revised: 11 November 2023
Accepted: 15 November 2023
Published: 20 November 2023

Copyright: © 2023 by the authors. Licensee MDPI, Basel, Switzerland. This article is an open access article distributed under the terms and conditions of the Creative Commons Attribution (CC BY) license (https://creativecommons.org/licenses/by/4.0/).

1. Introduction

Scheduling is the decision-making process used by many manufacturing and service industries to allocate resources to economic activities or tasks over he planning horizon [1,2]. This paper studies a scheduling model that is inspired by real-life applications, where supporting operations need to be prepared before regular jobs are processed. The specific application context is the scheduling of asoftware test at an IC design company, where the software system is modular and can be tested module by module and level by level. Before starting a module test, we need to install software utilities and libraries as well as adjust system parameters to shape an appropriate system environment. The setup operation corresponds to the installation of utilities and libraries, which are supporting tasks for the job. Different tests may require part of the same environment settings. If two jobs have common supporting tasks, the common setups are performed only once. The abstract model was also studied by Kononov, Lin, and Fang [3] as a single-machine scheduling problem formulated from the production scheduling of multimedia works. In the context of multimedia scheduling, when we want to play multimedia, we need to download their content first, including audio tracks, subtitles, and images, which can correspond to setup operations and jobs for this study, respectively. Once the setup operations of the multimedia objects are prepared, they can be embedded in upper-level objects without multiple copies, as in physical products. This unique property is different from the manufacture of tangible products, such as vehicles and computers. Following the standard three-field notation [4], we denote the model by $1|bp-prec|\sum_j C_j$, where the one indicates the single-machine setting, $bp-prec$ indicates the bipartite precedence relation between shared setups and test jobs, and $\sum_j C_j$ is the objective to minimize the total completion time.

This paper is organized into seven sections. In Section 2, the problem definition is presented with a numerical example for illustrations. The literature review follows. Section 3 introduces two integer programming models based on different formulation approaches. Section 4 is dedicated to the development of a branch-and-bound algorithm, including the development of upper bound, lower bound, and tree traversal methods. In Section 5, an ant colony optimization algorithm is proposed. Section 6 presents the computational experiments on the proposed methods. Finally, conclusions and suggestions for future works are given in Section 7.

2. Problem Definition and Literature Review

2.1. Problem Statements

We first present the notation that will be used in this paper. Note that all parameters are assumed to be non-negative integers.

n	number of jobs;
m	number of setup operations;
$T = \{t_1, t_2, \ldots, t_n\}$	set of jobs to be processed;
$S = \{s_1, s_2, \ldots, s_m\}$	set of setup operations;
$\mathcal{R} = \{(s_i, t_j) \mid s_i \in S \text{ supports } t_j \in T\}$	relation indicating whether the setup operation s_i is required for each job t_j;
p_j	processing time of job t_j on the machine;
sp_i	processing time of setup s_i on the machine;
$\sigma = (\sigma_1, \sigma_2, \ldots, \sigma_n)$	particular sequence of the jobs;
σ^*	optimal schedule sequence;
C_j	completion time of job t_j;
$Z(\sigma) = \sum_{j \in T}$	total job completion time under schedule σ.

The subject of our research is dedicated to studying the single-machine scheduling problem with shared common setup operations. The objective is to minimize the total completion time of the jobs, i.e., ΣC_j. The problem can be described as follows:

From time zero onwards, two disjoint sets of activities S and T are to be processed on a machine. Each job t_j has a set of setup operations that job t_j can only start after its setups are completed. All setup operations and jobs can be performed on the machine at any time. Although all setup operations need to be processed once, they do not contribute to the objective function because their role is only the preparatory operations for jobs under the priority relation. At any time, the machine can process at most one setup operation or job. No preemption of any processing is allowed. In software test scheduling, jobs t_j represent the software to be tested, and setups s_i refers to the preparation of a programming language or compilation environment that needs to be installed in advance so that the test software can be executed. For example, if t_1 is an Android application that needs to be tested, and t_1 needs setups s_1 and s_4, then s_1 could be JAVA, s_4 could be Android Studio, etc.

To illustrate the problem of our study, we give numerical examples of four setup operations, five test jobs, the relation $\mathcal{R}$, and its corresponding graph. The parameters and relation are shown in Figure 1.

Two example schedules are produced and shown below in the form of Gantt charts. The feasible schedule shown in Figure 2 is $\sigma = (t_1, t_2, t_3, t_4, t_5)$ with a total completion time of 115. Setups s_2, s_3 precede job t_1. The order of s_2 and s_3 is immaterial. Figure 3 shows schedule $\sigma^* = (t_4, t_2, t_1, t_3, t_5)$ associated with a total completion time of 101, which is optimal for the given instance. While both are feasible solutions, the objective value of Figure 3 will be better than that of Figure 2.

activities	s_1	s_2	s_3	s_4	t_1	t_2	t_3	t_4	t_5
length	2	4	3	2	5	3	6	2	7

$\mathcal{R}(s_i, t_j)$	t_1	t_2	t_3	t_4	t_5
s_1	0	1	0	1	0
s_2	1	1	0	0	1
s_3	1	0	0	1	0
s_4	0	0	1	0	1

(a) Parameters of five jobs.

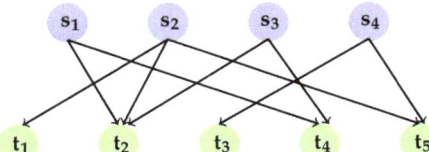

(b) Bipartite relation.

Figure 1. Example of 4 setups and 5 jobs.

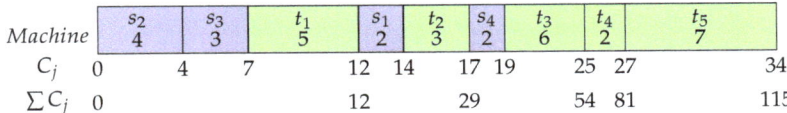

Figure 2. Feasible solution.

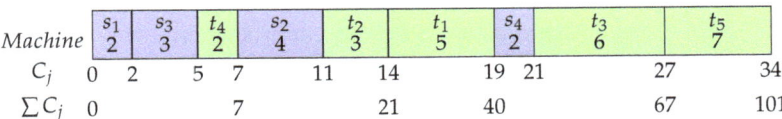

Figure 3. Optimal solution.

2.2. Literature Review

The scheduling problem studied by Kononov, Lin, and Fang [3] has a single machine that performs all setup operations and testing jobs. Referring to Brucker [5] and Leung [1], we know that precedence constraints play a crucial role in scheduling problems, especially when complexity status or categories are involved. Existing research works in the literature consider precedence relations presented in various forms. Bipartite graphs are often studied in graph theory. The graph shown in Figure 1 is bipartite because edges exist between nodes on one side and nodes on the other. Linear allocation problems can also be visualized by both supply and demand. Unfortunately, scheduling theory rarely addresses precedence constraints in bipartite graphs.

After formulation, Kononov, Lin, and Fang [3] studied two minimum sum objective functions, namely the number of late jobs and the total weighted completion time of jobs. As for the minimization of the total weighted completion time ($\sum_j w_j C_j$), Baker [6] is probably the first paper to address the existence of precedence constraints. Adolphson and Hu [7] proposed a polynomial time algorithm for the case in which rooted trees give priority. A fundamental problem for the jobs-per-unit execution time is $1|prec, p_i = 1|\sum w_j C_j$, where $w_j \in 1, 2, 3$ has been proven to be strongly NP-hard by Lawler [8]. The minimum latency set cover problem studied by Hassin and Levin [9] is the most relevant. The minimum latency set cover problem involves a subset of several operations. A subset is complete when all of their operations are finished. The objective function is the total weighted completion time of subsets. The minimum latency set cover problem is a special case of our $1|bp - prec|\sum w_j C_j$ problem, and the correspondence is as follows: In our problem, an operation is mapped to a setup operation (s_i), and a subset is interpreted as a testing job (t_j). Furthermore, Hassin and Levin [9] showed that the minimum delay set cover problem is strongly NP-hard even if all operations require the unit execution time (UET). Subsequently the $1|bp - prec|\sum w_j C_j$ problem is hard as well. By performing a pseudo-polynomial time reduction in Lawler's result about $1|prec, p_j = 1|\sum w_j C_j$, where $w_j \in 1, 2, 3$, Kononov, Lin and Fang [3] proved $1|bp - prec, s_i = t_j = 1|\sum C_j$ is strongly NP-hard. In other words, it is very difficult to minimize the total weighted completion time in our model, even though all setup operations and all testing jobs require unit execution time and all weights are one.

To solve the scheduling problem, Shafransky and Strusevich [10]; Hwang, Kovalyov, and Lin [11]; and Cheng, Kravchenko, and Lin [12] studied several special cases with fixed job sequences and solved these problems in polynomial time. Moreover, the branch-and-bound algorithm is an enumeration technique that can be applied to combinatorial optimization problems. Brucker and Sievers [13] deploy branch-and-bound algorithms on the job-shop scheduling problem and Hadjar, Marcotte, and Francois [14] do the same on the multiple-depot vehicle scheduling problem. To find approximate solutions to a hard optimization problem, various meta-heuristics have been designed. Kunhare, Tiwari, and Dhar [15] used particle swarm optimization for feature selection in intrusion detection systems. Kunhare, Tiwari, and Dhar [16] further used a genetic algorithm to compose a hybrid approach to intrusion detection. For solving a worker assignment bi-level programming problem, Luo, Zhang, and Yin [17] designed a two-level algorithm, which simulated annealing as the upper level to minimize the worker idle time and the genetic algorithm as the lower level to minimize the production time. For more general coverage, the reader is referred to Ansari and Daxini [18] and Rachih, Mhada, and Chiheb [19]. Ant colony optimization (ACO) is a meta-heuristic algorithm that can be used to find approximate solutions to difficult optimization problems. Many research studies in the literature also use ACO to solve scheduling problems, such as Blum and Sampels [20] on group shop scheduling problems; Yang, Shi, and Marchese [21] on generalized TSP problems; and Xiang, Yin, and Lim [22] on operating room surgery scheduling problems. According to the above, it is known that the branch-and-bound algorithm and ACO may be effective in solving the scheduling problem in our study.

3. Integer Programming Models

In this section, to mathematically present the studied problem $1|bp - prec|\Sigma_j C_j$, we formulate two integer programming models. Since the problem's nature is set on permutations of jobs, we deploy two common approaches, sequence-based decision variables and position-based decision variables, for shaping permutation-based optimization problems. The models will be then implemented and solved by the off-the-shelf Gurobi Optimizer.

3.1. Position-Based IP

In the section, we focus on the decision that assigns $m + n$ activities at $m + n$ positions. Activities $1, 2, \ldots, m$ are setups and activities $m + 1, m + 2, \ldots,$ and $m + n$ are jobs. Therefore, an activity could be either a job or a setup operation. In the model, there are six categories of constraints; $(m + n)^2$ binary variables x; and two subsets of $m + n$ integer variables, e_l and C_k. Index $k \in \{1, 2, \ldots, m + n\}$ indicates the positions. We use the binary relation $(i, j) \in \mathcal{R}$ to indicate whether the setup i should finish before the job j starts. The variables used in the model are defined in the following:
Decision variables:

$$x_{i,k} = 1 \text{ if the activity } i \text{ is in the position } k; 0, \text{ otherwise.}$$

Auxiliary variables:

$$p_l: \text{ processing time of the activity } l;$$
$$C_k: \text{ completion time of the job in the position } k.$$

Note that extra variables, C'_k, are introduced for extracting the completion times of jobs. If a position k is loaded with a setup, then $C'_k \geq -M$, where M is a big number.

Position-based IP:

$$\min \sum_{k=1}^{m+n} C'_k$$

$$\text{s.t.} \quad \sum_{k=1}^{m+n} x_{l,k} = 1, \qquad \text{activity } l \in \{1,\ldots,m+n\} \text{ is assigned to a position;} \quad (1)$$

$$\sum_{l=1}^{m+n} x_{l,k} = 1, \qquad \text{position } k \text{ accommodates one activity;} \quad (2)$$

$$\sum_{k=1}^{m+n} x_{i,k} \cdot k \leq \sum_{k=1}^{m+n} x_{j,k} \cdot k, \qquad (i,j) \in \mathcal{R}, 1 \leq i \leq m, m+1 \leq j \leq m+n; \quad (3)$$

$$C_1 = \sum_{l=1}^{m+n} x_{l,1} \cdot p_l, \qquad \text{completion time of the first position;} \quad (4)$$

$$C_k \geq C_{k-1} + \sum_{l=1}^{m+n} x_{l,k} \cdot p_l, \qquad \text{completion time of position } k \in \{1,\ldots,m+n\}; \quad (5)$$

$$C'_k \geq C_k - (\sum_{i=1}^{m} x_{i,k}) M, \qquad (6)$$

$$x_{l,k} \in \{0,1\}, \qquad 1 \leq l,k \leq m+n; \quad (7)$$

$$C_k \geq 0, C'_k \geq 0, \qquad 1 \leq k \leq m+n. \quad (8)$$

The goal is to minimize the total completion time of jobs. Constraint (1) lets each position accommodate exactly one job or one setup. Constraint (2) lets each activity be assigned to exactly one position. Constraint (3) ensures that any job j can start only after its setup operations, i, are all finished. Constraint (4) lets the completion time of the first position be greater than or equal to the processing time of the event that occupied the first position. Constraint (5) defines the completion time of the position k to be greater than or equal to the completion time of $k-1$ plus the processing time of the event that is processed in the position k. Constraint (6) defines the completion time k' if the position k contains a job. The reason we added a variable is that if the objective function computes the completion time of jobs in $\sum_{k=1}^{m+n} \sum_{j=m+1}^{m+n} C_k \cdot x_{jk}$; it becomes quadratic. Therefore, we add an extra variable, C', to make the objective function linear, i.e., $\sum_{k=1}^{m+n} C'_k$.

3.2. Sequence-Based IP

In this section, the formulation approach is to determine the relative positions between each two activities. The model consists of five categories of constraints; $(m+n)^2$ binary variables x; and two subsets of $m+n$ integer variables, p_j and C_k.

Decision variable:

$$x_{i,j} = 1 \text{ if activity } i \text{ precedes the activity } j; 0, \text{ otherwise.}$$

Auxiliary variables:

p_l : processing time of the activity l;

Sequence-based IP: C_k : completion time of the activity k.

$$\min \sum_{k=m+1}^{m+n} C_k$$

s.t. $x_{i,j} + x_{j,i} = 1,$ $\quad i \neq j \in \{1, \ldots, m+n\};\quad$ (9)

$x_{j,i} = 0,$ $\quad (i,j) \in \mathcal{R}, 1 \leq i \leq m, m+1 \leq j \leq m+n;\quad$ (10)

$C_j \geq C_i + p_j + (x_{i,j} - 1)M,$ $\quad i \neq j \in \{1, \ldots, m+n\};\quad$ (11)

$C_i \geq sp_i,$ $\quad 1 \leq i \leq m;\quad$ (12)

$C_j \geq p_j + \sum_{(i,j) \in \mathcal{R}} sp_i,$ $\quad m+1 \leq j \leq m+n;\quad$ (13)

$x_{i,j} \in \{0,1\},$ $\quad 1 \leq i,j \leq m+n;\quad$ (14)

$C_k \geq 0,$ $\quad 1 \leq k \leq m+n.\quad$ (15)

The objective value is to minimize the total completion time of jobs except for setup operations. Constraint (9) limits the precedence between the two events. Constraint (10) means that if job j needs setup i, then setup i should come before job j. Constraint (11) lets the completion time of job j be greater than or equal to the completion time of job i plus the processing time of job j if job i precedes job j. Constraint (12) defines the completion time of event i if it is a setup. Constraint (13) defines the completion time of event j if it is a job.

4. Branch-and-Bound Algorithm

In this section, we explore a search tree that generates all permutations of jobs. In the branch-and-bound algorithm, there will be an upper bound representing the current best solution during the search process. In the process of searching, each node will calculate the lower bound once, and if the lower bound calculated is not better than the upper bound, the subtree of the node will be pruned to speed up the search. Therefore, we propose an upper bound as the initial solution, a lower bound for pruning non-promising nodes, and a property to check whether each node satisfies the condition when pruning the tree.

4.1. Upper Bound

First, we use an ACO algorithm coupled with local search to find an approximate solution as an upper bound, sorted by the settings of pheromone and visibility. Details about the ACO algorithm will be introduced in Section 5. Implementing a branch-and-bound algorithm with tight upper bounds helps converge the solution process faster.

4.2. Lower Bound

Lower bounds can help cut unnecessary branches that will never lead to a solution better than the incumbent one. Different approaches can be used to derive lower bounds. In our study, we compute a lower bound by sorting the remaining processing times of unscheduled jobs. We can express it as the $1|r_j|\Sigma C_j$ problem. When the setup operations of the scheduled jobs are complete, we can release these setup times. Then, we denote the unfinished setup operations as the release date of each job and implement the shortest remaining processing time (SRPT) method. The process with the least amount of time remaining before completion is selected to execute. Finally, we add the total current completion time of scheduled jobs and the result of the SRPT mentioned above as a lower bound. The Lower Bound algorithm is shown in Algorithm 1.

Algorithm 1: LowerBound

1 **Function** LowerBound(σ):
2     $LB = 0$;
3   **if** $length(\sigma) == n$ **then**
4         $LB = sum(\sigma)$;
5   **else**
6   sort the unscheduled jobs by the shortest remaining processing time;
7         $LB = sum(\sigma) + \text{SRPT}(\sigma_{unscheduled})$;
8   **return** LB.

4.3. Dominance Property

In this section, after we use the lower bound to prune nodes, we also propose a property of the branch-and-bound algorithm (Algorithm 2), which can also speed up node pruning and reduce tree traversal time. The content description and proof of the property are as follows:

Lemma 1. *Let $J = \{j_1, j_2, ..., j_k\}$ be the unscheduled jobs at a node X in the branch-and-bound tree. For any unscheduled job j_a, if there is another unscheduled job j_b such that the setups of j_b are all scheduled and $p_b \leq p_a$, then the subtree $X + j_a$ by choosing j_a as the next job to schedule can be pruned off because j_b precedes j_a in some optimal solution.*

Proof. Let σ be the sequence of scheduled jobs. Assume that there is an optimal solution (σ, j_a, L, j_b), where L is a sequence of the unscheduled jobs. When the setups of job j_a are not yet completed, its completion time C_a would be $C_\sigma + \sum_{i \in unfinished}^{m\ i \to a} sp_i + p_a$, and, when the setups of job j_b are completed, its completion time C_b would be $C_\sigma + C_a + C_L + p_b$, where C_L is the completion time of all jobs of L. Assuming the positions of j_b and j_a are swapped as (σ, j_b, L, j_a), we denote their completion times as C'_b, C'_L, and C'_a. At this point, C'_b will be $C_\sigma + p_b$, and C'_a will be $C_\sigma + C'_b + C'_L + \sum_{i \in unfinished}^{m\ i \to a} sp_i + p_a$. Suppose that if p_b is less than p_a, it makes C'_b less than C_b, which also makes the completion time of L shorter, to the benefit of both job j_y and L. When both C'_y and C'_L move forward, the result of C'_a will also decrease accordingly. According to the assumption, we know that the total completion time of (σ, j_b, L, j_a) will be smaller than that of (σ, j_a, L, j_b). Therefore, we can prune off the branch of node j_a, which will not lead to a better solution without sacrificing the optimality. □

Algorithm 2: Check Property

1 **Function** CheckProperty(J):
2   **forall** $j_a \in J$ **do**
3   **forall** $j_b \in J$ and $j_a \neq j_b$ **do**
4   **if** *the setups of j_b have finished* and $p_b \leq p_a$ **then**
5   **return** False;
6   **return** True.

4.4. Tree Traversal

In this section, we use three different tree traversal methods, depth-first search (DFS), breadth-first search (BFS), and best-first search (BestFS), to perform the branch-and-bound algorithm. Moreover, we also added the upper bound, lower bound, and property mentioned above into our branch-and-bound algorithm.

4.5. Depth-First Search (DFS)

DFS is a recursive algorithm for searching all the nodes of a tree and can generate the permutations of all the solutions. It starts at the root node and traverses along each branch before backtracking. The advantage of DFS is that the demand for memory is relatively low, but the disadvantage is that because of recursion, there will be a heavier loading in the stack operation, and it will take more time to find all the solutions. The DFS algorithm is shown in Algorithm 3.

First, the algorithm will obtain the upper bound from Line 15 and call the recursive DFS function. When we encounter the deepest node or have visited all of its children, we move backward along the current path to find the unvisited node to traverse. In the search process, we use LowerBound() and CheckProperty() to test whether we should continue to search down or not. If the lower bound is greater than or equal to the upper bound, or if the property is not met, we will prune the branch because it does not yield a better solution than the current one. This method can reduce the number of search nodes.

Algorithm 3: Depth-First Search

1 **Function** DFS($sequence, ub, \sigma, \sigma^*$):
2   **if** $length(\sigma) == n$ **then**
3   **if** $sum(\sigma) < ub$ **then**
4             $ub = sum(\sigma)$;
5             $\sigma^* = \sigma$;
6   **return** ub, σ^*;
7   **forall** $t_j \in sequence$ **do**
8         $\sigma.append(t_j)$;
9   denote $sequence_{unscheduled}$ as $sequence$ without t_j;
10   **if** LowerBound(σ) $< ub$ **then**
11   **if** CheckProperty($t_j, sequence_{unscheduled}$) **then**
12                $ub, \sigma^* =$ DFS($sequence_{unscheduled}, ub, \sigma, \sigma^*$);
13   **return** ub, σ^*;
14 $ub =$ UpperBound($sequence$);
15 $ub, \sigma^* =$ DFS($sequence, ub, [], \sigma^*$);

4.6. Breadth-First Search (BFS)

BFS is a tree traversal algorithm that satisfies given properties. It starts at the root of the tree, traverses all nodes at the current level, and moves to the next depth level. Unlike DFS, which will find a solution first, it will wait until the last level is searched to find all suitable solutions. In particular, this method uses a queue to record the sequence of visited nodes. The advantage of BFS is that each node is traversed by the shortest path, but the disadvantage is that it requires more memory to store all of the traversed nodes. It thus takes more time to search deeper trees.

The BFS algorithm is shown in Algorithm 4. First, the algorithm will obtain the upper bound by UpperBound() from Line 25. The BFS function starts from Line 2; we create a queue that uses the First-In-First-Out strategy. Lines 3 through 5 are the initial settings that we use to set a root. From Lines 6 to 24, we enqueue the root node and then dequeue the values in order. Then, we enqueue the unvisited nodes and recalculate the lower bound until there is no value in the queue. Before each enqueue, it is necessary to use LowerBound() and CheckProperty() to check whether the lower bound is smaller than the upper bound and whether it satisfies the property. It can reduce the number of visited nodes and shorten the execution time. In Line 12, we use the Without() function to obtain the nodes that have not been visited yet. The loop stops when the queue is empty, indicating that all nodes have been traversed.

Algorithm 4: Breadth-First Search
---
1 **Function** BFS(*sequence, ub*):
2   Let Q be a queue;
3   **forall** $t_j \in sequence$ **do**
4   **if** LowerBound(t_j) $< ub$ **then**
5   Q.enqueue(t_j);
6   **while** Q *is not empty* **do**
7        $\sigma = Q$.dequeue();
8   **while** LowerBound(σ) $\geq ub$ **do**
9   **if** Q *is empty* **then**
10   break;
11           $\sigma = Q$.dequeue();
12   **forall** $t_k \in$ Without(σ) **do**
13   σ.append(t_k);
14   **if** $length(\sigma) == n$ **then**
15   **if** $sum(\sigma) < ub$ **then**
16                $ub = sum(\sigma)$;
17                $\sigma^* = \sigma$;
18   **else**
19   **if** LowerBound(σ) $< ub$ **then**
20   **if** CheckProperty(t_k, σ) **then**
21   Q.enqueue(t_j);
22   **if** Q *is empty* **then**
23   break;
24   **return** ub, σ^*;
25 $ub =$ UpperBound(*sequence*);
26 $ub, \sigma^* =$ BFS(*sequence, ub*);

4.7. Best-First Search (BestFS)

BestFS works as a combination of depth-first and breadth-first search algorithms. It is different from other search algorithms that blindly traverse to the next node, it uses the concept of a priority queue and heuristic search, using an evaluation function to determine to which neighbor node is the best to move. It is also a greedy strategy because it always chooses the best path at the time, rather than BFS using an exhaustive search. The advantage of BestFS is that it is more efficient because it always searches through the node with the smaller lower bound first. On the other hand, the disadvantage is that the structure of the heap is difficult to maintain and requires more memory resources. Since each visited node will be stored in the heap, we can directly obtain the node with the smallest lower bound bound by heapsort. Therefore, when the amount of data is large, there will be too many nodes growing at one time, which will occupy a relatively large memory space.

The concept of the BestFS algorithm is the same as Algorithm 4. The difference is that in the BestFS function, we change the queue to a priority queue by using a min-heap data structure, where the priority order is sorted using the calculated lower bound, instead of using the FIFO order. The smaller the lower bound is, the higher the priority. When we use a heap to pop or push values, we will perform the function of heapify at the same time to ensure the heap is in the form of a min-heap. Heapify is the process of creating a heap data structure from a binary tree. Similarly, before each element is pushed into the heap, we use `LowerBound()` and `CheckProperty()` to check whether the lower bound is smaller than the upper bound and whether it satisfies the property.

5. Ant Colony Optimization (ACO)

Ant colony optimization (ACO) was proposed by Dorigo et al. [23] and Dorigo [24]. It is a meta-heuristic algorithm based on probabilistic techniques and populations. ACO is inspired by the foraging behavior of ants, where the probability of an ant choosing a path is proportional to the pheromone concentration on the path, that is, a large number of ant colonies will give positive feedback. When ants are looking for food, they constantly modify the original path through pheromones and, finally, find the best path. Initially, Ant System (AS) was used to solve the well-known traveling salesman problem (TSP). Later, many ACO variants were produced to solve different hard combinatorial optimization problems, such as assignment problems, scheduling problems, or vehicle routing problems. In recent years, some researchers have focused on applying the ACO algorithm to multi-objective problems and dynamic or stochastic problems. In ant colony optimization, each ant constructs its foraging path (solution) node by node. When determining the next node to move on, we can use dominance properties and exclusion information to rule out the nodes that are not promising. In comparison with other meta-heuristics, this feature may save the time required for handling infeasible or inferior solutions. The pseudo-code of ACO that we adopt is shown in Algorithm 5.

Algorithm 5: Ant Colony Optimization

---

1 **Function** ACO():
2   initialize the ACO parameters;
3   **while** *stopping criteria is not met* **do**
4   **foreach** *ants in population* **do**
5   generate the first job randomly;
6   **foreach** *unselected job* **do**
7   choose next job by the transition rule;
8   update local pheromone;
9   LocalSearch(*sequence*$_{lbest}$);
10   update pheromone based on the best solution.

State transition rule: We treat each job as a node in the graph and all nodes are connected. To choose the next edge, the ant will consider the visibility of each edge available from its current location, as well as the pheromones. The formula for calculating the visibility value is given by $\eta_{ij} = \frac{1}{\sum_{i \to j} sp_i + p_j}$, where η_{ij} is the visibility value from node i to node j, defined as the inverse of the processing time of job j plus its unfinished setup operations. Then, we will calculate the probability of each feasible path; the probability formula is given as $p_{ij}^k = \frac{\tau_{ij}^\alpha * \eta_{ij}^\beta}{\sum_{k \in unselected_i} \tau_{ik}^\alpha * \eta_{ik}^\beta}$, where τ_{ij} is the pheromone on the edge from node i to node j, $\alpha \geq 0$ is a parameter for controlling the influence of the pheromone, and $\beta \geq 0$ is a parameter for controlling the influence of invisibility. The next node is determined by a roulette wheel selection.

Pheromone update rule: When all ants have found their solutions, the pheromone trails are updated. The formula for updating the pheromones is defined as $\tau_{ij} = (1 - \rho) * \tau_{ij} + \triangle \tau_{ij}^k$, where ρ is the pheromone evaporation rate, and $\triangle \tau_{ij}^k$, the incremental of the pheromone from node i to node j by the kth ant, is $\tau_{ij}^k = \frac{Q}{\Sigma C_k}$ if the ant k traverses $edge_{i,j}$; 0, otherwise, where ΣC_k is the total completion time in the solution of the kth ant, and Q is a constant.

Stopping criterion: We set a time limit of 1800 s for the ACO execution. Once the course reaches the time limit, the ACO algorithm will stop and report the incumbent best solution.

To close the discussion of ACO features, we note that local search algorithms can improve on the ACO solution at each iteration and make the result closer to the global optimal solution. At the end of each ACO generation, we deploy a 2-OPT local search procedure to the best solution of each generation so as to probabilistically escape the incumbent solution away from the local optimum.

6. Computational Experiments

In this section, we generate test data for appraising the proposed methods. The solution algorithms were coded in Python, and the integer programming models are implemented on Gurobi 9.1.2 interfaced with Python API. The experiments were performed on a desktop computer with Intel Core(TM) i7-8700K CPU at 3.70GHz with 32.0 GB RAM. The operating system is Microsoft Windows 10. We will describe the data generation design and parameter settings in detail and discuss the experimental results.

6.1. Data Generation Scheme

In the experiments, datasets were generated according to the following rules, and all parameters are integers:

1. Six different numbers of jobs $n \in \{5, 10, 20, 30, 40, 50\}$ and different numbers of setup operations $m \in \{4, 8, 18, 25, 35, 45\}$.
2. A binary support relation array $\mathcal{R}$ of a size $n * m$ is randomly generated. If (s_i, t_j) belongs to $\mathcal{R}$, denoted by $r_{ij} = 1$, then job t_j cannot start unless setup s_i is completed. The probability for $r_{ij} = 1$ is set to be 0.5, i.e., if a generated random number ≤ 0.5, then $r_{ij} = 1$. Note that when $r_{ij} = 1$ for all i and j, the problem can be solved by simply arranging the job in the shortest processing time (SPT) order.
3. The processing times of jobs p_j were generated from the uniform distribution $[1, 10]$.
4. The processing times of setups sp_i were generated from the uniform distribution $[1, 5]$.
5. For each job number, three independent instances were generated. In total, 18 datasets will be tested, as shown in Table 1.

Table 1. Categories of datasets.

Datasets	n	m
$\mathcal{D}_1, \mathcal{D}_2, \mathcal{D}_3$	5	4
$\mathcal{D}_4, \mathcal{D}_5, \mathcal{D}_6$	10	8
$\mathcal{D}_7, \mathcal{D}_8, \mathcal{D}_9$	20	18
$\mathcal{D}_{10}, \mathcal{D}_{11}, \mathcal{D}_{12}$	30	25
$\mathcal{D}_{13}, \mathcal{D}_{14}, \mathcal{D}_{15}$	40	35
$\mathcal{D}_{16}, \mathcal{D}_{17}, \mathcal{D}_{18}$	50	45

6.2. Results of Integer Programming Models

In the experiments of the integer programming models, we ran two integer programming models on the dataset with a time limit of 1800 s. The results are shown in Table 2. If an IP model did not complete its execution of a dataset in 1800 s, its run time is denoted as "−". In the table, the *gap* column indicates the relative difference between the feasible solution found upon termination and the best proven lower bound. The gap values were in the output of Gurobi. The gap value is defined as: $gap(\%) = \frac{|ObjBound - ObjVal|}{|ObjVal|} \times 100\%$, where $ObjBound$ and $ObjVal$ are a lower bound and the incumbent solution objective, respectively. When the gap is zero we have demonstrated optimality. The column *best solution* represents the best result of all our proposed methods on the same dataset.

When n_k is 10, the sequence-based IP takes more than 1800 s, even though both methods can obtain the optimal solution. The position-based IP takes less time and ends up with a gap of 0%. When n_k is greater than or equal to 20, neither model can find the optimal solution within 1800 s, but there are still some solutions that can find the same solution as the best solution, such as $\mathcal{D}_{17}$ of the position-based IP and $\mathcal{D}_{13}$ of the sequence-based IP. As

n_k increases, the gap of the position-based IP will be greater than that of the sequence-based IP. However, when we compare it with the best solution, even if the objective value is the same as the best solution, the gap value is still very large, such as the position-based IP of $\mathcal{D}_{17}$ and the sequence-based IP of $\mathcal{D}_7$ to $\mathcal{D}_9$. It means that their lower bounds are not tight i.e., they have a significant deviation from the final feasible solution.

Table 2. Results of different IP models.

n_k	Datasets	Position-Based			Sequence-Based			Best Solution
		obj.	Time	gap	obj.	Time	gap	
5	$\mathcal{D}_1$	101	0.09	0%	101	0.10	0%	101
	$\mathcal{D}_2$	128	0.09	0%	128	0.10	0%	128
	$\mathcal{D}_3$	122	0.08	0%	122	0.10	0%	122
10	$\mathcal{D}_4$	461	246.11	0%	461	-	19%	461
	$\mathcal{D}_5$	423	46.10	0%	423	-	21%	423
	$\mathcal{D}_6$	457	355.95	0%	457	-	25%	457
20	$\mathcal{D}_7$	2055	-	44%	2052	-	53%	2052
	$\mathcal{D}_8$	1822	-	34%	1820	-	58%	1820
	$\mathcal{D}_9$	1670	-	46%	1662	-	57%	1662
30	$\mathcal{D}_{10}$	3609	-	50%	3602	-	61%	3597
	$\mathcal{D}_{11}$	3985	-	50%	4007	-	62%	3985
	$\mathcal{D}_{12}$	4448	-	62%	4469	-	66%	4424
40	$\mathcal{D}_{13}$	8196	-	72%	8168	-	66%	8168
	$\mathcal{D}_{14}$	7395	-	68%	7402	-	67%	7390
	$\mathcal{D}_{15}$	7975	-	70%	7935	-	66%	7935
50	$\mathcal{D}_{16}$	12,882	-	76%	12,963	-	66%	12,880
	$\mathcal{D}_{17}$	12,305	-	73%	12,374	-	67%	12,305
	$\mathcal{D}_{18}$	10,891	-	72%	10,953	-	66%	10,871

6.3. Results of Branch-and-Bound Algorithm

Table 3 shows the results of the branch-and-bound algorithm with three different tree traversal methods. We set the time limit to 1800 s. In this table, the column *node_cnt* represents the number of visited nodes. The *dev* column is an abbreviation for deviation, expressed as a percentage of the difference between the objective value and the best solution. The calculation formula is as $dev(\%) = \frac{(obj - best\ solution)}{best\ solution} \times 100\%$.

When n_k is less than 20, DFS and BestFS successfully find the optimal solutions, but their execution times and the number of visited nodes of BFS are much larger than others. Even if n_k is 20, BFS cannot find the optimal solution within the time limit. In addition, we can see that the execution time of BestFS is faster than that of DFS for a small number of jobs. When n_k is greater than or equal to 30, the three methods fail to find the optimal solution within the time limit. The number of visited nodes and the deviation of DFS are clearly lower than those of BFS and BestFS. The results indicate that DFS is more efficient than BFS and BestFS because the DFS algorithm is not a layer-order traversal but will backtrack after finding the solution. Therefore, BFS and BestFS may not be able to find any feasible solution within the time limit. To sum up, the performance of DFS is better than those of BFS and BestFS, so we will analyze the experimental results of DFS in detail in the next section.

Table 3. Results of different tree traversal methods.

n_k	Datasets	DFS				BFS				BestFS			
		obj.	node_cnt	Time	dev	obj.	node_cnt	Time	dev	obj.	node_cnt	Time	dev
5	$\mathcal{D}_1$	101	25	0.00	0.00	101	67	0.00	0.00	101	16	0.00	0.00
	$\mathcal{D}_2$	128	22	0.00	0.00	128	44	0.00	0.00	128	12	0.00	0.00
	$\mathcal{D}_3$	122	27	0.00	0.00	122	68	0.01	0.00	122	20	0.00	0.00
10	$\mathcal{D}_4$	461	203	0.06	0.00	461	4141	0.39	0.00	461	283	0.04	0.00
	$\mathcal{D}_5$	423	246	0.04	0.00	423	2518	0.27	0.00	423	128	0.02	0.00
	$\mathcal{D}_6$	457	1055	0.25	0.00	457	34,646	2.57	0.00	457	1788	0.18	0.00
20	$\mathcal{D}_7$	2052	34,798	69.07	0.00	7839	1,940,323	-	2.82	2052	33,393	22.62	0.00
	$\mathcal{D}_8$	1820	44,844	77.49	0.00	6651	2,081,103	-	2.65	1820	44,166	22.03	0.00
	$\mathcal{D}_9$	1662	201,418	314.67	0.00	6211	2,078,269	-	2.74	1662	172,094	96.32	0.00
30	$\mathcal{D}_{10}$	3605	440,015	-	0.00	18,533	1,482,922	-	4.15	18,533	1,903,404	-	4.15
	$\mathcal{D}_{11}$	4053	385,433	-	0.02	22,005	1,083,532	-	4.52	22,055	1,064,974	-	4.53
	$\mathcal{D}_{12}$	4470	392,869	-	0.01	22,990	1,165,534	-	4.20	22,990	1,423,640	-	4.20
40	$\mathcal{D}_{13}$	8357	189,796	-	0.02	51,610	846,721	-	5.32	51,610	769,918	-	5.32
	$\mathcal{D}_{14}$	7564	176,723	-	0.02	44,779	873,638	-	5.06	44,779	1,112,645	-	5.06
	$\mathcal{D}_{15}$	8074	185,522	-	0.02	49,102	888,079	-	5.19	49,102	1,094,652	-	5.19
50	$\mathcal{D}_{16}$	13,007	74,873	-	0.01	106,541	856,905	-	7.27	106,541	954,605	-	7.27
	$\mathcal{D}_{17}$	12,527	84,980	-	0.02	97,383	933,536	-	6.91	97,383	1,047,559	-	6.91
	$\mathcal{D}_{18}$	11,255	90,908	-	0.04	87,545	1,055,329	-	7.05	87,545	1,181,533	-	7.05

6.4. Results of DFS Algorithm

In the experiment, we compare three different cases, including the original DFS algorithm, DFS with the lower bound, and DFS with the dominance property. Table 4 shows the experimental results of the different cases and also compares their objective values (*obj.*), numbers of visited nodes (*node_cnt*), execution times (*time*), and deviations (*dev*) from the best solution.

We can find that when the lower bound and properties are incorporated into DFS, the number of visited nodes is significantly reduced. Since this method will cut off unhelpful branches, it can also speed up the traversal, making it easier to find better solutions. Even when n_k is greater than or equal to 30, none of the three cases can find the best solution within the time limit. However, compared with the original DFS, DFS with a lower bound and DFS with a dominance property attained smaller deviations, indicating the capability of finding solutions closer to the best solution.

Table 4. Results of DFS algorithm.

n_k	Datasets	DFS				DFS + LB				DFS + LB + Property			
		obj.	node_cnt	Time	dev	obj.	node_cnt	Time	dev	obj.	node_cnt	Time	dev
5	$\mathcal{D}_1$	101	325	0.00	0.00	101	28	0.00	0.00	101	25	0.00	0.00
	$\mathcal{D}_2$	128	325	0.00	0.00	128	48	0.00	0.00	128	22	0.00	0.00
	$\mathcal{D}_3$	122	325	0.00	0.00	122	27	0.00	0.00	122	27	0.00	0.00
10	$\mathcal{D}_4$	461	9,864,100	173.53	0.00	461	614	0.11	0.00	461	203	0.07	0.00
	$\mathcal{D}_5$	423	9,864,100	174.60	0.00	423	626	0.09	0.00	423	246	0.05	0.00
	$\mathcal{D}_6$	457	9,864,100	182.09	0.00	457	2381	0.51	0.00	457	1055	0.25	0.00
20	$\mathcal{D}_7$	2174	27,177,572	-	0.06	2052	135,187	230.35	0.00	2052	34,798	69.07	0.00
	$\mathcal{D}_8$	2145	28,810,807	-	0.18	1820	287,087	429.71	0.00	1820	44,844	77.49	0.00
	$\mathcal{D}_9$	1904	29,472,356	-	0.15	1662	1,006,390	1405.52	0.00	1662	201,418	314.67	0.00
30	$\mathcal{D}_{10}$	4229	14,013,551	-	0.18	3679	426,340	-	0.02	3605	440,015	-	0.00
	$\mathcal{D}_{11}$	4757	13,668,237	-	0.19	4211	462,562	-	0.06	4053	385,433	-	0.02
	$\mathcal{D}_{12}$	5087	14,077,620	-	0.15	4530	443,418	-	0.02	4470	392,869	-	0.01

Table 4. *Cont.*

n_k	Datasets	DFS				DFS + LB				DFS + LB + Property			
		obj.	node_cnt	Time	dev	obj.	node_cnt	Time	dev	obj.	node_cnt	Time	dev
40	$\mathcal{D}_{13}$	9557	7,184,349	-	0.17	8405	169,550	-	0.03	8357	189,796	-	0.02
	$\mathcal{D}_{14}$	8505	7,327,087	-	0.15	7645	210,938	-	0.03	7564	176,723	-	0.02
	$\mathcal{D}_{15}$	9131	7,111,936	-	0.15	8250	210,891	-	0.04	8074	185,522	-	0.02
50	$\mathcal{D}_{16}$	14,629	4,136,372	-	0.14	13,196	104,445	-	0.02	13,007	74,873	-	0.01
	$\mathcal{D}_{17}$	14,272	4,189,689	-	0.16	12,911	119,416	-	0.05	12,527	84,980	-	0.02
	$\mathcal{D}_{18}$	12,901	4,254,099	-	0.19	11,522	114,774	-	0.06	11,255	90,908	-	0.04

6.5. Results of ACO Algorithm

In this section, we performed the ACO algorithm on the 18 datasets and set the time limit to 1800 s. Tables 5–7 summarize the results of the three branch-and-bound algorithms with ACO upper bounds. The results include objective values (*obj.*) and deviation (*dev*) of the ACO. The execution time of the ACO algorithm is much shorter than that of the branch-and-bound algorithm. In addition, we will compare the objective value (*obj.*), the number of visited nodes (*node_cnt*), and the execution times, (*time*), of the original algorithm and the algorithm with ACO as the upper bound. The ACO parameters used in the experiments are shown as follows: $generation = 300$; $population = 20$; $\alpha = 3$; $\beta = 1$, and $\rho = 0.1$.

As can be seen from the experimental table, the deviation of the ACO is small and an even better solution can be found than IP models within 1800 s. Therefore, we can use the ACO as the initial value of the upper bound (ub) to speed up the tree traversal time.

When the branch-and-bound algorithm is executing with the test $lb < ub$, the ACO can make ub smaller, cutting more unnecessary branches. According to the tables, when n_k is less than or equal to 20, the algorithm with an upper bound finds the best solution in a shorter time and visits fewer nodes; especially for the ACO in BFS, this is more obvious. As the value of n_k becomes larger, it increases the probability of the algorithm finding the best solution within the same time limit. In summary, using the ACO solution as an upper bound can make the branch-and-bound algorithm perform better.

Table 5. Results of DFS with ACO upper bounds.

n_k	Datasets	DFS			ACO		DFS + ACO		
		obj.	node_cnt	Time	obj.	dev	obj.	node_cnt	Time
5	$\mathcal{D}_1$	101	25	0.00	101	0.00	101	5	0.00
	$\mathcal{D}_2$	128	22	0.00	128	0.00	128	7	0.00
	$\mathcal{D}_3$	122	27	0.00	122	0.00	122	4	0.00
10	$\mathcal{D}_4$	461	203	0.06	461	0.00	461	112	0.06
	$\mathcal{D}_5$	423	246	0.04	427	0.01	423	75	0.04
	$\mathcal{D}_6$	457	1055	0.25	464	0.02	457	954	0.25
20	$\mathcal{D}_7$	2052	34,798	69.07	2058	0.00	2052	32,861	64.83
	$\mathcal{D}_8$	1820	44,844	77.49	1868	0.03	1820	43,257	72.69
	$\mathcal{D}_9$	1662	201,418	314.67	1668	0.00	1662	157,071	243.59
30	$\mathcal{D}_{10}$	3605	440,015	-	3616	0.01	3597	433,789	-
	$\mathcal{D}_{11}$	4053	385,433	-	3986	0.00	3985	373,573	-
	$\mathcal{D}_{12}$	4470	392,869	-	4424	0.00	4424	357,690	-
40	$\mathcal{D}_{13}$	8357	189,796	-	8282	0.01	8282	159,727	-
	$\mathcal{D}_{14}$	7564	176,723	-	7390	0.00	7390	131,500	-
	$\mathcal{D}_{15}$	8074	185,522	-	7967	0.00	7967	145,476	-
50	$\mathcal{D}_{16}$	13,007	74873	-	12,880	0.00	12,880	69,077	-
	$\mathcal{D}_{17}$	12,527	84,980	-	12,587	0.02	12,527	83,440	-
	$\mathcal{D}_{18}$	11,255	90,908	-	10,871	0.00	10,871	71,311	-

Table 6. Results of BFS with ACO upper bounds.

n_k	Datasets	BFS			ACO		BFS + ACO		
		obj.	node_cnt	Time	obj.	Deviation	obj.	node_cnt	Time
5	$\mathcal{D}_1$	101	67	0.00	101	0.00	101	4	0.00
	$\mathcal{D}_2$	128	44	0.00	128	0.00	128	3	0.00
	$\mathcal{D}_3$	122	68	0.01	122	0.00	122	4	0.00
10	$\mathcal{D}_4$	461	4141	0.39	461	0.00	461	96	0.04
	$\mathcal{D}_5$	423	2518	0.27	427	0.01	423	118	0.03
	$\mathcal{D}_6$	457	34,646	2.57	464	0.02	457	2578	0.40
20	$\mathcal{D}_7$	7839	1,940,323	-	2058	0.00	2052	43,231	33.67
	$\mathcal{D}_8$	6651	2,081,103	-	1868	0.03	1868	3,185,673	-
	$\mathcal{D}_9$	6211	2,078,269	-	1668	0.00	1662	79,117	124.83
30	$\mathcal{D}_{10}$	18,533	1,482,922	-	3616	0.01	3616	782,158	-
	$\mathcal{D}_{11}$	22,005	1,083,532	-	3986	0.00	3986	394,009	-
	$\mathcal{D}_{12}$	22,990	1,165,534	-	4424	0.00	4424	485,726	-
40	$\mathcal{D}_{13}$	51,610	846,721	-	8282	0.01	8282	649,800	-
	$\mathcal{D}_{14}$	44,779	873,638	-	7390	0.00	7390	532,584	-
	$\mathcal{D}_{15}$	49,102	888,079	-	7967	0.00	7967	702,847	-
50	$\mathcal{D}_{16}$	106,541	856,905	-	12,880	0.00	12,880	682,047	-
	$\mathcal{D}_{17}$	97,383	933,536	-	12,587	0.02	12,587	927,886	-
	$\mathcal{D}_{18}$	87,545	1,055,329	-	10,871	0.00	10,871	820,528	-

Table 7. Results of BestFS with ACO upper bounds.

n_k	Datasets	BestFS			ACO		BestFS + ACO		
		obj.	node_cnt	Time	obj.	Deviation	obj.	node_cnt	Time
5	$\mathcal{D}_1$	101	16	0.00	101	0.00	101	4	0.00
	$\mathcal{D}_2$	128	12	0.00	128	0.00	128	3	0.00
	$\mathcal{D}_3$	122	20	0.00	122	0.00	122	4	0.00
10	$\mathcal{D}_4$	461	283	0.04	461	0.00	461	96	0.04
	$\mathcal{D}_5$	423	128	0.02	427	0.01	423	61	0.02
	$\mathcal{D}_6$	457	1788	0.18	464	0.02	457	1333	0.18
20	$\mathcal{D}_7$	2052	33,393	22.62	2058	0.00	2052	13,380	24.48
	$\mathcal{D}_8$	1820	44,166	22.03	1868	0.03	1820	39,031	25.69
	$\mathcal{D}_9$	1662	172,094	96.32	1668	0.00	1662	71,082	100.10
30	$\mathcal{D}_{10}$	18,533	1,903,404	-	3616	0.01	3616	1,350,098	-
	$\mathcal{D}_{11}$	22,055	1,064,974	-	3986	0.00	3986	518,619	-
	$\mathcal{D}_{12}$	22,990	1,423,640	-	4424	0.00	4424	648,245	-
40	$\mathcal{D}_{13}$	51,610	769,918	-	8282	0.01	8282	790,216	-
	$\mathcal{D}_{14}$	44,779	1,112,645	-	7390	0.00	7390	971,168	-
	$\mathcal{D}_{15}$	49,102	1,094,652	-	7967	0.00	7967	1,087,057	-
50	$\mathcal{D}_{16}$	106,541	954,605	-	12,880	0.00	12,880	888,985	-
	$\mathcal{D}_{17}$	97,383	1,047,559	-	12,587	0.02	12,587	1,078,245	-
	$\mathcal{D}_{18}$	87,545	1,181,533	-	10,871	0.00	10,871	1,181,376	-

To summarize the computational study, we note that the two proposed integer programming approaches and the branch-and-bound algorithm, aimed at solving the problem to optimality, can complete their execution courses for 20 jobs or less. For larger instances, these exact two approaches become inferior. When reaching the specified time limit, the reported solutions are not favorable. Another observation is about the three traversal strategies. DFS has its advantages in its easy implementations (by straightforward recursions) and minimum memory requirement. The BFS and BestFS strategies are known to show their significance in maintaining acquired information about the quality of the unexplored nodes in a priority queue. On the other hand, they suffer from the memory space and heap manipulation work for the unexplored nodes. BFS and BestFS would be preferred when a larger memory is available and advanced data structure manipulations are available.

7. Conclusions and Future Works

In this paper, we studied the scheduling problem with shared common setups of the minimum total completion time. We proposed two integer programming models and the branch-and-bound algorithm, which incorporates three tree traversal strategies and the initial solutions yielded from an ACO algorithm. A computational study shows that the position-based IP outperforms the sequence-based one when the problem size is smaller. As the problem grows larger, the gap values for the sequence-based IP are smaller than those of the position-based IP. Similar to the branch-and-bound algorithm, the DFS performs best, regardless of whether lower bounds and other properties are used or not. Finally, we also observed that using ACO to provide an initial upper bound indeed speeds up the execution course of the branch-and-bound algorithm.

For future research, developing tighter lower bounds and upper bounds could lead to better performance. More properties can be found to help the branch-and-bound algorithm curtail non-promising branches. For integer programming models, tighter constraints can be proposed to reduce the execution time and optimality gaps to reflect a real-world circumstance in which multiple machines or servers are available for a software test project. In this generalized scenario, a setup could be performed on several machines if the jobs that it supports are assigned to distinct machines.

Author Contributions: Conceptualization, M.-T.C. and B.M.T.L.; methodology, M.-T.C. and B.M.T.L.; software, M.-T.C.; formal analysis, M.-T.C. and B.M.T.L.; writing—original draft preparation, M.-T.C. and B.M.T.L.; writing, M.-T.C. and B.M.T.L.; supervision, M.-T.C. and B.M.T.L.; project administration, B.M.T.L.; funding acquisition, B.M.T.L. All authors have read and agreed to the published version of the manuscript.

Funding: Chao and Lin were partially supported by the Ministry of Science and Technology of Taiwan under the grant MOST-110-2221-E-A49-118.

Data Availability Statement: The datasets analyzed in this study are be available upon request.

Conflicts of Interest: The authors declare no conflict of interest.

References

1. Leung, J.Y.T. *Handbook of Scheduling: Algorithms, Models, and Performance Analysis*; CRC Press: Boca Raton, FL, USA, 2004.
2. Pinedo, M. *Scheduling*; Springer: Berlin/Heidelberg, Germany, 2016.
3. Kononov, A.V.; Lin, B.M.T.; Fang, K.T. Single-machine scheduling with supporting tasks. *Discret. Optim.* **2015**, *17*, 69–79. [CrossRef]
4. Graham, R.; Lawler, E.L.; Lenstra, J.K.; Kan, A.R. Optimization and approximation in deterministic sequencing and scheduling: A survey. *Ann. Discret. Math.* **1979**, *5*, 287–326.
5. Brucker, P. *Scheduling Algorithms*; Springer: Berlin/Heidelberg, Germany, 2013.
6. Baker, K.E. Single Machine Sequencing with Weighting Factors and Precedence Constraints. Unpublished papers, 1971.
7. Adolphson, D.; Hu, T.C. Optimal linear ordering. *Siam J. Appl. Math.* **1973**, *25*, 403–423. [CrossRef]
8. Lawler, E.L. Sequencing jobs to minimize total weighted completion time subject to precedence constraints. *Ann. Discret. Math.* **1978**, *2*, 75–90.
9. Hassin, R.; Levin, A. An approximation algorithm for the minimum latency set cover problem. In *Lecture Notes in Computer Science*; Springer: Berlin/Heidelberg, Germany, 2005; Volume 3669, pp. 726–733.
10. Shafransky, Y.M.; Strusevich, V.A. The open shop scheduling problem with a given sequence of jobs on one machine. *Nav. Res. Logist.* **1998**, *41*, 705–731. [CrossRef]
11. Hwang, F.J.; Kovalyov, M.Y.; Lin, B.M.T. Scheduling for fabrication and assembly in a two-machine flowshop with a fixed job sequence. *Ann. Oper. Res.* **2014**, *27*, 263–279. [CrossRef]
12. Cheng, T.C.E.; Kravchenko, S.A.; Lin, B.M.T. Server scheduling on parallel dedicated machines with fixed job sequences. *Nav. Res. Logist.* **2019**, *66*, 321–332. [CrossRef]

3. Brucker, P.; Jurisch, B.; Sievers, B. A branch and bound algorithm for the job-shop scheduling problem. *Discret. Appl. Math.* **1994**, *49*, 107–127. [CrossRef]
4. Hadjar, A.; Marcotte, O.; Soumis, F. A branch-and-cut algorithm for the multiple sepot Vehicle Scheduling Problem. *Oper. Res.* **2006**, *54*, 130–149. [CrossRef]
5. Kunhare, N.; Tiwari, R.; Dhar, J. Particle swarm optimization and feature selection for intrusion detection system. *Sādhanā* **2020**, *45*, 109. [CrossRef]
6. Kunhare, N.; Tiwari, R.; Dhar, J. Intrusion detection system using hybrid classifiers with meta-heuristic algorithms for the optimization and feature selection by genetic algorithms. *Comput. Ind. Eng.* **2022**, *103*, 108383. [CrossRef]
7. Luo, L.; Zhang, Z.; Yin, Y. Simulated annealing and genetic algorithm based method for a bi-level seru loading problem with worker assignment in seru production systems. *J. Ind. Manag. Optim.* **2021**, *17*, 779–803. [CrossRef]
8. Ansari, Z.N.; Daxini, S.D. A state-of-the-art review on meta-heuristics application in remanufacturing. *Arch. Comput. Methods Eng.* **2022**, *29*, 427–470. [CrossRef]
9. Rachih, H.; Mhada, F.Z.; Chiheb, R. Meta-heuristics for reverse logistics: A literature review and perspectives. *Comput. Ind. Eng.* **2019**, *127*, 45–62. [CrossRef]
10. Blum, C.; Sampels, M. An ant colony optimization algorithm for shop scheduling problems. *J. Math. Model. Algorithms* **2004**, *3*, 285–308. [CrossRef]
11. Yang, J.; Shi, X.; Marchese, M.; Liang, Y. An ant colony optimization method for generalized TSP problem. *Prog. Nat. Sci.* **2008**, *18*, 1417–1422. [CrossRef]
12. Xiang, W.; Yin, J.; Lim, G. An ant colony optimization approach for solving an operating room surgery scheduling problem. *Comput. Ind. Eng.* **2015**, *85*, 335–345. [CrossRef]
13. Dorigo, M.; Maniezzo, V.; Colorni, A. *Positive Feedback as a Search Strategy*; Technical Report 91–016; Dipartimento di Elettronica, Politecnico di Milano, Milan, Italy, 1991.
14. Dorigo, M. Optimization, Learning and Natural Algorithms. Ph.D. Thesis, Dipartimento di Elettronica, Politecnico di Milano, Milan, Italy, 1992. (In Italian)

Disclaimer/Publisher's Note: The statements, opinions and data contained in all publications are solely those of the individual author(s) and contributor(s) and not of MDPI and/or the editor(s). MDPI and/or the editor(s) disclaim responsibility for any injury to people or property resulting from any ideas, methods, instructions or products referred to in the content.

Article

Several Goethals–Seidel Sequences with Special Structures

Shuhui Shen * and Xiaojun Zhang

School of Mathematical Sciences, University of Electronic Science and Technology of China, Chengdu 611731, China; sczhxj@uestc.edu.cn
* Correspondence: shshen@std.uestc.edu.cn

Abstract: In this paper, we develop a novel method to construct Goethals–Seidel (GS) sequences with special structures. In the existing methods, utilizing Turyn sequences is an effective and convenient approach; however, this method cannot cover all GS sequences. Motivated by this, we are devoted to designing some sequences that can potentially construct all GS sequences. Firstly, it is proven that a quad of ± 1 polynomials can be considered a linear combination of eight polynomials with coefficients uniquely belonging to $\{0, \pm 1\}$. Based on this fact, we change the construction of a quad of Goethals–Seidel sequences to find eight sequences consisting of 0 and ± 1. One more motivation is to obtain these sequences more efficiently. To this end, we make use of the k-block, of which some properties of (anti) symmetry are discussed. After this, we can then look for the sequences with the help of computers since the symmetry properties facilitate reducing the search range. Moreover, we find that one of the eight blocks, which we utilize to construct GS sequences directly, can also be combined with Williamson sequences to generate GS sequences with more order. Several examples are provided to verify the theoretical results. The main contribution of this work is in building a bridge linking the GS sequences and eight polynomials, and the paper also provides a novel insight through which to consider the existence of GS sequences.

Keywords: Goethals–Seidel sequences; k-block and k-partition; symmetry and antisymmetry

MSC: 05B05; 05B20

Citation: Shen, S.; Zhang, X. Several Goethal–Seidel Sequences with Special Structures. *Mathematics* **2024**, *12*, 530. https://doi.org/10.3390/math12040530

Academic Editors: Alexander A. Lazarev, Frank Werner and Bertrand M. T. Lin

Received: 12 January 2024
Revised: 4 February 2024
Accepted: 6 February 2024
Published: 8 February 2024

Copyright: © 2024 by the authors. Licensee MDPI, Basel, Switzerland. This article is an open access article distributed under the terms and conditions of the Creative Commons Attribution (CC BY) license (https://creativecommons.org/licenses/by/4.0/).

1. Introduction

A square matrix H of order n is called a Hadamard matrix (HM) if its entries are ± 1 and any two different rows (columns) are orthogonal. The order n satisfies $n = 1, 2, 4m$ with m being a positive integer, and a well-known conjecture related to HMs is whether a Hadamard matrix of order $4m$ exists for any m. HMs are widely applied in many fields, including signal processing, coding and cryptography, while the smallest order of an unconstructed HM is 668. More interesting properties and applications of HMs can be found in [1–4] and the references therein.

The construction of HMs is a classic problem in combinatorics, and many works have been devoted to it in past decades, such as Kronecker products [5], orthogonal designs [6], difference families [7] and many other methods [1,8–13]. In the existing methods, many are required to construct circulant matrices and then plug these constructed circulant matrices into some type of arrays such as the Williamson array and GS array [3,14]. In this paper, we will make use of a GS array taking the form of

$$G = \begin{pmatrix} A & BR & CR & DR \\ -BR & A & D^T R & -C^T R \\ -CR & -D^T R & A & B^T R \\ -DR & C^T R & -B^T R & A \end{pmatrix},$$

where A, B, C and D are four circulant matrices of order n satisfying

$$AA^T + BB^T + CC^T + DD^T = 4nI_n, \quad (1)$$

and R is the back-diagonal identity matrix of order n. The fact that A, B, C and D are circulant matrices implies that they are sufficient for the purposes of constructing the first rows of them, which are denoted by four sequences, i.e., a, b, c and d, respectively. If matrices A, B, C and D with entries ± 1 satisfy condition (1), then a, b, c and d are called a quad of GS sequences, and they are particularly said to be a quad of Williamson sequences if A, B, C and D are also symmetrical.

In [15], Goethals and Seidel conducted pioneering work on the GS array and obtained the HMs of a GS type with orders of 36 and 52. In [16,17], Whiteman utilized the Parseval relation to theoretically construct GS sequences of order $\frac{q_1+1}{4}$ and Williamson sequences of order $\frac{q_2+1}{2}$ in a finite field $GF(q_1^2)$ and $GF(q_2^2)$, respectively, where $q_1 \equiv (3 \mod 8)$ and $q_2 \equiv (1 \mod 4)$ are both prime powers. With the help of computers by exhaustive search, Doković studied the GS array and GS sequences in numerous works, where many different orders were obtained, as seen in [18–21] et al. Making use of Lagrange identity for polynomials (LIP), Yang—in [22]—proved that a quad of Williamson sequences of order n and a four-symbol δ-code of order m can be used to construct a quad of GS sequences of order mn. Yang also presented some other results [23–26], where the construction of GS sequences was mainly based on using two groups of sequences that were known beforehand.

In addition to the methods mentioned above, utilizing T-sequences directly is an alternative method, where a quad of GS sequences could be considered a linear combination of a quad of T-sequences, as shown in, e.g., [27]. The existing methods, however, have a slight drawback that not each GS sequences can be represented by a linear combination of T-sequences, as seen in Remark 1.

Motivated by this, we firstly defined the k-block and k-partition in this paper, which aid in dividing a quad of sequences into k parts. Next, we proved that a quad of ± 1 polynomials $\{F_i(\xi)\}_{i=1}^4$ associated with sequences $\{f_i\}_{i=1}^4$ can uniquely be considered a linear combination of eight polynomials $\{G_i(\xi)\}_{i=1}^8$ that are associated with sequences $\{g_i\}_{i=1}^8$ consisting of 0 and ± 1. For now, all of the GS sequences could be taken into consideration compared with the construction method by using T-sequences. In other words, the construction of GS sequences $\{f_i\}_{i=1}^4$ could be transformed into finding a group of k-partition $\{g_i\}_{i=1}^8$. Then, by supposing that $\{f_i\}_{i=1}^4$ are a quad of GS sequences, some relationships between associated polynomials $\{G_i(\xi)\}_{i=1}^8$ were revealed. To reduce the complexity of discussion, it is natural and necessary to impose some constraints on $\{G_i(\xi)\}_{i=1}^8$, e.g., the properties of symmetry or antisymmetry. Finally, by using k-partitions or k-blocks directly, we obtained some types of GS sequences with different symmetrical structures of $G_i(\xi)$. One was established by utilizing an eight partition, where three were based on nine partitions, and two used nine blocks. As an additional application, the eight partition mentioned above of order n, when combined with a quad of Williamson sequences of order m, can also lead to a quad of GS sequences with order mn. The theoretical results proposed in this paper are validated by some examples. This paper represents the first time that a quad of ± 1 sequences have been considered a combination of eight blocks, which ensures that all the "existing" GS sequences can be taken into consideration and that consequently more GS sequences can be potentially discovered. Moreover, when comparing with the results in [28] (where a rough discussion of GS sequences and k-partition was presented and there was no rigorous proof to reveal the bijective relation), in this paper, we extended the results that we not only proved the uniqueness of the linear combination, but also investigated some of the necessary conditions for the existence of these sequences.

The rest of the paper is organized as follows. In Section 2, we introduce some of the necessary notations and definitions needed in later analysis. In Section 3, it is proven that a quad of ± 1 sequences can be considered a linear combination of an eight block uniquely. Then, based on a k-block with (anti)symmetry properties, we constructed several

GS sequences and presented some examples to verify the theoretical results. In Section 4 by combining a quad of Williamson sequences of order m and an eight partition of order n (which was obtained above), a quad of GS sequences of order mn was constructed. Some conclusions will be made in Section 5.

2. Preliminaries

For a sequence $a = (a_0, a_1, \ldots, a_{n-1})$, its periodic autocorrelation function $R_a(\tau)$ is defined as

$$R_a(\tau) = \sum_{i=0}^{n-1} a_i \bar{a}_{i+\tau}, \quad \tau = 0, 1, \ldots, n-1,$$

where $\bar{a}_i$ is the conjugate of a_i, and the sum $i + \tau$ is evaluated as modulo-n. A polynomial

$$\Phi_a(\xi) = a_0 + a_1 \xi + a_2 \xi^2 + \cdots + a_{n-1} \xi^{n-1}$$

is called the associated polynomial of sequence a, where ξ is the n-th root of unity $e^{\frac{2\pi}{n}I}$ and $I = \sqrt{-1}$. The finite Parseval relation [17], also named the Wiener–Khinchin theorem [29,30], between $R_a(\tau)$ and $\Phi_a(\xi)$ is presented in the following identity

$$R_a(\tau) = \frac{1}{n} \sum_{j=0}^{n-1} \|\Phi_a(\xi^j)\|^2 \xi^{j\tau}, \quad \tau = 0, 1, \ldots, n-1,$$

and its inverse form is

$$\|\Phi_a(\xi^j)\|^2 = \sum_{\tau=0}^{n-1} R_a(\tau) \xi^{-j\tau}, \quad j = 0, 1, \ldots, n-1.$$

For the HMs of a GS type, their four circulant matrices possess the following property.

Lemma 1 ([16]). *Let A, B, C and D denote four circulant matrices of order n whose first rows are four sequences $a = \{a_i\}_{i=0}^{n-1}$, $b = \{b_i\}_{i=0}^{n-1}$, $c = \{c_i\}_{i=0}^{n-1}$ and $d = \{d_i\}_{i=0}^{n-1}$, respectively. Then, $AA^T + BB^T + CC^T + DD^T = 4nI_n$ if and only if*

$$\|\Phi_a(\xi^j)\|^2 + \|\Phi_b(\xi^j)\|^2 + \|\Phi_c(\xi^j)\|^2 + \|\Phi_d(\xi^j)\|^2 = 4n,$$

$j = 0, 1, \ldots, n-1$, *where ξ is the n-th root of unity.*

Hereafter, without special clarification, a capital letter such as $F_i(\xi)$ denotes the associated polynomial, the bold letter f_i represents the sequence and the lower case letter f_{ij} denotes the j-th element in f_i, where i and j rely on different cases. Before the discussion, some definitions are necessary to give.

Definition 1 (GS sequences, [22]). *Four ± 1 sequences $q_i = (q_{i0}, q_{i1}, \ldots, q_{i,n-1})$, $i = 1, 2, 3, 4$ are said to be a quad of GS sequences of order n if their associated polynomials $Q_i(\xi)$ satisfy*

$$\sum_{i=1}^{4} \|Q_i(\xi^j)\|^2 = 4n,$$

where ξ is the n-th root of unity for $j = 0, \ldots, n-1$.

Motivated by the definition of L-matrices ([3], Definition 4.15), we define a k-block and k-partition as follows.

Definition 2 (*k*-block and *k*-partition). *A class of sequences $g_i = (g_{i0}, \ldots, g_{i,n-1}), i = 1, \ldots, k$, is said to be a k-block of order n, if it holds*

$$
\begin{align}
&\text{(i)} \quad g_{ij} \in \{0, \pm 1\}, \quad j = 0, 1, \ldots, n-1, \ i = 1, 2, \ldots k, \\
&\text{(ii)} \quad \sum_{i=1}^{k} |g_{ij}| = 1, \quad j = 0, 1, \ldots, n-1.
\end{align}
\tag{2}
$$

If a k-block $\{g_i\}_{i=1}^{k}$ of order n additionally satisfies

$$
\text{(iii)} \quad \sum_{i=1}^{k} R_{g_i}(\tau) = n, \quad \tau = 0, \ldots, n-1,
\tag{3}
$$

we call $\{g_i\}_{i=1}^{k}$ a k-partition, where ξ is the n-th root of unity.

Definition 3 (symmetry and antisymmetry, [22]). *Let $F_i(\xi)$ be a polynomial associated with sequences $f_i = (f_{i0}, \ldots, f_{i,n-1})$. $F_i(\xi)$ is symmetrical (or antisymmetrical) if it satisfies*

$$\overline{F_i(\xi)} = F_i(\xi) \ (\text{or } \overline{F_i(\xi)} = -F_i(\xi)),$$

where ξ is the n-th root of unity. In other words, the coefficients $(f_{i0}, \ldots, f_{i,n-1})$ satisfy $f_{ij} = f_{i,n-j}$ (or $f_{ij} = -f_{i,n-j}), j = 1, 2, \ldots, n-1$.

3. Main Results

Inspired by [27], we extended the construction of GS sequences from four sequences to eight sequences. Then, we obtained the main result that a quad of ± 1 sequences can be uniquely considered a linear combination of an eight block, as stated in the following lemma.

Lemma 2. *The associated polynomials of sequences $\{f_i\}_{i=1}^{4}$ and $\{g_i\}_{i=1}^{8}$ are denoted by $\{F_i(\xi)\}_{i=1}^{4}$ and $\{G_i(\xi)\}_{i=1}^{8}$, respectively. Then, given a quad of ± 1 sequences $\{f_i\}_{i=1}^{4}$ of order n, there exists a unique eight block $\{g_i\}_{i=1}^{8}$ of order n such that the associated polynomials $\{F_i(\xi)\}_{i=1}^{4}$ can be uniquely written as a linear combination of the associated polynomials $\{G_i(\xi)\}_{i=1}^{8}$ that*

$$
\begin{align}
F_1(\xi) &= G_1(\xi) + G_2(\xi) + G_3(\xi) + G_4(\xi) + G_5(\xi) + G_6(\xi) + G_7(\xi) - G_8(\xi), \\
F_2(\xi) &= G_1(\xi) + G_2(\xi) - G_3(\xi) - G_4(\xi) + G_5(\xi) + G_6(\xi) - G_7(\xi) + G_8(\xi), \\
F_3(\xi) &= G_1(\xi) - G_2(\xi) + G_3(\xi) - G_4(\xi) + G_5(\xi) - G_6(\xi) + G_7(\xi) + G_8(\xi), \\
F_4(\xi) &= G_1(\xi) - G_2(\xi) - G_3(\xi) + G_4(\xi) - G_5(\xi) + G_6(\xi) + G_7(\xi) + G_8(\xi),
\end{align}
\tag{4}
$$

where ξ is the n-th root of unity.

Proof. We first prove the existence. In (4), it is evident that the coefficients on the left and right hand sides are equal to each other correspondingly. Thus, we can equivalently rewrite (4) in the form of the matrix multiplication

$$\mathbf{F} = (\widehat{H} \ \widetilde{H}) \begin{pmatrix} \widehat{\mathbf{G}} \\ \widetilde{\mathbf{G}} \end{pmatrix},$$

where we denote

$$\mathbf{F} = \begin{pmatrix} f_1 \\ f_2 \\ f_3 \\ f_4 \end{pmatrix}, \quad \widehat{\mathbf{G}} = \begin{pmatrix} g_1 \\ g_2 \\ g_3 \\ g_4 \end{pmatrix}, \quad \widetilde{\mathbf{G}} = \begin{pmatrix} g_5 \\ g_6 \\ g_7 \\ g_8 \end{pmatrix},$$

$$\widehat{H} = \begin{pmatrix} 1 & 1 & 1 & 1 \\ 1 & 1 & -1 & -1 \\ 1 & -1 & 1 & -1 \\ 1 & -1 & -1 & 1 \end{pmatrix}, \quad \widetilde{H} = \begin{pmatrix} 1 & 1 & 1 & -1 \\ 1 & 1 & -1 & 1 \\ 1 & -1 & 1 & 1 \\ -1 & 1 & 1 & 1 \end{pmatrix}.$$

Then, we split $\mathbf{F}$ into $\mathbf{F} = \widehat{\mathbf{F}} + \widetilde{\mathbf{F}}$ satisfying

$$\widehat{\mathbf{F}} = \widehat{H}\widehat{\mathbf{G}} \text{ and } \widetilde{\mathbf{F}} = \widetilde{H}\widetilde{\mathbf{G}},$$

which implies

$$\widehat{\mathbf{G}} = \frac{1}{4}\widehat{H}\widehat{\mathbf{F}} \text{ and } \widetilde{\mathbf{G}} = \frac{1}{4}\widetilde{H}\widetilde{\mathbf{F}}$$

since both $\widehat{H}$ and $\widetilde{H}$ are symmetrical Hadamard matrices.

Denote by $\mathbf{F}_j$ the j-th column of a Matrix $\mathbf{F}$, and by $p(j)$ the number of 1 in $\mathbf{F}_j$. Taking the structure of $\widehat{H}$ and the property of k-block (2) into consideration, it follows that $p(j) \in \{0, 2, 4\}$, and similarly we get $p(j) \in \{1, 3\}$ for $\widetilde{H}$. Then, it is natural to define

$$\widehat{\mathbf{F}}_j = \begin{cases} \mathbf{F}_j, & p(j) \in \{0, 2, 4\}, \\ 0, & p(j) \in \{1, 3\}, \end{cases} \text{ and } \widetilde{\mathbf{F}}_j = \begin{cases} \mathbf{F}_j, & p(j) \in \{1, 3\}, \\ 0, & p(j) \in \{0, 2, 4\}, \end{cases} \quad (5)$$

$j = 1, 2, \ldots, n$, which then guarantees the existence of the eight block $\{g_i\}_{i=1}^8$.

Further, we proceeded with the proof of uniqueness. Supposing that there exists another

$$\mathbf{G}^* = \begin{pmatrix} \widehat{\mathbf{G}}^* \\ \widetilde{\mathbf{G}}^* \end{pmatrix},$$

then we have

$$\widehat{\mathbf{F}}^* = \widehat{H}\widehat{\mathbf{G}}^* \text{ and } \widetilde{\mathbf{F}}^* = \widetilde{H}\widetilde{\mathbf{G}}^*.$$

Still, we considered it in view of each column. For a given j, either $\widehat{\mathbf{G}}_j^*$ or $\widetilde{\mathbf{G}}_j^*$ is equal to 0, because $\mathbf{G}^*$ also consists of an eight block $\{g_i^*\}_{i=1}^8$, which means only one of $\widehat{\mathbf{G}}_j^*$ or $\widetilde{\mathbf{G}}_j^*$ contains a non-zero element. This fact yields that either $\widehat{\mathbf{F}}_j^*$ or $\widetilde{\mathbf{F}}_j^*$ is equal to 0, and it must correspond to the splitting (5). Otherwise, the converse case $\widehat{\mathbf{F}}_j = \widetilde{\mathbf{F}}_j^*$ and $\widetilde{\mathbf{F}}_j = \widehat{\mathbf{F}}_j^*$ could not guarantee that the entries of $\mathbf{G}^*$ belong to $\{0, \pm 1\}$. As a result, we know $\widehat{\mathbf{F}} = \widehat{\mathbf{F}}^*$ and $\widetilde{\mathbf{F}} = \widetilde{\mathbf{F}}^*$, which eventually ensures the uniqueness of splitting (5). □

Next, we investigated the relationships between $G_1(\xi), G_2(\xi), \ldots, G_8(\xi)$. From (4), we arrive at

$$\sum_{i=1}^4 \|F_i(\xi)\|^2 = 4\sum_{i=1}^8 \|G_i(\xi)\|^2 + 2U(\xi) + 2\overline{U(\xi)}$$

with

$$\begin{aligned} U(\xi) = \; & G_1(\xi)\overline{G_5(\xi)} + G_1(\xi)\overline{G_6(\xi)} + G_1(\xi)\overline{G_7(\xi)} + G_1(\xi)\overline{G_8(\xi)} \\ & + G_2(\xi)\overline{G_5(\xi)} + G_2(\xi)\overline{G_6(\xi)} - G_2(\xi)\overline{G_7(\xi)} - G_2(\xi)\overline{G_8(\xi)} \\ & + G_3(\xi)\overline{G_5(\xi)} - G_3(\xi)\overline{G_6(\xi)} + G_3(\xi)\overline{G_7(\xi)} - G_3(\xi)\overline{G_8(\xi)} \\ & - G_4(\xi)\overline{G_5(\xi)} + G_4(\xi)\overline{G_6(\xi)} + G_4(\xi)\overline{G_7(\xi)} - G_4(\xi)\overline{G_8(\xi)}. \end{aligned} \quad (6)$$

Further, if $f_1, \ldots, f_4$ are a quad of GS sequences of order n, then we obtain

$$4n = \sum_{i=1}^{4} \|F_i(\xi)\|^2 = 4\sum_{i=1}^{8} \|G_i(\xi)\|^2 + 2U(\xi) + 2\overline{U(\xi)}. \tag{7}$$

Remark 1. *Note that the definition of the k-partition is actually the special case of L-matrices ([3], Definition 4.15). The reason why we emphasize it specifically in this paper is due to the important role it plays in the construction of GS sequences. After such construction has taken place, then it will be convenient to describe them. In particular, a quad of T-sequences [14] is a four partition.*

Remark 2. *In the existing works, e.g., [27], the method for constructing GS sequences is based on a quad of a four partition and the structure $\widetilde{H}$. In the proof of Theorem 2, it is seen that this method could not guarantee that all GS sequences can be taken into consideration. The result is extended that we construct the GS sequences from using a four partition into an eight partition.*

3.1. GS Sequences Based on a k-Partition

In this subsection, we begin with the identities (4) and (7) to construct GS sequences. From the definition of an eight partition, it is natural to obtain the following lemma.

Lemma 3. *For an eight partition $\{g_i\}_{i=1}^{8}$, $\{f_i\}_{i=1}^{4}$ are a quad of GS sequences if and only if*

$$U(\xi) + \overline{U(\xi)} = 0,$$

with ξ being the n-th root of unity, where $U(\xi)$ and $\overline{U(\xi)}$ are defined in (6).

Proof. A combination of (3) and (7) leads to the results immediately. □

Thus, we only need to construct an eight partition satisfying $U(\xi) + \overline{U(\xi)} = 0$. However, it is still challenging to find an eight partition directly, and—as a reduction—we imposed some conditions on the polynomials $G_i(\xi), i = 1, 2, \ldots, 8$, such as properties of symmetry or antisymmetry. We first recall an existing result.

Lemma 4 ([28]). *Let $\{g_i\}_{i=1}^{8}$ be an eight partition of order n and their associated polynomials $\{G_i(\xi)\}_{i=1}^{8}$ satisfy the following symmetry properties*

$$G_1(\xi) = \overline{G_1(\xi)}, \quad G_2(\xi) = \overline{G_2(\xi)}, \quad G_3(\xi) = \overline{G_3(\xi)}, \quad G_4(\xi) = \overline{G_4(\xi)},$$
$$G_5(\xi) = -\overline{G_5(\xi)}, \quad G_6(\xi) = -\overline{G_6(\xi)}, \quad G_7(\xi) = -\overline{G_7(\xi)}, \quad G_8(\xi) = -\overline{G_8(\xi)}, \tag{8}$$

where ξ is the n-th root of unity. Then, there exist a quad of GS sequences $\{f_i\}_{i=1}^{4}$ that are associated with the polynomials $F_1(\xi), \ldots, F_4(\xi)$ generated by (4).

It is evident that there exist a great deal of polynomial groups satisfying $U(\xi) + \overline{U(\xi)} = 0$. Here, we simply provide one more condition with different types of $\{G_i(\xi)\}_{i=1}^{8}$.

Theorem 1. *For an eight partition $\{g_i\}_{i=1}^{8}$, if their associated polynomials $\{G_i(\xi)\}_{i=1}^{8}$ satisfy the following symmetry properties*

$$G_1(\xi) = \overline{G_1(\xi)}, \quad G_2(\xi) = \overline{G_2(\xi)}, \quad G_3(\xi) = -\overline{G_3(\xi)},$$
$$G_4(\xi) = -\overline{G_4(\xi)}, \quad G_5(\xi) = -\overline{G_6(\xi)}, \quad G_7(\xi) = -\overline{G_8(\xi)}, \tag{9}$$

with ξ being the n-th root of unity, then $f_1, \ldots, f_4$ are a quad of GS sequences formed in (4).

Proof. It is easy to verify $U(\xi) + \overline{U(\xi)} = 0$ from (6) and (9). □

Two following groups of sequences are shown to verify Theorem 1. For $n = 8$,

$$g_1 = (+, 0, 0, 0, -, 0, 0, 0), \quad g_2 = (0, 0, 0, 0, 0, 0, 0, 0),$$
$$g_3 = (0, 0, 0, 0, 0, 0, 0, 0), \quad g_4 = (0, 0, +, 0, 0, 0, -, 0),$$
$$g_5 = (0, 0, 0, 0, 0, 0, 0, 0), \quad g_6 = (0, 0, 0, 0, 0, 0, 0, 0),$$
$$g_7 = (0, 0, 0, -, 0, 0, 0, -), \quad g_8 = (0, +, 0, 0, 0, +, 0, 0),$$

by (4), the GS sequences of order eight are

$$f_1 = (+, -, +, -, -, -, -, -), \quad f_2 = (+, +, -, +, -, +, +, +),$$
$$f_3 = (+, +, -, -, -, +, +, -), \quad f_4 = (+, +, +, -, -, +, -, -),,$$

for $n = 9$, they are

$$g_1 = (+, 0, 0, 0, 0, 0, 0, 0, 0), \quad g_2 = (0, 0, 0, 0, 0, 0, 0, 0, 0),$$
$$g_3 = (0, 0, 0, 0, 0, 0, 0, 0, 0), \quad g_4 = (0, 0, 0, 0, 0, 0, 0, 0, 0),$$
$$g_5 = (0, 0, 0, 0, +, -, 0, 0), \quad g_6 = (0, 0, 0, +, -, 0, 0, 0, 0),$$
$$g_7 = (0, 0, 0, 0, 0, 0, 0, -, -), \quad g_8 = (0, +, +, 0, 0, 0, 0, 0, 0),$$

and the GS sequences are

$$f_1 = (+, -, -, +, -, +, -, -, -), \quad f_2 = (+, +, +, +, -, +, -, +, +),$$
$$f_3 = (+, +, +, -, +, +, -, -, -), \quad f_4 = (+, +, +, +, -, -, +, -, -)..$$

In the process of creating the constructions above, discovering the relations between $g_1, g_2, \ldots, g_8$ still seemed complex. As such, we next changed the structure of $\{G_i(\xi)\}_{i=1}^{8}$ further. For a quad of Williamson sequences [31] $w_i = (w_{i0}, w_{i1}, \ldots, w_{i,n-1}), i = 1, 2, 3, 4$, it holds $w_{10} = w_{20} = w_{30} = w_{40} = 1$ and the associated polynomials potentially take the form of

$$W_1(\xi) = 1 - G_1(\xi) + G_2(\xi) + G_3(\xi) + G_4(\xi),$$
$$W_2(\xi) = 1 + G_1(\xi) - G_2(\xi) + G_3(\xi) + G_4(\xi),$$
$$W_3(\xi) = 1 + G_1(\xi) + G_2(\xi) - G_3(\xi) + G_4(\xi),$$
$$W_4(\xi) = 1 + G_1(\xi) + G_2(\xi) + G_3(\xi) - G_4(\xi),$$

where ξ is the n-th root of unity and the coefficients of $\{G_i(\xi)\}_{i=1}^{4}$ are of a four block. The associated polynomials $W_1(\xi), W_2(\xi), W_3(\xi), W_4(\xi)$ satisfy

$$4n = \sum_{i=1}^{4} \|W_i(\xi)\|^2 = \sum_{i=1}^{4} \|2G_i(\xi) + 1\|^2.$$

Inspired by this, it is reasonable to assume that the constant in (4) is contained in $G_1(\xi)$ and is 1, and following the analogous manner we can separate the constant 1 out. As a result, and slightly different from (4), the associated polynomials $F_1(\xi), \ldots, F_4(\xi)$ can be rewritten as

$$F_1(\xi) = 1 + G_1(\xi) + G_2(\xi) + G_3(\xi) + G_4(\xi) + G_5(\xi) + G_6(\xi) + G_7(\xi) - G_8(\xi),$$
$$F_2(\xi) = 1 + G_1(\xi) + G_2(\xi) - G_3(\xi) - G_4(\xi) + G_5(\xi) + G_6(\xi) - G_7(\xi) + G_8(\xi),$$
$$F_3(\xi) = 1 + G_1(\xi) - G_2(\xi) + G_3(\xi) - G_4(\xi) + G_5(\xi) - G_6(\xi) + G_7(\xi) + G_8(\xi), \quad (10)$$
$$F_4(\xi) = 1 + G_1(\xi) - G_2(\xi) - G_3(\xi) + G_4(\xi) - G_5(\xi) + G_6(\xi) + G_7(\xi) + G_8(\xi),$$

where ξ is the n-th root of unity and the coefficients of $G_1(\xi), \ldots, G_8(\xi)$ are of an eight block. Then, we have

$$\sum_{i=1}^{4} \|F_i(\xi)\|^2 = 4 + 4\sum_{i=1}^{8} \|G_i(\xi)\|^2 + 2U(\xi) + 2\overline{U(\xi)} + 2V(\xi) + 2\overline{V(\xi)}, \quad (11)$$

with

$$\begin{aligned}
U(\xi) = &\ G_1(\xi)\overline{G_5(\xi)} + G_1(\xi)\overline{G_6(\xi)} + G_1(\xi)\overline{G_7(\xi)} + G_1(\xi)\overline{G_8(\xi)} \\
&+ G_2(\xi)\overline{G_5(\xi)} + G_2(\xi)\overline{G_6(\xi)} - G_2(\xi)\overline{G_7(\xi)} - G_2(\xi)\overline{G_8(\xi)} \\
&+ G_3(\xi)\overline{G_5(\xi)} - G_3(\xi)\overline{G_6(\xi)} + G_3(\xi)\overline{G_7(\xi)} - G_3(\xi)\overline{G_8(\xi)} \\
&- G_4(\xi)\overline{G_5(\xi)} + G_4(\xi)\overline{G_6(\xi)} + G_4(\xi)\overline{G_7(\xi)} - G_4(\xi)\overline{G_8(\xi)}
\end{aligned}$$

and

$$V(\xi) = G_5(\xi) + G_6(\xi) + G_7(\xi) + G_8(\xi) + 2G_1(\xi).$$

Consequently, we only need to construct the eight block $\{g_i\}_{i=1}^{8}$ of order n, which together with $e := (1, 0, \ldots, 0)$ of order n actually makes up a nine partition.

Analogous to Lemma 3, $\{f_i\}_{i=1}^{4}$ are a quad of GS sequences if and only if $U(\xi) + \overline{U(\xi)} + V(\xi) + \overline{V(\xi)} = 0$. In this case, an observation of the structure of $V(\xi)$ led to some more concrete relationships between $G_1(\xi)$ and $G_5(\xi)$-$G_8(\xi)$. We still added some symmetry properties, as shown in the theorems below, and omitted the proof for compactness.

Theorem 2. *For a nine partition $e, g_1, \ldots, g_8$ of order n, if the associated polynomials $G_i(\xi)$ of sequences $g_i, i = 1, \ldots, 8$, satisfy*

$$G_1(\xi) = -\overline{G_1(\xi)}, \quad G_2(\xi) = \overline{G_2(\xi)}, \quad G_3(\xi) = \overline{G_4(\xi)},$$
$$G_5(\xi) = -\overline{G_5(\xi)}, \quad G_6(\xi) = -\overline{G_6(\xi)}, \quad G_7(\xi) = -\overline{G_7(\xi)}, \quad G_8(\xi) = -\overline{G_8(\xi)},$$

then we obtain a quad of GS sequences generated by (10).

In this case, note that all polynomials $G_i(\xi), i = 5, 6, 7, 8$, are antisymmetrical. The following two examples are shown to verify Theorem 2. For $n = 10$, we have

$$\begin{aligned}
g_1 &= (0,0,0,0,0,0,0,0,0,0), & g_2 &= (0,0,0,0,+,-,+,0,0,0), \\
g_3 &= (0,0,0,0,0,0,0,+,+,0), & g_4 &= (0,0,+,+,0,0,0,0,0,0), \\
g_5 &= (0,0,0,0,0,0,0,0,0,0), & g_6 &= (0,0,0,0,0,0,0,0,0,0), \\
g_7 &= (0,0,0,0,0,0,0,0,0,0), & g_8 &= (0,+,0,0,0,0,0,0,0,-),
\end{aligned}$$

which together with (10) lead to a quad of GS sequences of order 10 as follows

$$\begin{aligned}
f_1 &= (+,-,+,+,+,-,+,+,+,+), & f_2 &= (+,+,-,-,+,-,+,-,-,-), \\
f_3 &= (+,+,-,-,-,+,-,+,+,-), & f_4 &= (+,+,+,+,-,+,-,-,-,-).
\end{aligned}$$

For $n = 12$,

$$\begin{aligned}
g_1 &= (0,0,0,0,0,0,0,0,0,0,0,0), & g_2 &= (0,0,+,0,0,0,+,0,0,0,+,0), \\
g_3 &= (0,+,0,0,0,-,0,0,0,+,0,0), & g_4 &= (0,0,0,+,0,0,0,-,0,0,0,+), \\
g_5 &= (0,0,0,0,0,0,0,0,0,0,0,0), & g_6 &= (0,0,0,0,0,0,0,0,0,0,0,0), \\
g_7 &= (0,0,0,0,0,0,0,0,0,0,0,0), & g_8 &= (0,0,0,0,+,0,0,0,-,0,0,0),
\end{aligned}$$

we can obtain a quad of GS sequences of order 12

$$\begin{aligned}
f_1 &= (+,+,+,+,-,-,+,-,+,+,+,+), & f_2 &= (+,-,+,-,+,+,+,+,-,-,+,-), \\
f_3 &= (+,+,-,-,+,-,-,+,-,+,-,-), & f_4 &= (+,-,-,+,+,+,-,-,-,-,-,+).
\end{aligned}$$

Similarly, we can construct two more types of GS sequences in view of $V(\xi)$.

Corollary 1. *For $e, g_1, \ldots, g_8$ of order n being a nine partition, the associated polynomials satisfy*

$$G_1(\xi) = -\overline{G_1(\xi)}, \quad G_2(\xi) = \overline{G_2(\xi)}, \quad G_3(\xi) = -\overline{G_4(\xi)},$$
$$G_5(\xi) = -\overline{G_5(\xi)}, \quad G_6(\xi) = -\overline{G_6(\xi)}, \quad G_7(\xi) = -\overline{G_8(\xi)},$$

with the n-th root of unity ξ. Then, we obtain a quad of GS sequences $\{f_i\}_{i=1}^4$ defined by (10).

Here, in $G_i(\xi), i = 5, 6, 7, 8$, we obviously choose two of them as they were antisymmetrical and another two as they were antisymmetrical with each other. Again two examples are illustrated to verify Corollary 1. For $n = 6$, we have

$$g_1 = (0,0,0,0,0,0), \quad g_2 = (0,0,0,+,0,0),$$
$$g_3 = (0,0,0,0,-,0), \quad g_4 = (0,0,+,0,0,0),$$
$$g_5 = (0,0,0,0,0,0), \quad g_6 = (0,0,0,0,0,0),$$
$$g_7 = (0,0,0,0,0,-), \quad g_8 = (0,+,0,0,0,0),$$

which together with (10) leads to a quad of GS sequences of order 6

$$f_1 = (+,-,+,+,-,-), \quad f_2 = (+,+,-,+,+,+),$$
$$f_3 = (+,+,-,-,-,-,), \quad f_4 = (+,+,+,-,+,-).$$

For $n = 9$, we have

$$g_1 = (0,0,0,0,0,0,0,0,0), \quad g_2 = (0,0,0,0,0,0,0,0,0),$$
$$g_3 = (0,0,0,0,0,+,-,0,0), \quad g_4 = (0,0,0,+,-,0,0,0,0),$$
$$g_5 = (0,0,0,0,0,0,0,0,0), \quad g_6 = (0,0,0,0,0,0,0,0,0),$$
$$g_7 = (0,0,0,0,0,0,0,-,-), \quad g_8 = (0,+,+,0,0,0,0,0,0),$$

which we can use to obtain a quad of GS sequences of order 9

$$f_1 = (+,-,-,+,-,+,-,-,-), \quad f_2 = (+,+,+,-,+,-,+,+,+),$$
$$f_3 = (+,+,+,-,+,+,-,-,-), \quad f_4 = (+,+,+,+,-,-,+,-,-).$$

Corollary 2. *For a nine partition $e, g_1, \ldots, g_8$ of order n, the associated polynomials $G_i(\xi)$ satisfy*

$$G_1(\xi) = -\overline{G_1(\xi)}, \quad G_2(\xi) = \overline{G_2(\xi)}, \quad G_3(\xi) = \overline{G_4(\xi)},$$
$$G_5(\xi) = -\overline{G_6(\xi)}, \quad G_7(\xi) = -\overline{G_8(\xi)},$$

where ξ is the n-th root of unity. Then, the $\{f_i\}_{i=1}^4$ defined in (10) is a quad of GS sequences.

The last case is that in these four polynomials, two pairs are antisymmetrical with each other. We also provide two examples to verify Corollary 2. For $n = 6$, we have

$$g_1 = (0,0,0,0,0,0), \quad g_2 = (0,0,0,+,0,0),$$
$$g_3 = (0,0,0,0,+,0), \quad g_4 = (0,+,0,0,0,0),$$
$$g_5 = (0,0,0,0,0,-), \quad g_6 = (0,+,0,0,0,0),$$
$$g_7 = (0,0,0,0,0,0), \quad g_8 = (0,0,0,0,0,0).$$

(10) yields a quad of GS sequences of order 6

$$f_1 = (+,+,+,+,+,-), \quad f_2 = (+,+,-,+,-,-),$$
$$f_3 = (+,-,-,-,+,-), \quad f_4 = (+,+,+,-,-,+).$$

For $n = 9$, we have

$$g_1 = (0,0,0,0,0,0,0,0,0), \quad g_2 = (0,0,0,0,0,0,0,0,0),$$
$$g_3 = (0,0,0,1,0,0,0,1,0), \quad g_4 = (0,0,1,0,0,0,1,0,0),$$
$$g_5 = (0,0,0,0,1,0,0,0,-1), \quad g_6 = (0,1,0,0,0,-1,0,0,0),$$
$$g_7 = (0,0,0,0,0,0,0,0,0), \quad g_8 = (0,0,0,0,0,0,0,0,0),$$

which together with (10) results in a quad of GS sequences of order 9

$$f_1 = (+,+,+,+,+,-,+,+,-), \quad f_2 = (+,+,-,-,+,-,-,-,-),$$
$$f_3 = (+,-,-,+,+,+,-,+,-), \quad f_4 = (+,+,+,-,-,-,+,-,+).$$

3.2. GS Sequences Based on a Nine Block

In addition, if we only discuss the term $U(\xi) + \overline{U(\xi)}$ in (11), then we can obtain some results related to GS sequences.

Corollary 3. *For a nine block $e, g_1, \ldots, g_8$, the associated polynomials mentioned in (10) satisfy*

$$G_1(\xi) = -\overline{G_1(\xi)}, \quad G_2(\xi) = -\overline{G_2(\xi)}, \quad G_3(\xi) = \overline{G_3(\xi)},$$
$$G_4(\xi) = \overline{G_4(\xi)}, \quad G_5(\xi) = \overline{G_6(\xi)}, \quad G_7(\xi) = \overline{G_8(\xi)},$$

and

$$\sum_{i=1}^{4} \|F_i(\xi)\|^2 = 4 \sum_{i=1}^{4} \|G_i(\xi)\|^2 + \sum_{i=5}^{8} \|2G_i(\xi) + 1\|^2 = 4n,$$

where ξ is the n-th root of unity. Then, we have a quad of GS sequences by (10).

There is an example through which to verify Corollary 3. For $n = 5$, we have

$$g_1 = (0,0,0,0,0), \quad g_2 = (0,0,-,+,0),$$
$$g_3 = (0,0,0,0,0), \quad g_4 = (0,0,0,0,0),$$
$$g_5 = (0,0,0,0,0), \quad g_6 = (0,0,0,0,0),$$
$$g_7 = (0,+,0,0,0), \quad g_8 = (0,0,0,0,+),$$

which together with (10) leads to a quad of GS sequences

$$f_1 = (+,+,-,+,-), \quad f_2 = (+,-,-,+,+),$$
$$f_3 = (+,+,+,-,+), \quad f_4 = (+,+,+,-,+).$$

Corollary 4. *For a nine block $e, g_1, \ldots, g_8$, the associated polynomials satisfy*

$$G_1(\xi) = \overline{G_2(\xi)}, G_3(\xi) = \overline{G_4(\xi)}, G_5(\xi) = -\overline{G_6(\xi)}, G_7(\xi) = \overline{G_8(\xi)}$$

and

$$\sum_{i=1}^{4} \|F_i(\xi)\|^2 = 4 \sum_{i=3}^{6} \|G_i(\xi)\|^2 + \sum_{i \in \{1,2,7,8\}} \|2G_i(\xi) + 1\|^2 = 4n,$$

where ξ is the n-th root of unity. Then, a quad of GS sequences are generated by (10).

One example is presented to verify the results of Corollary 4. For $n = 9$, we have

$$g_1 = (0,0,0,0,0,0,0,0,0), \quad g_2 = (0,0,0,0,0,0,0,0,0),$$
$$g_3 = (0,0,0,+,-,0,0,0,0), \quad g_4 = (0,0,0,0,0,-,+,0,0),$$
$$g_5 = (0,+,+,0,0,0,0,0,0), \quad g_6 = (0,0,0,0,0,0,0,-,-),$$
$$g_7 = (0,0,0,0,0,0,0,0,0), \quad g_8 = (0,0,0,0,0,0,0,0,0).$$

which also yields a quad of GS sequences

$$f_1 = (+,+,+,+,-,-,+,-,-), \quad f_2 = (+,+,+,-,+,+,-,-,-),$$
$$f_3 = (+,+,+,+,-,+,-,+,+), \quad f_4 = (+,-,-,-,+,-,+,-,-).$$

Remark 3. *In order to construct the GS sequences, we transformed it into the construction of eight polynomials $G_1(\xi), \ldots, G_8(\xi)$. For some special cases, we were able to obtain $G_i(\xi)$ via a four partition such as through T-sequences and, in actuality, we also searched them directly with computers in some more general cases, where utilizing known symmetry and antisymmetry properties may significantly reduce the search range.*

4. GS Structures of Two Groups of Polynomials

We analyzed a quad of GS sequences with different structures in Section 3, and we now intend to utilize two groups of polynomials $\{E_i(\xi)\}_{i=1}^8$ and $\{G_i(\xi)\}_{i=1}^8$, which are associated with sequences $\{e_i\}_{i=1}^8$ and $\{g_i\}_{i=1}^8$ to construct several different GS sequences.

We changed the conditions from an eight partition to a four partition, which produced the following result.

Theorem 3. *Let $\{E_i(\xi)\}_{i=1}^4$ be the associated polynomials of Williamson sequences $\{e_i\}_{i=1}^4$ of order m, and let $G_1(\xi), G_2(\xi), G_7(\xi), G_8(\xi)$ of order n be chosen in Theorem 1, i.e., satisfying*

$$G_1(\xi) = \overline{G_1(\xi)}, G_2(\xi) = \overline{G_2(\xi)}, G_7(\xi) = -\overline{G_8(\xi)}.$$

Then, the four new polynomials, which are defined by

$$\begin{aligned} F_1(\xi) &= E_1(\xi)G_1(\xi) + E_2(\xi)G_2(\xi) + E_3(\xi)G_7(\xi) + E_4(\xi)G_8(\xi), \\ F_2(\xi) &= E_1(\xi)G_2(\xi) - E_2(\xi)G_1(\xi) + E_3(\xi)G_8(\xi) - E_4(\xi)G_7(\xi), \\ F_3(\xi) &= E_1(\xi)G_7(\xi) - E_2(\xi)G_8(\xi) - E_3(\xi)G_1(\xi) + E_4(\xi)G_2(\xi), \\ F_4(\xi) &= E_1(\xi)G_8(\xi) + E_2(\xi)G_7(\xi) - E_3(\xi)G_2(\xi) - E_4(\xi)G_1(\xi), \end{aligned} \quad (12)$$

satisfy

$$\sum_{i=1}^4 \|F_i(\xi)\|^2 = \sum_{i=1}^4 \|E_i(\xi)\|^2 \sum_{i=1}^4 \|G_i(\xi)\|^2 = 4mn.$$

Moreover, if $(m,n) = 1$, then the sequences $f_1, \ldots, f_4$ made up of the coefficients of $F_1(\xi), \ldots, F_4(\xi)$ are a quad of GS sequences.

Proof. Since Williamson sequences $\{e_i\}_{i=1}^4$ are symmetrical, it is easy to verify the results $\sum_{i=1}^4 \|F_i(\xi)\|^2 = 4mn$. Further, $(m,n) = 1$ guarantees that $\{f_i\}_{i=1}^4$ consists of ± 1. □

We now give an example for the sequences g_1, g_2, g_7, g_8 of the associated polynomials $G_1(\xi), G_2(\xi), G_7(\xi), G_8(\xi)$ in Theorem 3 of order $n = 8$,

$$g_1 = (+,0,0,0,+,0,0,0), \quad g_2 = (0,0,+,0,0,0,+,0),$$
$$g_7 = (0,0,0,+,0,0,0,-), \quad g_8 = (0,+,0,0,0,-,0,0)$$

and a quad of Williamson sequences e_i of order $m = 7$

$$e_1 = (+,+,-,-,-,-,+), \quad e_2 = (+,-,+,+,+,+,-),$$
$$e_3 = (+,+,-,+,+,-,+), \quad e_4 = (+,+,-,+,+,-,+).$$

As the application of (12), we can obtain a quad of GS sequences of order $mn = 56$ as follows

$$f_1 = (+,-,+,-,-,-,-,+,+,+,+,-,-,+,+,+,-,-,+,+,+,+,-,-,-,-,+,-,$$
$$+,+,+,+,-,+,-,-,+,-,+,+,-,-,+,-,-,+,+,-,+,-,-,+,-,+,+,+),$$
$$f_2 = (+,-,+,+,+,-,-,-,-,+,+,+,+,+,-,-,+,-,+,-,-,+,-,+,+,-,+,+,$$
$$+,+,+,-,+,+,-,+,-,-,+,-,+,-,-,+,+,+,+,+,-,-,-,-,+,+,+,-),$$
$$f_3 = (+,+,+,-,+,+,-,+,+,-,-,-,-,-,-,-,-,-,-,+,-,-,+,+,-,+,+,$$
$$+,-,+,+,+,-,-,-,+,+,-,+,-,+,-,+,-,+,-,+,+,+,-,-,+,+,+,-),$$
$$f_4 = (+,-,-,-,+,-,+,-,+,+,+,-,-,+,+,-,-,+,+,-,+,-,+,+,+,+,-,+,$$
$$+,+,-,+,+,+,+,+,+,-,+,+,-,-,+,+,-,-,+,+,+,+,+,-,+,-,-,-).$$

5. Conclusions

In this paper, we studied several special structures of a quad of GS sequences by using k-partitions or k-blocks with different symmetry properties. It has been rigorously proven that a quad of ± 1 sequences can be determined uniquely by an eight block. Then, we can write a quad of GS sequences into two forms (4) or (10), and we can then let $U(\xi) + \overline{U(\xi)} = 0$ in (7) or $U(\xi) + \overline{U(\xi)} + V(\xi) + \overline{V(\xi)} = 0$ in (11), respectively. This, consequently, reveals some of the relationships between these k-partitions or k-blocks, which are based on whether we can add some symmetry properties to obtain GS sequences with different structures. Moreover, through making use of some of the special structures of $\{G_i(\xi)\}_{i=1}^8$ of order n and Williamson sequences of order m, we managed to construct a quad of GS sequences of order $4mn$.

For now, to obtain the k-partitions and k-blocks, we completely made use of the computer by using an exhaustive search based on the symmetry and antisymmetry properties, which reduced the degree of computational consumption significantly. In the future, we will be devoted to discussing more sufficient or necessary conditions for the existence of a k-block in order to obtain more of the relationships between a k-block serving for the purposes of improving searching efficiency, and we will also try to determine the k-partition theoretically.

Author Contributions: Conceptualization, X.Z.; methodology, X.Z.; data curation, S.S.; writing—original draft, S.S.; writing—review & editing, S.S. and X.Z.; supervision, X.Z.; funding acquisition, X.Z. All authors have read and agreed to the published version of the manuscript.

Funding: This research was funded by National Natural Science Foundation of China, grant number 62371094.

Data Availability Statement: The authors confirm that the data supporting the findings of this study are available within the article.

Conflicts of Interest: We declare that we have no financial and personal relationships with other people or organizations that can inappropriately influence our work, there is no professional or other personal interest of any nature or kind in any product, service and/or company that could be construed as influencing the position presented in, or the review of, this paper.

References

1. Colbourn, C.J.; Dinitz, J.H. (Eds.) *Handbook of Combinatorial Designs*, 2nd ed.; Discrete Mathematics and Its Applications, Chapman & Hall/CRC: Boca Raton, FL, USA, 2007; pp. xxii+984.
2. Horadam, K.J. *Hadamard Matrices and Their Applications*; Princeton University Press: Princeton, NJ, USA, 2007; pp. xiv+263.
3. Seberry, J. *Orthogonal Designs*; Hadamard Matrices, Quadratic Forms and Algebras, Revised and Updated Edition of the 1979 Original [MR0534614]; Springer: Cham, Germany, 2017.

4. Seberry, J.; Yamada, M. *Hadamard Matrices Constructions Using Number Theory and Algebra*; John Wiley & Sons, Inc.: Hoboken, NJ, USA, 2020; pp. xxx+321.
5. Craigen, R. Constructing Hadamard matrices with orthogonal pairs. *Ars Combin.* **1992**, *33*, 57–64.
6. Baumert, L.D.; Hall, M., Jr. A new construction for Hadamard matrices. *Bull. Am. Math. Soc.* **1965**, *71*, 169–170. [CrossRef]
7. Turyn, R.J. A special class of Williamson matrices and difference sets. *J. Combin. Theory Ser. A* **1984**, *36*, 111–115. [CrossRef]
8. Farouk, A.; Wang, Q. Construction of new Hadamard matrices using known Hadamard matrices. *Filomat* **2022**, *36*, 2025–2042. [CrossRef]
9. Fitzpatrick, P.; O'Keeffe, H. Williamson type Hadamard matrices with circulant components. *Discret. Math.* **2023**, *346*, 113615. [CrossRef]
10. Harada, M.; Ishizuka, K. Hadamard matrices of order 36 formed by codewords in some ternary self-dual codes. *Discret. Math.* **2024**, *347*, 113661. [CrossRef]
11. Kratochvíl, J.; Nešetřil, J.; Rosenfeld, M. Graph designs, Hadamard matrices and geometric configurations. In *Graph Theory and Combinatorial Biology (BAlatonlelle, 1996)*; Bolyai Society Mathematical Studies; János Bolyai Mathematical Society: Budapest, Hungary, 1999; Volume 7, pp. 101–123.
12. Seberry, J. A résumé of some recent results on Hadamard matrices, (v, k, λ)-graphs and block designs. In *Combinatorial Structures and Their Applications (Proc. Calgary Internat. Conf., Calgary, Alta., 1969)*; Gordon and Breach: New York, NY, USA; London, UK; Paris, France, 1970; pp. 463–466.
13. Xia, T.; Zuo, G.; Lou, L.; Xia, M. Hadamard matrices of composite orders. *Trans. Comb.* **2024**, *13*, 31–40.
14. Seberry, J.; Yamada, M. Hadamard matrices, sequences, and block designs. In *Contemporary Design Theory*; John Wiley and Sons: Hoboken, NJ, USA, 1992; pp. 431–560.
15. Goethals, J.M.; Seidel, J.J. A skew-Hadamard matrix of order 36. *J. Aust. Math. Soc.* **1970**, *11*, 343–344. [CrossRef]
16. Whiteman, A. Skew Hadamard matrices of Goethals—Seidel type. *Discret. Math.* **1972**, *2*, 397–405. [CrossRef]
17. Whiteman, A. An infinite family of Hadamard matrices of Williamson type. *J. Comb. Theory A* **1973**, *14*, 334–340. [CrossRef]
18. Doković, D.V. Construction of some new Hadamard matrices. *Bull. Aust. Math. Soc.* **1992**, *45*, 327–332. [CrossRef]
19. Doković, D.V. Ten new orders for Hadamard matrices of skew type. *Univ. Beograd. Publ. Elektrotehn. Fak. Ser. Mat.* **1992**, *3*, 47–59.
20. Doković, D.V. Two Hadamard matrices of order 956 of Goethals-Seidel type. *Combinatorica* **1994**, *14*, 375–377. [CrossRef]
21. Doković, D.V.; Kotsireas, I. Goethals-Seidel difference families with symmetric or skew base blocks. *Math. Comput. Sci.* **2018**, *12*, 373–388. [CrossRef]
22. Yang, C.H. Hadamard matrices, finite sequences, and polynomials defined on the unit circle. *Math. Comp.* **1979**, *33*, 688–693. [CrossRef]
23. Yang, C.H. Hadamard matrices and δ-codes of length $3n$. *Proc. Am. Math. Soc.* **1982**, *85*, 480–482. [CrossRef]
24. Yang, C.H. A composition theorem for δ-codes. *Proc. Am. Math. Soc.* **1983**, *89*, 375–378. [CrossRef]
25. Yang, C.H. Lagrange identity for polynomials and δ-codes of lengths $7t$ and $13t$. *Proc. Am. Math. Soc.* **1983**, *88*, 746–750. [CrossRef]
26. Yang, C.H. On composition of four-symbol δ-codes and Hadamard matrices. *Proc. Am. Math. Soc.* **1989**, *107*, 763–776.
27. Cooper, J.; Wallis, J. A construction for Hadamard arrays. *Bull. Aust. Math. Soc.* **1972**, *7*, 269–277. [CrossRef]
28. Shen, S.; Zhang, X. Constructions of Goethals–Seidel Sequences by Using k-Partition. *Mathematics* **2023**, *11*, 294. [CrossRef]
29. Doković, D.V.; Kotsireas, I. Compression of periodic complementary sequences and applications. *Des. Codes Cryptogr.* **2015**, *74*, 365–377. [CrossRef]
30. Fletcher, R.; Gysin, M.; Seberry, J. Application of the discrete Fourier transform to the search for generalised Legendre pairs and Hadamard matrices. *Australas. J. Combin.* **2001**, *23*, 75–86.
31. Williamson, J. Hadamard's determinant theorem and the sum of four squares. *Duke Math. J.* **1944**, *11*, 65–81. [CrossRef]

Disclaimer/Publisher's Note: The statements, opinions and data contained in all publications are solely those of the individual author(s) and contributor(s) and not of MDPI and/or the editor(s). MDPI and/or the editor(s) disclaim responsibility for any injury to people or property resulting from any ideas, methods, instructions or products referred to in the content.

Article

Approximation of the Objective Function of Single-Machine Scheduling Problem

Alexander Lazarev [1], Nikolay Pravdivets [1,2,*] and Egor Barashov [1]

[1] V.A. Trapeznikov Institute of Control Sciences of Russian Academy of Sciences, 65 Profsoyuznaya Street, 117997 Moscow, Russia; jobmath@mail.ru (A.L.); barashov.eb@gmail.com (E.B.)
[2] Department of Mathematics, Faculty of Economic Sciences, HSE University, 11 Pokrovsky Boulevard, 109028 Moscow, Russia
* Correspondence: pravdivets@ipu.ru

Abstract: The problem of the approximation of the coefficients of the objective function of a scheduling problem for a single machine is considered. It is necessary to minimize the total weighted completion times of jobs with unknown weight coefficients when a set of problem instances with known optimal schedules is given. It is shown that the approximation problem can be reduced to finding a solution to a system of linear inequalities for weight coefficients. For the case of simultaneous job release times, a method for solving the corresponding system of inequalities has been developed. Based on it, a polynomial algorithm for finding values of weight coefficients that satisfy the given optimal schedules was constructed. The complexity of the algorithm is $O(n^2(N+n))$ operations, where n is the number of jobs and N is the number of given instances with known optimal schedules. The accuracy of the algorithm is estimated by experimentally measuring the function $\varepsilon(N,n) = \frac{1}{n}\sum_{j=1}^{n} \frac{|w_j - w_j^0|}{w_j^0}$, which is an indicator of the average modulus of the relative deviation of the found values w_j from the true values w_j^0. An analysis of the results shows a high correlation between the dependence $\varepsilon(N,n)$ and a function of the form $\alpha(n)/N$, where $\alpha(n)$ is a decreasing function of n.

Keywords: scheduling theory; single machine scheduling; total weighted completion times; approximation

MSC: 90B35

Citation: Lazarev, A.; Pravdivets, N.; Barashov, E. Approximation of the Objective Function of Single-Machine Scheduling Problem. *Mathematics* 2024, 12, 699. https://doi.org/10.3390/math12050699

Academic Editor: Javier Alcaraz

Received: 31 January 2024
Revised: 21 February 2024
Accepted: 23 February 2024
Published: 28 February 2024

Copyright: © 2024 by the authors. Licensee MDPI, Basel, Switzerland. This article is an open access article distributed under the terms and conditions of the Creative Commons Attribution (CC BY) license (https://creativecommons.org/licenses/by/4.0/).

1. Introduction

Scheduling theory is a branch of discrete optimization devoted to planning operations over time. The problems of scheduling theory are diverse, including, but not limited to, production scheduling, including human-robot collaborations [1], classical Resource-Constrained Project Scheduling Problem (RCPSP) [2], creating smart planning eco-systems [3], distributed scheduling problems [4], and dynamic systems [5]. However, classical problems for a single machine remain relevant, still capture the attention of the scientific community [6] and are also used in modern approaches of Industry 4.0 [7].

In the classical single-machine scheduling problem, there is a set of jobs with given release times, processing times and due dates. The goal is to schedule the jobs to proceed on the machine, minimizing some objective functions. A wide variety of studies of this problem can be found for such objective functions as the total or maximum lateness [8,9], the weighted number of tardy jobs [10], the total (weighted) completion time [11,12] or any arbitrary non-decreasing function of the completion time [13]. The idea is that the objective function is known and should be maximized or minimized.

In practice, the quality criterion and, therefore, the objective function are not defined for some applied scheduling problems. Let some optimal schedules be pre-given. The goal is to construct an optimal schedule for the new input data and to estimate unknown objective function. To apply the methods of scheduling theory to this problem, it is necessary to determine the objective function. The task of the objective function approximation arises as a sub-task in the scheduling automation process, so the approximation algorithm must be fast enough compared to the required frequency of scheduling. An indicator of the quality of the approximation algorithm is the quality of the schedule obtained for the approximated objective function.

A linear approximation for a single-machine scheduling problem is considered: it is assumed that there exists an objective function that is linear in job-weighted completion times, and the previously constructed schedules are optimal with respect to this objective function. The initial problem is reduced to solving a system of linear inequalities with respect to the unknown values of the weight coefficients of the objective function. A detailed review of the results of the algebraic theory of linear inequalities was given by [14], which also includes an algorithm for finding a general formula for non-negative solutions of [15] based on the principle of boundary solutions. General results on this topic were also presented by [16,17], who also used some properties of convex cones in the solution space Refs. [18,19] obtained results for a set of solutions (redundancy and dimension) of a certain class of systems of inequalities–normal systems.

The main contribution of this paper is an algorithm for approximating the weight coefficients for the case of simultaneous job release times. The system of linear inequalities in this case has a sparse matrix (most of the elements are zero), which contains a significant number of dependent inequalities. The solution method is primarily based on the exclusion of dependent inequalities from the system and using some general properties of linear inequality systems.

The structure of this paper is organized as follows. In Section 2 the mathematical formulation of the problem $1 \parallel \sum w_j C_j$ will be given and thereupon mathematical statement of the problem of approximation of objective function weight coefficients is formulated; in Section 3 a method for solving the problem is proposed; in Section 4 a numerical study of the constructed approximation algorithm is carried out and its final complexity is calculated. Section 5 contains a brief conclusion.

2. Mathematical Problem Formulation

The problem studied in this article is in some way the inverse of one of the classic problems in scheduling theory, the problem of minimizing the total weighted completion time $1 \mid r_j \mid \sum w_j C_j$. To describe the main problem, problem $1 \mid r_j \mid \sum w_j C_j$ should be introduced first. There is a single machine and a set $J = \{1, 2, \ldots, n\}$ of n jobs that need to be processed on the machine. For each job $j \in J$, the release time r_j and processing time p_j are given. There are no precedence relations of jobs, and interruptions of the job processing are prohibited. The order in which the jobs $(j_1, \ldots, j_n)$ are processed is called a schedule. In problem $1 \mid r_j \mid \sum w_j C_j$, it is necessary to find a schedule π^0 minimizing the total weighted completion time $\sum w_j C_j$, where C_j is the completion time of job j, and $w_j > 0$ is a weight coefficient of the completion time of the corresponding job j. Completion times of jobs under schedule $\pi = (j_1, \ldots, j_n)$ are defined as follows:

$$C_{j_1}(\pi) = r_{j_1} + p_{j_1};$$

$$C_{j_k}(\pi) = \max\{r_{j_k}, C_{j_{k-1}}(\pi)\} + p_{j_k}, k = 2, \ldots, n.$$

Remark 1. *The case of problem $1 \mid r_j \mid \sum w_j C_j$ with zero weight coefficients can be solved trivially: all corresponding jobs are processed last and are excluded from the consideration. The case with negative weight coefficients does not make sense from a practical point of view. In this regard, it is assumed in this paper that all weight coefficients are positive.*

Remark 2. *Note, that the problem $1 \mid r_j \mid \sum w_j L_j$ about the total weighted lateness $L_j = C_j - d_j$, where d_j is the due date for job $j \in J$, is equivalent to problem $1 \mid r_j \mid \sum w_j C_j$ and the optimal schedule π^0 in problem $1 \mid r_j \mid \sum w_j L_j$ does not depend on the values of due dates d_j. Further,* the problem $1 \mid r_j \mid \sum w_j C_j$ will be considered, implying that all the results obtained can be applied to the problem $1 \mid r_j \mid \sum w_j L_j$.

Definition 1. *A set of job release times and processing times $I = \{r_1, \ldots, r_n, p_1, \ldots, p_n\}$ is called a problem instance I of problem $1 \mid r_j \mid \sum w_j C_j$.*

The general case of problem $1 \mid r_j \mid \sum w_j C_j$ with weight coefficients w_j is NP-hard in the strong sense [20]. An analysis of the approaches and methods for solving single-machine scheduling problems can be found in [21]. According to generalized Smith theorem [22], a polynomially solvable special case of problem $1 \mid r_j \mid \sum w_j C_j$ is problem $1 \mid\mid \sum w_j C_j$, in which, despite the general case, a simultaneous release times $r_1 = \ldots = r_n = r$ are assumed. An optimal schedule in this case will be a schedule constructed in order of non-decreasing values $p_j/w_j, j \in J$.

Definition 2. *A set of job processing times $I = \{p_1, \ldots, p_n\}$ is called a problem instance I of problem $1 \mid\mid \sum w_j C_j$.*

Now, the problem of approximation of objective function weight coefficients can be formulated as follows.

Problem 1. *N instances I_k, $k = 1, \ldots, N$, of the problem $1 \mid\mid \sum w_j C_j$ (or the problem $1 \mid r_j \mid \sum w_j C_j$ in the general case) are given, and corresponding optimal schedules π_k^0 are known. The goal is to approximate values of unknown weight coefficients w_j, $j \in J$.*

Thus, the problem considered in this paper is inverse to the problem $1 \mid\mid \sum w_j C_j$. A linear approximation is considered for the problem for a single machine: it is assumed that there is an objective function that is linear with respect to the completion times, the optimal schedule is known, but the weight coefficients of the objective function are unknown. This problem may arise, for example, at the initial stages of automating individual processes at enterprises where there is a long experience in scheduling "manually", but modeling the entire production process and the analytical formulation of the optimality criterion is, for some reason, impossible or not obvious.

3. Approximation Problem Solving Method

The method for solving the problem of approximating weight coefficients (both for general and for particular cases) is based on determining the optimality of schedules $\pi_k^0, k = 1, 2, \ldots, N$:

$$\sum_{j=1}^{n} C_j^k(\pi) w_j \geq \sum_{j=1}^{n} C_j^k(\pi_k^0) w_j, \ \forall \pi.$$

Therefore,

$$\sum_{j=1}^{n} \left(C_j^k(\pi) - C_j^k(\pi_k^0) \right) w_j \geq 0, \ \forall \pi, k = 1, 2, \ldots, N. \quad (1)$$

Thus, the values of w_j are generally determined by a system of $N(n! - 1)$ inequalities of the form (1), i.e., the dependence of the number of inequalities in the system on the number of jobs is not polynomial, because for any instance there are $n!$ possible schedules. The non-polynomial complexity of the approximation algorithm can be avoided if among the $N(n! - 1)$ inequalities there is a polynomial number m of independent ones, while the remaining inequalities are consequences of these m inequalities.

In case $N = 1$ the following approximation problem can be considered: one instance I of problem $1 \mid r_j \mid \sum w_j C_j$ of dimension n is given, i.e., for n jobs, the release times r_j and processing times p_j are defined, and the optimal schedule π^0 is also known. Then, for an arbitrary acceptable schedule π the following inequality holds:

$$\sum_{j=1}^{n}\left(C_j(\pi) - C_j(\pi^0)\right)w_j \geq 0. \qquad (2)$$

Repeating the arguments about the non-polynomial number of inequalities, the following proposition can be formulated. The proposition is sufficient for the polynomial approximation algorithm.

Proposition 1. *For an arbitrary instance I of problem $1 \mid r_j \mid \sum w_j C_j$ in a system of $(n! - 1)$ inequalities of the form (2) there is a subsystem of m inequalities, the solution of which coincides with the solution of the initial system, and the number m depends polynomially on n.*

Each of the strict inequalities of the form (2) corresponds to some non-optimal schedule π. In this case, Proposition 1 means that among $(n! - 1)$ non-optimal schedules there are m schedules $\Pi = \{\pi_1, \ldots, \pi_m\}$ such that the solution of this system of inequalities of the form (2) corresponding to the schedules π_i, $i = 1, \ldots, m$, coincides with the solution of the initial system, and the number m depends polynomially on n. In other words, for any schedule $\pi \notin \Pi$, an inequality of the form (2) corresponding to schedule π is a consequence of the system of inequalities corresponding to schedules π_i, $i = 1, \ldots, m$. Finding proof (or inconsistency) of the Proposition 1 is the key to solving the approximation problem for the $1 \mid r_j \mid \sum w_j C_j$.

3.1. The Initial and Efficient System of Inequalities for the Problem $1 \mid\mid \sum w_j C_j$

Consider approximating the weight coefficients of the problem $1 \mid\mid \sum w_j C_j$. According to the generalized Smith theorem [22], for problem instance $I = \{p_1, \ldots, p_n\}$ of $1 \mid\mid \sum w_j C_j$ there exists an optimal schedule $\pi^* = (j_1, j_2, \ldots, j_n)$, for which

$$\frac{p_{j_1}}{w_{j_1}} \leq \frac{p_{j_2}}{w_{j_2}} \leq \ldots \leq \frac{p_{j_n}}{w_{j_n}}. \qquad (3)$$

Remark 3. *If one or more adjacent non-strict inequalities of set (3) turn into equality, that is, the ratios $\frac{p_j}{w_j}$ are equal for jobs $j \in \{j_k, \ldots, j_{k+l}\}$, all those schedules $\tilde{\pi}^*$ are also optimal, in which the jobs $j_k, \ldots, j_{k+l}$ are placed in any other arbitrary order $\sigma(j_k, \ldots, j_{k+l})$:*

$$\pi^* = \left(j_1, \ldots, j_{k-1}, j_k, \ldots, j_{k+l}, j_{k+l+1}, \ldots, j_n\right),$$

$$\tilde{\pi}^* = \left(j_1, \ldots, j_{k-1}, \sigma(j_k, \ldots, j_{k+l}), j_{k+l+1}, \ldots, j_n\right),$$

$$\sum w_j C_j(\tilde{\pi}^*) = \sum w_j C_j(\pi^*) = \min_\pi \sum w_j C_j(\pi).$$

An inequality of the form (3) is valid for all N given instances $I_k = \{p_1^k, \ldots, p_n^k\}$ of the problem and the corresponding optimal schedules $\pi_k^0 = (j_1^k, j_2^k, \ldots, j_n^k)$, $k = 1, \ldots, N$.

Definition 3. *The system of inequalities for weight coefficients w_j*

$$\frac{p_{j_1}^k}{w_{j_1^k}} \leq \frac{p_{j_2}^k}{w_{j_2^k}} \leq \ldots \leq \frac{p_{j_n}^k}{w_{j_n^k}}, \quad k = 1, \ldots, N, \qquad (4)$$

*we will call the **initial system** of inequalities of the problem of approximation of weight coefficients for the case $r_1 = \ldots = r_n$.*

The initial system (4) contains $N(n-1)$ inequalities. To reconstruct the system to a more convenient form for solving, the following notation will be used.

Let $K = \{1, \ldots, N\}$ be the set of indices $k \in K$ corresponding to the given pairs (I_k, π_k^0) of problem instances and their optimal schedules, and let $\tilde{K} \subset K$ be some subset of the set K. Further, the record of the form

$$\min_{k \in \tilde{K}} \ (\text{or} \max_{k \in \tilde{K}})$$

will mean the minimum (maximum) for all possible pairs (I_k, π_k^0) such that $k \in \tilde{K}$.

For an arbitrary pair of jobs $i, j \in \{1, \ldots, n\}$, $i \neq j$, the set K can be divided into two subsets $K_{i,j}$ and $K_{j,i}$ depending on the relative position of the jobs i, j in the schedule π_k^0:

$$K_{i,j} = \{k \in K : \pi_k^0 = (\ldots, i, \ldots, j, \ldots)\},$$

$$K_{j,i} = \{k \in K : \pi_k^0 = (\ldots, j, \ldots, i, \ldots)\}.$$

Then, from the inequalities (4) of the initial system for the corresponding weight coefficients w_i, w_j the following inequalities can be constructed:

$$\frac{p_i^k}{w_i} \leq \frac{p_j^k}{w_j}, \ k \in K_{i,j},$$

$$\frac{p_j^k}{w_j} \leq \frac{p_i^k}{w_i}, \ k \in K_{j,i},$$

or, more conveniently,

$$\frac{w_j}{w_i} \leq \frac{p_j^k}{p_i^k}, \ k \in K_{i,j}, \tag{5a}$$

$$\frac{w_j}{w_i} \geq \frac{p_j^k}{p_i^k}, \ k \in K_{j,i}. \tag{5b}$$

Remark 4. *Obviously, $K_{i,j} \cap K_{j,i} = \varnothing$, $K_{i,j} \cup K_{j,i} = K$ for all $i, j \in J$, $i \neq j$. Consequently, in inequalities (5a) and (5b) all inequalities of the initial system related to w_i, w_j occurred.*

Let

$$Y(i,j) = \min_{k \in K_{i,j}} \left(\frac{p_j^k}{p_i^k}\right),$$

$$X(i,j) = \max_{k \in K_{j,i}} \left(\frac{p_j^k}{p_i^k}\right),$$

then the system of inequalities (5a) and (5b) for the chosen i, j is equivalent to the double inequality:

$$X(i,j) \leq \frac{w_j}{w_i} \leq Y(i,j). \tag{6}$$

Remark 5. *Consider the case when one of the sets $K_{i,j}, K_{j,i}$ is empty. Let, for example, $K_{i,j} = \varnothing$, that is, there were no inequalities of the form (5a) in the initial system. In this case, it will be assumed that $Y(i,j) = \infty$ for the uniformity of the algorithm, and the inequality (6) will have form*

$$X(i,j) \leq \frac{w_j}{w_i} < \infty.$$

Similarly, if $K_{j,i} = \varnothing$, then it will be assumed that $X(i,j) = 0$ and the inequality (6) will have form

$$0 \leq \frac{w_j}{w_i} \leq Y(i,j).$$

Jobs i, j were chosen arbitrarily; therefore, the inequality (6) can be written for any pair of different jobs $i, j \in J$.

Definition 4. *A system of inequalities*

$$X(i,j) \leq \frac{w_j}{w_i} \leq Y(i,j), \qquad (7)$$

where:
$X(i,j) = \max\limits_{k \in K_{j,i}} \left(\frac{p_j^k}{p_i^k}\right),$
$Y(i,j) = \min\limits_{k \in K_{i,j}} \left(\frac{p_j^k}{p_i^k}\right),$
$K_{i,j} = \{k \in K : \pi_k^0 = (\ldots, i, \ldots, j, \ldots)\},$
$K_{j,i} = \{k \in K : \pi_k^0 = (\ldots, j, \ldots, i, \ldots)\},$
$i, j \in J,\ i \neq j,$
*we call the **efficient system** of inequalities of the weight coefficient approximation problem for the case $r_1 = \ldots = r_n$.*

Lemma 1. *The initial and efficient systems of inequalities (4) and (7) are equivalent.*

Proof. The efficient system is the result of equivalent transformations of the inequalities of the initial system and, taking into account the Remark 4, includes all the inequalities of the initial system related to w_i, w_j for all possible pairs $i, j \in J, i \neq j$, that is, it contains all the inequalities of the initial system. Therefore, the efficient system of inequalities is equivalent to the initial system. □

Thus, the solution sets of the efficient and initial systems will coincide. Lemma 1 allows us to turn to the efficient system consisting of $n(n-1)$ inequalities of the form (6) from the initial system consisting of N inequalities of the form (4). To find solutions to an efficient system, the following two lemmas are necessary.

Lemma 2. *The set of solutions of the initial (and efficient) system is a convex polyhedral cone in n-dimensional space.*

Proof. The initial system for the case $r_j = r$, $j \in J$, consists of inequalities of the form (4):

$$\frac{p_{j_1}^k}{w_{j_1}^k} \leq \frac{p_{j_2}^k}{w_{j_2}^k} \leq \ldots \leq \frac{p_{j_n}^k}{w_{j_n}^k},\ k = 1, \ldots, N.$$

Thus, the initial system of inequalities is a system of $N(n-1)$ linear inequalities. The general solution of this system, as well as a solution of any system of linear inequalities, is a convex cone with a finite number of faces. □

Corollary 1. *Any plane section of the set of solutions is also a convex set as the intersection of two convex sets: the solution of the initial system and the cutting plane.*

Lemma 3. *Let $\mathcal{P}$ be a rectangular parallelepiped in n-dimensional space $\mathbb{R}^n$, $n \in \mathbb{N}$. Let a convex set $\mathbf{M} \subset \mathbb{R}^n$ of hyperspace points touch each face of $\mathcal{P}$. Then, the center O of the parallelepiped $\mathcal{P}$ is an interior point of the set $\mathbf{M}$.*

Proof. Obviously, the proof must be based on the property of convexity of the set **M**. If the assertion of Lemma 3 for the subset **M'** of the set **M**, which is limited only by the tangency points of the hyperspace by the initial set will be proved, then it will also be proved for the whole set **M**. Next, consider arbitrary n tangency points of the hyperspace by the set **M'**. The hyperplane drawn through these points will always "cut off" part of the hyperspace without its center. Thus, no matter what points are chosen, the center of the hyperspace will always be in the "non-cut-off" part, and therefore, will be an internal point of the set **M'**. Figure 1 shows an illustration for the lemma in space $\mathbb{R}^3$. The statement of the lemma in this case takes the following form: the center of the parallelepiped, inside which there is a convex figure touching each of the sides of the parallelepiped, is an interior point of this figure. As can be seen from the figure, the points of contact of the convex set K, L and M form a plane that "cuts" the initial parallelepiped into two parts, one of which contains its center O. Since the convex set is tangent to each side of the parallelepiped, the point O will always be interior. □

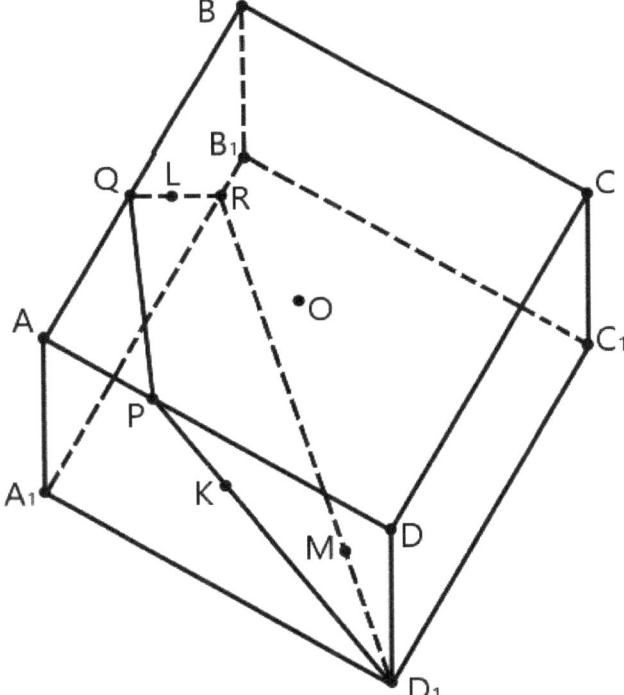

Figure 1. Illustration for Lemma 3 in space $\mathbb{R}^3$.

3.2. Method for Solving the Efficient System of Inequalities

Details of the efficient system of inequalities solution method are described in this section. Input is a system $\frac{n(n-1)}{2}$ of double inequalities of the form

$$X(i,j) \leq \frac{w_j}{w_i} \leq Y(i,j), \quad i,j \in J, \ i \neq j. \tag{8}$$

This system can also be written as $n(n-1)$ simple linear inequalities:

$$\begin{cases} w_j - Y(i,j)w_i \leq 0, \\ -w_j + X(i,j)w_i \leq 0, \end{cases} \quad i,j \in J, \ i \neq j,$$

Thus, the approximation problem has been reduced to a system of linear homogeneous inequalities. For such systems, there are many algorithms for finding a system of generating vectors sufficient to write a general formula for non-negative solutions. However, the resulting system has a special form, significantly different from the general one. In addition, the goal of the approximation problem is not to find all possible solutions to the system. Thus, a fast algorithm for finding a particular solution to the system of inequalities of the obtained form will be described.

The inequality (8) for three pairs formed from the jobs $\{f, g, h\}$ will take the following form:

$$X(f,g) \leq \frac{w_g}{w_f} \leq Y(f,g), \tag{9a}$$

$$X(g,h) \leq \frac{w_h}{w_g} \leq Y(g,h), \tag{9b}$$

$$X(h,f) \leq \frac{w_f}{w_h} \leq Y(h,f). \tag{9c}$$

The idea of the method is that one or more of the inequalities from (9a)–(9c) can be strengthened using the others. For example, multiplying the inequalities (9a) and (9b) gives:

$$X(f,g)X(g,h) \leq \frac{w_h}{w_f} \leq Y(f,g)Y(g,h)$$

or

$$\frac{1}{Y(f,g)Y(g,h)} \leq \frac{w_f}{w_h} \leq \frac{1}{X(f,g)X(g,h)}. \tag{10}$$

So, the inequality (10), which is a consequence of the inequalities (9a) and (9b), can improve the estimate of the ratio w_f/w_h in the inequality (9c). Indeed, if the values $X(h,f)$, $Y(f,g)$, $Y(g,h)$ are such, that

$$X(h,f) \leq \frac{1}{Y(f,g)Y(g,h)},$$

then the inequality (9c) can be transformed by setting

$$X(h,f) = \frac{1}{Y(f,g)Y(g,h)}.$$

We use the definition of matrices from the efficient system of inequalities:

$$\frac{1}{X(i,j)} = \frac{1}{\max\limits_{k \in K_{j,i}} \left(\frac{p_j^k}{p_i^k}\right)} = \min\limits_{k \in K_{j,i}} \left(\frac{p_i^k}{p_j^k}\right) = Y(j,i). \tag{11}$$

If $X(h,f) \leq X(h,g)X(g,f)$, then, taking into account the ratio (11), the inequality (9c) can be strengthened, setting $X(h,f) = X(h,g)X(g,f)$, as a result of which the set of solutions of the system (9) and the efficient system of inequalities remain unchanged.

Similarly, all the inequalities of the efficient system can be strengthened:

$$X(i,j) := \max\left\{X(i,j); \max\limits_{l=1,\ldots,n, l \neq i, l \neq j} \{X(i,l)X(l,j)\}\right\}, \ i,j \in J, \ i \neq j. \tag{12}$$

The procedure (12) must be repeated for all possible pairs of jobs i, j. On some steps after the change of $X(i,j)$ it can appear that some of $X(k,j)$ or $X(i,k)$ can also be updated, and the inequality with $X(i,j)$ can be strengthened again, where $k = 1, \ldots, n$, $i \neq k \neq j$. Therefore, it is necessary to repeat the procedure (12) until none of the inequalities of the efficient system can be strengthened during the whole iteration. As will be shown in Section 4.3.3, this procedure will need to be repeated not more than $O(n^3)$ times. After that, the values of $Y(j,i)$ must also be updated according to the relation (11). The matrices X, Y obtained after a sufficient number of repetitions of the procedure (12) will be denoted by $\tilde{X}, \tilde{Y}$.

Thus, if $w_j/w_i = z \in [\tilde{X}(i,j); \tilde{Y}(i,j)]$ for any pair $i,j \in J$, $i \neq j$, then among the inequalities of the system remaining after the corresponding simplifications, there are no pairs that contradict each other. Therefore, for each $z \in [\tilde{X}(i,j); \tilde{Y}(i,j)]$ there exists a solution to the initial system (4) of inequalities such that $w_j/w_i = z$.

The solution of the system, as shown in Lemma 2, is a convex cone. Therefore, the weight coefficients can be scaled: problems $1 \parallel \sum w_j C_j$ and $1 \parallel \sum (\gamma w_j) C_j$, where $\gamma > 0$, are equivalent, and if the set of coefficients $w = \{w_1, \ldots, w_n\}$ is a solution of a system of inequalities (initial or efficient), then the coefficients $\gamma w = \{\gamma w_1, \ldots, \gamma w_n\}$ are also a solution to this system. Due to this fact, one of the weight coefficients can be chosen arbitrarily, then the system can be solved for the remaining weight coefficients, and the resulting solution can be scaled. The resulting solution will correspond to the solution of the initial system of inequalities.

Let, for example, $w_1 = 1$. By Corollary 1 the cross section of the set of solutions of the initial system by the plane $w_1 = 1$ is also a convex set. Then, for arbitrary $j \in \{2, \ldots, n\}$ a parallelepiped in a hyperspace of dimension $(n-1)$ can be described:

$$\tilde{X}(1,j) \leq w_j \leq \tilde{Y}(1,j). \tag{13}$$

Moreover, as was proved above, for all w_j and $z \in [\tilde{X}(1,j); \tilde{Y}(1,j)]$ there exists a solution to the system such that $w_j/w_1 = z$ or $w_j = z$. In particular, for $w_1 = 1$ there exists a solution such that $w_j = \tilde{X}(1,j)$ and such that $w_j = \tilde{Y}(1,j)$. In other words, the section of the set of solutions by the plane $w_1 = 1$ lies inside the parallelepiped described by the inequalities (13) and has at least one common point with each of its faces. Therefore, by Lemma 3 the center of this parallelepiped is an interior point of the set of solutions to the initial system of inequalities and is a solution to the initial system.

The discussion given above can be summarized as the following theorem.

Theorem 1. *A vector $w = (w_1, \ldots, w_j, \ldots, w_n)$, where*

$$w_j = \begin{cases} 1, & j = l; \\ (\tilde{X}(l,j) + \tilde{Y}(l,j))/2, & j \neq l, \end{cases}$$

is a solution of the efficient system (7) of inequalities (index l can be chosen arbitrarily).

Any value within the interval $[\tilde{X}(l,j); \tilde{Y}(l,j)]$ can be taken as w_j, $j \in J$. We used the value in the middle of the interval $w_j = (\tilde{X}(l,j) + \tilde{Y}(l,j))/2$.

3.3. Algorithm for Solving the Approximation Problem

This section describes the algorithm for solving the problem $1 \parallel \sum w_j C_j$, $j \in J$, with unknown weight coefficients w_j. N instances of this problem are given: $I_k = \{p_1^k, \ldots, p_n^k\}$, $k \in N$, and for each instance the optimal schedule $\pi_k^0 = (j_1^k, j_2^k, \ldots, j_n^k)$ is known. It is necessary to approximate unknown values of the weight coefficients w_j, $j \in J$.

The algorithm for approximating the weight coefficients of the objective function is based on solving the efficient system of inequalities:

$$X(i,j) \leq \frac{w_j}{w_i} \leq Y(i,j), \tag{14}$$

where:

$$X(i,j) = \max_{k \in K_{j,i}} \left(\frac{p_j^k}{p_i^k}\right), \quad (15)$$

$$Y(i,j) = \min_{k \in K_{i,j}} \left(\frac{p_j^k}{p_i^k}\right), \quad (16)$$

$$K_{i,j} = \{k \in K : \pi_k^0 = (\ldots, i, \ldots, j, \ldots)\}, \quad (17)$$

$$K_{j,i} = \{k \in K : \pi_k^0 = (\ldots, j, \ldots, i, \ldots)\}, \quad (18)$$

$$i, j \in J, \ i \neq j.$$

To approximate the coefficients w_j it is necessary:

1. construct sets $K_{i,j}$, $K_{j,i}$ according to Formulas (17) and (18);
2. construct matrices X and Y according to Formulas (15) and (16);
3. calculate matrices $\tilde{X}$ and $\tilde{Y}$ by repeating procedure (12) as it is described in Section 3.2;
4. calculate $w_j = \begin{cases} 1, & j = l \\ (\tilde{X}(l,j) + \tilde{Y}(l,j))/2, & j \neq l \end{cases}$, where index l is chosen arbitrarily.

4. Numerical Study

4.1. Description of Numerical Experiment

To study the efficiency of the constructed method for approximating the objective function of problem $1 \mid\mid \sum w_j C_j$, the solution algorithm described in Section 3.3 was programmed in a *Python* environment and computational experiments were carried out for various numbers of jobs n and numbers of given instances N with known optimal schedules. For each experiment, $n \in \{10, 50, 100, 150, 200, 250\}$ weight coefficients $w_j^0, j \in J$ and $N \in [5, 100]$ (with a step of 5) problem instances $I_k = \{p_1^k, \ldots, p_n^k\}, k = 1, \ldots, N$, (values p_j^k and w_j^0 have a uniform distribution on the interval $[0;1]$) were generated, and the constructed approximation algorithm was executed. The algorithm output is a set of the weight coefficients $w_j, j \in J$. To compare the found values of w_j and the true weight coefficients w_j^0, both sets are normalized (scaling is allowed due to the linearity of the objective function):

$$\|w\| = \sqrt{\sum_{j=1}^n w_j^2},$$

$$w_j := \frac{w_j}{\|w\|}, \ w_j^0 := \frac{w_j^0}{\|w^0\|}.$$

Measure of efficiency $\varepsilon(N, n)$ of the algorithm is the modulus of the relative deviation of the found normalized values w_j (averaged over $j \in J$) from their true normalized values w_j^0:

$$\varepsilon(N, n) = \frac{1}{n} \sum_{j=1}^n \frac{|w_j - w_j^0|}{w_j^0}. \quad (19)$$

The results of a series of experiments for the dependence of the approximation efficiency measure $\varepsilon(N, n)$ on N for different values of n are shown in Figures 2–5.

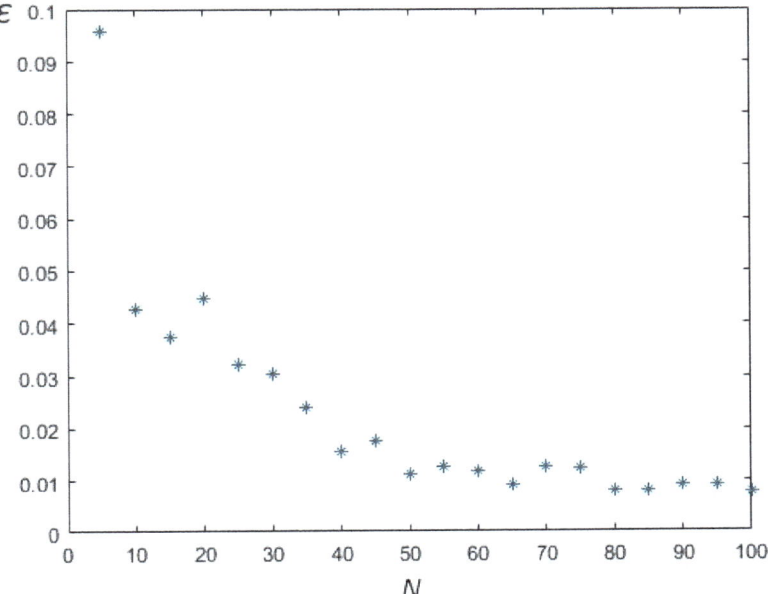

Figure 2. Modelling results, $n = 10$.

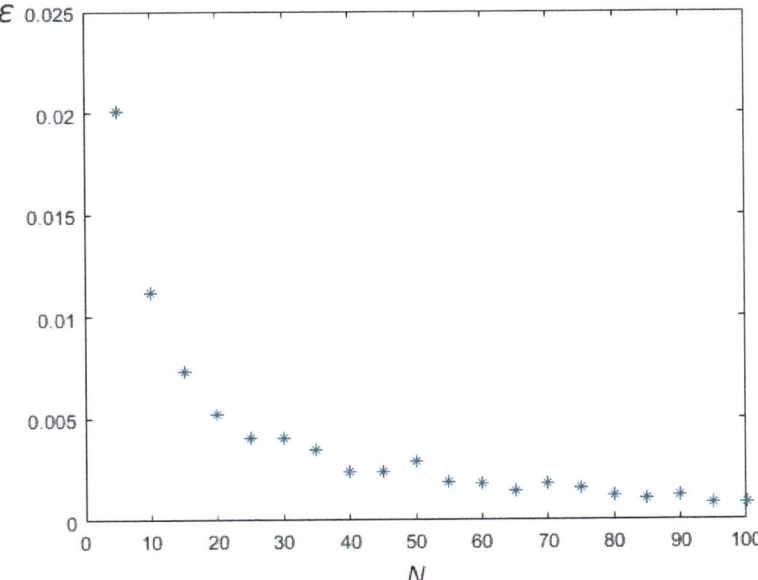

Figure 3. Modelling results, $n = 50$.

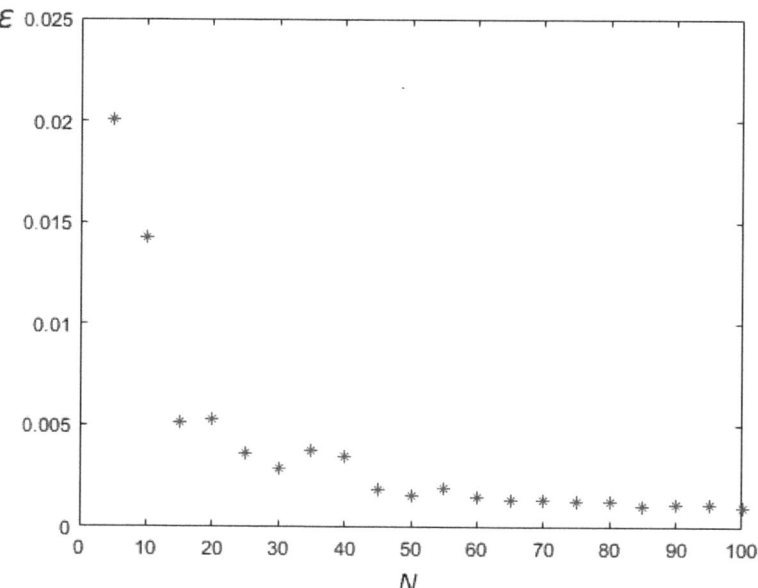

Figure 4. Modelling results, $n = 100$.

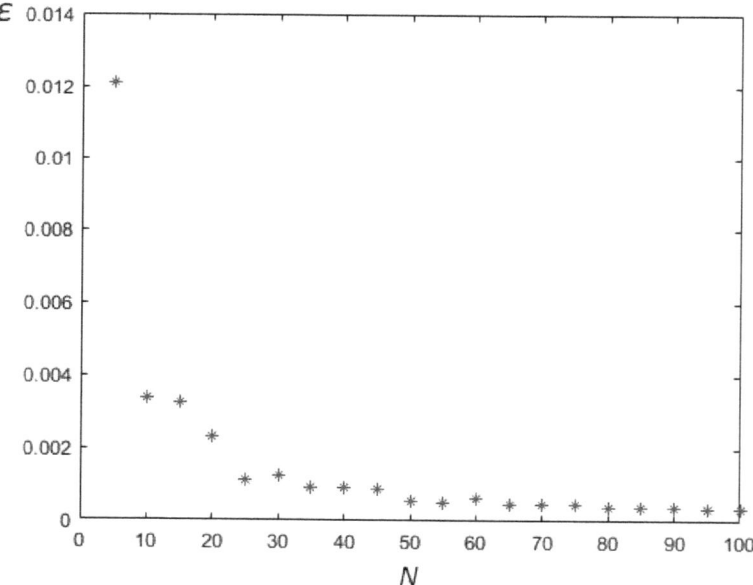

Figure 5. Modelling results, $n = 250$.

4.2. Analysis of Experiment Results

Function $\varepsilon(N, n)$ decreases as the number of known optimal schedules N increases. Moreover, the least squares (LSM) approximation of the dependence of $1/\varepsilon$ on N by the line $y = ax$ in all cases with a sufficiently large number of repetitions of the experiment, gives a high linear correlation coefficient $r > 0.9$. In Figure 6 a graphical representation of the result of a linear approximation with a linear correlation coefficient of $r = 0.93$ is presented.

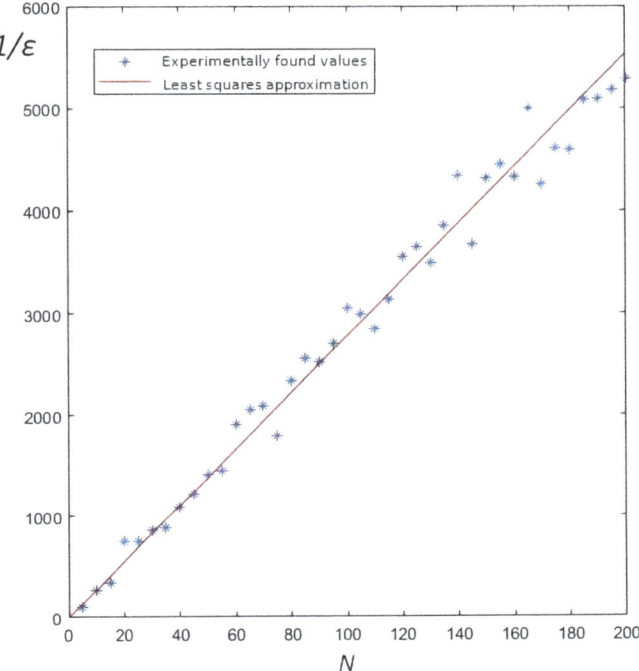

Figure 6. Modelling results, $n = 200$.

Due to the described correlation, the following hypothesis about the type of dependence $\varepsilon(N, n)$ is made:

$$\varepsilon(N, n) = \frac{a(n)}{N}. \qquad (20)$$

This hypothesis possibly depends on the distribution of the input parameters with the growth of the number n of jobs and number N of given instances with known optimal schedules.

Moreover, as can be seen from the diagrams above, with a greater number of jobs n, more accurate results of the algorithm can be obtained. That is, the function $a(n)$ tends to be decreasing. For accurate statistical verification of the hypothesis, it is necessary to conduct a large number of computational experiments.

4.3. Computational Complexity Estimation

The approximation algorithm consists of four sequential procedures:

1. construction of sets $K_{i,j}$, $K_{j,i}$;
2. calculation of matrices X and Y;
3. calculation of matrices $\tilde{X}$ and $\tilde{Y}$;
4. calculation of w_j.

The computational complexity of each of these procedures will be as follows.

4.3.1. Construction of Sets $K_{i,j}$, $K_{j,i}$

As it was described in Section 3.1, sets $K_{i,j}$ and $K_{j,i}$ are defined as follows:

$$K_{i,j} = \{k \in K \,:\, \pi_k^0 = (\ldots, i, \ldots, j, \ldots)\},$$

$$K_{j,i} = \{k \in K \,:\, \pi_k^0 = (\ldots, j, \ldots, i, \ldots)\}.$$

To construct these sets, it is necessary to determine the position of each requirement $j \in J$ in each schedule $\pi_k^0, k = 1, \ldots, N$. Then, for each pair of different jobs $i, j \in J$ it is necessary to compare their positions in schedule π_k^0. Therefore, the construction of sets $K_{i,j}$, $K_{j,i}$ requires the following number of operations:

$$N \cdot \left(O(n) + O\left(\frac{n(n-1)}{2}\right)\right) = O(n^2 N),$$

where n is a number of jobs, N is a number of schedules.

4.3.2. Calculation of Matrices X and Y

The $n \times n$ matrices X and Y are calculated as follows:

$$X(i,j) = \max_{k \in K_{j,i}} \left(\frac{p_j^k}{p_i^k}\right), \quad Y(i,j) = \min_{k \in K_{i,j}} \left(\frac{p_j^k}{p_i^k}\right), \quad i, j \in J, \; i \neq j.$$

For each instance I_k of the problem and all possible pairs (i,j), $i \neq j$, the ratio p_j^k/p_i^k is calculated, which requires $O(Nn(n-1))$ operations. Then, for each set $K_{j,i}$, the largest value is chosen, which is placed in $X(i,j)$, which requires $O(n(n-1) \cdot O(N))$ operations. After all, finding $Y(i,j)$ taking into account the relation (11) requires $O(n(n-1))$ operations. Therefore, to calculate the matrices X and Y, it is required to perform the following number of operations:

$$O(Nn(n-1)) + O(n(n-1) \cdot O(N)) + O(n(n-1)) = O(n^2 N).$$

4.3.3. Calculation of Matrices $\tilde{X}$ and $\tilde{Y}$

Calculation of the matrices $\tilde{X}$ and $\tilde{Y}$ is the most time-consuming part of the algorithm in terms of computational complexity. Indeed, a procedure of the form (12):

$$X(i,j) := \max\left\{X(i,j); \max_{l \in J, i \neq l \neq j}\{X(i,l)X(l,j)\}\right\}, \quad i, j \in J, \; i \neq j, \quad (21)$$

for each pair i, j involves $(n-2)$ computing the product $X(i,l)X(l,j)$ and finding the maximum of $(n-1)$ values. Thus, the number of operations required to perform the procedure (12) once is

$$O\left((n-2) + (n-1)\right) = O(n).$$

To find the matrices $\tilde{X}$ and $\tilde{Y}$, it is necessary to repeat the procedure (12) in a loop for all possible pairs of jobs i, j until there will be no such pair i, j so that the element $X(i,j)$ can be increased. However, after each repetition of the procedure, the element $X(i,j)$ either is increased or unchanged, so the number of repetitions of the procedure can be significantly reduced. This can be conducted by choosing a special order in which the pairs $i, j \in J$ are considered such that the procedure (12) will be executed for each pair of jobs no more than two times. In this case, the number of operations required to calculate the matrices $\tilde{X}$ and $\tilde{Y}$, is

$$O\left(2 \cdot \frac{n(n-1)}{2} \cdot n\right) = O(n^3).$$

4.3.4. Calculation of w_j

Computational complexity of finding all values

$$w_j = \begin{cases} 1, & j = l; \\ (\tilde{X}(l,j) + \tilde{Y}(l,j))/2, & j \neq l, \end{cases} \quad j \in J,$$

is $O(n)$ operations.

4.3.5. Resulting Complexity

Thus, the computational complexity of the algorithm can be estimated with the following number of operations:

$$O(n^2N) + O(n^2N) + O(n^3) + O(n) = O(n^2N + n^3) = O(n^2(N+n)).$$

5. Conclusions

The result of the work is an algorithm for approximating the values of the weight coefficients of the problem $1 \ || \ \sum w_j C_j$ using N given instances of the problem with known optimal schedules. The result of the algorithm is a set of weight coefficients w_j, $j \in J$ such that for each of the N given instances, the optimal schedule found for the approximate values of the weights either is equal to the given optimal schedule corresponding to the unknown true set of weights w_j^0, or has the same objective function value with it. The results described in this paper are also relevant to the problem $1 \ || \ \sum w_j L_j$.

The computational complexity of the algorithm is limited to $O(n^2(N+n))$ operations, where n is the number of jobs and N is a number of initial instances with known optimal schedules.

A numerical experiment was carried out to study the efficiency of the method. All shown examples have $N \in [5, 100]$ given instances of the problem $1 \ || \ \sum w_j C_j$, where the number of jobs n is the same for all instances in each set and were given from the interval $[10, 250]$ to check the correlation. The accuracy of the algorithm is estimated by experimentally measuring the function $\varepsilon(N,n) = \frac{1}{n}\sum_{j=1}^{n}\frac{|w_j - w_j^0|}{w_j^0}$, which is an indicator of the average modulus of the relative deviation of the found values w_j from the true values w_j^0. An analysis of the results shows a high correlation between the dependence $\varepsilon(N, n)$ and a function of the form $\alpha(n)/N$, where $\alpha(n)$ is a decreasing function of n. So, based on the result of the experiment, it is clear that a greater number of jobs n, more accurate results of the algorithm can be obtained. In Section 4.2 it is shown that the dependence of $1/\varepsilon$ on N is approximated by the line $y = ax$; the least squares method shows a high linear correlation coefficient $r > 0.9$ in all cases with a sufficiently large number of repetitions of the experiment.

Based on the current results, further work is planned in the following areas:

- searching for a formal proof of the hypothesis about the form of dependence $\varepsilon(N, n)$ from Section 4.2 when $r_j = const$, $j \in J$;
- continue studying the general case $1 \ | \ r_j \ | \ \sum w_j C_j$, where jobs can have different release times; it is necessary to find either a subsystem of inequalities with a polynomial number of inequalities, equivalent to the original system, or the strongest subsystem with a polynomial number of inequalities with an estimate of the approximation error;
- trying to adapt the results to solve the problem of approximating more complex objective functions.

Author Contributions: Conceptualization, A.L.; methodology, A.L. and N.P.; software, E.B.; validation, A.L. and N.P.; formal analysis, A.L. and N.P.; investigation, E.B and N.P.; data curation, E.B.; writing—original draft preparation, E.B. and N.P.; writing—review and editing, A.L. and N.P.; visualization, E.B.; supervision, A.L.; project administration, A.L. All authors have read and agreed to the published version of the manuscript.

Funding: This research received no external funding.

Data Availability Statement: The paper describes a theoretical research. No new data were created or analyzed in this study. Data sharing is not applicable to this article.

Acknowledgments: Authors gratefully thank Nikolay A. Loginov, who took an active part at the initial stage of the work.

Conflicts of Interest: The authors declare no conflicts of interest.

References

1. Vahedi-Nouri, B.; Tavakkoli-Moghaddam, R.; Hanzálek, Z.; Dolgui, A. Production scheduling in a reconfigurable manufacturing system benefiting from human-robot collaboration. *Int. J. Prod. Res.* **2024**, *62*, 767–783. [CrossRef]
2. Lazarev, A.A.; Nekrasov, I.; Pravdivets, N. Evaluating typical algorithms of combinatorial optimization to solve continuous-time based scheduling problem. *Algorithms* **2018**, *11*, 50. [CrossRef]
3. Rzevski, G.; Skobelev, P.; Zhilyaev, A. Emergent Intelligence in Smart Ecosystems: Conflicts Resolution by Reaching Consensus in Resource Management. *Mathematics* **2022**, *10*, 1923. [CrossRef]
4. Lei, D.; Liu, M. An artificial bee colony with division for distributed unrelated parallel machine scheduling with preventive maintenance. *Comput. Ind. Eng.* **2020**, *141*, 106320. [CrossRef]
5. Zhao, X.; Liu, H.; Wu, Y.; Qiu, Q. Joint optimization of mission abort and system structure considering dynamic tasks. *Reliab. Eng Syst. Saf.* **2023**, *234*, 109128. [CrossRef]
6. Koulamas, C.; Kyparisis, G.J. A classification of dynamic programming formulations for offline deterministic single-machine scheduling problems. *Eur. J. Oper. Res.* **2023**, *305*, 999–1017. [CrossRef]
7. Martinelli, R.; Mariano, F.C.M.Q.; Martins, C.B. Single machine scheduling in make to order environments: A systematic review *Comput. Ind. Eng.* **2022**, *169*, 108190. [CrossRef]
8. Tanaka, K.; Vlach, M. Minimizing maximum absolute lateness and range of lateness under generalized due dates on a single machine. *Ann. Oper. Res.* **1999**, *86*, 507–526. [CrossRef]
9. Mosheiov, G.; Oron, D.; Shabtay, D. Minimizing total late work on a single machine with generalized due-dates. *Eur. J. Oper. Res.* **2021**, *293*, 837–846. [CrossRef]
10. Hermelin, D.; Karhi, S.; Pinedo, M.; Shabtay, D. New algorithms for minimizing the weighted number of tardy jobs on a single machine. *Ann. Oper. Res.* **2021**, *298*, 271–287. [CrossRef]
11. Janiak, A.; Kovalyov, M. Single machine group scheduling with ordered criteria. *Ann. Oper. Res.* **1995**, *57*, 191–201. [CrossRef]
12. Rudek, R. The single machine total weighted completion time scheduling problem with the sum-of-processing time based models Strongly NP-hard. *Appl. Math. Mod.* **2017**, *50*, 314–332. [CrossRef]
13. Lazarev, A.; Pravdivets, N.; Werner, F. On the dual and inverse problems of scheduling jobs to minimize the maximum penalty *Mathematics* **2020**, *8*, 1131. [CrossRef]
14. Chernikov, S. Linear Inequalities. In *Itogi Nauki i Tekhniki. Series 'Algebra. Topology. Geometry'*; VINITI: Moscow, Russia, 1968. (In Russian)
15. Chernikova, N.V. Algorithm for finding a general formula for the non-negative solutions of a system of linear inequalities. *USSR Comput. Math. Math. Phys.* **1965**, *5*, 228–233. [CrossRef]
16. Zhu, Y. Generalizations of some fundamental theorems on linear inequalities. *Acta Math. Sin.* **1966**, *16*, 25–40.
17. Fan, K. On infinite systems of linear inequalities. *J. Math. Anal. Appl.* **1968**, *21*, 475–478. [CrossRef]
18. Eckhardt, U. Theorems on the dimension of convex sets. *Linear Algebra Appl.* **1975**, *12*, 63–76. [CrossRef]
19. Eckhardt, U. Representation of Convex Sets. In *Extremal Methods and Systems Analysis*; Springer: New York, NY, USA, 1980.
20. Lenstra, J.; Rinnooy Kan, A.; Brucker, P. Complexity of Machine Scheduling Problems. *Ann. Discret. Math.* **1977**, *1*, 343–362.
21. Lazarev, A. *Scheduling Theory: Methods and Algorithms*; ICS RAS: Moscow, Russia, 2019. (In Russian)
22. Smith, W. Various optimizers for single-stage production. *Nav. Res. Logist. Q.* **1956**, *3*, 59–66. [CrossRef]

Disclaimer/Publisher's Note: The statements, opinions and data contained in all publications are solely those of the individual author(s) and contributor(s) and not of MDPI and/or the editor(s). MDPI and/or the editor(s) disclaim responsibility for any injury to people or property resulting from any ideas, methods, instructions or products referred to in the content.

MDPI
St. Alban-Anlage 66
4052 Basel
Switzerland
www.mdpi.com

Mathematics Editorial Office
E-mail: mathematics@mdpi.com
www.mdpi.com/journal/mathematics

Disclaimer/Publisher's Note: The statements, opinions and data contained in all publications are solely those of the individual author(s) and contributor(s) and not of MDPI and/or the editor(s). MDPI and/or the editor(s) disclaim responsibility for any injury to people or property resulting from any ideas, methods, instructions or products referred to in the content.

www.ingramcontent.com/pod-product-compliance
Lightning Source LLC
LaVergne TN
LVHW070747100526
838202LV00013B/1319